STRIKING A
BALANCE

AEI-Hoover
policy studies

The studies in this series are issued jointly
by the American Enterprise Institute
for Public Policy Research and the Hoover
Institution on War, Revolution and Peace.
They are designed to focus on
policy problems of current and future interest,
to set forth the factors underlying
these problems and to evaluate
courses of action available to policy makers.
The views expressed in these studies
are those of the authors and do not necessarily
reflect the views of the staff, officers
or members of the governing boards of
AEI or the Hoover Institution.

STRIKING A BALANCE

Environment and Natural Resources
Policy in the Nixon-Ford Years

John C. Whitaker

American Enterprise Institute for Public Policy Research
Washington, D.C.

Hoover Institution on War, Revolution and Peace
Stanford University, Stanford, California

HC
110
.E5
W53

Library of Congress Cataloging in Publication Data

Whitaker, John C   1926–
  Striking a balance.

  (AEI-Hoover policy studies ; 21) (Hoover Institution
studies ; 57)
  1. Environmental policy—United States. 2. United
States—Politics and government—1969–1974. 3. United
States—Politics and government—1974–   I. Title.
II. Series. III. Series: Hoover Institution stud-
ies ; 57.
HC110.E5W53   301.31'0973   76-53775
ISBN 0-8447-3226-5

Printed in United States of America

To

Betty and the boys: John, Bob, Steve, Bill and Jim—
my six best reasons for a better environment.

Contents

Preface

In a way this book really began when my recently widowed mother moved our family from my birthplace on pristine Vancouver Island in British Columbia to the unsightly clutter, noise, and grime of a large U.S. eastern seaboard city. I was then an eight-year-old boy. The shock from seeing as a small child what seemed like mountains of rusting automobiles in junk yards, trash in gutters, and streams chock-full of cans and tires made a searing impression. I resolved to get back to the unspoiled world I had come from, never for a second accepting the challenge of cleaning up the new world that had been thrust upon me.

A way back to the wilderness was my goal, first as a child at summer camp in the rural beauty of Nova Scotia, then as a college student learning geology and seeing the wilderness wonders of Alaska on summer field trips with the United States Geological Survey. Later my career in geology gave me the opportunity to enjoy the breathtaking beauty of the high desert country of the Great Basin, the unspoiled sky and clear streams of the Rockies, the Cascades and the primeval rain forests of the Pacific Northwest, and, still later, the Andes, the Amazon jungles, the Nile, and the clean unspoiled beaches of West Africa.

First, I saw the environment only in traditional terms—seeking to conserve it as Teddy Roosevelt had done. But, by the late 1960s, like so many other Americans, I began to realize the obvious. Man could no longer retreat to ever-shrinking unspoiled areas to renew himself, but instead he must turn and face the challenge of improving the quality of life in our cities. Mother Nature had been abused perhaps to her limits. As Theodore White put it in an essay for *Life* magazine (June 26, 1970), "The two natural containers of the environment, the air and the water, finally vomited back on Americans the filth they could no longer absorb."

It has been one of life's great privileges to have served at the White House and the Department of Interior and to have had the chance to try to do something about the problem—to help lay out the legislative and administrative strategies for correcting the environmental abuses and to chart a natural resources development policy with environmental safeguards.

This book tries to tell that story. It focuses on the policy options available, explains why the decisions were made the way they were, and tries to sketch the political realities that sometimes limited the available courses of action.

Bethesda, Maryland
October 1976

Acknowledgments

Although I alone am responsible for the views expressed in this book, it could not have been written without the help of many people to whom I am most grateful. Some of them were participants in the weary but exhilarating succession of twelve-hour days needed to chart a new environmental and natural resources development policy. There is a curious tradition that authors never write down the names of *all* the people that helped them, either because space is at a premium or because someone may be forgotten. Neither reason is a good one when so many have been so generous with their time.

DEPARTMENT OF AGRICULTURE: Claude Gifford and Don Paarlberg.

COUNCIL ON ENVIRONMENTAL QUALITY: Edwin Clark, Steven Jellinek, and William Matuszeski.

ENVIRONMENTAL PROTECTION AGENCY: Elouise Agee, Alvin Alm, Thomas Alexander, John Quarles, Fred Smith, Jr., Eric Stork, and Roger Strelow.

FEDERAL ENERGY ADMINISTRATION: John Hill and Eric Zausner.

FEDERAL POWER COMMISSION: James Watt.

DEPARTMENT OF INTERIOR: William Avery, Dale Bajema, Mary Dee Beal, Gary Bennethum, Curt Berklund, Richard Bernknopf, Leonard Bikowski, Kenneth Brown, Austin Burke, Frank Clarke, Jared Carter, Henry Cooper, Henry Coulter, Richard Curry, Robert Davis, Hazel Dawson, Priscilla Dodenhoff, Dennis Drabelle, Walter Dupree, Frank Edwards, Hermann Enser, Gary Everardt, Warren Fairchild, Frederick Ferguson, James Flannery, Charlotte Floyd, Ruth Friedman, Hugh

Garner, Joseph Gorrell, Gerrie Green, Bernardo Grossling, Theodore Heintz, Lawrence Hoese, Betty Johnson, Dale Johnson, Gable Johnson, Betty Jones, Frank Kelly, Peter Kelsey, Sharon Kissel, Montis Klepper, Doris Koivula, John Kyl, Robert Landau, Hans Larsen, Signe Larson, Robert Lawton, Cleo Layton, David Lindgren, Norma Lodico, Percy Luney, William Lyons, Margaret Markert, Lance Marston, Harry McKittrick, Robert Milne, William Moffat, Charles Montgomery, John Morgan, Thomas Moritz, David Page, Dwight Patton, Ray Peck, John Powell, Allan Powers, Robert Presley, Leigh Ratiner, Nathaniel Reed, Heather Ross, Robert Schoen, Richard Schoepf, Eleanor Schwartz, John Spinks, Sondra Stevens, Thomas Teisberg, Edna Thompson, Ronald Walker, Peter Ward, David Watts, Russell Wayland, Douglas Wheeler, Ralph Williams, Kenneth Witt, Lee Woodbury, and Marie Zunic.

NATIONAL OCEANIC AND ATMOSPHERIC ADMINISTRATION: Richard Gardner and Robert White.

OFFICE OF MANAGEMENT AND BUDGET: Thomas Barry, Charles Bingman, Donald Crabill, James Currie, Earl Darrah, Norman Harkness, James Hyde, Roy Niemela, Wesley Sasaki, and Jim Tozzi.

DEPARTMENT OF STATE: Christian Herter, Jr.

WHITE HOUSE (past and present): Sally Dahler, Christopher DeMuth, Michael Duval, Daniel Kingsley, John Ehrlichman, Richard Fairbanks, Royston Hughes, Ray Price, Glenn Schleede.

OUTSIDE THE FEDERAL GOVERNMENT: David Branand of the American Mining Congress; Clarence Davies and Boyd Gibbons of Resources for the Future, Inc.; Mary Eldridge of Yarmouth, Nova Scotia; Darius Gaskins, assistant professor of economics, University of California (Berkeley); William Reilly, president of the Conservation Foundation; and William Vogley, professor of mineral economics, Pennsylvania State University.

I am also grateful to the two institutions that have supported the publication of this book—the American Enterprise Institute for Public Policy Research and the Hoover Institution on War, Revolution and Peace.

Finally, I want to thank my wife Betty, who shared my experiences at the White House, the Department of Interior, and in the writing of this book. She was profoundly loyal and my best constructive critic in her subtle, wifely way. While I labored over the manuscript, she used her considerable maternal talents to keep our five young boisterous boys at bay—boys who hopefully will never have to try to explain to their children how come there is an automobile tire in a trout stream.

1

Conservation/Environment:
Theodore Roosevelt to Richard Nixon

On October 18, 1968, near the climax of his presidential campaign, Richard Nixon spoke in Illinois and then flew on to a political rally in New Jersey. His thoughts, like those of his opponent Hubert Humphrey, were on the large issues of peace, prosperity, the rising crime rate, and inflation. On that day CBS aired a network radio address that Nixon had already recorded about "America's Natural Resources." It was one of eighteen radio addresses published near the end of the campaign in *Nixon Speaks Out*, a compendium of thirty-four position papers and statements covering the major issues of the campaign.[1] One radio speech on natural resources and the quality of our environment seemed adequate to cover an issue that stirred little interest among the electorate at the time. Attention was needed for the more important issues.

Nixon Speaks Out contained six major statements on foreign affairs, three on law and order, and five on the pocketbook issues.

In another Nixon campaign publication containing speeches, statements, issue papers, and answers to questions from the press, 64 pages were devoted to foreign policy and 110 pages to domestic policy, with only five of these covering environment, natural resources, and energy.[2] If the President-to-be showed little interest in the issue, so did the press. In fact, Nixon staff members do not recall even one question to the candidate about the environment.

---

[1] Richard M. Nixon, *Nixon Speaks Out: Major Speeches and Statements in the Presidential Campaign of 1968*, published by the Nixon-Agnew Committee, New York, N.Y., October 25, 1968.

[2] Richard M. Nixon, *Nixon on the Issues*, published by the Nixon-Agnew Committee, New York, N.Y., October 17, 1968.

1

In the Humphrey camp, things were just as quiet. The vice-president dedicated a park in San Antonio, Texas, on August 10 and the John Day Dam in Oregon on September 28, using both occasions to discuss the environment and conservation. Otherwise he said nothing on the issue.[3]

It seems hard to believe that only seventeen months after the election, on April 22, 1970, the country would celebrate Earth Day, a national outpouring of concern for cleaning up the environment. The next morning's *Washington Post* carried a page-one story headlined "Earth Day Stirs Nation," along with a picture of 5,000 people at the Washington Monument for a rock concert.[4] The *New York Times* proclaimed, "Millions Join Earth Day Observances across the Nation," over a page-one picture of thousands of New Yorkers walking in the spring sunshine on auto-free Fifth Avenue.[5] Union Square became the ecological headquarters of the city. The crowd heard speeches and visited booths on conservation, peace, clean air, water pollution, voluntary sterilization. According to the *New York Times,* "Thousands crowded into a block-long polyethylene bubble on 17th Street to breathe pure, filtered air. Before the enclosure had been open to the public half an hour the pure air carried unmistakable whiffs of marijuana."[6]

Earlier on Earth Day morning, Sacred Heart fourth graders participated in a Union Square clean-up—the brooms, shovels, and rakes provided by one of the city's major polluters, Consolidated Edison, which had braced for demonstrators outside its headquarters at Irving Place and 14th Street.[7]

Earth Day rolled on with lighthearted celebration all over the New York area. White Plains high school students painted the railroad station and landscaped its grounds.[8] Finch College students washed windows on a Lexington Avenue subway.[9] Thirty girls from Washington Irving High School, wearing surgical masks, collected trash and dragged clean white sheets along sidewalks to show how dirty they got.[10]

---

[3] Democratic National Committee news releases of August 10 and September 28, 1968.

[4] *Washington Post,* April 23, 1970, p. 1.

[5] *New York Times,* April 23, 1970, p. 1.

[6] Ibid., p. 30.

[7] Ibid., p. 1.

[8] Ibid., p. 30.

[9] Ibid.

[10] Ibid.

On the other side of the Hudson in Hoboken, a crowd dumped a coffin into the river. The coffin contained the names of America's polluted rivers.[11] At Fairleigh Dickinson University in Rutherford, New Jersey, students gathered to eulogize the "dead" Passaic River.[12]

And so it went across the nation. University of New Mexico students collected signatures on a plastic globe and presented it as an "enemy of the earth" award to twenty-eight state senators accused of weakening a recent environmental law.[13] In Syracuse, New York, students made plans to beat a car "to death." [14] At Indiana University, coeds tossed birth control pills at Earth Day crowds.[15] In Denver a parade of over 500 bicyclists and hikers rallied at the state capitol.[16] In Birmingham, Alabama, one of the worst air-polluted cities in the nation, the Greater Birmingham Alliance to Stop Pollution (GASP) held a "right to live rally." [17] At the University of Texas in Austin, the campus paper came out with a make-believe April 22, 1990, headline, "Noxious Smog Hits Houston: 6,000 Dead." [18] At Logan Airport in Boston, thirteen persons were arrested for defying orders to end demonstrations protesting noise pollution and the development of the SST, one of the few disturbances in an otherwise overwhelmingly peaceful and often forceful crusade of millions of people over the nation.[19]

The American business community endorsed Earth Day with some gimmicks (Consolidated Edison loaned New York Mayor John Lindsay an electric car) [20] and some practical actions of its own to deal with pollution abatement. Sun Oil announced plans to make throwaway containers that could be destroyed easily.[21] Texas Gulf Sulphur promised to reduce emissions from natural gas processing plants,[22] and Scott Paper announced plans to spend large sums on pollution abatement for plants in Maine and Washington State.[23] Reynolds Metal paid one-half

---

[11] Ibid.
[12] Ibid.
[13] Ibid.
[14] Ibid.
[15] *Washington Post,* April 23, 1970, p. 20.
[16] *Denver Post,* April 23, 1970, p. 1.
[17] *Washington Post,* April 23, 1970, p. 20.
[18] Ibid.
[19] *Washington Post,* April 23, 1970, p. 20.
[20] *New York Times,* April 23, 1970, p. 1.
[21] *Washington Post,* April 23, 1970, p. 20.
[22] Ibid.
[23] Ibid., p. 1.

cent for each salvaged aluminum can and sent trucks to fourteen states to pick up aluminum cans.[24]

But industry bore the brunt of the Earth Day criticism. A "grim reaper" picketed a Minneapolis auditorium and, inside, University of Minnesota students tried to interrupt a General Electric stockholders' meeting to read a denunciation of the corporation over a coffin filled with G.E. appliances.[25] In Philadelphia, Ralph Nader called industry the worst polluter, one that could be curbed only by a "radical militant ethic" among consumers.[26] The "polluters of the month" award from New Orleans college students went to the oil industry.[27]

So many politicians were on the stump that Congress closed down. The oratory, one of the wire services observed, was "as thick as smog at rush hour." [28] Earth Day attracted support from the entire political spectrum. Here is a sampling drawn from the *Washington Post* and *New York Times* the morning after Earth Day.

In a Bloomington, Indiana high school, Hubert Humphrey who, like Nixon, had barely touched on the issue in the 1968 campaign, urged that the United Nations "establish a global agency to strengthen enforcement and monitor pollution abatement throughout the world." [29] (A year and two months later in Stockholm, Sweden, the United Nations did take some of the steps Humphrey suggested.) Senator Gaylord Nelson, Democrat of Wisconsin and originator of the idea of Earth Day, told Denver college students "to campaign nationwide to elect an 'Ecology Congress' this year." [30]

Senator Edmund Muskie, Democrat of Maine, speaking at the University of Pennsylvania said, "The power of the people is in the cash register and we can resolve to purchase only from those companies that clean themselves up." [31] The man who was to become a presidential contender in 1972 continued: "A cleaner environment will cost heavily in foregone luxuries, in restricted choices, in higher prices for certain goods and services and in hard decisions about our national priorities." [32]

---

[24] *New York Times,* April 23, 1970, p. 30.
[25] *Washington Post,* April 23, 1970, p. 20.
[26] Ibid.
[27] Ibid.
[28] Ibid.
[29] *New York Times,* April 23, 1970, p. 30.
[30] *Washington Post,* April 23, 1970, p. 20.
[31] *New York Times,* April 23, 1970, p. 30.
[32] *Washington Post,* April 23, 1970, p. 20.

Senator George McGovern, Democrat of South Dakota, said to students at Purdue University that the government and industry would have to spend $150 billion in the next two decades to stamp out pollution.[33] McGovern was short of the mark—later the Council on Environmental Quality (CEQ) estimated that the nation would spend $217.7 billion from 1974 through 1983 for environmental improvement.[34]

Senator Birch Bayh, Democrat of Indiana, called for a "National Environmental Control Agency."[35] A few months later, on July 9, 1970, President Nixon proposed to Congress the establishment of the Environmental Protection Agency (EPA), and he presided at the swearing-in ceremony for the agency's first administrator, William D. Ruckelshaus, on December 4, 1970.

Paddling against the political current that day, Senator Gordon Allott, Republican of Colorado, voiced concern that "some extremists want to use the environment issue as one more club with which to beat America."[36] Many political observers felt that Allott's less-than-enthusiastic embrace of the environmental issue contributed significantly to his defeat in 1972 by Senator Floyd Haskell, Democrat of Colorado, who campaigned vigorously in favor of the environmental issue.

Nor were state officials about to let a good thing go by. In Annapolis, Maryland, Governor Marvin Mandel signed twenty-one bills and legislative resolutions dealing with the environment.[37] Illinois Attorney General William Scott announced that he would sue Milwaukee for polluting Lake Michigan.[38] The Michigan legislature voted citizens legal standing to press for suits on environmental grievances.[39] Massachusetts gave preliminary approval to a constitutional amendment to facilitate action against pollution.[40]

Governor Nelson Rockefeller was pictured in the *New York Times* riding a bicycle after speaking in Prospect Park in Brooklyn. The picture was captioned "a non-polluting vehicle." Earlier in the day, he had signed a bill coordinating state government pollution-abatement

---

33 Ibid.
34 Council on Environmental Quality (CEQ), *Sixth Annual Report* (Washington, D.C.: U.S. Government Printing Office, December 1975), p. 534, Table 10.
35 *New York Times,* April 23, 1970, p. 30.
36 Ibid.
37 Ibid.
38 *Chicago Tribune,* April 23, 1970, p. 1.
39 *New York Times,* April 23, 1970, p. 30.
40 Ibid.

and preservation functions under a Department of Environmental Conservation. New Jersey's Governor William Cahill signed a similar measure,[41] and Lt. Governor Paul Simon of Illinois urged the formation of an environmental institute at one of the state universities.[42]

Some audiences, students in particular, had a feeling they were being used by politicians trying to catch up to an already snowballing issue. Former Secretary of Interior Stewart Udall was heckled until he agreed to donate his $1,000 lecture fee to a Michigan State campus environmental action group.[43] Senator Edward Kennedy, Democrat of Massachusetts, was heckled at Yale [44] and Senator Charles Goodell, Republican of New York, was greeted at New York University with leaflets calling his speech "the biggest cause of air pollution." [45]

But, in general, everybody embraced this newest "motherhood" issue. Mayor Lindsay's reaction in New York was probably representative: "This is the first time I've walked down Fifth Avenue without getting booed half the distance." [46]

The Nixon administration reacted to Earth Day in many ways. Those around the President responded with the same kind of frenzied activity that characterized members of Congress. Cabinet and subcabinet members spoke across the country. The week ended with a televised symbolic clean-up of the Potomac River by White House staff members.[47] But Nixon remained aloof. That week White House proclamations appeared for National Archery Week and National Boating Week, but no proclamation for Earth Day. The President's reasons were clear. He felt his detailed thirty-seven point environmental message to Congress a few months earlier had substantively dealt with the pollution problem. A proclamation on Earth Day could be construed as grandstanding. He also saw in the environment issue a potential backlash effect in fewer jobs, slower economic development, and higher prices. He decided to remain quiet. In fact, a few days before Earth Day he had directed Secretary of Interior Walter Hickel to endorse the construction of the Alaskan pipeline, something that was

[41] Ibid.
[42] *Washington Post,* April 23, 1970, p. 20.
[43] Ibid.
[44] Ibid.
[45] *New York Times,* April 23, 1970, p. 30.
[46] Ibid.
[47] CBS-TV Evening News, April 25, 1970.

6

anathema to the activist core of dedicated environmentalists, in a speech Hickel was giving in Alaska on Earth Day.[48]

Hickel, who personally favored building the pipeline, was in a difficult position. As chief spokesman for the environment he would lose creditability by endorsing the Alaska pipeline. But as former governor of Alaska, he knew the majority of Alaskans favored the pipeline because of the large number of jobs involved. Typical of the sentiment were bumper stickers which appeared around the state saying, "Sierra Club, Go Home!"

There was little doubt that the Nixon administration took its licks on Earth Day. In a one-hour CBS-TV special, Walter Cronkite called Earth Day crowds "predominantly white, predominantly young, and predominantly anti-Nixon." Daniel Schorr noted that whereas the issue "could have united the young and the Administration," instead, "they went their polarized ways." Dennis Hayes, the twenty-five-year-old national coordinator of Earth Day who had "already hitchhiked his way around the earth and seen firsthand what man has done to his environment in the name of progress," told crowds that "we cannot save the environment as long as the war goes on." One young girl, who had publicly sworn never to bear children as part of her environmental crusade, called on a local rally to "dump Nixon. Maybe it won't work, but it's worth a try," and correspondent Dan Rather characterized the White House attitude toward Earth Day as "benign neglect." [49] But back on Capitol Hill, Congressman John Anderson, Republican of Illinois, chairman of the House Republican Conference, called on Democrats to "get down to earth" on Earth Day and to start congressional action on environmental quality bills introduced by President Nixon two months ago.[50]

How had it all happened and why? When Rachel Carson wrote *Silent Spring* in 1962,[51] few would have guessed that by the end of the decade the environment would erupt into a significant issue. Two candidates for President and the legion of newsmen that followed them had barely mentioned the issue in the campaign of 1968. Yet by the

---

[48] Department of Interior press release, April 23, 1970, accompanying Hickel's speech, "Be Part of the Solution—Not the Problem," delivered to University of Alaska students, April 22, 1970.

[49] CBS-TV Network Special, April 22, 1970.

[50] *New York Times,* April 23, 1970, p. 30.

[51] Rachel Carson, *Silent Spring* (Boston, Mass.: Houghton Mifflin Company, 1962).

Table 1
INCREASE IN PUBLIC CONCERN OVER POLLUTION, 1965–1970

Q: Compared with other parts of the country, do you think the problem of air/water pollution in your area is very serious or somewhat serious?

Year	Sample Size	Air	Water
1965	2,128	28%	35%
1966	2,033	48	49
1967	2,000	53	52
1968	2,079	55	58
1970	2,168	69	74

Source: Hazel Erskine, "The Polls: Pollution and Its Cost," *Public Opinion Quarterly,* Spring 1972, p. 121 (from Opinion Research Corporation).

Table 2
MOST IMPORTANT DOMESTIC PROBLEMS

Q: Aside from the Vietnam War and foreign affairs, what are some of the most important problems facing people here in the United States?

Problem	May 1971 Survey	May 1969 Survey	Significant Changes
Inflation/cost of living/taxes	44%	34%	+10%
Pollution/ecology	25	1	+24
Unemployment	24	7	+17
Drugs/alcohol	23	3	+20
Racial problem	22	39	−17
Poverty/welfare	20	22	
Crime/lack of law and order	19	15	+4
Unrest among young people	12	6	+6
Education	8	5	+3
Housing	6		

Source: Opinion Research Corporation, "Public Opinion on Key Domestic Issues," mimeographed (Princeton, N.J., May 1971), p. 17. May 1969 and May 1971 polls based on 1,508 and 1,506 interviews, respectively.

spring of 1970 there was this national outpouring called Earth Day. The polls trace the transformation.

It was not until 1965 that the issue was deemed important enough for the pollsters to ask about it. Over the five-year period leading up to Earth Day, the increase in public awareness of air and water pollution is striking (see Table 1).

Similarly, a comparison of Opinion Research surveys taken during May 1969 and May 1971 showed how concern for pollution and ecology had increased (see Table 2). In May 1971 fully a quarter of the public thought the issue of pollution and ecology was important, whereas only 1 percent had thought so just two years earlier. Also, "pollution/ecology" showed the most significant increase in public concern (24 percentage points) over the two-year period of any of the four top-rated domestic issues.

The public's concern over air and water pollution jumped in the Gallup polls from tenth place in the summer of 1969 to fifth place in the summer of 1970 and was perceived by the American public at that time as more important than race, crime, and teenage problems.[52] In December 1970, a Harris poll showed that Americans rated pollution as "the most serious problem" facing their communities.[53] And *Time* magazine named the environment as the issue of the year for 1970.[54]

To test further the public's awareness of environmental and related problems, Opinion Research Corporation sampled views on twenty-five such problems and recorded a sharp rise in public awareness over the year and a half from December 1969 to May 1971 (see Table 3). The foremost environmental problems in the public mind were air pollution, smog, pollution of lakes, rivers, and seas, mercury residue in fish and other foods, earthquakes, oil spills, and fish kills. In each case there was a significant shift upward in the public's awareness, with the increases ranging between a strong 21 percent and a very strong 73 percent.

Opinion Research also tested the importance of the environment issue along with nineteen important domestic issues (see Table 4). "Reducing air and water pollution" ranked fourth out of nineteen issues. It was considered very important by 79 percent of the total public and

[52] Gallup Poll, August 29, 1970.

[53] Louis Harris and Associates, December 26, 1970.

[54] *Time* Magazine, "Issue of the Year: The Environment," January 4, 1971, pp. 21-22.

9

Table 3

AWARENESS OF ENVIRONMENTAL PROBLEMS

Q: Which of these subjects have you heard or read a lot about in recent months?

Subject	May 1971 Survey	Dec. 1969 Survey	Significant Change
Unsafe drugs	92%	74%	+18%
Air pollution, smog	88	67	+21
Violent crimes	84	67	+17
Pollution of lakes, rivers, and seas	81	57	+24
Mercury residues in fish and other foods	76	3	+73
Earthquakes	75	33	+42
Automobile accidents	71	65	+6
Oil spills	66	30	+36
Fish kills	65	26	+39
DDT in animals and humans	51	45	+6
Cyclamates (artificial sweeteners)	51	62	−11
Coal mine explosions	48	22	+26
Changes in weather or climate	42	29	+13
Lead poisoning of children	39	16	+23
Radioactive wastes	29	16	+13
Thermal (heat) pollution of rivers	28	13	+15
Nuclear fallout	28	17	+11
Train or truck accidents involving dangerous substances	28	26	
Sonic booms due to aircraft	27	25	
Mid-air collisions of aircraft	25	32	−7
Underground nuclear explosions	23	26	
Silt build-up in harbors	21	13	+8
Military accidents involving poison gas	18	16	
Soil pollution of farms due to salt	13	8	+5
Strontium-90 in milk	11	8	

Source: Opinion Research Corporation, "Public Opinion on Key Domestic Issues," p. 17, based on 1,506 interviews.

Table 4
IMPORTANCE OF SELECTED DOMESTIC PROBLEMS

Q: As I read each of the items on this list, please tell me if you personally think it is very important, fairly important, or not too important.

Item	Very Important	Fairly Important	Total Important	Not Too Important	No Opinion
Combatting crime	89%	9%	98%	1%	1%
Holding down inflation	82	14	96	2	2
Holding down the unemployment rate	79	16	95	3	2
Reducing air and water pollution	79	14	93	5	2
Solving state and local problems like crime rates, run-down local services, or poor school systems	78	16	94	4	2
Providing adequate health care services for the American people	71	21	92	7	1
Training enough doctors	71	20	91	7	2
Making federal government operate more efficiently	69	22	91	4	5
Reforming the federal welfare system	67	18	85	8	7
Making federal operations more responsive to public needs	64	23	87	7	6
Working to restore and enhance the natural environment	63	25	88	8	4
Working to see that the people get more voice in how the country is run	62	24	86	10	4
Providing increased federal aid to education	59	24	83	13	4
Providing adequate living standards for the needy through welfare programs	48	29	77	17	6
Creating a national compulsory health insurance program	37	25	62	29	9
Sharing tax revenues with state and local governments	32	34	66	16	18

11

Table 4 *(continued)*

Item	Very Impor- tant	Fairly Impor- tant	Total Impor- tant	Not Too Impor- tant	No Opinion
Requiring zoning laws in suburban communities that permit lower or moderate income housing	30	33	63	25	12
Extending federal busing legislation to the whole country, not just the South	26	19	45	40	15
Passing laws to speed up racial integration of suburban communities	25	26	51	40	9

Source: Opinion Research Corporation, "Public Opinion on Key Domestic Issues," p. 17, based on 1,506 interviews.

fairly important by an additional 14 percent. "Working to restore and enhance the natural environment" ranked eleventh in importance, was regarded as very important by 63 percent of the total public and fairly important by an additional 25 percent.

Another index of the public's interest in the environment was a willingness to spend more government money on federal programs to improve the environment (see Table 5). Opinion Research showed that about three-fourths of the public support more government spending for air and water pollution abatement programs, that support exists in all population groups, and that it was particularly high among the young.

However, heightened concern and awareness over pollution and a desire for more government spending for pollution abatement programs did not mean that taxpayers had committed themselves to spending their own money to improve the quality of the environment. Spending for government programs never seems to equate with spending one's own money. Opinion Research reported that in May 1971 three-fourths of the public would pay *small* price increases for pollution control, but six out of ten people opposed *large* price increases for pollution control (see Table 6A).

But the phrase "large increase," without being specific about how much increase, may have scared off the respondent because a Roper poll asking respondents if they would pay 10 percent more for various pollution control measures received a favorable response (see Table 6B).

Table 5
SPENDING ON GOVERNMENT PROGRAMS

Q: Here is a list of various government programs. For each one would you tell me whether you think government spending should be kept at the present level, if spending should be increased, or if spending should be decreased.

Item	Spending Should Be Increased	Spending Kept at Present Level	Spending Should Be Decreased	No Opinion
Finding a cure for cancer	81%	16%	1%	2%
Air and water pollution	74	18	3	5
Anti-crime and law enforcement programs	74	19	2	5
More doctors and hospitals	72	22	2	4
Aid to education	69	23	5	3
Programs to enhance and restore our environment	56	30	4	10
Medicare	55	34	4	7
Low-income housing	50	30	12	8
Financial help to the cities	44	35	9	12
Farm support program	38	30	17	15
Highway building program	32	48	13	7
Rural development	32	39	9	20
Welfare programs	30	32	30	8
National defense	29	47	17	7
Space program	11	30	55	4
Financing Vietnam War	6	17	70	7
Foreign aid	2	23	68	7

Source: Opinion Research Corporation, "Public Opinion on Key Domestic Issues," p. 73, based on 1,506 interviews.

A Harris poll in 1971 indicated that 78 percent of the public would be willing to pay (how much was not specified) to have air and water pollution cleaned up and 48 percent would be willing to accept a 10 percent reduction in jobs for a cleaner environment.[55]

Poll editor Hazel Erskine indicated that individuals were not "personally anxious" to foot the bill for correcting pollution damage,

---

[55] Louis Harris and Associates, October 1971.

Table 6A
PERSONAL SPENDING FOR POLLUTION CONTROL

Q: Would you be for or against companies spending large sums of money on pollution control if this means a small increase [or large increase] in the prices they charge for their products or services?

	For	Against	No Opinion
A *small increase* in their prices	76%	17%	7%
A *large increase* in their prices	30	60	10

Source: Opinion Research Corporation, "Public Opinion on Key Domestic Issues," p. 134, based on 1,506 interviews.

although willingness to pay for pollution control is growing.[56] According to a Harris survey in 1965, only three or four out of ten were personally willing to spend any money at all for correction of air and water pollution. From 1967 to 1971, Harris surveys reported the numbers "willing to pay $15 a year more in taxes to finance a federal program to control air pollution" had moved from 44 percent to 56 percent.[57] Most other surveys showed that the proportion which would commit small amounts to battle pollution had risen well above half.

Congress received even stronger messages. Twenty-two congressmen, in a survey that reached about 300,000 Americans in varying kinds of congressional districts, asked their constituents if they were willing to pay more for pollution control. Respondents in all but three congressional districts answered affirmatively. Then-Congressman Gerald Ford asked, "Should the federal government expand efforts to control air and water pollution even if it costs you more in taxes and prices?" The message was clear: 68.3 percent yes, and 27.5 percent, no.[58] Congressman Ford voted to override President Nixon's veto on the Federal Water Pollution Control Act Amendments of 1972.[59] Nixon vetoed the

---

[56] Hazel Erskine, "The Polls: Pollution and Its Cost," *Public Opinion Quarterly,* Spring 1972, p. 120.

[57] The Council on Environmental Quality estimated 1973 per capita pollution abatement costs at $35 to $40 and projected 1976 costs of $80 per person. CEQ, *Fifth Annual Report* (Washington, D.C.: U.S. Government Printing Office, December 1974), pp. 176-177.

[58] *Christian Science Monitor,* December 23, 1971, p. 1.

[59] *Congressional Record,* October 18, 1972, pp. 37060-61; the vote was 247 to override, 23 to sustain. P.L. 92-500 (86 Stat. 816).

Table 6B
PERSONAL SPENDING FOR POLLUTION CONTROL

Q: A good many products in one way or another are contributing to the pollution of our air and water—and it will probably cost quite a lot to develop methods to prevent the pollution effects. Would you be willing to pay 10 percent more for [each proposition listed below] or do you think the problem is not that serious?

Item	Willing to Pay 10 Percent More	Problem Not Serious	Undecided
Detergents, if it turns out to be the only way to eliminate the pollution of water supplies	69%	17%	13%
Gasoline, if it turns out to be the only way to eliminate the pollution caused by automobile exhausts	68	16	15
An automobile, if it turns out to be the only way to eliminate the pollution caused by the exhausts	67	17	17
Electricity, if it turns out to be the only way to eliminate the pollution caused by power plants	64	22	14
Magazines and newspapers, if it turns out to be the only way to eliminate pollution caused by paper mills	60	20	20
Airplane tickets, if it turns out to be the only way to eliminate pollution caused by airplane exhausts	59	18	22

Source: The Roper Organization, Inc., October 1971, based on 2,000 interviews.

bill largely because of the very heavy federal expenditures included for sewage treatment plants. Not surprisingly, because the perspective almost always changes once in the oval office, President Ford tried unsuccessfully to hold down sewage treatment expenditures.[60]

The 1972 elections ended any speculation that the environmental issue lacked clout. New Yorkers approved $1.15 billion in bonds for

[60] In a January 24, 1975 letter to Environmental Protection Agency (EPA) Administrator Russell Train, President Ford allotted only $4 billion of the $9 billion available to the states for sewage treatment plant construction under the 1970 Federal Water Pollution Control Act. Later the Supreme Court ruled the allotment illegal and the remaining $5 billion was released to the states.

pollution control, Washington State voters backed $265 million, and Floridians $240 million, to clean up the environment.[61] The movement had come of age. Writing in the spring of 1972, poll editor Hazel Erskine summed up the rapid growth of the environmental issue this way: "A miracle of public opinion has been the unprecedented speed and urgency with which the ecological issues have burst into the American consciousness. Alarm about the environment sprang from nowhere to major proportions in a few short years." [62]

The Beginning: Unlimited Abundance

It is relatively easy, with the aid of polls, to trace the sudden emergence of the environmental issue, but why Earth Day, and what it symbolized in shifting public opinion, ever happened in the first place is harder to explain. The recent environmental movement in America is impossible to separate from its earlier relative, the conservation movement.

For about 300 years, successive generations of colonists and Americans methodically assaulted their environment without regard to what they were doing or for what would be left after they had done it. Americans were no different from their ancestors through 5,000 years of civilization who had abused their natural surroundings by over-cutting, overgrazing, overcropping, and even overcrowding. After all, America had 3 million or more square miles of the richest, most fertile land on the face of the earth. To conserve such abundance seemed pointless and so the pioneers cut, slashed, dug, and burned their way across the new nation, taking pride in a development mentality of "fruitful farms and flourishing cities." Indeed, the empty wilderness was viewed with the aversion present-day observers reserve for the inner-city ghetto.

Here and there, a few voices were raised in defense of nature. George Catlin first proposed a national park in 1832,[63] and George March in 1864 developed a notably perceptive analysis of man's widening impact upon ecological systems, particularly the effect of over-cutting on water, wildlife, and soil.[64]

---

[61] *Washington Post,* November 20, 1972, editorial page.

[62] Erskine, "The Polls: Pollution and Its Cost," p. 120.

[63] Roderick Nash, ed., *The American Environment: Readings in the History of Conservation* (Reading, Pa.: Addison Wesley Publishing Company, 1968), p. 5.

[64] Nash, *American Environment,* p. 13.

But by and large the unrestrained development of our natural resources, actively encouraged by government policy, continued well into the last quarter of the nineteenth century. The Homestead Act [65] induced settlers by the millions to invade the West, and the 1872 Mining Law [66] was a homestead act for prospectors with no provisions for environmental protection while mining the public lands.

End of an Era

By the 1880s, the damage to the land was beginning to show. Vast areas of timber had fallen victim to settlement, lumbering, and forest fires, which in turn led to soil erosion and loss of wildlife. Market hunters had killed off most buffalo, wild turkey, and all passenger pigeons. The 1890 census announced the closing of the frontier, a symbol of American opportunity and abundance for 300 years. No longer was the continent open-ended. For the first time America had boundaries. The earlier stirrings of conscience were reinforced by a more practical motive: the growing conviction that, after all, there really was a limit to our natural resources, a bottom to the barrel.

There were second thoughts about the period of vast industrial expansion that followed the Civil War, and a new and troubled mood spread. Society developed some ugly cracks: the inhuman treatment of the immigrants crowded in the slums of the eastern cities, the exploitation of western settlers by the railroads, and violence on the labor front. These were problems that earlier generations had escaped by removing themselves a few hundred miles to the West. But there was no longer any place to run. Disillusionment set in in the late 1880s, as it did much later in the 1960s when reactions against unrestricted growth seemed to be stirring. The meaning of "progress," as it had been touted for so many years, came to be questioned.

Conservation: First Movement

The conservation movement appeared, in a troubled time as a welcome opportunity for many Americans to involve themselves in a

---

[65] Chapter 75 (12 Stat. 392), May 20, 1862.

[66] Formally known as "An Act to Promote the Development of Mining Resources of the United States," Chapter 152 (17 Stat. 91), May 10, 1872.

positive, constructive effort. It was a chance to do battle with the forces of evil in defense of the good, the true, and the beautiful.

Such were the modest beginnings of the conservation movement in America. It materialized slowly with the joining of a number of separate environmental concerns, each moved by its own constituency, each concerned primarily with a single aspect of the whole problem. Carl Schurz, secretary of interior from 1877 to 1881, showed great concern for forest management although it would be ten years before Congress moved to set aside our first national forest reserve.

Protection of wildlife, of interest to both sportsmen and naturalists, led to the formation of the New York Audubon Society, which soon had a counterpart in every state. But it remained for a forester, Gifford Pinchot, to see first that conservation was an ecological system and not a series of separate problems championed by competing advocates. By Pinchot's own account:

> In plain words, a man by the name of Pinchot was riding a horse by the name of Jim on the Ridge Road in Rock Creek Park near Washington. And while he rode, he thought. . . .
>
> The forest and its relation to streams and inland navigation, to water power and flood control; to the soil and its erosion; to coal and oil and other minerals; to fish and game; and many other possible uses or wastes of natural resources—these question would not let him be. What had all these to do with Forestry? And what had Forestry to do with them?
>
> . . . Suddenly the idea flashed through my head that there was a unity in this complication—that the relation of one resource to another was not the end of the story. Here were no longer a lot of different, independent, and often antagonistic questions, each on its own separate little island, as we had been in the habit of thinking. In place of them, here was one single question with many parts. Seen in this new light, all these separate questions fitted into and made up the one great central problem of the use of the earth for the good of man.[67]

Pinchot and Theodore Roosevelt

More than any single individual, Gifford Pinchot deserves to be called the father of the conservation movement. This movement began at the turn of the century, flowered with Theodore Roosevelt's strong interest,

---

[67] Gifford Pinchot, *Breaking New Ground* (New York, N.Y.: Harcourt, Brace and Company, 1947), p. 322.

continued until it fell victim to the indifference of the Taft administration, and later became lost in the nation's larger concerns of World War I.

Pinchot's father was a founder of the Yale School of Forestry, and Gifford Pinchot followed his father into the profession, studying at the Ecole Nationale Forestière in Nancy, France. Returning to America in 1891, Gifford Pinchot made forest surveys in Arizona and Pennsylvania, became forester for the Vanderbilt estate at Biltmore, North Carolina, and opened a successful forestry consulting business. In 1898 he became chief of the Bureau of Forestry in the Department of Agriculture. At that time, however, the administration of national forests was vested in the Department of Interior, and it was not until 1905 that Pinchot was able to persuade Congress to transfer the federal forest reserves to the Department of Agriculture. He became chief forester of the newly named United States Forest Service.[68]

Under Pinchot, the national forests expanded from 38 million acres to more than 172 million acres.[69] Regulations were adopted on stream pollution, overcutting, forest fire prevention, and reforestation. In all these activities, Pinchot soon became the recognized leader of the American conservation movement.

Pinchot, a born showman and a gifted politician,[70] attracted the active interest and support of Theodore Roosevelt. In 1908, Pinchot prevailed on Roosevelt to call a White House Conference of Governors on Conservation. Roosevelt's welcoming address stated the growing national concern:

> This conference on the conservation of natural resources is in effect a meeting of the representatives of all the people of the United States called to consider the weightiest problem now before the nation; and the occasion for the meeting lies in the fact that the natural resources of our country are in danger of exhaustion if we permit the old wasteful methods of exploiting them longer to continue.
>   ... We have become great in a material sense because of the lavish use of our resources, and we have just reason to be proud of our growth. But the time has come to inquire seri-

---

68 Several attempts have been made by the executive branch to put the Forest Service back into the Department of Interior. Interior Secretary Ickes tried to do this but never received really strong support from Franklin Roosevelt. Later, President Nixon firmly advocated it but Congress did not respond (see Chapter 3).
69 By 1976, the national forest lands included 187 million acres.
70 Later, Pinchot was twice elected governor of Pennsylvania.

ously what will happen when our forests are gone, when the coal, the iron, the oil, and the gas are exhausted, when the soils shall have been still further impoverished and washed into the streams, polluting the rivers, denuding the fields, and obstructing navigation.[71]

The key feature of the conservation movement as articulated by Roosevelt and Pinchot was its utility. Its central theme was the proper management of natural resources for commercial purposes. But while this was the dominant theme, a number of discordant notes were contributed by John Muir and others, the philosophical antecedents of David Brower and Michael McCloskey,[72] who championed the cause of preservation as opposed to utilization. Muir emphasized that the conservation movement should be as much concerned with the quality of the environment as with the stock of physical resources to be managed.

John Muir, Scottish geologist, naturalist, and author, seemed a conventional although very bright young man. He was raised on a Wisconsin farm and graduated from the University of Wisconsin. But then he vanished into the grand American wilderness for virtually a lifetime, coming to sight occasionally when his "bread money" gave out. He walked around the Great Lakes, covered the Ohio Valley south to the Gulf of Mexico, and penetrated the swamps of Florida. He visited Cuba, crossed the Isthmus of Panama, and came to California in 1868. For ten years, he led an isolated life in the Sierra Nevadas making the Yosemite Valley his home. More than anyone, Muir developed the theory of glacial scouring to account for the origins of Yosemite Valley, and he discovered sixty-five residual glaciers in the Sierra Nevadas. For two years he was part of a geodetic survey team exploring the Great Basin of the West. In 1879, he went to Alaska and discovered Glacier Bay. In 1881, he pushed north to the Arctic Ocean. He saw the headwaters of the Yukon and the MacKenzie. He published about 150 articles, most of them in popular periodicals like *Harper's* and *Century* magazines and in the *San Francisco Bulletin*.

John Muir is best remembered as the foremost advocate of protecting our trees through the preservation of wilderness areas. He

---

[71] Theodore Roosevelt's Opening Address, *Conference of Governors Proceedings May 13-15, 1908* (Washington, D.C.: U.S. Government Printing Office, 1908), pp. 3 and 8.

[72] David R. Brower was executive director of the Sierra Club (its first) from 1952 until 1969 and is now president of Friends of the Earth. J. Michael McCloskey is currently the executive director of the Sierra Club.

helped establish Yosemite and Sequoia National Parks, and the large Sierra forest reservation. He and other exponents of wilderness preservation articulated the largely unspoken views held by a great number of people. Their ideas included the notion that natural beauty is important to man and must be preserved, that the solitude and tranquility of nature are needed by people who have little enough of it in their daily lives, and that humans need to remind themselves occasionally that they are kin to every living thing. There was instinctive concern among many people for preserving the quality of the environment. Some support came from the more utilitarian leaders of the conservation movement interested in resource management, but not enough to satisfy the demands of the preservationists. Muir, who had originally joined with Pinchot to fight the timber interests on overcutting, watershed protection, and reforestation, later split with him, regarding Pinchot as hopelessly utilitarian.

Nothing could have divided the two groups as much as the issue of damming a pristine river, and that is the way it is today. The early conservation movement eventually came apart at the high-noon confrontation over damming the Hetch Hetchy Valley at the lower end of Yosemite Park to create a drinking-water reservoir and site for hydro-electric power for San Francisco.

By this time, 1913—with Teddy Roosevelt gone from the White House—much of the steam had gone out of the movement. In terms of public concern, it was never to reach the same peak again until Earth Day, 1970. Yet, in spite of a decline in public concern, the environmental ethic had taken root and much of importance had been accomplished. Nationwide forest-fire protection became a reality. Federal soil conservation work began. Major flood-control programs got under way along the Mississippi. Construction started on the Boulder Canyon project—the first federally sponsored, large-scale, multiple-purpose river basin development. A network of migratory bird sanctuaries was organized. And, in 1916, the National Park Service was created.

Franklin D. Roosevelt

The second Roosevelt in the White House put thousands of idle people back to work on the land in the 1930s, in what was one of the best conservation investments this country ever made. The top soil remaining on drought-ridden farms from Texas to North Dakota was blowing

21

away rapidly, and Roosevelt embarked on a wholesale effort to repair the mounting damage to the nation's land, forests, and watercourses. Within a month of his inauguration he established the Civilian Conservation Corps that at various times employed 300,000 to 400,000 workers. Thousands of miles of roads and trails were built, more than a billion trees were planted, thousands of roadside parks were created, trail shelters were built, and millions of acres benefitted from soil erosion and flood control measures.

The Tennessee Valley Authority (TVA) was another landmark in the utilitarian conservation era of Franklin Roosevelt. It was the most ambitious project ever taken in government planning. Ironically, the Boulder Canyon project, nurtured by individualist Herbert Hoover, served as a precedent and something of a limited prototype for TVA. Even for the New Deal, TVA was an extraordinary intrusion of centralized government planning into the preserve of the private sector. It transformed a whole region—its economy, the living habits of the people, its population balance and social structure. TVA became a byword for regional planning throughout the world.

World War II and Later

Conservation remained in limbo during World War II. When activity resumed, it was focused at first, as it had been in Theodore Roosevelt's time, on supposedly impending shortages of resources. The President's Materials Policy Commission of 1952 made recommendations to avert the shortages it foresaw.[73] But supplies of commodities remained ample and, in some cases, excessive, so no fundamental policy changes occurred. With immense economic progress following World War II, the problem in the 1950s and 1960s did not seem to be related to shortages but, if anything, to sheer abundance. Pollution became unconscionable. Each year America was throwing away 80 million tons of paper and paper products, 100 million automobile tires, 60 billion cans, 30 billion glass bottles, and millions of junked automobiles and major appliances; and in 1969 the total solid wastes produced by the United States reached 4.3 billion tons.[74]

---

[73] U.S. President's Materials Policy Commission, *Resources for Freedom: A Report to the President* (Washington, D.C.: U.S. Government Printing Office, 1952), 5 volumes.

[74] CEQ, *First Annual Report* (Washington, D.C.: U.S. Government Printing Office, August 1970), pp. 107-108.

Americans acted as if their rivers and lakes could absorb sewage and industrial wastes indefinitely. In the middle 1960s one of three Americans was not served by a sewage system at all and of the two-thirds who did have a sewage system, 60 percent had inadequate treatment.[75] In 1948, in the industrial coal town of Donora in western Pennsylvania, thousands became ill and twenty deaths were attributed to air pollution.[76] In London in 1952 a "killer smog" settled over the city and deaths mounted to 1,600 above normal.[77] By 1968, the United States was choking from air pollution. Over 200 million tons of the five main classes of pollutants (carbon monoxide, particulates, sulfur oxides, hydrocarbons, and nitrogen oxides) were being pumped into the nation's air each year. Episodes of heavy air pollution in New York, in Los Angeles, and in the supposedly pristine mountain air of Denver and Salt Lake City caused genuine concern, discomfort, increases in illness and even deaths, especially among older people.

Noise and pesticides, although less obvious, were becoming vaguely menacing to Americans. The roar of the jet age and the din of freeways and city traffic pounded ears unceasingly, and an estimated 16 million American workers were threatened with ear damage.[78] Evidence mounted that pesticides killed shellfish, fish, and birds, and had caused cancer in test animals. The very development of pesticides, one of man's greatest achievements in increasing agricultural productivity, gave pause for concern.

Open space was dwindling in the tide of suburban sprawl. Two million acres of land a year were being taken out of agricultural use. Each year about 160,000 acres were being paved over by highways and airports, about 420,000 acres became reservoirs and flood control projects, and another 420,000 acres were being developed for urban use.[79]

As Americans traveled in their automobiles, which had doubled in number from 1950 to 1970, they saw garish road signs, fields of junked automobiles, choked and dying streams, overgrazed and eroded hills and valleys, and roadsides lined with endless miles of beer cans, pop bottles, and the tinfoil from candy wrappers and cigarette packages.

[75] Ibid., p. 35.
[76] Ibid., p. 67.
[77] Ibid.
[78] Ibid., p. 124.
[79] Ibid., pp. 173-174.

They could no longer move a few hundred miles West; the frontiers were gone.

The idea of conservation was replaced by campaigns for environmental protection. Concern for the quality and preservation of the environment finally overcame the strict utilitarian concept of conservation. The ghost of John Muir was at work and a good deal more.

Rachel Carson's *Silent Spring* had set loose an avalanche of literature on the effects of various man-made compounds upon the ecological systems of the earth. Everything was aired, discussed, debated, and shouted about: pesticides, fertilizers, oil spills, sulfur dioxide emissions, acid drainage from mines, thermal pollution from nuclear power plants, plus just about everything bad said about radioactivity since Los Alamos.

But why? Why, for example, had the environmentalist awakening been so long delayed? Why when it came was it so much more advanced in the United States than in other countries? What factors motivated millions to so much activity? Where did the movement get its support?

First, the environmental movement probably bloomed at the time it did mainly because of affluence. Americans have, of course, been relatively much better off than people of other nations for the past hundred years, but nothing in all history compares even remotely to the prosperity we have enjoyed since the end of World War II, and which became visibly evident by the mid-fifties. An affluent economy yields things like the forty-hour week, three-day weekends, the two-week paid vacation, plus every kind of labor-saving gadget imaginable to shorten the hours that used to be devoted to household chores. The combination of spare money and spare time created an ambiance for the growth of the causes that absorb both money and time. Another product of affluence has been the emergence of an "activist" upper middle class—college-educated, well-heeled, concerned, and youthful for its financial circumstances. The nation has never had anything like it before. It is, in fact, a conflict in terms—a mass elite. It is sophisticated, resourceful, politically potent, and compulsively dedicated to change, to "involvement." It forms the backbone of the environmentalist movement in the United States.

There are, of course, things besides affluence that have contributed to the movement during the past decade. One is television and the opportunities it provides for advocacy journalism. It will be years before we can assess the full impact of this medium upon the thinking of the American public. Science has contributed another—and

24

unique—dimension to the national agitation. To the obvious signs of pollution that people could see, feel, and smell, science added a whole panoply of invisible threats: radiation, heavy metal poisons, chlorinated hydrocarbons in the water, acidic radicals in the atmosphere—all potentially more insidious, more pervasive, and more dangerous than the familiar nuisances. This could happen only in a country able to support a large, advanced scientific community. It takes an immense laboratory infrastructure, marvelously sensitive instruments, intensive funding, computers, data banks, and vast interchanges of information to be able to isolate and trace the progress through the ecosystem of elements and compounds at concentrations measured in parts per billion, and to establish their effects upon living organisms in the biosphere. Only a handful of nations even could aspire to do it.

The press served the pollinating function of a honey bee, transporting the latest scientific findings to the public which reacted with fear and misgivings. These were relayed by the press back to the scientific community which was stimulated by public concern to intensify its investigations, leading to more discoveries of new perils, and so on. The result was that vastly more was known and noted about pollution in the United States than in any other country, and this in itself provided a climate in which support for environmentally related causes could be elicited.

Finally, one can speculate, there was the absence during this period of any competing great challenge to capture and mobilize the energies of the people—no frontiers to be tamed, no more empires to be built, no great patriotic war to be fought, not even any hard times to be shared and endured. The effort to save the environment offered purpose and commitment to millions of people, old and young, who very much needed to be doing something positive to relieve the feelings of guilt, boredom, and rootlessness that seemed to be the unwanted by-products of the prosperity and economic security of the fifties and sixties.[80]

The feverish pitch of Earth Day was to pass. By 1976 the environmental movement had not gone away but, instead, like the civil rights movement of the sixties, had begun to succeed, at least to be institutionalized, and there was simply less and less to talk about. But even

[80] For additional background speculating on the reason for the tide of public opinion favoring environmental issues, see Robert Leider, *Nothing but Blue Skies* (Annapolis, Maryland, Proceedings of the United States Navy, June 1972), pp. 27-34; and Clarence Davies, *Setting the Agenda* (in publication).

more fundamental, the way of thinking changed. The old custom of endorsing growth without regard to the quality of that growth seemed forever behind us. The failure of the economy to take into full account the social costs of environmental pollution was beginning to be rectified. Not only were environmental considerations now factored into federal government decision making through the National Environmental Policy Act, but over and over again Americans paid for low-polluting or pollution-free products like low-sulfur heating oil, unleaded gasoline, and coal from fully reclaimed strip mines, for automobile emission controls, for electricity from cleaner fuels, and for more parklands. More fundamentally, the nation began to understand what Gifford Pinchot thought as he rode a horse in Rock Creek Park in the nation's capital—that the environment was an interdependent whole of which man was only a part.

2
The Beginning

At this writing it has been seven years since President Nixon handed the author the job of putting together the first presidential message to Congress on the environment. Surely seven years is sufficient time to reflect and let emotions cool. Yet there is still only one word, *hysteria*, to describe the Washington mood on the environment issue in the fall of 1969. The words *pollution* and *environment* were on every politician's lips. The press gave the issue extraordinary coverage,[1] Congress responded by producing environment-related bills by the bushel, and the President was in danger of being left behind.

On May 29, 1969, Nixon announced the formation of a cabinet committee called the Environmental Quality Council.[2] Dr. Lee DuBridge, science adviser to the President, was named executive secretary, and the staff to support the cabinet committee was provided by the Office of Science and Technology, which DuBridge also directed.

Nixon held cabinet meetings on such subjects as pesticides, outdoor recreation, air pollution standards, and development of a low-pollution unconventional automobile engine. But the meetings left him dissatisfied. There was too much scientific jargon. Only bits and pieces of issues were tossed at him. There was no overall strategy. Should enforcement be by regulation, or by user fees, or a combination of both? What were the overall costs to industry and the consumer, in terms of

---

[1] According to the Public Issues Research Bureau, even a year later, for the twelve-month period October 1970 to September 1971, a survey of 20,904 editorials in five leading newspapers showed that the environment was the major domestic issue of editorial concern. (*New York Times,* January 16, 1972, p. 65.)

[2] Created by Executive Order 11472, which also established the Citizens' Advisory Committee on Environmental Quality, with Laurance S. Rockefeller as chairman.

the increased price of products for various pollution abatement schedules under varying standards and regulations? Finally, what effects would the various clean-up scenarios have upon the federal budget? None of these fundamental questions was being answered.

There are several reasons why this cabinet committee, like nearly all others, was ineffective in recommending a comprehensive program to the President. First, cabinet officers are likely to be ineffective because they lack time to do creative homework, and often have a tendency simply to reject or endorse options given to them by their staffs, rather than participating in the creation of alternative strategies. Even more serious, with a broad issue like that of the environment, no one is in charge. No single department has enough expertise to take overall leadership. Finally, in the specific case being considered here, the Office of Science and Technology failed in its role of staff coordinator because it was working on so many projects that efforts on the environmental issue tended to be diluted and because it lacked the necessary expertise. Its staff, although of high scientific capability, did not include scientific specialists who could deal with each discrete environmental issue. Nor did it include legal experts to deal with enforcement strategies or economists to assist in cost-benefit studies. Most important, the federal establishment had to have a signal that the environment issue was a concern of the President—that a maximum effort was needed. The Office of Science and Technology was not perceived to be close to the President, but John Ehrlichman was.

Putting Ehrlichman in charge, with the author reporting to him, gave the system "clout." Ehrlichman saw the President regularly and came back with firm yes or no answers or, more often, requests for still more analysis. Probably equally important, Ehrlichman was "pro environment." A land-use lawyer in Seattle before joining the Nixon administration, he understood the complexities of the environmental issue and the various regulatory strategies that could be employed and had a healthy respect for the cost of these alternatives. Whatever else history may say about John Ehrlichman, those who worked closest to the oval office on the environment issue know that he was a staunch advocate of environmental quality and that a great deal was accomplished by his effective advocacy. Like Nixon, he had no illusions about the politics of the environmental concern. The activist core of the environmental movement could always outpromise the administration, either on federal spending or on "stiff and tough" (even if tech-

28

nologically impossible) legislative proposals. However, there was broad-based support for environmental quality among both sexes, in all age and income groups, and among both liberals and conservatives. And as we have seen (Chapter 1), next to the two traditionally highest-ranking issues, foreign affairs and the pocketbook concerns, environment ranked as one of the most important issues. Finally, the President had an even chance with the press on the issue. He might not get much credit, but without strong action there would be plenty of blame.

The President's Environmental Message
Task Force

The author did not put together the environment task force, he inherited one, a very good one. The credit should go to Egil Krogh, who handled the environment issue under Ehrlichman for the President briefly in the summer of 1969, when it became apparent to Nixon that neither the cabinet committee nor the staff of the Office of Science and Technology was progressing on the issue to his satisfaction. The author took over leadership of the task force in late August 1969. Its members were bright and young, with the stamina routinely to put in twelve- to fourteen-hour days. They were led by the author's assistant, Christopher DeMuth, a recent A.B. from Harvard who had been brought to the White House by Patrick Moynihan, a former Harvard professor. DeMuth later became a lawyer and served on the Secretary of State's Advisory Committee on the 1972 United Nations Conference on the Human Environment. Other members went on to distinguished careers in the federal government. James Hyde, who handled hours of tedious negotiations for the Bureau of the Budget on what ultimately became twenty-three legislative proposals, later became deputy assistant director of the Office of Management and Budget (OMB) for legislative reference. Glenn Schledee, an examiner with the Bureau of the Budget, later became an associate director of the White House Domestic Council staff. John Quarles, then an assistant to Interior Undersecretary Russell Train, became deputy administrator of the Environmental Protection Agency (EPA). Others who went to EPA were Alvin Alm, then a budget examiner for water pollution and water resource development programs for the Bureau of the Budget, who became assistant administrator for planning and management; Roger Strelow, then on the staff of

29

the National Air Pollution Control Administration at the Department of Health, Education, and Welfare (HEW), who became assistant administrator for air and waste management; and Charles Elkins, also a budget examiner at the Bureau of the Budget, who became deputy assistant administrator of EPA for noise control; Darrell Trent, on the White House staff at that time, who later became executive director of the Property Review Board and deputy director of the Office of Emergency Preparedness; Daniel Kingsley, then with the General Services Administration (GSA), who later became a member of the White House staff and then associate administrator for operations at the Small Business Administration; Raymond Price, who wrote drafts of the President's first environment message and later was promoted to direct all presidential speech writing. Other members were James Schlesinger, then assistant director for the Bureau of the Budget who became, successively, chairman of the Atomic Energy Commission, director of the Central Intelligence Agency, and then secretary of defense; and James Lynn, then general counsel of the Department of Commerce who became, successively, the undersecretary of commerce, secretary of housing and urban development, and director of the Office of Management and Budget.

The task force system worked where the cabinet committee administered by the Office of Science and Technology had failed because (1) it had access to the President through Ehrlichman, and, when necessary, directly to the President; (2) each member was either a specialist in his field or had at his disposal for as long as needed the particular specialist required; (3) each member was close enough to his secretary so that the cabinet officer knew what was going on and what issues were in contention; and finally (4) speaking with the President's backing, the author made it clear to each cabinet officer that the task force member from his department was on call full time and that completing the President's environment section of the state of the union message and his special message to Congress on the environment were their highest, and if necessary, only priorities.

The task force system did have shortcomings that the creation of a Council on Environmental Quality (CEQ) eliminated. Task force members often had to let other work in their departments slip, and at times they had to take positions against the interests of their departments, knowing that they had to go back and "live" with people of different persuasions.

30

By the long Thanksgiving weekend in November 1969, the task force was able to supply President Nixon with a sixty-five-page outline of preliminary recommendations for his environmental message to Congress, scheduled for early February 1970. Mr. Nixon studied the recommendations over the weekend at Key Biscayne, scribbled marginal notes, and gave the task force its first guidance. Five major areas were covered in the report.

1. A New Department of Environment and Natural Resources. President Nixon was acutely aware of the extent to which responsibility for the environment was dispersed throughout the government. At cabinet meetings he had watched Secretary Robert H. Finch at HEW and Secretary John A. Volpe at the Department of Transportation (DOT) argue over which department should take the lead in developing an unconventional low-polluting automobile. On pesticides, Secretary Walter J. Hickel at Interior and Secretary Finch at HEW had argued for tighter pesticide controls, while Secretary Clifford M. Hardin at Agriculture emphasized the increased crop productivity resulting from the application of pesticides. Secretary of State William P. Rogers was concerned that one effect of a ban on the use of DDT in this country might be to restrict the supply of DDT to the developing countries. Hickel wanted vastly larger amounts of money and a new method of financing for water pollution control, but was opposed by Robert Mayo, director of the Bureau of the Budget, and other economic advisers. Maurice Stans at Commerce was wary of tighter pollution controls and what effect this might have on corporate profits. Dr. Paul McCracken, chairman of the Council of Economic Advisers, had the same concern plus another one: Would the United States be at an economic disadvantage competing in the international market if its product prices reflected the costs of pollution abatement standards that were more stringent than those of other countries? And so it went. There was hardly a cabinet officer around the table who did not have a stake in the pollution issue. Even the postmaster general joined the debate, offering to use postal cars to test an experimental fleet of low-pollution vehicles.

The task force report to the President highlighted the problem of fragmented responsibility.

> The federal government spends billions of dollars annually on programs to protect or enhance the environment. It spends

31

billions more on activities which are not so designed but which nonetheless have profound environmental consequences (highways and location of federal facilities, for example). Yet there is no single member of the President's Cabinet with responsibility for the environment, and programs are dispersed almost haphazardly among the departments. In recent years the Secretary of the Interior has become de facto Secretary of the Environment, yet these concerns have not penetrated far into the Department—beyond the Secretary's Office. At any rate, he does not have control over many of the most important environmental programs, and he has many unrelated responsibilities.[3]

To emphasize the archaic government organization pattern, the report added that "the emblem of the Department [of Interior] is still the bison, a species decidedly remote from the most urgent current environmental problems."

The task force report also presented the case against establishing a Department of Environment and Natural Resources.

There are many who believe that, while an Environment Department is wholly desirable and probably inevitable, it would be premature to establish the department at this time. Briefly stated, the argument is that we have not yet developed sufficiently a precise idea of what we mean by "environmental protection and development," and that the creation of a single department in such circumstances could lock the federal government into a course which could, in time, prove obsolete or even counterproductive.

In addition, the proposal might create political difficulties for the administration. A truly comprehensive department would include the Forest Service from the Department of Agriculture and the Corps of (Civil) Engineers from the Department of Defense, both politically sensitive agencies with powerful and possessive congressional patrons. A less politically risky alternative was offered to Nixon—"at a minimum, the name of the Department of Interior could be changed and its statement of purposes revised, the Bureau of Indian Affairs transferred to HEW, and the Air Pollution Control Administration transferred to the new department." But Nixon scribbled "good idea" next to the full Department of Environment and Natural Resources option, thus signaling

---

[3] This quotation and all others in this chapter from the task force report are contained in a November 25, 1969, memorandum for the President, "Recommendations for Environment Message," by Christopher DeMuth.

that he was prepared to take the political heat. Later (see Chapter 3) the concept was altered: an Environmental Protection Agency and a Department of Natural Resources were proposed, and the idea of a Department of Environmental and Natural Resources was dropped.

2. Air Pollution. President Nixon agreed to a recommendation to begin federal development and procurement of unconventionally powered low-pollution experimental automobiles. The task force advised him that, given available and foreseeable technology, automotive emissions could be reduced gradually until the late 1970s and early 1980s, but that thereafter, barring unforeseen developments in the internal combustion engine, total emissions would begin to increase again because of the increased numbers of vehicles in use. In the cabinet, Transportation Secretary John Volpe, Health, Education, and Welfare Secretary Robert Finch and Science Adviser Lee DuBridge all backed the program, but Nixon had doubts. He believed the federal effort would lack the technical competence and funds that Detroit could bring to bear to solve the problem.[4] Besides, he was fed up with the infighting to control the proposed program between Finch, whose department had authority to set auto emission standards, and Volpe, whose department already had a program to design experimental cars to improve safety and study alternative power sources.[5] But the task force's view—ultimately accepted by Nixon—was that, left to itself, the automobile industry was unlikely, because of its enormous investment in the internal combustion engine, to make a heavy investment in alternative low-pollution power sources. So, an outside force was needed to demonstrate to the public that a very low-pollution vehicle was possible. Finally, federal sponsorship might stimulate commercial production of such vehicles in competition with the existing automobile industry.

In addition, Nixon backed a plan to reduce substantially the emissions from existing automobiles by authorizing the secretary of HEW to regulate automobile fuel consumption and additives and by strengthening the inspection procedures. The plan included (1) requiring auto manufacturers to make emission tests of a statistically repre-

---

[4] After seven years and $54 million, there has been no significant breakthrough in reducing emissions using unconventional power sources. Nixon may have been proved right.

[5] Nixon finally decided to put Russell Train, at the time chairman of the Council on Environmental Quality, in charge of the program to avoid giving control to either Finch or Volpe.

sentative sample of vehicles coming off the assembly line, (2) testing vehicles at assembly plants and dealerships with federal equipment, and (3) requiring certification of all new vehicles for compliance with federal emission standards. The President also agreed to a tightening of the 1973 and 1975 model-year emission standards. He invited automobile executives to a cabinet meeting to comment on the proposed standards, and although they protested that the standards could not be met because the technology was lacking, he stood by the task force recommendations. In his environmental message he said: "These new standards represent our best present estimate of the lowest emission levels obtainable by those years." [6] As we shall see (Chapter 5), Congress legislated even more stringent emission standards, which it later had to rescind when it became clear that the technology for achieving them did not exist.

Nixon also endorsed recommendations to control pollution from stationary sources, like industrial and electric power plants. These two sources, combined, were responsible for about 85 percent of the sulfur oxides that cause respiratory irritation and threaten human health at certain concentrations. They also were generating over half of the particulate matter that contributes significantly to dirty air.

Yet, under existing law,[7] enforcement was cumbersome and slow. The enforcement method, like that employed for water pollution, consisted of convening a conference of state and federal pollution control agencies, and, if subsequent recommendations were ignored, bringing federal suits against polluters. Unless pressed by the force of public opinion, states seemed unwilling to use adequate enforcement powers. Industrial polluters could threaten to move their facilities— meaning jobs and taxes—to other states if tough standards were enforced. At best, the most an industrial polluter feared from the federal government was a cease-and-desist order which carried an inconsequential fine and could be delayed for years. So Nixon backed a task force recommendation for nationwide air quality standards, rather than standards applying only within air quality regions. No longer, then, would an industrial polluter be able to threaten to move

---

[6] *Public Papers of the Presidents of the United States, Richard Nixon, 1970,* Special Message to the Congress on Environmental Quality, February 10 (Washington, D.C.: U.S. Government Printing Office, 1971), p. 101.

[7] The Clean Air Act of 1963, P.L. 88-206 (77 Stat. 392), December 17, 1963, as amended in 1965; P.L. 89-272 (79 Stat. 992), October 20, 1965; and P.L. 90-148 (81 Stat. 485), November 21, 1967.

to a state with more lax air quality standards. The states would have the option of providing standards even tighter than the national standards. Under the task force recommendation, they would have nine months to give the federal government a plan to meet at least the national standards; and if the plan were judged inadequate, the federal government was authorized to design a state-wide plan and enforce the standard. The President also backed a legislative proposal, over the protests of the Department of Commerce, giving the federal government the authority to levy fines up to $10,000 per day for noncompliance.

In addition, Nixon supported national emission standards for new stationary sources emitting pollutants like asbestos, beryllium, and cadmium that could be harmful to health. More funds were added for manpower training to strengthen state air control agencies. Finally, research funding in the control of sulfur dioxide emissions was increased when the task force report pointed out that fossil fuels used in electric power plants generated about 45 percent of the sulfur dioxides and industrial facilities produced another 40 percent. Despite increases in the number of nuclear power plants, the number of fossil fuel power plants was expected to triple by the end of the year 2000.

3. Water Pollution. The task force pointed out that, unlike the situation in air pollution where the technology was lacking to reduce auto emissions and to lower sulfur dioxides in fossil fuels, no technological breakthroughs were required to clean up the nation's waters. All that was needed was money, huge amounts of it. In the four years since the Clean Waters Restoration Act of 1966,[8] federal appropriations for constructing municipal treatment plants had totaled only about one-third of authorizations. Not until FY 1970 had federal funding taken any major leap upward—from $214 million to $800 million.[9] The report argued that much more money was needed. It recommended an investment of about $10 billion in federal, state and local funds over a five-year period, to be provided either by increasing appropriations in the existing grant program or, as Secretary Hickel wanted, through federal contracting authority in the amount of $10 billion to repay

---

[8] P.L. 89-753 (80 Stat. 1246), November 3, 1966.

[9] A strong campaign for increased funding was carried out by organized labor, the League of Women Voters and environmental groups. The House appropriated $600 million, the Senate $1 billion, and the conference compromised on $800 million.

the principal on municipal bonds sold to finance waste treatment plants (see Chapter 4).

Other major task force recommendations called for:

—Changing the rigid allocation formula for municipal waste treatment plants, so that the secretary of the interior could disperse funds to those areas where facilities were most in demand or where the greatest improvement in water quality would result, for example, by construction of large regional waste treatment plants.

—Requiring as a condition of receiving a federal grant to construct a municipal waste treatment plant that a user fee be charged to industries sufficient to cover the cost of treating industrial wastes. There was no reason why the general public should support the cost of treating industrial waste and user charges would provide incentives to reduce pollution and excessive water use.

—Providing authority for the secretary of the interior to oversee state water quality standards for "all navigable waters" rather than only interstate waters.

—Extending authority over water quality standards to include interstate ground waters as well as surface waters.

—Requiring that municipal treatment plants be built to prescribed design, operation and maintenance standards, because in the past many federally financed plants were poorly designed, without plans for expansion and improvements in technology, while other plants had not been operated to full capacity or properly maintained.

—Increasing financial support for state water pollution agencies.

—Most fundamental of all, taking action to increase and speed up enforcement powers against polluters. As in the case of air pollution, the task force reported that the states had little incentive, except for public opinion, to stop water pollution. They would have to impose large costs on local governments and industries. Industries could pack up and take their payrolls and taxes elsewhere if strong standards were enforced. Also, states were timid about enforcing tough water pollution standards on large interstate rivers and lakes unless they were sure that other states bordering the same waters had similar standards. As the President later put it in his environmental message to Congress: "As controls over interstate waters are tightened, polluting industries will be increasingly tempted to locate on intrastate lakes and rivers—with a consequently increased threat to those waterways—unless they, too, are brought under the same strictures. I propose . . . a simple but profoundly significant principle: that the nation's waterways belong to all of us, and that neither a municipality nor an industry should be allowed to discharge wastes into those waterways beyond their capacity to absorb the wastes without becoming polluted." [10]

But the federal government's ability to take action was not much better than that of the states. Federal enforcement was impossibly cumbersome. First, the secretary of the interior had to call conferences and hearings and wait one year before he could request the attorney general to bring suit to secure a pollution abatement schedule. Even then, any industry or municipality with reasonably competent legal help could stall on a cease-and-desist order for months, even years, knowing that an ultimate contempt-of-court citation was a minor inconvenience compared to the cost of installing the pollution abatement equipment needed to comply with water quality standards.

The task force recommended, and Nixon agreed to, quicker enforcement actions, including fines up to $10,000 per day for failing to meet water quality standards or implementation schedules, and authority for the secretary of the interior to seek immediate injunctive relief in emergency situations (including water pollution hazards or irreversible damage to water quality).

4. Cleaning Up Federal Facilities. A task force idea that Nixon strongly endorsed was the issuing of an executive order requiring that all federal facilities conform to then-existing air and water quality standards. The order stated that all facilities had to comply by the end of 1972—and thus committed the federal government to a $359 million program to achieve this objective.[11] The order also required that all

---

[10] *Public Papers of the Presidents, Nixon, 1970,* Special Message to the Congress on Environmental Quality, pp. 99-100.

[11] At the time, the cost of cleaning up federal facilities was underestimated. The task force did not anticipate the stringent standards and tight timetables, with the resulting escalating costs, of the Clean Air Amendments of 1970 and Water Pollution Control Act Amendments of 1972. In FY 1972 outlays for air and water pollution abatement in federal facilities were $488.4 million, while outlays for all forms of pollution abatement were $570.7 million.

federal facilities built in the future must be pollution-free and that funds must be included for air and water pollution control at time of construction. The task force report made the point bluntly:

> This is not simply an abstract issue: local newspaper articles on pollution often carry photographs of federal installations belching black clouds of soot into the air, or polluting the rivers. Presumably, the meaning of this is not lost on industrial polluters or citizens' conservation groups. If the Administration undertakes a major commitment to reduce air and water pollution without accelerating abatement of federal facilities, opposition leaders could well be handed an embarrassing issue, which could undermine both the Administration's credibility and its chances of succeeding in what it sets out to do. In such situations, arguments about "cost effectiveness" are unlikely to be widely persuasive.

"A must," the President wrote. "We can't ask industry and states and cities to act if we don't set an example." [12]

5. Outdoor Recreation. The task force reported that only about 3 percent of federal lands and 25 percent of federal recreational areas were situated within convenient reach of large metropolitan areas; parks were simply not near where most people lived. Moreover, only middle and upper income groups could enjoy them: the "minimum entrance fee" was a family car and $200 in your pocket to get there and home again. As Nixon later said in his environmental message to Congress,

> Thousands of acres in the heart of metropolitan areas were reserved for only minimal use by Federal installations. . . . Until now the uses to which Federally-owned properties were put has largely been determined by who got them first. As a result, countless properties with enormous potential as recreation areas linger in the hands of agencies that could just as well—or better—locate elsewhere. [13]

The solution to this problem adopted subsequently (see Chapter 9) was to create the Property Review Board but, at the time, the task force proposed the appointment of a Presidential Commission on Utilizing Military Lands for Parks to recommend ways for making certain military reservation lands available for parks or new towns, and perhaps, in

---

[12] Noted in the margin of Christopher DeMuth's memo to the President on the environmental message, November 25, 1969.

[13] *Public Papers of the Presidents, Nixon, 1970,* Special Message to the Congress on Environmental Quality, p. 106.

some cases, turning the land back for private development. Nixon had his eyes on the jewel of the United States Army's properties, San Francisco's Presidio, which he wanted to see turned into a city-owned park. However, Bryce Harlow, his chief congressional liaison adviser, told him that the Armed Services committees of both the House and Senate would oppose this adamantly. Instead of a piecemeal approach that focused on military lands only, a better strategy would be to establish a full-time presidential commission with a full-time staff to convert military and other federal properties into urban parklands, Harlow suggested. The President, however, was less concerned about the Armed Services committees and determined to go ahead. "Sounds OK—but don't let this be an excuse to delay actions on items which obviously should be disposed of," he wrote.[14]

Converting federal property into urban parks, although a good way to bring parks closer to where people lived, was only a partial answer. Much more money to acquire lands and to develop recreational facilities was needed. The Land and Water Conservation Fund, established in 1964,[15] was authorized annual appropriations of $200 million to buy lands for the National Park System and to establish a matching grant program for states and cities to acquire and develop their own parks, but in the Johnson years obligations to the fund had lagged far below authorizations (see Table 7). Nixon increased the Land and Water Conservation Fund from $200 to $300 million. Later he proposed establishment of the first urban national parks in New York and San Francisco harbors. But by 1976 even the $300 million annual funding level seemed inadequate to finance the growing need for urban parks (see Chapter 9).

The President's Environmental Message to Congress

During December and January, as the February deadline for the President's environmental message to Congress approached, internal squabbles became more intense. Interior Secretary Hickel wanted long-term financing of parks (Chapter 9) and municipal waste treatment plants (Chapter 4), but President Nixon, although sympathetic to the idea,

---

[14] Noted in the margin of Christopher DeMuth's memo to the President on the environmental message, November 25, 1969.
[15] P.L. 88-579 (78 Stat. 897), September 3, 1964.

Table 7

OBLIGATIONS TO LAND AND WATER CONSERVATION FUND,
FY 1965–FY 1969

(in thousands of dollars)

	1965	1966	1967	1968	1969 [a]
Federal	$1,458	$13,726	$ 47,233	$ 43,381	$147,653
State grants	204	14,064	81,498	72,097	71,750
Total	$1,662	$27,790	$128,731	$115,478	$219,403

[a] The sudden increase in federal obligations in FY 1969 is because P.L. 90-545 permitted the obligation of $85,513 million to purchase much of Redwoods National Park.

Source: Personal communication from OMB.

finally rejected it on the advice of his economic advisers. Secretary Stans at the Commerce Department voiced opposition to the injunctive procedures and stiff fines in the proposed water and air pollution legislation. Nixon turned him down but did go along with Stans's idea for a National Industrial Pollution Control Council, a group of industrial executives and their engineers to consult with government on pollution abatement.[16] Everybody had pet proposals, including the President, who wanted a special fee or tax placed on cars to cover the cost of moving abandoned or junked cars to steel mills. Several times Nixon ended meetings on his environmental message to Congress by asking how his proposal was coming along. Ehrlichman, DeMuth and the author resisted the idea because there was no way of establishing a proper fee, given fluctuations in the price of steel. When steel prices were high, no incentive was needed to get cars to steel mills, but when prices were low the incentive fee would have to be very high—perhaps $50 per car, politically a painfully high price. But the President insisted the matter not be dropped, and his message said, "I have asked the Council on Environmental Quality to take the lead in producing a recommendation

---

[16] Later the council was discontinued, when Congress failed to appropriate FY 1974 funds. Many members felt there was a potential for conflict of interest ("fox in the chicken coop" or "sending the goat to guard the cabbage patch") in asking industrial polluters to advise federal regulators on pollution abatement. However, the author thought the council performed the worthwhile function of bringing federal and corporate pollution control abatement engineers together, better to understand their mutual technical problems.

for a bounty payment or other system to promote scrapping of all junked automobiles." [17]

Arguments have a way of getting resolved by deadlines. By 3 A.M. on February 10 the President's final draft of the environmental message went to the mimeograph machine so that it could be in the hands of the press by 9:30 A.M. (but embargoed until 12 noon when Congress would receive it). All the arguments were over, at least for a few weeks.

In retrospect, the proposals of the Nixon task force might seem modest. Strip mining, land use, control of pesticides and noise, and a tax to reduce sulfur dioxide, for example, had been either incompletely studied or not even thought of at the time of the President's message. Nor were any very useful cost-benefit studies of various pollution abatement scenarios available. That came later when Congress began to increase the environment budget and tighten pollution standards beyond what the President proposed. However, what was completely missed during the study was how proposed air pollution legislation would ultimately come into conflict with energy requirements. The task force report made only vague reference to the problem, but with an emphasis on pollution control rather than potential energy shortages: "The President should . . . promote coal gasification and give the highest priority to air pollution problems in its decisions regarding the use of natural gas. Finally, since oil imports could provide a substantial quantity of low-sulphur oil, any decision on oil imports should carefully consider effects on reducing air pollution." No one understood then that natural gas would be in such short supply in a few years that, rather than promoting its use to improve air quality (as the task force report suggested), the administration would be advocating, because of energy shortages, a switch from clean natural gas to high-sulfur coal and a lowering of air quality in the process. Nor was any concern expressed that tighter automobile emission standards would mean poorer gasoline mileage—after all, gasoline was plentiful and cheap. And why not suggest to the President more imports of low-sulfur oil? Imported oil was cheap, plentiful, and the Persian Gulf suppliers seemed dependable enough.

In spite of these shortcomings, it was a beginning and, in the author's opinion, a remarkable one. A set of conditions existed simultaneously that allowed the federal government to do something that

---

[17] *Public Papers of the Presidents, Nixon, 1970,* Special Message to the Congress on Environmental Quality, p. 95.

it rarely does well—respond quickly to a problem. The President was interested and wanted to move, and so did Congress. A dedicated group of fine young people was able to work long hours to pull together a bewildering set of issues that were the responsibility of agencies scattered throughout the federal bureaucracy. The group produced a coherent set of recommendations that emerged as a comprehensive, thirty-seven-point program encompassing twenty-three separate pieces of legislation and fourteen administrative actions. Nixon could say without exaggeration on television and radio the day he sent his environmental message to Congress: "This is the most far-reaching and comprehensive message on conservation and restoration of natural resources ever submitted to Congress by a President of the United States." [18]

---

[18] Ibid.

3

New Federal Institutions for Energy and Environment

Reorganization of the federal government has been a concern of modern American presidents. President Eisenhower took a group of scattered agencies and formed the Department of Health, Education, and Welfare (HEW). After "Sputnik" had pricked America's pride in its scientific supremacy, he also created the Office of Science and Technology in the Executive Office of the President. President Kennedy gave the chairman of the Civil Service Commission the lead role in establishing government-wide personnel policies. President Lyndon Johnson took the fiercely competitive bureaus, offices, and other fiefdoms that had grown up over the years to represent the various modes of transportation and molded them into one Department of Transportation (DOT).[1] He drew together another group of agencies to form the Department of Housing and Urban Development (HUD) and created the Office of Economic Opportunity (OEO), the advocacy agency for the poor.

But President Nixon went the furthest. He eliminated the Department of the Post Office, replacing it with a public corporation free of political patronage. He merged the Peace Corps and Vista into one agency called Action. He created the Environmental Protection Agency (EPA), the National Oceanic and Atmospheric Administration (NOAA), the Federal Energy Office (FEO), and later the Federal Energy Administration (FEA). Finally he proposed that the Atomic Energy Commission (AEC) be abolished, with most of its functions going to two new agencies, a Nuclear Regulatory Commission and an Energy Research and Development Administration; both were created by

---

[1] However, Johnson was unable to get Congress to move the Maritime Administration into the new Department of Transportation.

law after Mr. Ford became President. In the Executive Office of the President, Nixon created the Office of Management and Budget (OMB), the Domestic Council, the Office of Telecommunications Policy, and the Council on International Economic Policy. Just as important as creating new institutions, he eliminated from the Executive Office of the President the Office of Science and Technology,[2] the National Council on Marine Resources and Engineering Development, the National Aeronautics and Space Council, and the Office of Emergency Preparedness. Nixon also accepted and used effectively a Council on Environmental Quality (CEQ), which was established in the Executive Office of the President on the initiative of Congress.

But Nixon's most ambitious proposal failed. He proposed that the Departments of State, Defense, Treasury, Justice, and a smaller version of Agriculture be retained,[3] and that the remaining seven departments and several agencies should be combined into four new ones: Community Development, Human Resources, Natural Resources, and Economic Affairs. When Congress failed to act, Nixon moved administratively to appoint four "super cabinet" officers—reflecting the four functional departments he had in mind.[4] He then installed them in the Executive Office Building to serve as his major advisers and, above all, as referees and coordinators of a government that had become so big and complex that it was nearly impossible to run it in the old style. Theodore White describes Nixon's view:

> the President shared a central recognition that the Office has become the Administrative center of too many conflicting interests. Congress has, over generations, solved too many problems by establishing special bureaus, special commissions, special agencies—and then dumped them all on the President for resolution of conflicts. Bureaus, Commissions and Agencies have become so numerous, so captive to the interests they were set up to guide, so fossilized in statutes, that their supervision

---

[2] But in June 1975 President Ford proposed legislation to create a similar organization, the Office of Science and Technology Policy, and on May 11, 1976, he signed the National Science and Technology Policy Organization and Priorities Act of 1976, P.L. 94-282 (90 Stat. 459), thus reversing Nixon's decision.

[3] Nixon had originally proposed eliminating the Department of Agriculture, then modified the proposal under constituency political pressure, but still recommended reducing the department's proposed size from 85,600 employees and annual outlays of $8.7 billion to 28,000 employees and annual outlays of $5.2 billion.

[4] See Richard Nathan, *The Plot That Failed* (New York, N.Y.: John Wiley and Sons, 1975), for a good description of Nixon's attempts to use his cabinet members as managers of the broad functions of government.

by a solitary individual executive is impossible—no single cabinet officer can supervise the energy problem, for example—not Interior, not Commerce, not Defense, not Agriculture, not State. Only the President can put it all together. No single office can make policy on the clash of American races—not HEW, not HUD, not the Department of Justice, not the Labor Department, not the Civil Rights Commission. Only the President can make national policy which is at once moral, wise and workable. No single Federal agency can master wages, prices, inflation—not Treasury, not the Federal Reserve Board, not the Labor Department, not the Council of Economic Advisers, not Agriculture. Only the President can.

All of which means that the Office has become one in which greater and greater power has to be concentrated—some such reorganization must take place—whether by elevating the Constitutional Vice-President to Executive Vice-President, or by repackaging all agencies and departments into groups linked by functions, or by means yet to be devised.[5]

In his book on political reform, *Washington Post* reporter David Broder quotes John Gardner, former secretary of HEW, on why government reorganization plans have often failed:

As everyone in this room knows, but few people outside Washington understand, questions of public policy nominally lodged with the Secretary are often decided far beyond the Secretary's reach by a trinity consisting of (1) representatives of an outside lobby, (2) middle-level bureaucrats, and (3) selected members of Congress, particularly those concerned with appropriations. In a given field, these people may have collaborated for years. They have a durable alliance that cranks out legislation and appropriations on behalf of their special interests. Participants in such durable alliances do not want the departmental secretaries strengthened. The outside special interests are particularly resistant to such change. It took them years to dig their particular tunnel into the public vault, and they don't want the vault removed.[6]

This "iron triangle"—composed of the vested interest, select members of Congress, and the middle-level bureaucracy—runs the federal government. To attempt fundamental reorganization of the government is to take on a political fight almost impossible to win. The lobbyists do not want change. After all, many have spent their adult

---

[5] Theodore White, *Breach of Faith—The Fall of Richard Nixon* (New York, N.Y.: Atheneum Publishers and Reader's Digest Press, 1975), pp. 338-339.

[6] David Broder, *The Party's Over* (New York, N.Y.: Harper and Row, 1971), p. 163.

lives getting to know the players in the other two corners of the triangle. The bureaucrats do not want change. No matter how often they are assured that they will not lose their jobs when they are transferred to some new and strange department, they are bound to worry. Then there is the uncertainty of who their new boss will be. Finally, the members of the congressional committees resist change since the longer they hold their committee assignments, the more influence they can exert on the departments under their jurisdiction. Jamie L. Whitten, Democrat of Mississippi, twenty years in the House and chairman of the Agriculture Subcommittee of the Committee on Appropriations, saw four secretaries of agriculture come and go. The turnover in that post is usually much higher: two secretaries, Ezra Benson and Orville Freeman, each served for the unusually long period of eight years. Otto Passman, Democrat of Louisiana, assumed the chairmanship of the Foreign Affairs Subcommittee of the House Committee on Appropriations in 1955 and, in the next two decades, worked with five secretaries of state, including one, Dean Rusk, who served an eight-year term. Cabinet officers typically serve three or four years,[7] whereas the ranking senators and congressmen on the authorization and appropriations committees usually work their way up the congressional seniority ladder over a ten- or fifteen-year period. Consequently, if they do their homework they probably know more about a department than its cabinet officer, and their staffs generally know precisely where to go in the department to get the information they want, often before the secretary knows.

Nixon believed government should be organized around functions rather than on the basis of programs heaped on programs, many outmoded and often unconnected. He wanted his cabinet officers to be less the special pleaders, reflecting narrowly based interest groups, and more the broad-based officials setting priorities. This thinking was at odds with the tendency of the Congress to divide and redivide its body into narrower and narrower interest areas. The number of standing congressional committees had grown from 34 in 1946 to 297 in 1975.[8] Broder attributed this phenomenon in Congress to "new demands on

---

[7] President Nixon appointed thirty-one cabinet officers to the twelve major departments and gave cabinet status to seventeen more advisers. President Truman made twenty-two cabinet appointments, President Eisenhower twenty-one, President Kennedy thirteen, and President Johnson twenty.

[8] The Legislative Reorganization Act of 1946 reduced the number of standing committees in the House and Senate from eighty-one to thirty-four: Chapter 753 (60 Stat. 812), August 2, 1946. The 1975 figure is from *Congressional Monitor,* April 30, 1975.

government, combined with the insatiable empire-building of individual lawmakers, the desire of every man to be a king of his own dunghill." [9] As a result, the congressman—like the other two corners of the "iron triangle," the middle-level bureaucrat and the special-interest lobbyist— has little or no chance to think and choose in terms of broad priorities. He can only perfect and fertilize, through the appropriation process, a few blades of grass—never seeing the whole lawn.[10]

As the lawmaker perfects his narrow specialty, the President, acutely aware of the problem of priority setting, is robbed of the balanced advice he should receive from his cabinet officers who have also become captured in the iron triangle. Presidents react like any manager. They want to put one person in charge of a job—one person for the environment, another for energy. But it cannot be done without government reorganization, and presidents are left bewildered and frustrated.

Joseph Califano, President Johnson's chief domestic adviser, set up a ceremony for the signing of the 1964 Wilderness Act. Secretary of Interior Udall was invited, but Secretary of Agriculture Freeman was overlooked because the White House staff forgot that wilderness areas could be carved out of national forests (under the Department of Agriculture) just as they could from national parks (under the Department of Interior).[11] In a cabinet meeting the author saw President Nixon direct Attorney General John Mitchell to take charge of the drug problem, thinking in terms of law enforcement. Secretary Robert Finch of HEW had to remind the President that his department had responsibility for the rehabilitation phase of drug control. It is almost impossible to put one man in charge. Seldom if ever in modern government can a problem be solved by only one department, unless the departments have been enlarged to encompass broader functions.

This chapter reviews the decision-making process within the administration that led to the creation of various environment and energy-oriented organizations.

---

[9] Broder, *The Party's Over*, p. 163.

[10] Congress took steps in 1974 to reform its piecemeal budget process. Pursuant to the Budget Act of that year (P.L. 93-344, July 12, 1974), Congress began in the spring of 1975 to set an overall spending target and to estimate the surplus or deficit for the next fiscal year. Under the required procedure, if by the fall of the year the total of all individual spending bills exceeds the spending target, Congress must cut spending, or raise new revenues, or increase the budget.

[11] Joseph Califano, Jr., *A Presidential Nation* (New York, N.Y.: W. W. Norton and Company, Inc., 1975), p. 22.

The Council on Environmental Quality (CEQ)

The Council on Environmental Quality was invented by Congress, not the administration, but it served the President's needs well. As we have seen (Chapter 2), the interagency task force formed to work full time on Nixon's first environmental message to Congress had its problems. The members had to devote much of their time to other responsibilities in their agencies. Often they had to take positions against the interest of their departments, knowing this would not be forgotten by their departmental colleagues once the President's message was delivered to Congress and the heady days of working in the White House office complex were over. But most important, year-round, thoughtful staff work was needed to create sound environmental legislation.

Early in May of 1969 Nixon created a cabinet-level Environmental Quality Council, staffed primarily by the Office of Science and Technology. But here, too, neither the cabinet members and their staffs, nor the experts drawn from the Office of Science and Technology, were able to give the task their single-minded attention. As a result, the cabinet committee also proved to be an ineffective vehicle for addressing the environmental issue.

The National Environmental Policy Act of 1969,[12] which passed Congress in December, established within the Executive Office of the President a full-time, three-member CEQ, appointed by the President and confirmed by the Senate. The act provided for: (1) preparation by CEQ of an annual report assessing the quality of the environment; (2) review by CEQ of the programs of the federal government to implement the policy of the bill "to use all practicable means—to create and maintain conditions under which man and nature can exist in productive harmony and fulfill the social, economic and other requirements of present and future generations of Americans"; (3) the sleeper requirement that an environmental-impact statement should be prepared by any agency proposing "major federal actions significantly affecting the quality of the human environment"; [13] (4) appropriations of $300,000

---

[12] P.L. 91-90 (83 Stat. 852), January 1, 1970.

[13] At the time the bill was signed, no consideration was given to the federal costs of preparing environmental-impact statements, to the cost to consumers of the added environmental stipulations for federally sponsored construction, nor to how the new law could be used as an instrument of litigation to delay or stop federal projects that required federal permits.

in FY 1970, $700,000 in FY 1971, and $1,000,000 per year thereafter. (The budget reached $2,750,000 by FY 1976.)

Within the White House there was little debate about recommending that the President sign the bill. A three-person council was an inefficient form of organization—one head of the operation would have been preferable—but it was hardly worth a veto, especially because the veto would probably be overridden.

There was the inevitable jurisdictional dispute in Congress. The bill was primarily the work of Senator Henry Jackson, Democrat of Washington, chairman of the Senate Interior and Insular Affairs Committee, and Congressman John D. Dingell, Democrat of Michigan, chairman of the House Merchant Marine and Fisheries Committee. But the Senate Public Works Committee had demanded a major role in the environmental action since it had jurisdiction over federal water and air quality legislation. Presidential politics was also involved since Senator Edmund Muskie, Democrat of Maine, chaired the Public Works Subcommittee dealing with air and water quality and did not want the credit to go to Jackson, his rival for the presidential nomination. Muskie had his own bill, which provided for establishing in the Executive Office of the President an Office of Environmental Quality, headed by a director and deputy director appointed by the President and confirmed by the Senate. The administration opposed the creation of two statutory bodies in the Executive Office of the President, both serving as advisers to the President. This would only increase confusion, conflict, and duplication of effort. Finally, Senators Jackson and Muskie worked out a compromise. Its essence, apart from preserving their respective committee jurisdictions, was to create a complementary organization that would supposedly mesh into an integrated agency in the Executive Office of the President. Thus, the CEQ created in the Jackson bill would be concerned with policy considerations, while the proposed Office of Environmental Quality in the Muskie bill would function as a staff for the new council. In the signing statement on Jackson's bill (the National Environmental Policy Act), the President tried to get Muskie to back off:

> I know that Congress has before it a proposal to establish yet another staff organization to deal with environmental problems in the Executive Office of the President. I believe this would be a mistake. No matter how pressing the problem, to over

organize, to over-staff, or to compound the levels of review and advice, seldom brings earlier or better results.[14]

Later, when Muskie's bill passed,[15] Nixon signed it anyway because it contained many favorable provisions relating to pollution from oil and ships. The problem of the duplicative Office of Environmental Quality in the Muskie bill was solved by simply not activating the office.

Nixon signed the National Environmental Policy Act on New Year's Day in the middle of a holiday weekend—traditionally a time of little news when bowl games, and year-end wrap-up stories leave editors still struggling for hard news. So when Nixon called reporters into his San Clemente office and signed the bill, he made front-page news around the country. He gave credit to Jackson and Dingell and then said, "It is particularly fitting that my first official act of the new decade is to approve the National Environmental Policy Act—the 1970's absolutely must be the years when America pays its debt to the past by reclaiming the purity of the air, its waters and our living environment. It is literally now or never." [16]

The President had only one reservation about the bill. He already was planning to propose the establishment of an Environmental Protection Agency or a Department of Environment and Natural Resources. If these plans worked out, there would be less need for a coordinating function for environmental policy in the White House. Nixon did not particularly like the idea of institutionalizing into the law a permanent council whose advisers, over the long run, could be counted on to be pushed by their natural constituency always to advocate an environmental position, and probably an extreme one. Eventually their advice would become predictable and therefore likely to be useless to future presidents. Also, if there were a council of advisers for the environment, why not a council for transportation, civil rights, Indians, blacks, welfare planning—indeed why not for any issue that required coordination between departments? It would be better, in Nixon's view, to recast the departments around broad functions to reduce the coordination needed and thereby reduce the size of the White House staff.

---

[14] *Public Papers of the Presidents, Nixon, 1970,* Statement about the National Environmental Policy Act of 1969, January 1, 1970, p. 3.

[15] The Water Quality Improvement Act of 1970, P.L. 91-244 (84 Stat. 91), April 4, 1970.

[16] *Public Papers of the Presidents, Nixon, 1970,* Statement about the National Environmental Policy Act of 1969, p. 2.

In retrospect, CEQ was a success. Three good men were appointed to get it off to a good start: Russell Train, a well-known conservationist who, besides being an articulate advocate of the environmental concerns, had a talent for picking bright young people for his staff; Robert Cahn, a respected conservation reporter with the *Christian Science Monitor*; and Dr. Gordon MacDonald, a brilliant atmospheric physicist and former vice-chancellor for research and graduate affairs of the University of California, Santa Barbara.[17]

CEQ's strength was that it had very little operational responsibility. Its thoughtful professional staff could spend its time creating sound environmental legislation and conducting or contracting for research on important environmental questions. CEQ also played the lead role in negotiating international commitments on the environment for the administration.

Some environmental groups and some members of Congress felt that CEQ members should always advocate the environmental view and speak out on issues regardless of the President's policy. But advisers to the President who allow themselves the luxury of advocating a narrow constituency viewpoint will soon find their influence diminishing.

CEQ in fact fought many battles within the administration and won. Its guidelines for environmental-impact statements, much to the chagrin of other departments, often delayed federal construction projects until more stringent environmental controls were applied and a better understanding of the environmental consequences of particular federal actions had been obtained. The Cross-Florida barge canal construction was halted by President Nixon at the urging of CEQ Chairman Russell Train, John Ehrlichman, and the author, over the protests of the Army Corps of Engineers. CEQ also influenced the decision to halt construction of the Tocks Island reservoir on the Delaware River, again over Corps of Engineer objections. CEQ studies of poisons used to kill predators led to an executive order barring the use of poisons on all public lands except for emergency situations.[18] This order was strongly opposed by the Department of Agriculture and elements of the Department of Interior. Another CEQ study led to a presidential proposal on limiting ocean dumping that later became law, and ultimately it led to an international convention to control ocean dumping. At CEQ's urging,

---

[17] MacDonald, along with classmates Secretary of State Henry Kissinger and former Defense Secretary James Schlesinger, graduated summa cum laude at Harvard.
[18] Executive Order 11643, signed February 8, 1972.

the secretary of transportation agreed to reject the Minarets road proposal, which could have led to development of the environmentally fragile high Sierra country in California. The chairman of the CEQ also served on the Property Review Board and forcefully advocated, over other departments' objections, the transfer of federal properties to local governments to be converted into park lands.

By 1976 CEQ probably passed the zenith of its influence on the Executive Office of the President, primarily because so much had been accomplished that the institution had tended to work itself out of a job. Nearly all the major legislation, much of it created by CEQ and sent to Congress, had either become law or was under active congressional consideration by the time Nixon left office. The advice CEQ gave to President Ford did, as Nixon had expected, become so routinely predictable as to be discounted or taken for granted. In the author's opinion a time will come, probably by 1980, when CEQ should cease to exist. By then, if the job has been well done, protection of the environment will be built into federal decision making and the executive branch will not need an environmental watchdog. But almost anyone from the Washington-based iron triangle environmental constituency would disagree with this statement and that is why, Washington being what it is, the CEQ will probably exist long after its useful life is over.

The Environmental Protection Agency (EPA)

In the task force studies in the winter of 1969–70 that led to Nixon's February 1970 environmental message to Congress, considerable thought was given to reorganizing the government to handle environmental problems better (see Chapter 2). At that time the author favored sending legislation to Congress to create a Department of Environment and Natural Resources (DENR) that would include the existing Department of Interior, the water planning functions from the Corps of Engineers, the Rural Electrification Administration, the Soil Conservation Service and the Forest Service from the Department of Agriculture, the oceanic and atmospheric agencies of the government (later to become the National Oceanic and Atmospheric Administration, NOAA), and finally, the environmental monitoring, research, standard-setting and enforcement functions of pollution abatement throughout the government (later to become the Environmental Protection Agency). But the

President's Advisory Council on Executive Organization, better known as the Ash Council after its chairman, Roy L. Ash,[19] was not ready to move. It had just completed a study on NOAA.[20] It had not yet completed studies on other options under consideration, the main ones being to create a Department of Natural Resources (DNR), which would encompass all of the above except the pollution abatement functions, or to create an independent Environmental Protection Agency, which would encompass the pollution functions and much of the environmental monitoring, research, standard-setting and enforcement activity of the federal government. Specifically, EPA would include: the Federal Water Quality Administration from Interior, the National Air Pollution Control Administration from HEW, the Environmental Control Administration from HEW, the Pesticides Registration Program from the Agricultural Research Service of the Department of Agriculture, and elements of the Radiation Protection Standards functions from AEC.[21]

Finally, a recommendation on what to do with NOAA was put off while the DNR and DENR options were studied to see if NOAA would fit into either organization. But the matter did not get sorted out early enough to be included in the February 1970 environmental message to Congress. The President had to be content to ask the Ash Council "to make an especially thorough study of the organization of Federal environmental, natural resources and oceanographic programs and to report its recommendations to me." [22] In addition to the options of DNR, DENR and EPA, another possibility was to assign environmental protection responsibilities to HEW, forming a separate administration within HEW for this purpose. The argument was that, given HEW's strong public and personal health capability, this arrangement would stress the health-related aspects of environmental protection. On the other hand, such a solution would be likely to subject the standard-setting and enforcement functions to the inherent bias of HEW, to the disadvantage of other departments. The fifth possibility was to form a small agency within the Executive Office of the President to establish

---

[19] Ash was president of Litton Industries at the time and later was named director of the Office of Management and Budget.

[20] *Memorandum of the President's Advisory Council on Executive Organization, April 1969 to November 1970*, pp. 53-56.

[21] After EPA was created, an Office of Noise Abatement was established by the Clean Air Act of 1970. Offices of toxic substances and land use were established administratively.

[22] *Public Papers of the Presidents, Nixon, 1970*, Special Message to Congress on Environmental Quality, p. 108.

pollution abatement standards, leaving the operational aspects of air, water, solid waste, pesticides, et cetera, in their respective departments. This option had the advantage of being least disruptive to the organizational structure of the departments, but it was unlikely to result in the kind of strong central management that most observers perceived to be necessary.

Once these options were fleshed out, they were discussed with the affected cabinet officers, one by one, first in a visit by the Ash Council staff and the author and later in a more formal hearing in which each cabinet officer stated his views to the Ash Council. The process set off the inevitable bureaucratic maneuvering, leaks to members of Congress, and contacts with special interest groups as the iron triangle began to function. From the departments and the subcommittees of Congress the advice was predictable, depending on the option and how it would affect parochial interest: do nothing—if the proposal would take a program away from the department or subcommittee in question; or, by all means, move ahead—if the proposal would give more responsibility to the department or greater jurisdiction to the subcommittee.[23]

Secretary Hickel, with the most to gain, favored DENR built around the existing Department of Interior. He rejected the "fox in the chicken coop" argument—that there would be an inherent conflict of interest if pollution research, monitoring, standard-setting, and enforcement were lodged in the same department that was charged with using and developing our natural resources. On the contrary, Hickel argued, this would result in balanced and knowledgeable standards and enforcement.

Secretary Hardin at Agriculture, with the most to lose, favored the status quo. He opposed moving pesticide registration programs out of his department, contending that regulation of pesticides and development of crops were compatible and desirable. DENR was totally unacceptable to him, for it would mean that Agriculture would lose the Forest Service, the Rural Electrification Administration, and water planning functions, including budget control for the Soil Conservation Service. Above all, Hardin felt the plan to dismantle the Department of Agriculture would so alienate the farmer that it would be a severe political liability for the President.

[23] President Johnson's chief domestic aide, Joseph Califano, who was involved in numerous government reorganization plans, remembers only one time when a cabinet officer favored a reorganization plan that called for his department to lose a program. See *A Presidential Nation*, p. 25.

HEW Secretary Robert Finch, although his department stood to lose three bureaus if either the DENR or EPA options were chosen by the President, was not nearly so bureaucratically possessive. He favored the creation of EPA and subscribed to the "fox in the chicken coop" argument.

Treasury Secretary John B. Connally, whose advice the President listened to because he was the only member of the Ash Council with political experience, joined Hardin in opposing the DENR option for fear of alienating the farmers. But Connally favored EPA, reasoning that moving the pesticide registration functions to EPA would be only a minor irritation to farmers.

The Ash Council itself, in its memorandum of April 29, 1970, unanimously recommended the EPA option to the President,[24] but was split on whether the Environmental Science Services Administration (ESSA) should become part of EPA or remain in the Department of Commerce. Some members argued that ESSA was basically an environmentally oriented agency and that its scientific, institutional base would serve as a valuable core for EPA's environmental monitoring functions. Others saw ESSA as a service agency that could be located in any one of several agencies or departments without harming its mission.

The President decided upon the EPA alternative. In the author's view, several factors influenced his decision. First, the status quo was unacceptable. Better coordination of pollution control in the federal government was clearly needed: there were forty-four agencies located in nine separate departments with responsibilities in the fields of environment and resources.[25] Second, agreeing with Hardin and Connally, the President wanted to avoid the political heat that would be generated by moving a great deal of the Department of Agriculture to DENR.[26] He also subscribed to the "fox in the chicken coop" argument. Finally, the President had reservations about Secretary Hickel's ability to manage DENR, which would be an expanded version of Interior. It seemed to Nixon that Hickel had his hands full just with Interior. There had been speculation that Nixon decided in favor of EPA and against DENR, and in favor of putting NOAA in the Depart-

---

[24] *Memorandum of the President's Advisory Council on Executive Organization, April 1969 to November 1970,* pp. 121-29.

[25] Amory Bradford, Ash Council staff unpublished draft memorandum, April 8, 1970.

[26] Yet, in January 1971, Nixon decided to propose the abolishment of the Department of Agriculture.

ment of Commerce rather than in Interior, because of pique over the leaking of Hickel's letter to him criticizing his decision to send American troops into Cambodia. While there may be some truth to this, the author believes that the letter's main effect upon Nixon was to confirm his opinion that Hickel—who had allowed the leak, either on purpose or inadvertently—was a poor manager. Probably President Nixon's main reason for favoring EPA was that he did not want to undertake major departmental reorganization, including that entailed in the DNR proposal, until an overall plan had been perfected. This took another eight months to prepare and was not ready until the state of the union message in January 1971.

The EPA reorganization plan was submitted to Congress in July 1970,[27] the sixty-day period for congressional objections expired in September, and the new agency came into being on December 2, 1970.

The National Oceanic and Atmospheric Administration (NOAA)

The Stratton commission report,[28] delivered just as President Johnson left office, had proposed NOAA as an independent agency, largely as a result of impetus from the oceanographic institutions and the marine technology industries, which were pressing for an increased federal budget for marine science research and development. The Ash Council later slightly modified the commission's original NOAA proposal to include ESSA from the Department of Commerce, the U.S. Lake Survey from the Corps of Engineers, the National Oceanographic Data and Instrumentation Centers from the Navy Department, the Sea Grant program from the National Science Foundation, and Marine Fish and Anadromous Fish programs and the Bureau of Commercial Fisheries from the Department of Interior.

Whereas a large number of congressmen were concerned about the environmental issue, few of them showed much interest in ocean research and development. But more to the point, few had much reason to oppose it. As a result, it became apparent during 1969 that, unless the administration served up an alternative, Congress would eventually pass a bill establishing a new independent NOAA respon-

---

[27] *Public Papers of the Presidents, Nixon, 1970,* Special Message to Congress about Reorganization Plans to Establish the Environmental Protection Agency and the National Oceanic and Atmospheric Administration, July 9, 1970, pp. 578-586.

[28] Commission on Marine Science, Engineering, and Resources (chairman, Julius Stratton), *Our Nation and the Sea* (Washington, D.C.: U.S. Government Printing Office, January 1969), p. 270.

sible directly to the President. The Ash Council was directed to suggest options. The fundamental objection to elevating NOAA to the status of a separate agency was that it was organized around the ocean as a medium rather than around any purposes or objectives. No advantage was inherent in elevating oceanic and atmospheric research and development to the status of a separate agency reporting directly to the President—and providing just the sort of narrow institutional advice the President did not want.

Under the options presented by the Ash Council, the President could: (1) reaffirm lead agency designations and assign lead agencies to program areas not yet covered; (2) establish a new division for marine technology within the National Science Foundation; (3) reorganize Interior by adding to it all the elements encompassed in the NOAA proposal (less the Coast Guard) and by consolidating these under an assistant secretary of the interior; (4) place all the NOAA elements under an assistant secretary of commerce; and (5) include NOAA in the new DENR. The council recommended in favor of option (3)— with the proviso that an internal study be undertaken to assist Interior in learning to deal effectively with the sophisticated scientific activity transferred to it.

Nixon, adding the Ash Council's concern over Interior's ability to assimilate scientific expertise to his own concern about whether Hickel could manage additional responsibilities, decided to put NOAA into Commerce rather than Interior. Also, ESSA, with 10,020 employees already established in Commerce, represented about 82 percent of the 12,313 employees in the proposed NOAA. It did not seem productive to move such a large group from Commerce to Interior when only 1,933 employees would have to be transferred the other way.

Although most congressmen, perceiving NOAA's mission as primarily environmental protection of the oceans, might want NOAA in Interior and removed from the largely industry-oriented development mission of the Department of Commerce, Nixon correctly judged that the iron triangle would work its will. The Subcommittee on Oceanography [29] of the Senate Commerce Committee and its counterpart in the House, the Oceanography Subcommittee of the Merchant Marine and Fisheries Committee, both sponsored NOAA. Lacking the votes to establish NOAA as an independent agency, they made sure that the

---

[29] In 1970 the Commerce Subcommittee on Oceanography was renamed the Subcommittee on Oceans and Atmosphere.

new organization was placed in the Department of Commerce where they had jurisdiction. Thus the NOAA reorganization plan sailed through Congress and took effect October 3, 1970.

Department of Natural Resources (DNR)

It was far from a new idea when the Ash Council, in May 1970, recommended to President Nixon that the "principal natural resource programs of the Executive Branch be consolidated within the Department of the Interior, and that the department be renamed the Department of Natural Resources (DNR)." [30]

In 1937, President Roosevelt's Committee on Administrative Management, chaired by Louis Brownlow, journalist, teacher and, at the time, director of the Public Administration Clearing House in Chicago, recommended that the Department of Interior be renamed the Department of Conservation. The Brownlow Committee did not recommend specific agencies and bureaus to constitute the Department of Conservation, but said its purposes should be: "To advise the President with regard to protection and use of the natural resources of the Nation and the Public Domain." [31] By 1939, Interior Secretary Harold Ickes was trying hard to persuade President Roosevelt to move the Forest Service and the Rural Electrification Administration from the Agriculture Department to Interior. In fact, Ickes thought he had Roosevelt's assurances on moving the Forest Service. By his account, the bureaucratic intrigue was apparent.

> When he [Roosevelt] got around to the subject, he said right away that, of course, Forestry would be transferred to Interior. I found, to my great pleasure, that there was no thought of transferring Forestry except as an entity. I was glad of this because I believe that Silcox [then Chief of the Forest Service] would almost certainly fight any piecemeal transfer. He may fight anyhow, but he is less likely to do so if the whole organization comes over, especially since I may still be in a position to offer him the position of Under Secretary. Naturally we are all keeping very quiet about this transfer because we do not want to stir up the Forest Service and farm lobbies. [32]

[30] *Memorandum of the President's Advisory Council on Executive Reorganization, April 1969 to November 1970,* p. 147.

[31] *President's Committee on Administrative Management* (Washington, D.C.: U.S. Government Printing Office, 1937), p. 35.

[32] Harold Ickes, *The Secret Diary of Harold Ickes,* "The Lowering Clouds, 1939-1941," vol. 3 (New York, N.Y.: Simon and Schuster, 1954), pp. 77-78.

To Ickes's everlasting frustration, President Roosevelt never backed him on the reorganization plan.

In 1949, a majority of the Hoover Commission overrode the advice of its task force and its Committee on Natural Resources, which recommended a consolidation of water resources and public land management functions in a Department of Natural Resources. Instead the commission recommended that public land management be consolidated by transferring the Bureau of Land Management to the Department of Agriculture and the civil functions of the Corps of Engineers to the Department of Interior.[33] In 1953, the Temple University studies on federal reorganization recommended transfer of the Bureau of Land Management from the Department of Interior to Agriculture, but no comprehensive reorganization of natural resource functions was contemplated.[34] The second Hoover Commission, in 1955, recommended that a Water Resources Board be created and that the Corps of Engineers assume the Soil Conservation Service function of constructing headwater dams for flood control.[35] The Water Resources Council[36] later organized the kind of coordinating mechanism advocated by the Hoover Commission.

President Johnson appointed two task forces to study government organization. In 1964 the Price task force[37] recommended creating five new executive departments including a Department of Natural Resources. It offered Johnson two options: (1) merge the Departments of Interior and Agriculture, distributing nonresource programs to other agencies or (2) retain a Department of Agriculture but transfer the Forest Service and the Soil Conservation Service to the Interior Department, distributing the nonresource programs in Interior to other agencies. Under either option the task force recommended moving some water resources functions of the Federal Power Commission and the Corps of Engineers civil works program to the new Department of Natural

---

[33] Commission on Organization of the Executive Branch of the Government, *Concluding Report and Index to Commission Reports and Task Force Reports*, vol. 5 (Washington, D.C.: U.S. Government Printing Office, 1949), p. 65.

[34] This study group was designed to serve as a link between the Truman and Eisenhower administrations. The report was presented to the Rockefeller task force in 1953.

[35] Commission on the Organization of the Executive Branch of the Government, *Water Resources and Power*, vol. 1 (Washington, D.C.: U.S. Government Printing Office, 1955), pp. 39 and 71.

[36] Established under section 101 of the Water Planning Resources Act, P.L. 89-80 (79 Stat. 244), July 22, 1965.

[37] President's Task Force on Government Organization, chaired by Don K. Price, November 6, 1964.

Resources. In 1967 the Heineman task force,[38] operating under the principle of submerging special interest departments into multi-interest departments, proposed a very large Department of Natural Resources and Development including Interior, the Corps of (Civil) Engineers, HUD, Transportation, and Agriculture.

President-elect Nixon, in 1968, asked a transition team to study the organization of the executive branch. The team was chaired by his former law partner, Franklin A. Lindsay. It recommended establishing a President's Advisory Council on Executive Organization (which became the Ash Council) to investigate the creation of large broad-interest departments, including a Department of Natural Resources.

Congress also had its say. In June 1970, the Public Land Law Review Commission published a report strongly urging a unified department to administer the public lands and recommending specifically that "the Forest Service should be merged within the Department of the Interior into a new Department of Natural Resources." [39] The commission was chaired by Congressman Wayne Aspinall, chairman of the House Interior and Insular Affairs Committee, and weighted with congressmen and senators from the two committees with jurisdiction over the Department of Interior. Consequently it was expected that the group would favor moving the Forest Service from Agriculture to Interior. Their rationale had merit:

> The Forest Service is the only major public land agency not now in the Department of the Interior. We believe that the fact that the Forest Service is not under the same policy direction as the public land agencies has lead to unnecessary differences in policies between Forest Service and bureaus within Interior; to conflicts between them, particularly over the use of national forest lands for National Parks, that have been a source of embarrassment to national administrations; to confusion on the part of the using public; and to expensive duplication of staff, offices, programs and facilities.

---

[38] President's Task Force on Government Organization, chaired by Ben Heineman, June 1967.

[39] A Report to the President and to the Congress by the Public Land Law Review Commission, *One-third of the Nation's Land* (Washington, D.C.: U.S. Government Printing Office, June 1970), p. 282.

The Public Land Law Review Commission, authorized by P.L. 88-606 (78 Stat. 982) and signed by President Johnson September 19, 1964, consisted of six senators and six House members of the Interior and Insular Affairs committees and six members chosen by the President to study laws and administration of the public lands. The study cost $7 million, took six years, and was presented to President Nixon in a Rose Garden ceremony on June 23, 1970.

60

The original reasons for placing the administration of the national forests in the Department of Agriculture may have been sound. But the uses of the national forests have changed in recent years with increasing emphasis being placed on outdoor recreation and environmental quality. We think these charges justify separating the administration of national forests from the farm enterprise orientation of the Department of Agriculture and placing it in a closer relationship to the public lands functions of the Department of the Interior.[40]

President Nixon formally received the Public Land Law Review Comission's report in a Rose Garden ceremony, saying, "It is essential to plan now for the use of that land, not to do it simply in a case-by-case basis, but to have an overall policy, a strategy rather than simply the tactics dealing with case-by-case matters when they come up." [41]

By that time Nixon had received and studied the Ash Council proposal for reorganizing the major natural resource functions of the federal government, including the management of public lands, into a Department of Natural Resources. This proposal was much more extensive and specific than similar recommendations made to earlier presidents—and with good reason: there was no doubt that the existing government organization for managing the nation's natural resources had become chaotic. For example, four federal water resource, research and development programs were scattered through three departments—Agriculture, Interior, and Army.[42] To reduce the confusion, the Water Resources Council had been created in 1962, but it had made little headway. Nonmilitary public lands were managed by four agencies in two departments: [43] Agriculture's national forests and grasslands were often adjacent to Interior's public lands, and needlessly different policies and procedures were often followed. Federal recreation and land

---

[40] Ibid.

[41] *Public Papers of the Presidents, Nixon, 1970,* Remarks on Receiving the Report of the Public Land Law Review Commission, June 23, 1970, p. 515.

[42] The four programs are: (1) the watershed development functions of the Soil Conservation Service in Agriculture; (2) the Corps of Engineers, which, under the civil works program of the Department of the Army plans, constructs, and maintains projects for flood control, navigation, water supply, irrigation, et cetera; (3) the Bureau of Reclamation in Interior; and (4) the Office of Water Research and Technology in Interior. The latter office was formed from a consolidation, in November 1974, of the Office of Saline Water and the Office of Water Resources Research.

[43] The four agencies are: (1) the Bureau of Land Management, (2) Fish and Wildlife Service's National Wildlife Refuge lands, (3) the National Parks in Interior, and (4) the Forest Service in Agriculture.

61

use was administered by six agencies in four departments,[44] with very little coordination. Finally, energy programs were scattered among several departments and agencies, with no single focal point of responsibility for developing energy policy.

The Ash Council gave the President some examples of difficulties caused by the chaotic government organization of natural resources management:

> In Kansas, proposed watershed developments (Agriculture) threaten to undermine the rationale for a reclamation project (Interior) downstream.
>
> In Montana, the Corps of Engineers and the Bureau of Reclamation are studying separate projects for the same site. Who, if anyone, should build which project awaits an uncertain resolution through existing interagency or other procedures.
>
> In California, development of a ski and summer mountain resort on Forest Service lands (Agriculture) in the Mineral King Basin was stymied by refusal to grant public access across National Park land by Interior. The interagency dispute was finally settled at the White House level (although action has been held up by an injunction obtained by conservation interests). Regardless of the merits of the case, resolution of the public access issue might have been accomplished during the planning stage had the lands been managed by the same department.
>
> In the Southeastern States, widespread stream channel straightening and deepening has been protested vigorously by the Department of the Interior, supported by conservation interests. The process of balancing fish and wildlife and scenic values against economic development needs is unnecessarily frustrated by fragmented planning and evaluation responsibility within the Federal Government.[45]

The Ash Council's final DNR plan proposed a department with four divisions.

1. Land and recreation. The council endorsed the principle of multi-purpose management of the public lands, including such functions

---

[44] The six agencies are: (1) recreation facilities at Corps of Engineer Reservoir sites, (2) the Open Spaces program at HUD, (3) the Forest Service in the Department of Agriculture, (4) the Bureau of Outdoor Recreation, (5) the National Park Service in the Department of the Interior, and (6) the Coastal Zone Management Office in the Department of Commerce. Both Interior and EPA have set up land-use offices in anticipation of being designated the lead agency in land-use legislation pending before Congress.

[45] *Memorandum of the President's Advisory Council on Executive Organization, April 1969 to November 1970,* p. 149.

as forestry, recreation facility development, visitor services, fire protection, grazing and range management, and wildlife management. Land and recreation components proposed for transfer to DNR from Interior included the National Park Service, the Fish and Wildlife Service, the Bureau of Outdoor Recreation, the Bureau of Land Management, and the Conservation Division of the Geological Survey. These were grouped with the Forest Service from Agriculture and the Coastal Zone Management program at that time pending before Congress.[46]

2. *Water resources.* The council's report stated that the key to an integrated national water policy was central control over the fragmented water planning and project evaluation functions of the Bureau of Reclamation, the Corps of (Civil) Engineers, and the Soil Conservation Service. It proposed that the secretary of DNR be responsible for evaluating cost benefits and environmental concerns and for making the final decisions on what projects should be implemented. In addition, the Water Resource Council should cease to exist, because interagency coordination would no longer be a vexing problem when responsibility for all major policy and project evaluation activities related to water resource projects was placed within one department.

3. *Energy and mineral resources.* The council pointed out that, over the years, both Congress and the executive branch had created separate bureaus and even agencies to promote competing forms of energy—like the Office of Oil and Gas, the Office of Coal Research, and the Atomic Energy Commission (AEC). Other agencies, like the Rural Electrification Administration and the Bonneville Power Administration, had been created to meet specific energy needs. But in no one place in the federal government was the responsibility vested to judge the impact of one program on another. Instead, special interests, congressional committees, and middle-level bureaucracies were each "digging their separate tunnels"—to paraphrase John Gardner's remark—to the Treasury in the name of coal, or oil, or nuclear development, but, unwittingly, never in the interest of a balanced, cohesive national energy policy. The council recommended combining the Bureau of Mines, the Geological Survey (except the Conservation Division), the Office of Oil and Gas, the Oil Import Administration and Appeals Board, the Office of Coal

---

[46] Later Congress placed Coastal Zone Management in the Department of Commerce—another victory for the iron triangle. The legislation was sponsored primarily by the Senate Commerce Committee and the House Merchant Marine and Fisheries Committee. Both committees had jurisdiction over the Department of Commerce.

Research, and the power marketing agencies [47]—all from the Department of Interior—with the Rural Electrification Administration from the Department of Agriculture. Finally, the Ash Council recommended combining all these energy agencies with the civilian energy programs of AEC.[48] With all these agencies in DNR, one department would be responsible for assessing mineral resources and conducting research and development on minerals extraction and processing; for operating uranium raw material and enrichment programs; for marketing federal electric power; for administering rural electrification and telephone programs; and, most important for modern needs, for setting overall policy for research and development on both fossil fuel and nuclear energy.

4. Oceanic, atmospheric, and earth sciences. The council originally and tentatively recommended two more divisions. One, Marine Resources and Technology, would have contained some of the functions of NOAA.[49] The other, Geophysical Science Services, whose general mission was described as increased knowledge of the physical environment and improved ability to predict and modify geophysical phenomena, would have included the data-gathering portions of NOAA,[50] the Environmental Science Services Administration, the Geological Survey (except the Conservation Division) from Interior, and the Coast Guard Data Buoy Program from the Department of Transportation. But before the DNR legislation was announced, NOAA became law,[51] so the two divisions were combined into one—called Oceanic, Atmospheric, and Earth Sciences—and the Geological Survey (except for the Conservation Division) was moved to the Energy and Mineral Resources component of DNR.

---

[47] Alaska Power Administration, Bonneville Power Administration, Southeastern Power Administration, Southwestern Power Administration, and the power-marketing functions of the Bureau of Reclamation.

[48] Uranium Raw Materials, Uranium Enrichment, Plowshare Programs, Power Reactor Development, Controlled Thermonuclear Reactions, and the Pacific Northwest Laboratory.

[49] Office of the Sea Grant Program from the National Science Foundation and the Marine Mining Program of the Bureau of Mines and the Bureau of Commercial Fisheries, both from Interior.

[50] National Oceanographic Data and Instrumentation Centers from the navy and the U.S. Lake Survey from the army.

[51] By the time DNR and the other components of the four major new departments were announced in the state of the union message on January 22, 1971, Secretary Rogers Morton had replaced Hickel at the Interior Department. Nixon, who had confidence in Morton's management capability, agreed to move NOAA to DNR.

Cabinet members and department personnel reacted even more strongly to the DNR plan than they had to EPA, because the plan's implications were more unsettling for the status quo of the iron triangle. Again, Agriculture Secretary Hardin did not want to lose the Forest Service or the Rural Electrification Administration. His greatest concern was over the change proposed for the Soil Conservation Service. The DNR plan would have split this agency, leaving its cost-estimating, engineering, construction, and maintenance functions in Agriculture, while transferring its policy and budget authority to DNR. The Soil Conservation Service is probably one of the most efficient "precinct" organizations in America. With offices in almost every county in the United States, its bureaucratic roots penetrate deep into the local communities; it ranks, along with the Corps of (Civil) Engineers and the Bureau of Reclamation, as one of the strongest members of the iron triangle.

Interior Secretary Morton favored the proposal since DNR would be an enlargement of his department, but Secretary Stans at Commerce, having just acquired NOAA, was not anxious to lose it and opposed the proposal. Secretary Romney at HUD was for it, except, predictably, he argued that HUD's Open Space program was uniquely tied to urban needs and did not require any special coordination with recreation policy in DNR.[52]

Secretary of Defense Melvin Laird, at first opposed to moving the Corps of [Civil] Engineers, relented when Nixon decided to move to DNR only the water planning, budget, and project evaluation functions of the Corps of Engineers, leaving responsibility for cost estimating, engineering, construction, and maintenance with the army. This way, Laird was assured that the army would have standby mobilization capacity for construction requirements in the event of war. Also, from the President's view, such a compromise might take some of the political sting out of this particular iron triangle relationship, but not much. Irrigation, flood control, and canal construction projects bring solid economic benefits and high federal subsidies to congressional districts. As a result, the Corps of Engineers, along with the Bureau of Reclamation, represent two of the great pork barrel sources in the federal government. For a congressman just to announce that a water resources

---

[52] But because the National Park Service was increasingly involved in servicing urban areas and because of the prospect of establishing Gateway East National Recreation Area in New York Harbor and the Golden Gate Recreation Area in San Francisco, Nixon did not accept Romney's argument.

project has been authorized by Congress often helps ensure his reelection.

President Nixon, recognizing the uphill battle that he would surely face, almost decided in the fall of 1970 not to fight for DNR—or for any of the proposed large multi-purpose departments. Over the Atlantic enroute back from French President de Gaulle's funeral in November, he told John Ehrlichman that "he had other fish to fry." He planned to challenge the iron triangle even more fundamentally by proposing special revenue sharing so that governors and state legislators, not members of Congress, would be setting domestic priorities over large groups of categorical grants. Nixon saw this proposal as the centerpiece of his state of the union message coming up in January, and he did not want to antagonize Congress with a reorganization plan as well.

But in late November the President changed his mind. He was impressed that John Connally, the only member of the Ash Council with political experience, was now ready to back DNR even though it could alienate the farm bloc. Each of the President's principal advisers—George Shultz of Treasury, Robert Finch of HEW, Robert Haldeman, John Ehrlichman, Bryce Harlow, and Donald Rumsfeld of the White House—backed not only DNR, but three more multi-purpose major departments as well—Community Development, Human Resources, and Economic Affairs. Press reaction to Nixon's overall organization plan, which included DNR, was almost euphoric, but the iron triangle shrugged it off. The 92nd Congress did no more than hold a few hearings.

DENR, ERDA, FEO, FEA, NRC, and Energy Czars

The next two years saw a bewildering procession of new agencies for managing the energy crisis and of new energy czars—nine in a row— each struggling manfully to untangle the organizational jungle of agencies. In June 1973, with energy supplies becoming shorter, President Nixon sent his third energy message to Congress.[53] Hoping to capitalize on the growing importance of the energy issue, he included in the message a proposal for a Department of Energy and Natural Resources, a modified version of DNR.

As proposed, DENR contained an Energy and Minerals Administration, including three recently created Interior Department offices—

[53] Office of the White House Press Secretary, June 29, 1973.

Data and Analysis, Energy Conservation, and Energy Research and Development—as well as several older-line Interior agencies—the Office of Oil and Gas, the Bureau of Mines (except for the research centers) and the power-marketing administrations. Also included was the Mining Enforcement and Safety Administration, which had recently been split off from the Bureau of Mines so that development and enforcement functions would not be in the same bureau. Finally, the uranium and thorium assessment programs of AEC and the Office of Pipeline Safety from the Department of Transportation were added to DENR.

Also in his third energy message, Nixon proposed the new Energy Research and Development Administration (ERDA)—an attempt to bring the main energy research and development functions of the government under one roof. AEC functions going to ERDA included nuclear materials production, reactor development, military applications, physical research, biomedical and environmental research, controlled thermonuclear research, non-nuclear energy research and development, and other nonregulatory functions. From Interior would come most of the fossil fuel research, including the Office of Coal Research, the energy research centers of the Bureau of Mines, the synthane coal conversion plant at Bruceton, Pennsylvania, and underground power electrical transmission research and development. From the National Science Foundation would come solar and geothermal power research and from EPA, alternative automobile power systems and fossil fuel power-plant emission control.[54] Finally, AEC would cease to exist. What was not transferred to ERDA and DENR was to become the Nuclear Energy Commission (NEC), a five-member commission to head the licensing, regulatory and related functions of AEC. Congress later renamed NEC the Nuclear Regulatory Commission (NRC).

The decision to try to move ERDA and NEC onto a faster legislative track than DENR revolved around two reasons.

The first was that DENR was going nowhere. The iron triangle spoke for the status quo, and the jurisdictional conflict was too much to overcome. The members of the Interior and Insular Affairs committees of the House and Senate wanted to move most of the energy functions from AEC to Interior, while the Joint Committee on Atomic Energy wanted to move most of Interior's energy-related functions to

---

[54] However, in a compromise worked out in conference committee, these functions were retained by EPA and the Senate dropped a provision for federal financial and technical assistance to citizen intervenors against nuclear power plants.

AEC. Members of the joint committee were adamantly opposed to DENR because, in their view, nuclear energy interests might be dominated by the fossil fuel interests at Interior. They were, however, willing to see AEC dismantled as long as their committee held jurisdictional sway over ERDA. And, in turn, members of the Interior and the Insular Affairs committees were willing to lose supervision of energy research and development to ERDA as long as they kept near-term energy development and the leasing of public lands for fossil and nuclear fuels and minerals, and gained the oceanic, water resources, and public land and recreation functions scattered throughout the remainder of government.

Second, President Nixon wanted to increase the federal energy research and development budget to $10 billion over five years and thought a special agency like ERDA was needed to manage the undertaking. He decided to build this new agency around the highly qualified AEC national laboratories system, which had a far greater research and development capability than the Department of Interior. Over the years, Interior had become top-heavy with political appointments from the coal states of West Virginia and Pennsylvania and the oil states of Texas and Oklahoma.

Predictably, Secretary of the Interior Morton and AEC Chairman Dixy Lee Ray objected to the ERDA proposal, Morton because he thought Interior should keep its full energy research and development capability, which was after all so closely related to the fuel development and leasing functions already in the department, and Ray because her agency was to cease to exist.

ERDA and NRC were established by law on October 11, 1974.[55] It is possible, though far from likely, that DENR might have passed Congress in some form had not the Arab boycott in late 1973 and early 1974 convinced President Nixon that he needed yet another energy organization, a specialized crisis management unit, to handle the crippling gasoline, propane, and heating fuel shortages that the country had to face. Instead of DENR, the Federal Energy Office was born (see below) and the search continued for an energy czar.

The designation of one man positioned to handle the energy problem eluded both President Nixon and President Ford. In the fall of 1970 and spring of 1971, when the administration first grappled with energy policy and began work on Nixon's first energy message to Congress in

---

[55] P.L. 93-438 (88 Stat. 1233).

June 1971, Dr. Paul McCracken, chairman of the Council of Economic Advisers, headed an energy task force to prepare the text. Following the message, the task force went out of existence, and General George Lincoln, director of the Office of Emergency Planning (OEP), held operating responsibility in the Executive Office of the President for energy policy. When Nixon abolished OEP in 1973, oversight responsibilities for the oil import program moved to the Treasury Department under the newly appointed deputy secretary, William Simon, who was also named by the President to head the Oil Policy Committee. For a brief period in 1973, Secretary of Agriculture Earl Butz appeared in the newly created role of counsellor to the President on natural resources, serving as yet another energy czar.

As the energy shortages became more acute in 1973 and the need for White House coordination even more apparent, Charles DiBona was brought to the White House to work under Ehrlichman. He developed a small staff that finished preparing Nixon's April 1973 energy message to Congress. That message announced more energy-coordinating entities, established a special energy committee composed of Treasury Secretary Shultz, Secretary of State Henry Kissinger, and Ehrlichman of the White House,[56] and formally annointed DiBona as the President's special consultant for energy matters. In addition, a new Division of Energy and Science was established in OMB. Just two months later, on June 29, in another energy message to Congress, Nixon created an Energy Policy Office headed by John Love, governor of Colorado,[57] and DiBona became his chief of staff. Governor Love also replaced Simon as chairman of the Oil Policy Committee. On December 4, 1973, as the Arab boycott deepened the crisis, President Nixon announced the creation of the Federal Energy Office, headed by William Simon. Governor Love promptly quit in a huff—leaving Washington the same day—so Simon became the sixth energy czar. Soon after, Nixon submitted legislation to Congress to create a Federal Energy Administration (FEA). FEA was established by law on May 7, 1974,[58] taking over the functions of fuel allocation and energy conservation, the Office of Oil and Gas, and the Office of Energy Data and Analysis from the Department of Interior, and most of the energy functions of the Cost

---

[56] Executive Order 11712, April 18, 1973.

[57] Executive Order 11726, June 29, 1973.

[58] The Federal Energy Administration Act of 1974, P.L. 93-275 (88 Stat. 96), May 7, 1974.

of Living Council. When Simon became secretary of the Treasury,[59] his FEA deputy, John Sawhill, became administrator of FEA.[60] Sawhill became the seventh energy czar, following Messrs. McCracken, Lincoln, Butz, DiBona, Love, and Simon.

After Gerald Ford became President, his close friend, Rogers Morton, became chairman of the Energy Resource Council, a new interagency coordinating committee, and Frank Zarb was named to head FEA. When Morton became secretary of commerce in May 1975, he remained titular energy czar, but in fact Zarb became the key adviser to the President and spokesman for the administration on energy matters. However, when Elliot Richardson became secretary of commerce, President Ford gave him Morton's former role as chairman of the Energy Resource Council. Thus, Richardson became the ninth energy czar since 1970.

Through it all, the idea of an energy czar tended to be over-rated. The federal government's energy responsibilities are in several departments (Treasury, Interior, State, and Transportation), in independent regulatory commissions (like the Interstate Commerce Commission, the Federal Power Commission, and the new Nuclear Regulatory Commission), and in the newly created FEA and ERDA. To establish a czar in any real sense would mean to centralize direction of all these agencies, and Congress is not likely to change all these laws so that a czar can reign supreme. In fact, Congress reacted by legislating more regulation and control, not by providing for the unbridled freedom of a czar.

Between 1970 and 1974 much had been accomplished to reorganize the environmental and energy functions of the government—EPA, NOAA, FEA, NRC, and ERDA were functioning. But by March 1975, DENR was dead. Until that time, Morton had hoped to get President Ford behind DENR, but Ford decided there were too many political obstacles in the iron triangle. He was comfortable with Frank Zarb in charge of energy policy and he did not want to complicate further the confused and often bitter energy battle with Congress by proposing still another reorganization plan involving energy.

David Broder speculated that the Democrats might champion President Nixon's idea of fundamentally reshaping the federal government, but that it would take a Democratic President with a strong

---

[59] May 8, 1974.
[60] July 10, 1974.

congressional majority to pull it off: "Just as it took the Nixon administration to end the costly, out-of-date policy of ignoring China, which had been invented and imposed by Republican ideologues, it may well take a Democratic administration to begin the work of reorganizing and rationalizing the crazy quilt of federal agencies created by Democratic Congresses and Presidents." [61]

---

[61] "Democratic Curbing of Government," *Washington Post,* October 1, 1975, editorial page.

4

Clean Water–How Soon, How Clean, How Costly?

When the administration turned its attention to the problem of obtaining clean water in the fall of 1969, its first task was to choose a pollution abatement strategy and decide how to finance it.

Choosing a Strategy

To attempt to control water pollution by regulation, standard setting, and judicial procedure is a cumbersome process that tends to produce inefficiency and more bureaucracy. Recognizing this, the administration gave serious consideration to the concept of effluent fees.

An effluent fee system is a market-administered alternative to regulation by enforcement that relies on financial rather than legal incentives to achieve compliance. Under the system, fees are set for levels of the various pollutants, like suspended solids, temperature, BOD (biochemical oxygen demand), pH, et cetera. The concept is appealingly simple: The more an enterprise pollutes, the more it pays. By charging effluent fees that cover the full social cost of pollution, the system creates a powerful incentive not to pollute—that is, the polluter is induced to pay the capital, operation, and maintenance costs of pollution abatement in order to avoid the more costly effluent fees. The system would be administered by some sort of water authority, such as a lake or a river basin commission, which would establish a schedule of fees for various kinds and amounts of pollutants. Each polluter would report his discharges and pay the required fees to the commission. It in turn would use the funds to provide pollution control facilities and to pay the administrative costs of establishing and collecting fees and ensuring against discharge of toxic pollutants. The fees could be raised or lowered, depending on the desired water quality.

An intriguing alternative to the effluent fee system is the concept of a "pollution rights" market, that is, a market in which only enough "pollution rights" are sold to keep a given waterway at an acceptable water quality level. In such a free market, theoretically, the optimum price for the rights would be set automatically, as are optimum prices for equities in a stock market, and would be automatically adjusted to take account of economic growth. Anyone would be able to buy "pollution rights." As J. H. Dales, a University of Toronto economist and proponent of the idea wryly pointed out, "Conservation groups might well want to buy up some rights merely in order to prevent them from being used. In this way, at least part of the guerrilla warfare between conservationists and polluters could be transferred into a civilized 'war with dollars'; both groups would, I think, learn something in the process." [1]

The effluent fee system has some advantages over the regulatory program that was being contemplated at the time by the administration. In theory, if the fee is high enough, it results in a greater reduction in waste discharged into waterways than does either regulation or a combination of regulation and effluent fees. Each polluter can choose his own method of pollution control and presumably employ the most cost-effective method. For example, firms with low treatment costs would have an incentive to treat wastes to very high levels, while firms with high treatment costs would treat to lower levels and pay the fee. Hence the costs of achieving a fixed total reduction in pollutants would be less under the effluent fee system than under regulation based on across-the board reduction requirements. The variety of techniques used should result in more experimentation, leading to new and less expensive pollution control methods. Finally, groups of dischargers would be likely to band together to promote cost-effective regional methods for pollution control.

Although the President later proposed effluent fees for air pollution control,[2] the idea of using the system for water pollution never

[1] J. H. Dales, *Pollution, Property and Prices* (Toronto, Ontario: University of Toronto Press, 1968), pp. 95-96.
[2] In his 1971 environment message to Congress, Nixon proposed taxing the sulfur content of fossil fuels discharged into the air. The fee was designed to encourage utilities and industrial plants to burn low-sulfur oil and coal and develop technologies to reduce sulfur emissions. In essence, the proposal was a charge on sulfur-oxide emissions. Companies would receive a rebate for reducing emissions below prescribed levels.

received his serious attention. There were serious disadvantages to the idea and the political ones were probably fatal. Neither the Democrats nor the Republicans in the congressional establishment of the Public Works Committee had ever given the proposal serious consideration, even though Senator William Proxmire, Democrat of Wisconsin, favored it. A regulatory strategy had been employed for years and the leaders of both the Senate and House Public Works Committees had a vested interest in this approach. Also, since an effluent fee is a form of taxation, congressional jurisdiction would have been claimed by the Ways and Means Committee in the House and the Finance Committee in the Senate—thus removing a lively political issue from the jurisdiction of the Public Works Committee. Finally, if the administration had sent proposed effluent fee legislation to the Ways and Means and Finance committees it is doubtful that they would have ever acted. Members of these committees view taxation primarily as a device for raising revenues and are reluctant to use it for curing all manner of social ills, including water pollution. In line with this philosophy the Ways and Means Committee never acted on a later Nixon proposal for a sulfuroxide tax on utility or industrial air emissions.

Moreover, an effluent fee program entails certain administrative problems. Probably hundreds of state and regional commissions encompassing lake and river systems would have to be created. Also, the setting of fee schedules would be complicated and expensive and perhaps not as clearly understandable to the public as a regulatory strategy, especially one with fines against polluters, a politically attractive approach. Finally, some environmental groups called the effluent fee system "a license to pollute" because, in theory at least, although highly unlikely in practice, a discharger could pay very high effluent fees and continue to pollute rather than install proper pollution control equipment.

Given the complex technical problems and the great political difficulties of radically changing the view of a congressional establishment wedded to a regulatory approach, the administration abandoned the effluent fee strategy. But an EPA study paper later concluded that the "effluent fee is the most effective alternative for meeting national water quality objectives. It promises to be the most effective and simultaneously requires the least national cost. In addition, it is the most desirable on the basis of equity and economic impact considerations." [3]

---

[3] Environmental Protection Agency, "Alternative Strategies in Water Quality Management," January 4, 1972, mimeographed, p. 18.

Financing

A spirited battle took place between Interior Secretary Hickel and the President's financial advisers on how to finance the huge costs of municipal waste treatment plants. Cumulatively, through the FY 1970 budget (President Johnson's last), funding for municipal treatment plants lagged more than $1.5 billion below annual authorizations, a shortfall of two-thirds over the previous four years. The Interior Department had given tentative estimates to the environmental message task force that $9.5 to $10 billion was needed to achieve satisfactory water quality standards for the period 1971–1975, and there was some thought that the costs could go as high as $15.5 billion.[4] Some of the variables that made cost predictions so tentative were regional cost differences, greater use of regional treatment plants that could reduce costs, and higher levels of treatment which would increase costs.

Hickel proposed to the President that, instead of continuing annual appropriations of lump-sum grants for financing municipal waste treatment plants, the administration should provide federal contracting authority of $10 billion in payments to be made over a period of up to thirty years to cover the principal amount of bonds issued by local public bodies to finance the full capital costs of municipal waste treatment facilities. Hickel wrote the President,

> I visualize the development of new contractual authority that incorporates the combined efforts of federal, state and local governments and private industry. Let us acknowledge the failure of the sterile cycle of annual Congressional appropriations. To follow this procedure is no less foolhardy than it would be for a manufacturing concern to purchase a new lot, build a new plant, redesign an assembly line process, tool the operation and hope to finance it out of a single year's petty cash.[5]

The rhetoric was good, and Nixon was sympathetic to financing both park acquisition (see Chapter 9) and waste treatment plants with the same long-term methods. But Treasury Secretary David Kennedy

---

[4] However, these estimates did not anticipate the larger federal share, higher standards and tighter deadlines eventually written into the Federal Water Pollution Control Act Amendments of 1972. In a July 31, 1975 letter from EPA Administrator Russell Train to OMB Director James Lynn, Train estimated that, based on the 1974 EPA needs survey, the cost of funding by 1983 of secondary treatment, required advance treatment, and interceptor sewers would be $60.4 billion.

[5] Letter from Secretary Hickel to President Nixon, October 29, 1969.

was cool to the plan, citing the adverse effect it would have on the municipal bond market. Nixon remained sympathetic, however, taking the position that this plan was the only way to stop a major budget busting spree in this field.[6] Budget Director Robert Mayo, aided by staff work done by Alvin Alm of the environmental message task force, presented a strong case against Hickel's proposal. In a final meeting with Ehrlichman and Mayo, Nixon decided in favor of a proposal made by Alm and backed by Mayo and Assistant Budget Director James Schlesinger for funding the federal share of the $10 billion program— $4 billion—through lump-sum grants to be authorized in FY 1971 and to be allocated over the next four years at the rate of $1 billion per year, with another assessment of needs in 1973 for FY 1975 and later years. Because the bond market was so weak (509 issues worth $2.9 billion proved unsalable in 1969),[7] Nixon also proposed an Environmental Financing Authority, so that if a municipality were unable to sell waste treatment plant construction bonds, then, as a means of last resort, the federal government would buy them and sell its bonds on the taxable market.

Hickel's proposal, though politically tempting as a way to remove the immense cost of financing waste treatment plants from the federal budget process, had too many flaws. First, there was the matter of budget integrity. The use of long-term contracts instead of annual appropriations to avoid showing in the budget the total amount of sewage treatment plant construction stimulated by federal funds would undermine the budget as a tool for allocating resources. Although Hickel's proposal required small federal outlays in the short run, it would have imposed a short-term pressure on capital markets and the construction industry. Borrowing for waste treatment plant funds would compete with borrowing to meet the nation's housing goals. Another danger was the precedent. If the administration backed Hickel's method of financing for waste treatment plants, how could it resist similar proposals for mass transit, municipal airports, hospitals, education, and other public facilities where the total demand could not be met through the normal budget process? Third, the proposal would mean that Nixon would be asking the Appropriations committees of the House and Senate

---

[6] Memorandum to John Ehrlichman from John R. Brown III, White House staff secretary, December 29, 1969.

[7] *Public Papers of the Presidents, Nixon, 1970,* Special Message to Congress on Environmental Quality, p. 98.

to grant the executive branch one-time authority, good for thirty years, to enter into $10 billion worth of construction contracts without any further congressional review—something Congress was highly unlikely to do.

Also from a comparative net cost standpoint, using OMB's analysis and assuming a $9.5 billion total federal, state, and local program that took into account the cost of federal borrowing, the estimated cost of Hickel's program was $9.5 billion and that of the lump-sum grant program finally endorsed by Nixon was only $6.4 billion. In other words, Hickel's program was almost 50 percent more costly. This was particularly significant because there was already concern that the future borrowing requirements of the state and local governments were so high that the tax-exempt bond markets would not be able to meet them at reasonable interest rates.

In addition, Hickel's program, by providing federal assistance for the full construction costs of waste treatment plants, destroyed the incentive provision in the law under which a 20 percent bonus was given if states provided 25 percent of the matching funds to local projects. On this basis, many states had passed sizable bond issues.

Finally, Hickel did not help his cause with the President by talking about his proposal to the press when he knew it was still an open issue. The *New York Times,* for example, reported on January 11, 1970, "Mr. Hickel has passed the word to friends that White House officials have informed him that the President looks favorably on his plan."

Although disappointed with Nixon's decision, Hickel never lost his sense of humor. During the arguments over the merits of his program he told Ehrlichman, Mayo, and the author that the combination of the lump-sum grant program and the Environmental Financing Authority was like a little fat girl who could not sing or dance. "Give me my program and she will dance like Shirley Temple," Hickel used to say. After the President's decision, he sent them a picture of himself awkwardly trying to dance with a baby monkey with the initials "EFA," for Environmental Financing Authority, written across her chest. Mayo wrote, "She may not be able to dance and sing, but, boy, can she buy tax-exempt bonds."[8]

---

[8] Actually, Hickel turned out to be right. EFA never financed a single project. It was set up as a lender of last resort and the Treasury Department required such stringent criteria that bonds could be guaranteed more easily in the private market. As a result, at the administration's request, Congress did not renew EFA's authority.

The Legislative Battle with Congress

President Nixon made water pollution legislation the centerpiece of his first environmental message to Congress.

> First, to clean up our nation's waters, I am proposing a five-year, $10 billion Clean Water Act to provide the municipal treatment plants needed to meet our water quality standards nationwide; and I am proposing a comprehensive enforcement plan with strong new legal weapons to insure that no city and no industry is allowed to continue polluting lakes and rivers.[9]

Incredibly, Congress did not get down to serious business on water pollution legislation for another year. During the spring of 1970, the Senate Public Works Subcommittee on Air and Water Pollution (later called the Environmental Pollution Subcommittee) held a few hearings but dropped the subject in order to complete legislation on solid waste,[10] air quality (which took most of its time),[11] and ocean pollution.[12]

Lacking congressional action on a comprehensive water pollution enforcement plan, the President moved administratively in December 1970,[13] using the permit authority in the Refuse Act of 1899 as a vehicle to control industrial pollution of waterways.[14] Under the executive order, EPA was directed to require that, in order to obtain a permit to discharge effluents into navigable waters, industries had to disclose the amount and kinds of effluents being discharged. Thus, much more accurate data on the precise nature and quantities of pollutants being discharged into the nation's waterways could be obtained and the cost of obtaining the data was borne by industry. Effective as the program ultimately proved to be, after a shaky administrative start, it was stopped by court action temporarily in December 1971.[15] Later the 1972 Amend-

---

[9] *Public Papers of the Presidents, Nixon, 1970,* Remarks on Transmitting a Special Message to Congress on Environmental Quality, February 10, 1970, p. 95. The federal share of the proposed program was $4 billion.

[10] The Resource Recovery Act of 1970, P.L. 91-512 (84 Stat. 1227), October 29, 1970.

[11] The Clean Air Amendments of 1970, P.L. 91-604 (84 Stat. 1676), December 31, 1970.

[12] The Water Quality Improvement Act, P.L. 91-224 (84 Stat. 91), April 3, 1970.

[13] *Public Papers of the Presidents, Nixon, 1970,* Statement on Signing Executive Order Establishing a Water Quality Enforcement Program, December 23, 1970, p. 1153.

[14] Ch. 425 (30 Stat. 1151), March 3, 1899.

[15] Kalur v. Resor, D.C. District Court, December 21, 1971, ruled that each permit had to be accompanied by an environmental-impact statement in accordance with

ments to the Water Pollution Control Act provided the authority to reinstate the permit program. With the benefit of hindsight, the author believes the institution of a permit program was the single most important step the administration took to improve water quality. It is doubtful that Congress ever would have established the program firmly in law if the administration had not already been "out front." The permit program eventually was accepted by environmental groups, and it gave industry a greater sense of certainty in its pollution abatement planning.

In February 1971, Nixon included in his second environmental message to Congress,[16] several proposals to strengthen the administration bill submitted the previous year. The request for municipal waste treatment financing was increased from a level of $1 billion annually for four years to $2 billion annually for three years. Mandatory use of the best available treatment technology for new sources and federal toxic discharge standards was proposed. Authority for legal actions by private citizens to enforce water quality standards was proposed, as well as broader enforcement authority and stiffer fines. The enforcement proposals were updated to track with the enforcement provisions that Congress had provided in the Clean Air Amendments of 1970.

By that time, after a year of inaction, Congress was ready to give water pollution its full attention. The Senate began hearings in February and the House in May. In October the Senate Public Works Committee reported out a bill—S. 2770, the Federal Water Pollution Control Act Amendments—that gave the President and his economic advisers considerable concern.

First, the total price tag, which included $14 billion over a four-year period to finance waste treatment plants, was a budget-busting $18 billion, compared to a three-year cost of $6 billion for Nixon's proposal. Second, the stated policy of the bill, "that the discharge of all pollutants into navigable waters would be eliminated by 1985," could be construed literally to mean zero discharge, not only an impossible goal to achieve, but also an unreasonable limitation because it did not permit

the National Environmental Policy Act of 1969—an impractical requirement since thousands of permits were required. In the same case, the Court also ruled that no permits could be issued for discharge into non-navigable tributaries of navigable waters. Later in U.S. v. Pennsylvania Chemical Corporation, the Third Circuit Court of Appeals held that until the permit program was fully operational, which could take years, a company could not be prosecuted criminally for discharging pollutants.

[16] *Public Papers of the Presidents, Nixon, 1971,* Special Message to Congress Proposing the 1971 Environmental Program, February 8, 1971, pp. 128-130.

consideration of the costs of removing the last few percent of effluent in relationship to the benefit of that result. The stated goal reflected a lack of understanding of the scientific and technical aspects of water pollution control. For example, a zero discharge provision that is unrelated to a consideration of the quality of the receiving water could lead to absurd results: water distilled to the no-discharge standard at great cost could be dumped into naturally saline streams; discharges that were actually beneficial to marine life could be eliminated; and agricultural irrigation in arid western states could be ended.

Third, the so-called fishable, swimmable waters provision of the bill provided for "an interim goal of water quality which provides for the protection and propagation of fish, shellfish, and wildlife and provides for recreation in and on water to be achieved by 1981." [17] This goal was qualified by the words "wherever attainable." In this spirit, the bill called for federal effluent standards requiring utilization of the best *practical* control technology by industries and secondary treatment by municipalities by 1977 and the use of the best *available* pollution abatement technology by 1981. In spite of the qualifying language, the fact was that the policy statement extended a promise that could not be fulfilled.

Another objection to the bill was that, in providing for federal guidelines and 100-percent federal financing of waste water management planning, it would give the federal government a dominating position in the planning process. State authority would be severely curtailed.

Finally, in the administration's view the standards incorporated in the Senate bill not only were unrealistic, but also were inequitable and costly. If the no-discharge requirement should apply to industries but not to municipalities, it would be grossly inequitable. Also, there could be inequities among industrial sources of pollution, since some industries could discharge into municipal treatment facilities while others could not. Moreover, if the no-discharge requirement was intended to apply to municipal facilities, then the added costs would be astronomical—bearing no reasonable relationship to benefits in terms of improved water quality.

EPA Administrator William Ruckelshaus, CEQ Chairman Russell Train, and Chairman of the Council of Economic Advisers McCracken all testified for the administration before the House Public Works Committee, objecting to the Senate bill because it diminished the states' role,

---

[17] S. 2770, sec. 101(a)(1) and (2).

abandoned the flexibility of varying water uses, created arbitrary and inflexible deadlines that could not physically be met and for which there was no demonstrated need, and created inflationary pressures in the construction industry.[18] In addition, Paul McCracken testified that, based on CEQ and EPA staff estimates, the twenty-five-year costs, including both capital and operating expenses necessary in order to reach a 95 percent effluent reduction, would be about $119 billion for both municipal sewage treatment plants and private industry. The cost of achieving about the last 3 percent reduction, that is, to reach zero discharge, would require approximately $200 billion more.[19] In general, the cost of water pollution escalates greatly as the amount of pollution reduction increases. The cost of the last 10 percent reduction could be many times that of the first 90 percent.

On November 2, 1971, over administration protests, the Senate passed the bill with a vote of 86 to 0.[20] The political climate created by the environmental revolution was such that if the President had sent out airplanes to fetch the missing fourteen senators, the vote could well have been 100 to 0 against his position.

In spite of this rebuff, the administration pushed hard to make the House version of the bill more to its liking. It met with only modest success. Whereas the Senate bill asked for "fishable, swimmable waters" by 1981 and provided for the elimination of all pollutants (zero discharge) by 1985, the House bill left room for flexibility by providing for a national study commission authorized to contract with the National Academy of Sciences to evaluate and report after three years on the social, environmental and economic goals of the bill. Only then would implementation be considered by Congress.

In some respects, the administration's arguments were effective. In conference, the House members were largely successful in selling their provision for a mid-course correction study, thus softening the zero discharge and the absolute standards contained in the initial Senate bill. Table 8 gives the schedule set forth in the act: By July 1977, industry would be required to have in place the "best practicable" technology,

18 Paul McCracken, chairman, Council of Economic Advisers, Russell Train, chairman, CEQ, and William Ruckelshaus, administrator, EPA, in remarks about the Senate bill before the House Public Works Committee, *Hearings on H.R. 11896, H.R. 11895 to Amend the Federal Water Pollution Control Act* (Washington, D.C.: U.S. Government Printing Office, December 7, 1971), pp. 200-352.

19 Paul McCracken, in ibid., p. 213.

20 *Congressional Record,* vol. 117, part 30 (November 2, 1971), p. S38865.

Table 8

SCHEDULE OF WATER POLLUTION CONTROL TECHNOLOGY IMPLEMENTATION UNDER FEDERAL WATER POLLUTION CONTROL ACT AMENDMENTS OF 1972 (P.L. 92-500)

Phase	Goal	Time	Control Technique	
			Municipal	Industrial
1	Meet existing water quality standards	1977	Secondary	Best practical
2	Fishable and swimmable waters	1983	Best practical	Best available
3	Zero discharge	1985	A goal not legally enforceable	

Source: Data from P.L. 92-500.

with practicability defined in terms of "total costs"—that is, both the internal costs to the company and the external costs to society, including such costs as unemployment. By July 1983, industry would be required to use the "best available technology" to meet a national water quality standard of "fishable, swimmable waters."

An exemption was provided wherever the discharge could demonstrate that the benefits of this standard did not bear a reasonable relationship to the cost. In other words, in spite of the rhetoric and promises, the final bill implicitly recognized the possibility that the costs would be so high that it was highly unlikely that anyone would be swimming in the Cuyahoga River or the Houston ship channel by 1983. Nevertheless, by July 1985, the national goal of no discharge of pollutants into navigable waters would come into place.

The House-Senate conference bill gave a firm statutory base for the permit program. It authorized EPA to issue permits for the discharge of pollutants from any point-source into U.S. waters.[21] This authority could be delegated to any state whose permit program met detailed statutory criteria. However, the provision for delegation was somewhat meaningless because a state would have to notify EPA of all

---

[21] Point-source refers to an effluent discharge from a specific location, such as a pipe from an industrial plant emptying into a stream. Non-point-sources include pollutants and siltation derived from runoff from fields, timber harvesting, denuded surface mine areas, and acid production from exposed chemical reactive areas. Non-point-sources are significant because they may negate the pollution control reduction achieved through point-source effluent limitations.

applications and submit proposed permits to EPA sixty days before issuance, enabling EPA to require inclusion of any conditions it determined were needed to meet the statutory criteria.[22]

But it was the bill's provisions for financing the water pollution program that gave Nixon and his advisers the greatest concern and eventually drew his veto. Whereas the administration had proposed a $6 billion program over three years, the final bill authorized $18 billion—$5 billion in FY 1973, $6 billion in FY 1974, and $7 billion in FY 1975. Further, the use of contract obligational authority meant that outlays under the program would bypass the normal budgetary and appropriation process. The administration believed that the requirement for an annual review of priorities and needs should be retained, particularly because of the program's large size. Also, it did not seem that contract authority was needed to demonstrate the intent of the federal government to continue to provide high funding levels to state and local governments.

Understanding the public's overwhelming demand for clean water, yet sensitive to the charge of overspending, Congress inserted the words "not to exceed" before the dollar amounts in the contract authority provisions, and the floor debate suggested that the executive branch would have the authority to make allotments to the states below the levels the contract authority specified.[23] The "not-to-exceed" language was construed by some of the President's legal advisers to mean that discretionary spending below the maximum limits would be sustained in courts. But in his veto message Nixon recognized the inevitable political pressures to spend to the authorized limits.

> Certain provisions of S. 2770 confer a measure of spending discretion and flexibility upon the President, and if forced to administer this legislation I mean to use those provisions to put the brakes on the budget-wrecking expenditures as much as possible. But the law will still exact an unfair and unnecessary price from the public. For I am convinced on the basis of twenty-six years' experience with the political realities here in Washington, that the pressure for full funding under this bill would be so intense that funds approaching the maximum authorized amount could ultimately be claimed and paid out,

---

[22] Although it could exercise a federal veto, in practice EPA clearly sought opportunities to delegate its authority, and by 1976 over half the states were handling their permit programs.

[23] *Congressional Quarterly Almanac,* 92nd Congress, 2nd session, vol. 28 (1972), p. 720.

no matter what technical controls the bill appears to grant the Executive.[24]

As previously noted, the bill authorized expenditures of $5 billion, $6 billion, and $7 billion for fiscal years 1973, 1974, and 1975. Later, after his veto had been overridden, the President announced allotments, over the protest of environmental groups, of half the total amount— $2 billion for the remainder of 1973, $3 billion for 1974, and $4 billion for 1975. Nixon's proposed program, in which the average federal share of expenditures was 40 percent, foresaw construction for waste treatment plants of $4 billion a year. Congress raised the maximum federal share to 75 percent. Thus, the $5 billion figure set out in the bill as a maximum for FY 1973 contemplated a maximum yearly construction rate of nearly $7 billion. EPA clearly did not believe that the relatively specialized segment of the construction industry that is capable of building sewage treatment plants could absorb new construction in the first years of the program at a rate much higher than $4 billion a year.[25] According to its testimony, EPA expected that attempts to spend money faster would merely fuel inflation and would not provide any more sewage treatment plants, only more expensive ones.[26]

It was for those reasons that Nixon refused to allot $9 billion of the maximum $18 billion in contract authority that Congress provided for under the original bill. In January 1975, President Ford released $4 billion for FY 1976.[27] On February 18, 1975, the Supreme Court ruled the executive branch could not curtail the eventual $18 billion obligation authorized under the act by reducing initial allotments to the states.[28]

---

[24] *Public Papers of the Presidents, Nixon, 1972,* Veto of the Federal Water Pollution Control Act Amendments of 1972, October 17, p. 992.

[25] William Ruckelshaus, EPA administrator, Testimony before the House Public Works Committee, *Hearings on Construction Capability, Inflation and S. 2770 and H.R. 11896 Targets* (Washington, D.C.: U.S. Government Printing Office, December 7, 1971), pp. 310-315.

[26] In fact, the construction grant program had no discernible effect on inflation in the initial years. First, significant sewage treatment plant construction was not under way until the nation was in an economic downturn that left the general construction industry with excess capacity. Second, it turned out that the sewage treatment construction industry was not as specialized as EPA had thought it was, and a wide variety of general construction firms proved capable of building sewage treatment plants.

[27] Letter from President Ford to Environmental Protection Administrator Russell Train, January 24, 1975.

[28] Train v. City of New York and Train v. Campaign Clean Water, Inc., 416 U.S. 969, February 18, 1975.

In retrospect, the original EPA estimate of the optimum construction rate still seems sound. EPA was unable to obligate even $2 billion per year in FY 1973 or 1974 (see Table 9), and obligations reached $3.6 billion in FY 1975 and were estimated at about $4.8 billion in FY 1976 (including the transitional quarter). Therefore, the funding level anticipated by Congress, at least for the early years of the program, proved to be unattainable. One of the chief reasons for the slower pace of the program was that the law created a larger number of new and complex requirements that state and local governments were required to meet in order to get construction grants.

As we have seen, the bill increased the federal share to 75 percent. The administration took the position that a higher share than was permitted under the previous legislation (55 percent) would reduce local incentive to construct and maintain sewage treatment plants in an economical and efficient manner. Eligibility for federal financing was also significantly expanded. Under the old law eligibility was restricted to treatment plants and interceptors, but the new bill also provided for federal financing of collection sewers, treatment of combined sewers, treatment of storm waters, and rehabilitation of existing sewers.

Nor were the provisions for areawide waste treatment planning to the administration's liking. Under the bill, the EPA administrator would designate areas with significant water pollution problems, and governors, in cooperation with local officials, would designate regional boundaries and create planning agencies to develop areawide water pollution abatement plans. EPA would pay 100 percent of the first two year's cost of developing the plans and up to 75 percent thereafter. Also the Corps of Engineers could provide technical assistance to any designated state planning agency. Although the concept of areawide planning and management was desirable, the administration held that the approach taken in the bill was much too narrow. It was thought that it would lead to establishing special purpose plans and special purpose agencies for water quality, with no necessary relationship to plans and institutional arrangements for broader but closely related planning and management requirements, such as land use, transportation, urban planning, and so on. There was also concern that there would be a lack of incentive to develop realistic plans and implement them. Finally, in the administration's view, there was no need for a statutory role for the Corps of Engineers, which could assist EPA and local water quality agencies under EPA

86

criteria. Separate appropriations were likely to lead to different operating criteria and possible duplication.

There were also strong objections to the retroactive reimbursement feature of the construction grant program. The bill authorized retroactive reimbursement of up to 55 percent of the eligible project costs of all municipal waste treatment projects built after June 30, 1966. It also authorized retroactive reimbursement of up to 30 percent of the cost of waste treatment plants constructed between 1956 and 1966. These provisions provided no real pollution-control benefits and in some cases represented a windfall. Nixon hit it hard in his veto message:

> Ironically, however, only a portion of the $18 billion by which my bill was fattened on Capitol Hill would actually go to buy more pollution control than the Administration bill would have done. One backward-looking provision, for example, would provide $750 million to reimburse State and local governments for work already completed on sewage treatment plants *between 1956 and 1966.* The precedent this would set for retroactive reimbursement in other matching grant programs is an invitation to fiscal chaos.[29]

Congress was scheduled to adjourn on October 17 and the President had until that day to sign the bill. Advocates of the bill, however, wanted Congress to stay in session beyond midnight so that Nixon would not have the opportunity for a "pocket veto." Actually, Nixon had almost made up his mind to veto the bill. However, he wanted a last-minute chance to see if Congress would enact a $250 billion spending ceiling before going home for the election. If it did, there was a possibility, depending on the language, that the legislation would give the President the right to withhold expenditures at least through FY 1973.

Nixon gave Ehrlichman instructions: if Congress fails to pass the spending ceiling, send the veto message that is already prepared and signed; if Congress passes the spending ceiling, check back, and be ready with an analysis of the precise authority under which it will be possible to withhold water pollution funds in order to stay within a spending ceiling of $250 billion. Late in the evening, while Ehrlichman, his assistant Kenneth Cole, and the author watched from the gallery, the Senate rejected the President's proposal for a ceiling on spending.

Nixon knew there was no chance his veto would be sustained, but he could not in conscience go along with what he called "charge-account

---

[29] *Public Papers of the Presidents, Nixon, 1972,* Veto of the Federal Pollution Control Act Amendments of 1972, October 17, pp. 991-992.

congressmen." He wrote, "I am prepared for the possibility that my action on this bill will be overridden. The defeat of my proposal for a spending ceiling showed that many Senators and Congressmen are simply AWOL in our fight against higher taxes." [30]

Ehrlichman and Caspar Weinberger, director of the Office of Management and Budget, held a midnight press conference in an effort to drive home the President's veto message. "Unfortunately," Ehrlichman said, "the bill which finally, after two and one-half years, has been enacted by Congress is some $18 billion over the President's budget. The long and the short of that is that a vote to sustain the President's veto will be a vote for fiscal responsibility. A vote to override the President's veto will be a vote for higher taxes and inflation." [31] Less than two hours later the Senate adjourned, voting to override the President by 52 to 12.[32] The next afternoon, the House chose the same course by a lopsided vote of 247 to 23.[33] Thus S. 2770, one of the major and most controversial pieces of environmental legislation during the Nixon years, became law.[34]

The Water Pollution Control Act Amendments of 1972 in Retrospect

With the benefit of hindsight the author believes that President Nixon's veto was justified. As was clear when it became law, the plan to clean up the nation's waterways was bound to run behind schedule. Both the National Commission on Water Quality Report [35] and the data on projected grants for municipal sewage treatment plants summarized in CEQ's *Sixth Annual Report* [36] indicated clearly that the 1977 deadline—secondary treatment for municipal waste—was far from being achieved. On the other hand, the 1977 goal—best practical pollution abatement technology for industrial pollutants—will be met substantially on schedule.

---

[30] Ibid., p. 992.

[31] Office of the White House Press Secretary, Transcript of a news briefing by John D. Ehrlichman, assistant to the President for domestic affairs and Caspar W. Weinberger, director, Office of Management and Budget, October 17, 1972.

[32] *Congressional Record*, vol. 118, part 28 (October 17, 1972), p. S 36879.

[33] *Congressional Record*, vol. 118, part 28 (October 18, 1972), p. H 37061.

[34] P.L. 92-500 (86 Stat. 816), October 18, 1972.

[35] National Commission on Water Quality, "Staff Draft Report," mimeographed, November 1975, p. I-9.

[36] CEQ, *Sixth Annual Report*, p. 68.

Table 9

EPA'S PROPOSED OBLIGATION AND OUTLAY SCHEDULE
(AS OF OCTOBER 1976) FOR THE $18 BILLION
MUNICIPAL WASTE TREATMENT GRANT PROGRAM
(in millions of dollars)

Fiscal Year	Obligations		Outlays	
	Annual	Cumulative totals	Annual	Cumulative totals
1973	$1,592	$ 1,592	$ 0	
1974	1,384	2,976	160	$ 160
1975	3,616	6,592	880	1,040
1976	4,265	10,857	1,770	2,810
1976 (transition quarter)	549	11,406	800	3,610
1977	6,594	18,000	3,370	6,980
1978			4,300	11,280
1979			3,400	14,680
1980			1,500	16,180
1981			1,190	17,370
1982			630	18,000

Source: Personal communications with OMB.

Although Nixon's attempts to impound funds may have slowed to a very limited extent the process of achieving these legislatively set deadlines, and although EPA was a new organization saddled with a cumbersome grant-dispensing system under the new law, there seems little doubt that the $18 billion initially authorized could have been obligated efficiently during the three-year life of the law. As a matter of fact, by the end of FY 1975 only about $6.6 billion of these funds had been obligated and only about $1 billion actually spent. By the end of FY 1976 (including the transitional quarter) only an estimated $3.6 billion was expected to be spent and an estimated $11.4 billion obligated (see Table 9). Over the three-year life of the law, EPA—even after Nixon's impoundments of part of its funds—had unobligated balances each year well over $1 billion. However, EPA still expected to increase annual obligations so that the entire originally appropriated $18 billion could be obligated by September 1977 (see Table 9). There is some question, in the author's opinion, as to whether the funds could ever have been obligated that rapidly without serious deterioration in the quality of the planning and design of municipal waste treatment construction projects. However, the main reason for the inability to obligate funds was not lack of contracting capacity or construction bottlenecks, as Nixon originally thought it would be, but cumbersome provisions of the law that made it impossible to gear up quickly for such a large construction grant program. Not only were the administrative procedures too complicated but there were not enough people to process the grants. Some 250 new people had to be added to EPA's staff to assist communities in completing their grant applications and expediting construction schedules. In addition, EPA reprogrammed over 150 positions for this purpose. One change needed in the law was to give the states a larger role in the grant certification process, and the administration supported the Wright-Cleveland bill (H.R. 2175), introduced January 28, 1975, which would achieve this purpose and also allow the states to use some of their grant funds to pay the administrative costs of processing grant applications.

But the vast underestimation of the program's cost made one wonder if EPA could ever catch up with the goals set in the Federal Water Pollution Control Act Amendments of 1972. EPA Administrator Russell Train, in a letter of July 31, 1975, to OMB Director James Lynn, put in an advanced FY 1977 budget request.[37] He proposed a six-year commitment (1977 through 1983) of $7 billion annually for a total of $42 billion, which EPA estimated to be the federal share of a construction grant program for the more critical facilities needed to bring municipal sources (but by no means all of the facilities) into compliance with the 1983 goals set forth in the law. This funding level would result in completion of the municipal point-source facilities by the mid-1980s but would not provide funding for storm water overflow problems. Train also proposed legislative amendments that would reduce the federal grant share to 60 percent for facilities to control combined sewer overflows and 45 percent for collection sewers and major sewer rehabilitation projects. In addition, an amendment would be offered to eliminate the eligibility of storm-

---

[37] "Recommendations by EPA to OMB on the Construction Grant Program," *Environment Reporter,* vol. 6, no. 16 (August 15, 1975), pp. 622-625.

sewer control projects. The federal share for construction grants for treatment plants and interceptors would remain unchanged at 75 percent.

The difficulty was, as in the case with the original law, that even the more modest objectives cited in Train's proposal were not likely to be achieved—because $7 billion annually is an enormous rate of expenditure, considering all our other national priorities.

It eventually became clear—and all recognized it—that the objectives of the 1972 act would not be achieved. Industrial pollution abatement deadlines would be partially met, but full compliance with municipal waste treatment deadlines was not likely even by the mid-1980s. Thus, the industrial pollution abatement goal appeared to have been fairly realistic and the municipal waste treatment goal quite unrealistic. A policy debate on amending the 1972 law was under way. The key questions it addressed were the advisability of trying to achieve the 1983 application of "best available" technology requirements and, to a lesser extent, the "fishable, swimmable waters" goal. While the national Water Quality Commission Report indicated that the 1983 "best available" technology goal was, in general, technologically achievable, the task before the full commission and the Congress was to evaluate the additional benefits against the additional cost.

After a three-year $17 million investigation with a forty-member professional staff and ninety-seven individual contract studies, the National Commission on Water Quality advised Congress that the requirements for meeting the "fishable, swimmable waters" goal in 1983 should be postponed, and it recommended mid-course legislative changes in the Federal Water Pollution Control Act Amendments of 1972, including "alterations in the implementing strategy to give the program a stability and continuity of funding and facilities design." [38] Its major recommendations included:

—Case-by-case and category-by-category extensions of the uniform treatment requirements for compliance with the 1977 deadline for both municipal and industrial plants.

—Postponement of the 1983 requirement for the use of the best available pollution control technology for five to ten years, with a new evaluation by 1985 by a new National Commission on Water Quality.

[38] Memorandum to commissioners of the National Commission on Water Quality from F. J. Clarke, executive director, March 2, 1976, p. 5.

—A new legislative authority which would require compliance as soon as possible but not later than 1980 in reducing poisons like PCBs, mercury, cyanide, kepone, cadmium, et cetera, in water.

—Decentralization of the program by granting more administrative and regulatory control through selective certification based on satisfactory state plans for control of pollution from both point- and non-point sources.

This left the question of the level of financing of the water pollution control program still unresolved. As noted above, EPA Administrator Train had recommended a six-year level of $7 billion annually. The National Commission on Water Quality sought a construction grant program (75 percent federally financed) of between $5 and $10 billion annually for five to ten years for priority treatment needs. The administration had requested zero budget authority for waste treatment construction grants in FY 1977. In order to bring the program within reasonable reach of federal budgetary resources, the administration proposed amendments to reduce or eliminate certain categories of facilities, thus reducing the federal share of projected needs from about $318 billion to $48 billion.

The framing of a sound water pollution program requires that Congress and the administration explicitly address the question of how much given levels of water quality are worth, with consideration given to balancing water pollution control and other national priorities. Estimates of benefits, though admittedly incomplete and hard to calculate, are needed in order to understand the relationship between increased expenditures for water pollution control and increased expenditures for water quality improvement. It is time that the facts become known—and the rhetoric cooled—so that a President is never again deluded into making the promise Lyndon Johnson made when he signed the Water Quality Act of 1965: "We are going to reopen the Potomac for swimming by 1975." [39]

[39] *Public Papers of the Presidents of the United States, Lyndon B. Johnson, 1965,* Remarks at the Signing of the Water Quality Act of 1965, October 2, 1965 (Washington, D.C.: U.S. Government Printing Office, 1966), p. 1035.

5

Clean Air—Technology or Not?

On the last day of 1970, Richard Nixon signed the Clean Air Amendments into law.[1] Curiously, in retrospect, there was little debate within the administration about the wisdom of signing the bill. Besides, given the nearly hysterical support for the environmental movement, a veto would have been futile: Congress would have promptly overridden it. Still, as he did in the case of the Water Pollution Control Act Amendments of 1972, Nixon could at least have had the satisfaction of vetoing the bill and pointing out its deficiencies—deficiencies that have become more obvious over the years.

Introduction

OMB, CEQ, EPA, HEW, Commerce, Transportation, and the AEC had all advised the President to sign the Clean Air Amendments. Justice, Defense, and GSA had "no objection," Labor and the Office of Science and Technology voted a drowsy "no comment," and Interior was so sleepy it failed to vote. Only the Federal Power Commission, OMB, and Commerce expressed some reservations (the same ones which had already been stated in a letter to the Congress from HEW Secretary Elliot Richardson),[2] but in the end they recommended signing. The author also thought the President should sign.

In the amendments, Congress gave Nixon much of what he had asked for in his first environmental message to Congress, including: (1)

---

1 Public Law 91-604 (84 Stat. 1676), December 31, 1970.
2 Letter of November 17, 1970, from HEW Secretary Elliot Richardson to Harley Staggers, chairman, House Committee on Interstate and Foreign Commerce.

national air quality standards, (2) emission standards applicable to major, newly constructed stationary sources of air pollution and to hazardous emissions from stationary sources, (3) expanded and stream-lined enforcement powers, (4) authority for assembly-line testing of auto emission control systems, and (5) authority to regulate fuels and fuel additives.[3] However, by trying to legislate technologies that were not yet perfected and by arbitrarily fixing deadlines for the control of auto emissions and stationary polluting sources, deadlines that in some cases required unproven technology, Congress started a process that led in the ensuing years to costly solutions for cleaning our air. On the other hand, there is no doubt that the pace of improvement in air pollution abatement technology increased because of this legislation.

The administration had advocated that auto emission standards be related to judgments about the best technology available within a given timetable for implementing the standards. However, the bill passed by Congress set forth auto emission levels based not on any demonstration of available technology but rather on the degree of air quality thought to be necessary in urban areas. Auto manufacturers were required to reduce emissions from 1975 model cars 90 percent below the standards applicable to 1970 vehicles. A one-year extension of this deadline could be granted by EPA's administrator under certain conditions, but further delays required congressional approval. Congress ignored the administration's concern that if good faith efforts failed to produce the technology required to meet the 1975 standards, successive deadline extensions would be advisable.

Nor did Congress adequately take into account known technology or the full range of economic and institutional factors when it set what proved to be unrealistically tight deadlines for meeting stationary source emission standards. The bill permitted states to achieve primary health standards and secondary aesthetic standards at the same time, but in some cases this proved to be technologically unfeasible, as could have been foreseen at the time. Both Congress and the administration failed to foresee that the nation would be so short of natural gas and low-sulfur residual oil that the bill's standards and compliance timetables would be impossible to achieve.

Still, the President signed the bill. No one advised him that even the auto emission levels already set by HEW under the old law, before

---

[3] *Public Papers of the Presidents, Nixon, 1970,* Special Message to the Congress on Environmental Quality, pp. 100-104.

catalytic converter technology was developed to achieve the tighter standards required by the new law, had decreased gas mileage in the short run. Heavier cars, automatic transmissions, and air conditioners also increased gas consumption—but, then, gas was plentiful and cheap. No one told the President that the new clean air law would accentuate a trend that would later be hard to reverse. That trend moved toward expanded use of cleaner and scarcer natural gas—as well as of cleaner, and almost four times more expensive, low-sulfur imported oil; and it moved away from our most abundant resource, coal, which at that time could not be burned cleanly enough to meet the standards of the new law.

Thus by legislating standards that required nonexistent technology and by hoping that the technology would come along in time to meet the rigid deadlines, Congress forced the federal government to try to meet idealistic deadlines for auto emissions in 1975 and for stationary sources of pollution in 1975–1977. As we shall see, the effort failed on both counts.

Auto Emissions

As early as the late 1940s, automobiles were recognized as a major cause of air pollution in our cities. Dr. A. Hagen-Smit, who first discovered that Southern California smog was related to auto emissions, outlined the problem to President Nixon and his cabinet at San Clemente in the late summer of 1969. California had taken the lead in auto emission research and was the first state to regulate auto emissions. Beginning with the 1963 model, it required crankcase ventilation systems, and later the auto industry voluntarily installed this system on all cars. In 1966 California began to control unburned hydrocarbons and carbon monoxide tailpipe emissions, and in 1968 the federal government applied about the same standards to the rest of the country.

Over the years, before the Clean Air Amendments of 1970 became law, emission standards were based on known technology and included consideration of penalty factors—such as cost, vehicle performance, and mileage—balanced against the benefits of cleaner air. Nixon, in his first environmental message to Congress, had the same philosophy in mind when he asked for emission level standards for 1973 and 1975 significantly lower than existing standards but still within the bounds of known technology. As the President wrote, "These new standards represent our best present estimate of the lowest emission levels obtainable by those years." [4] The House reacted quickly, and on June 10, 1970, voted 375 to 1 for a bill generally along the lines of the administration bill.[5]

In the Senate, Edmund Muskie was under intense pressure from environmental groups to produce a "tough" clean air bill. According to Clarence and Barbara Davies, "the President appeared to be taking the leadership on the pollution issue, threatening to undercut one of Muskie's strong points as a presidential contender." [6] Ralph Nader, in the foreword to a 1970 Nader report that was strongly critical of past air pollution legislation and enforcement, referred to "the collapse of the federal air pollution effort starting with Senator Edmund Muskie and continuing to the pathetic abatement efforts and auto pollution policies of the National Air Pollution Control Administration." [7] Muskie and the Public Works Committee staff, stung by this sort of criticism, needed a "tough" bill. Part of their strategy was to change the well-publicized air emission standard-setting procedure. Coincidentally, Dr. Delbert Barth of the National Air Pollution Control Administration of HEW (the Environmental Protection Agency had not yet been formed) set forth the levels of pollution control he estimated would be needed by automobiles by 1980 to achieve air quality goals.[8] Barth made no attempt to evaluate the technological questions of emission controls. Muskie and the Public Works Committee staff, in their bill, provided for reductions in hydrocarbons, carbon monoxide, and nitrogen oxide vehicular-exhaust emissions at about the same levels that Dr. Barth had roughly calculated would be required by 1980. But the committee telescoped the timetable for meeting these theoretical standards from 1980 to 1975/1976, which meant a 90 percent reduction by 1975 in hydrocarbons and carbon monoxide compared to standards for 1970 cars, as well as a 90 percent reduction by 1976 in nitrogen oxide emissions compared to average uncontrolled emissions of 1971 model year cars.

In this way, the 1975/1976 standards, based mainly on desirable air quality goals for 1980, were included in the Senate bill without

[4] Ibid., p. 101.

[5] *Congressional Record*, vol. 116, part 14 (June 10, 1970), p. H 19244.

[6] Clarence and Barbara Davies, *The Politics of Pollution* (Indianapolis, Indiana: Pegasus, 1975), p. 54.

[7] John Esposito, *The Ralph Nader Study Group Report on Air Pollution: Vanishing Air* (New York, N.Y.: Grossman Publishers, 1970), pp. VII-VIII.

[8] Delbert Barth, "Federal Motor Vehicle Emission Goals for CO, HC and NO_x Based on Desired Air Quality Levels," *Journal of the Air Pollution Control Association*, vol. 20, no. 8 (August 1970), pp. 519-523.

adequate demonstration that they could in fact be achieved technologically. These goals were then arbitrarily compressed to the 1975 and 1976 timetables.

The administration convinced the House-Senate conference committee to make a few changes in the bill. One was to order a National Academy of Sciences study on the feasibility of meeting the 1975 hydrocarbon and carbon monoxide standards and another was to set a more reasonable time frame within which a manufacturer might seek a deadline extension.

As passed by Congress and signed by the President, the bill did recognize that the auto industry might be unable to meet the emission standards on time. It provided that a one-year extension of the 1975/1976 standards could be granted if four conditions were met: (1) the auto manufacturers made a good-faith effort to meet the standards, (2) technological alternatives were not available in time, (3) the extension was backed by the National Academy of Sciences' study, and (4) suspension was essential to the public interest or public health and welfare of the nation.

In 1972, during March and April, five companies exercised their right under the law and asked for a one-year suspension of the 1975 hydrocarbon and carbon monoxide standards.[9] On May 12, EPA Administrator William Ruckelshaus denied the application. To grant a suspension, the law required that all four conditions must be met. In addition, Ruckelshaus interpreted the law to say that there was a presumption to deny an application where the technical information supplied was not clear.

> I reject the argument of some applicants that standards may lawfully be suspended where the effectiveness of available control technology cannot itself be affirmatively established or has not been "proved." . . . Under the law it is the applicant who must establish the ineffectiveness or nonavailability of control technology by which compliance may be achieved. I am not permitted by the Act to suspend the standards simply because additional testing and evaluation, which may be desirable, has not been completed by manufacturers at the time of my decision.[10]

[9] The five companies were Chrysler, Ford, General Motors, International Harvester, and Volvo.

[10] William Ruckelshaus, "Application for Suspension of the 1975 Motor Vehicle Exhaust Emission Standards, Decision of the Administrator," EPA, mimeographed, May 12, 1972, pp. 7-8.

For all practical purposes Ruckelshaus also ruled out cost as a significant factor in his decision. At the time, the Ford Motor Company estimated the incremental cost to the consumer of a 1975 car equipped with two catalytic converters to be $290. Later the National Academy of Sciences estimated that the total cost to achieve statutory emission levels would range from $5 billion to $11 billion in 1985, depending on whether nitrogen oxide standards were set at 2.0 grams per mile or 0.41 grams per mile and on whether catalyst changes were included. It also estimated that total benefits would range from $3.6 billion to $14.3 billion.[11] EPA held that the $11 billion figure for costs was too high, and instead estimated costs at $8 billion—and at only $4.8 billion if the 2.0 grams per mile rather than 0.41 grams per mile were adopted as the nitrogen oxide emission standard. EPA estimated benefits at $7.2 billion, while cautioning that it was difficult to measure environmental benefits in dollar amounts.[12] At any rate EPA agreed with the National Academy of Sciences' report that, "weighing all of these estimates, and their uncertainties, we conclude that the benefits in monetary terms that could reasonably be expected to accrue from implementing the federal statutory emission control standards for automobiles are commensurate with their expected cost." [13] Even if this information had been available to Ruckelshaus, his decision probably would have been the same. He wrote:

> Cost considerations are of limited relevance in judging whether technology effective to meet the 1975 standards is to be deemed available to the manufacturers. Assuming without deciding that cost considerations are intended by Congress to have some weight, I believe it is clear that the cost of the catalyst devices is not so high that they can properly be deemed to be not available to manufacturers within the meaning of section 202(b)(5).[14]

---

[11] National Academy of Sciences, *Air Quality and Automobile Emission Control, the Cost and Benefits of Automobile Emission Control—A Report by the Coordinating Committee on Air Quality Studies,* vol. 4, prepared for the Committee on Public Works, United States Senate, pursuant to S. Res. 135, approved August 3, 1973 (Washington, D.C.: U.S. Government Printing Office, 1974), p. 78, table 2-14 and p. 417, table 6-1.

[12] March 31, 1975, letter from Mr. Alvin L. Alm, assistant administrator, EPA, to the author.

[13] National Academy of Sciences, *Air Quality and Automobile Emission Control—A Report by the Coordinating Committee on Air Quality Studies,* vol. 1 of the summary report, September 1974, p. 3.

[14] Ruckelshaus, "Application for Suspension," p. 15.

Ruckelshaus denied the requests because the applicants had, in his opinion, not established that satisfactory emission control technology for 1975 model cars was not available. He argued there was sufficient lead time and that available technology was probably adequate.

Based on an analysis of the entire record, I conclude that emission reduction required to meet the 1975 standards can probably be achieved in a number of current engines suitable for use on most popular varieties of automobiles. My best analysis of the available data indicates that maximum reductions can be achieved by modification and improvements to the engine itself and by use of noble metal catalysts in the exhaust system.[15]

In effect, Congress had "legislated technology." Because of the short lead time, Ruckelshaus's decision locked the auto companies into the catalyst technology and foreclosed, for all practical purposes, several other technological approaches for reducing emissions. It turned out, as we shall see, that the decision to use the catalyst may have created health hazards that were as great as, or greater than, those involved in continuing to use the 1973–1974 emission control systems without catalysts. On the other hand, the use of catalysts produced significant economic benefits in terms of fuel economy.

The auto manufacturers promptly sued. The court denied the manufacturers' request for suspension of the 1975 deadline but, relying primarily on a National Academy of Sciences' report which had concluded the technology was not available to meet the 1974 emission standards, remanded the case to EPA for further consideration.[16] The court said that "the risk of an 'erroneous' denial of suspension outweigh[s] the risk of an 'erroneous' grant of suspension." [17] Based on the court's remand, Ruckelshaus wrote that, in his opinion,

the Court has required a high degree of confidence that the 1975 standards can be achieved and has cautioned that a decision to deny suspension, to the extent it is based on predictions of technological availability as opposed to direct evidence of such availability, must be supported by a detailed

---

15 Ibid., p. 17.

16 International Harvester v. Ruckelshaus, District of Columbia Court of Appeals, February 10, 1973.

17 William Ruckelshaus, "Application for Suspension of the 1975 Motor Vehicle Exhaust Emission Standards, Decision of the Administrator on Remand from the United States Court of Appeals for the District of Columbia Circuit," EPA, mimeographed, April 11, 1973, p. 4.

showing that the methodology underlying the prediction is reasonable and reliable.[18]

The court suggested that the administrator of EPA might establish higher standards if the deadline were suspended.

Another set of EPA hearings began on March 12, 1973. During the year that had elapsed since Ruckelshaus's original decision not to grant a suspension of the 1975 standards, substantial progress had been made. Both the rotary engine without a catalyst and the carbureted version of the stratified charge engine had shown under test that they could meet the 1975 standard. However, to meet the basic mass-production demand that the court had ruled was the real measure of technological feasibility, it was clear that conventional internal combustion engines would be needed. According to Ruckelshaus, "the principal questions before me on this remand are whether conventional engines equipped with catalysts can meet applicable emission standards and can be produced in 1975 in sufficient numbers to satisfy basic demand in a manner consistent with public interest." [19]

Without exception, all manufacturers testified that catalyst technology was not then available to meet the 1975 standards. Chrysler and American Motors testified that, even if catalyst-equipped vehicles could be mass produced in the 1975 model year, many would break down, resulting in severe financial penalties to the companies under the act's recall and warranty provisions. But General Motors was more optimistic about the reliability of the catalyst and proposed interim standards requiring catalyst-equipped cars for California in order to gain more reliability experience.[20] Ruckelshaus endorsed this suggestion in his decision and ordered a two-standard system: (1) a very tight standard for California that required catalysts and (2) a slightly less stringent standard (although tighter than the auto industry recommended) for the rest of the nation that did not require catalysts. This meant Ruckelshaus had decided that the risk of possible economic disruption if the catalyst failed after being adopted nationwide far outweighed the minimal losses in air quality resulting from a one-year extension of the interim standards that he proposed.

Although unhappy with the decision, the auto makers decided not to go to court. Presumably they weighed the odds of gaining a suspen-

---

[18] Ibid., p. 16.
[19] Ibid., p. 2.
[20] Ibid., pp. 9-13.

sion against the time the appeal would take and the uncertainties over the emission system needed in the 1975 model cars. Also it was clear that General Motors and Ford were more optimistic about the reliability of catalysts than were Chrysler and American Motors, and General Motors began to install catalysts on most of its cars, not just those destined for the California market. Moreover, tests were beginning to show that often the 50,000-mile warranty required under the law could be met with one catalyst or only one replacement. Finally, tests were showing that the fuel efficiency of catalyst-equipped 1975 model cars would be better than that of the 1973 models as well as what was predicted for the 1974 non-catalyst cars.

With the Arab boycott in late 1973 and the sudden rise in imported oil prices, the trade-off between clean air and gas mileage came under increasing scrutiny. In late 1973 EPA estimated that the 1975 model cars would have a 7 percent better fuel efficiency than the 1973/1974 models, but later EPA found its estimates too conservative. The final fuel economy improvement for 1975 models was 13.5 percent above that of the 1973/1974 models, on a fleet-wide sales-weighted average. As it turned out, weight and air conditioning contributed more to poor gas mileage than did auto emission controls. There was also a controversy about the additional amount of crude oil needed to make the unleaded gasoline required for catalysts. It was true that, for equivalent octane ratings, more oil was required to make unleaded gas. But the increase in oil consumption resulting from the low octane unleaded gas used in compact cars was very small—only about 1 percent. This modest increase would be more than offset by the fuel economy of smaller cars.

The 1976 nitrogen oxide standard specified in the Clean Air Amendments of 1970 also proved unrealistic, but this time there was no argument about it. EPA discovered that the monitoring data given to Congress and used by Congress as the basis for setting the 1976 nitrogen oxide standards was incorrect: there was no near-term need for such strict nitrogen oxide emission control to meet health standards. Also the standard set by Congress involved a considerable fuel penalty. So, without controversy, in June 1973 EPA granted a one-year suspension of the 1976 nitrogen oxide standard and approved an interim standard that did not require catalyst technology.

Up to this point the advocates of "legislating technology" appeared to have had the record on their side. There had been no disruption of the auto assembly lines by the failure of the catalysts. On the contrary, the plan was working better than many had dared hope, and the companies were being "pushed to the limits" as planned. In brief, the regulatory strategy seemed to be working for the benefit of the public. Congress, it turned out, had fixed the timetable too tightly but it had had the foresight to build in a one-year delay—or so almost everyone thought at the time Ruckelshaus made his decision.

But, then, the Ford Motor Company reported small amounts of sulfuric acid (H_2SO_4) emissions from their catalytic-equipped cars. After testing, EPA concluded that some of the sulfur that was emitted as sulfur dioxide oxidized into sulfates (SO_3), which then mixed with water vapor in the exhaust, resulting in a sulfuric acid mist from the tailpipe. The result could be a significant health hazard. More testing was conducted. In November 1973 the new EPA administrator, Russell Train, testified before Congress that sulfate emissions from catalyst-equipped vehicles were about 0.05 grams per mile and that, along heavily traveled multi-lane highways, there could be significant adverse health effects at the end of a model year in which about 25 percent of the cars would be equipped with catalysts.[21] Still, the data was sketchy at best and, in many parts of the country, medical scientists estimated that existing ambient sulfate levels already constituted a health hazard. So Train concluded that the health hazard from sulfate emissions, at least until further research was done, did not justify abandoning catalysts, which would have meant reversing the downward trend in hydrocarbons and carbon monoxide emissions. Meanwhile, Train promised that further testing would take place.

On March 22, 1974, because of concern over the energy crisis and uneasiness over the sulfate situation, President Nixon proposed a package of thirteen amendments to the Clean Air Amendments of 1970, including the freezing of auto emission interim 1975 standards for two additional years, 1976 and 1977. In June the Congress, sharing the administration's concern, changed the auto emission laws by providing for: (1) continuation of the 1975 interim standards for carbon monoxide, hydrocarbons, and nitrogen oxide through model year 1976; (2) the limitation of nitrogen oxide emissions to 3.1 grams per mile in model year 1975 and 1976, 2.0 grams per mile in 1977, and 0.4 grams

[21] Russell Train, EPA administrator, *Hearings on Compliance with Title II (Auto Emission Standards) of the Clean Air Act before the Senate Committee on Public Works,* 93d Congress, 1st session (November 6, 1973), pp. 431-436.

per mile in 1978; and (3) petition by manufacturers to the EPA administrator for suspension of the 1977 hydrocarbon and carbon monoxide emission limitations for one year and for prescription of alternative limitations.[22]

The automobile manufacturers again petitioned for a one-year extension of the 1977 standards, and hearings began in January 1975. Meanwhile, President Ford was not satisfied with the modest extension in deadlines that Congress had given in the Energy Supply and Coordination Act. In his state of the union address he proposed legislation that would put the national emission standards for hydrocarbons and carbon monoxide at the same level as California's for the 1975 model year cars, with a limit of 3.1 grams per mile nitrogen oxide emissions.[23] There would be a freeze on these standards for five years and the auto industry would enter into a voluntary agreement to achieve a 40 percent fuel economy improvement. This would provide a steady technological target for a known and fixed period of time and, at the same time, it would avoid any significant adverse effect on improving air quality. But just as the suspension hearing started, the extensive studies that Train had promised Congress on sulfate and sulfuric acid emissions became available. Their basic conclusion was that, over a two-to-four-year period, the then-estimated emissions of sulfuric acid from catalyst-equipped cars could potentially have a cost, in terms of harm to health, that more than offset the benefits of greater control of hydrocarbon and carbon monoxide emissions.

The unreasonableness of the statutory provision requiring a decision from the administrator of the EPA sixty days after a request for suspension became apparent, and the weakness in the entire concept of legislating technology lay exposed. Train had to make a decision in spite of very shaky scientific evidence. Questions were raised about EPA's procedures in estimating the incremental exposure of sulfuric acid from catalyst-equipped vehicles. There was no general agreement on the threshold for adverse health effects from sulfuric acid. But medical scientists at EPA felt so strongly about the admittedly unquantifiable health hazards of sulfuric acid emissions from catalyst-equipped cars that one alternative Train had to consider was to give up completely on

[22] The Energy Supply and Environmental Coordination Act of 1974, P.L. 93-319 (88 Stat. 246), June 22, 1974.
[23] Office of the White House Press Secretary, State of the Union, January 15, 1975.

catalysts. He refused to do this, and although only time and technological improvement will tell for sure, in the author's opinion, given the law under which Train had to operate, he made the correct decision. If he had removed catalysts, then emissions in 1975 model cars would have reverted to about the standards of the early 1970s. It was already too late to do anything about 1976 cars, or even to make major changes in 1977 cars. Also, until the potential sulfuric acid problem emerged, catalysts had performed quite well. As Train wrote in his decision:

> In many ways, catalysts have performed far better than some predicted when the 1975 interim standards were first published two years ago. Contrary to many predictions, both the production of catalysts and their installation on automobiles is proceeding without difficulty. The President of the National Academy of Sciences has stated that as of November, 1974, "significant advances have made catalytic emission control systems much more satisfactory for the control of automotive emissions than we anticipated in 1973." [24]

Boxed into a corner, Train decided to keep sulfuric acid emission reduced by allowing auto manufacturers to continue using catalysts, but making it unnecessary for them to employ air pumps. The pump device used injects air into the exhaust stream just before it enters the catalyst, and this additional oxygen permits the catalyst to convert hydrocarbons and carbon monoxide more completely to harmless carbon dioxide and water. But it is the extra oxygen that encourages the conversion of sulfur dioxide (SO_2) to sulfate (SO_3), which unfortunately reacts with water available in the exhaust to form a sulfuric acid (H_2SO_4) mist. No one knows yet whether the sulfuric acid emission phenomenon will turn out to be a problem. Further tests are required to determine the actual rates of sulfuric acid emissions from various types of cars, with and without an air pump, and the rates of dispersion, from which can be obtained possible maximum ambient concentrations. And a medical judgment must be obtained on what concentration levels may be harmful. It is possible that the whole sulfuric acid issue may turn out to be spurious, but until one can be sure, caution is required and increases in sulfuric acid emissions should be avoided.

So Train granted the application for suspension of the 1977 standards and established as an interim standard the 1975 hydrocarbon

---

[24] Russell Train, "Application for Suspension of the 1975 Motor Vehicle Exhaust Emission Standards, Decision of the Administrator," EPA, mimeographed, March 5, 1975, p. 5.

and carbon monoxide standards for all states except California. Thus auto makers could use a technology short of the best one available to reduce emissions, but still stringent enough to continue the downward trend in hydrocarbon and carbon monoxide emissions. Many vehicles could meet the standard without catalysts, and those that used catalysts could do so without the sulfuric-acid-producing air pump.

In mandating specific emission levels that were required to be achieved by rigidly fixed dates, Congress had clearly chosen to endorse the popular notion that major technological breakthroughs were there for the asking—if industry were only pushed hard enough and forced to spend enough money. Yet clearly the notion is suspect. Given strong public support for reduction in auto emissions, it is hard to support the conspiratorial theory that industry is not itself motivated to achieve technological breakthroughs.

Thus we have traveled full circle. By legislating technological breakthroughs that failed to materialize on timetables fixed by law, rather than authorizing a knowledgeable administrator to make decisions when he had enough information, Congress forced industry to embrace the catalytic converter technology. Six years after the passage of the act, serious doubts were raised over the health effects of the catalytic converter. Years had been lost that might have been devoted to other approaches to solving the emissions problem. While progress and benefits had been achieved at an acceptable cost, the time had come to freeze emission standards until a reliable technology could be confirmed.

Stationary Source Standards

Even without the Arab oil embargo, it is probable that the huge price increases the OPEC cartel placed on imported oil eventually would have forced administration policy makers to propose changes in the Clean Air Amendments of 1970. Deadlines that were coming due in the 1975–1977 time frame could not be met. In trying to achieve them, power plants and industrial users were using more cleaner-burning natural gas and low-sulfur residual fuel oil, both in short supply, and they were using less higher-sulfur coal, the United States's most abundant fuel. By the spring of 1974, after the fall and winter of the Arab boycott, with OPEC oil flowing again but at a staggering cost of $11 or more per barrel, the need to change the clean air laws became compelling. Although estimates varied widely even within the administration, there was general agreement that compliance with the State Air Implementation Plans would have a significant impact on the demand for various kinds of fuels and the ability of the market to supply them. The major problem was how to meet the sulfur oxide standards for industry and power plants. Without amending the law, it appeared that there would be a projected shortage of about 200 million tons of low-sulfur coal (0.6 lbs. sulfur per million BTU) per year to meet the projected requirement, or roughly one-third of the total national production. The projected oil shortage was about 435 million barrels of low-sulfur fuel oil (.56 lbs. sulfur per million BTU). Natural gas would be short by about 3.3 trillion cubic feet in 1975 and there would be even more serious shortfalls in subsequent years.[25]

In February, President Nixon, concerned that the balance had tipped too far in the direction of clean air at the expense of an adequate energy supply, instructed Treasury Secretary Simon, EPA Administrator Train, and the staffs of OMB and the Domestic Council to outline amendments to the 1970 act that would ensure the development of adequate sources of energy. On March 22, 1974, the administration sent a package of thirteen amendments to Congress.[26] Very few of them were acted on and less than a year later President Ford sent almost the identical list back to Congress.[27] The major amendments, designed to ease the supply problem by allowing the burning of higher-sulfur fuels, were as follows:

(1) Extension of Compliance Dates. This amendment, which provided that EPA and the states be allowed to issue enforcement orders for individual sources, in effect extended the deadline under the 1970 act for meeting air quality requirements but only when the source was on a fixed schedule of achieving full compliance. The reason for this proposed change was that many sources could not possibly meet the requirement and the mid-1975 deadline, because supplies of low-sulfur fuel were not adequate nationwide and stack-gas scrubber equipment was not available in sufficient quantity.

---

[25] Actually interstate natural gas fell short of promised deliveries by 2.7 trillion cubic feet in 1975.

[26] Contained in a March 22, 1974, letter from EPA Administrator Train to the President of the Senate Gerald Ford and Speaker of the House Carl Albert.

[27] January 30, 1975.

(2) Alternative and Intermittent Control Measures. Initially the administration was split on this issue. Most agencies favored an amendment to authorize the use of alternative or intermittent controls, such as adjusting power plant operations, switching from low- to high-sulfur fuels when weather conditions were favorable, or using tall smoke stacks for dispersion of pollutants—as long as ambient air quality standards were met. EPA opposed this amendment on the grounds that dispersal rather than reduction of sulfur-oxide emissions was inappropriate for indefinite use. EPA found accumulating evidence that sulfate compounds formed by sulfur dioxide caused adverse health effects. Because intermittent control systems would not reduce the total emission of sulfur dioxide, EPA believed they would be only marginally successful in reducing health damage from sulfates.[28]

The balance of the administration, notably the Department of Interior, the Federal Energy Administration, the Federal Power Commission, and the Tennessee Valley Authority, supported the use of alternative systems because they could operate at significantly less cost with a smaller fuel penalty. Also, they could avoid the costs associated with the solid waste problem created by using scrubbers. A March 1975 study by the National Academy of Sciences cast serious doubt on the wisdom of a policy *then* to require eventual permanent controls on all stationary sources of pollutants.[29] The report indicated that while scrubbers were commercially available for low-sulfur (less than 1 percent) coal where the coal used had a uniquely low-chlorine content (which retards corrosion and sludge buildup), no adequate demonstration had been made of scrubber technology applied to medium- or high-sulfur coals that contained higher-chlorine content. Costs, according to the National Academy of Sciences, had been seriously underestimated in a previous EPA study.[30]

For example, the EPA report estimated that a 500 megawatt unit burning 3.5 percent-sulfur coal cost about $100 per kilowatt hour, not $45 as EPA had estimated. Nor did EPA's estimates include

---

[28] For a complete report on the status of the potential adverse effects of sulfates see EPA's *Position Paper on the Regulation of Atmospheric Sulfates,* Office of Air and Waste Management, September 1975.

[29] National Academy of Sciences, National Academy of Engineering, and National Research Council, *Air Quality and Stationary Source Emission Control,* March 3, 1975.

[30] Environmental Protection Agency, *Implications of Alternative Policies for the Use of Permanent Controls and Supplemental Control Systems,* November 18, 1974.

107

sludge disposal, which cost about $4.50 per ton of coal for sludge fixation. Also, to refit older plants with scrubbers was estimated to be more expensive than to build new plants, and land acquisition could be a major difficulty. The report concluded that costs attributed to the use of tall stacks and/or intermittent control systems were substantially lower than alternative strategies. A later study by a contractor for EPA indicated that the cost of application of scrubber technology was somewhat lower than assumed in the National Academy of Sciences' study, but that it would still be in the $65 to $75 per kilowatt range and for some plants would be as high as $96 per kilowatt.[31]

Finally, in an administration compromise, FEA Administrator Frank Zarb and EPA Administrator Train agreed to an amendment that allowed the temporary use of intermittent control systems for isolated rural electrical power plants. All urban plants requiring further controls in order to meet air quality standards would need to install scrubbers or use low-sulfur fuel as quickly as practicable. New sources would have to meet the new source performance standards. All plants would have to achieve continuous reduction of sulfur dioxide no later than 1985, but urban plants would be expected to be in compliance by 1980.

(3) Significant Deterioration. This amendment was designed to provide legislative relief from court interpretations of the act that required EPA to take actions to prevent "significant deterioration" of air quality in those areas already cleaner than required to meet national air quality standards. EPA had contended originally that if air quality could not be lowered at all, efforts to move pollution sources out of areas already severely polluted would be impaired. The Sierra Club sued EPA, and on May 30, 1972, the district court ruled that EPA could not approve state air implementation plans that degraded existing air quality even if the air would be better than the national standards. EPA appealed, but on June 11, 1973, the Supreme Court deadlocked 4 to 4, thus upholding the district court ruling.

On August 16, 1974, in an effort to comply with the Court's ruling, EPA proposed regulations for preventing "significant deterioration" of air quality in areas where air was already cleaner than required by federal standards. In effect, EPA proposed three zones of air quality: Class I would designate those areas of a state where almost no change in current air quality patterns is desirable; Class II would designate

---

[31] EPA Contract No. 68-01-3150 by Pedco-Environmental, "Flue Gas Desulfurizing Process Cost Assessment," mimeographed, May 6, 1975.

those areas of a state where moderate change is desirable, but where stringent air quality constraints are nevertheless required; and Class III would designate those areas in states where major industrial or other growth is desired and where pollution concentrations up to the secondary standards would be allowed.

Environmentalists again disapproved, causing further uncertainties as to whether the EPA proposal would withstand a court test. EPA opposed the amendment backed by the rest of the administration, and instead asked Congress to review the issue and the regulatory approach that EPA had proposed. "We need legislation," Train wrote Congress, "which achieves a reasonable degree of certainty, including the minimization of litigation, so that vital national interests are not left in jeopardy." [32]

Other executive branch agencies believed the "significant deterioration" amendment was necessary because the effect of the Court's interpretation was to extend federal involvement beyond what is required to protect public health. Another effect was to limit the range of choice in land use and economic development decisions at the state and local level. If "no significant deterioration" should be held to mean almost no deterioration, which for practical purposes means none at all, then air quality considerations almost alone would control land use decisions and decide where economic development could take place and where it could not.

(4) Review of the State Air Quality Implementation Plans. This amendment would have authorized EPA to determine what changes could be made in state air implementation plans to make the deficit in clean low-sulfur fuels less than it otherwise would be. This analysis was needed because many state air quality implementation plans were more stringent than necessary to meet national primary health-related standards. If these plans were enforced they could prevent the use of an estimated 200 million tons of relatively high-sulfur coal annually—about one-third of the nation's total annual coal production. In fact, EPA had urged states to reduce limitations that were more stringent than necessary to protect public health so that the annual deficit was reduced from 200 to 185 million tons by the fall of 1974 and to 130 million tons by the end of 1975.

---

[32] Letter from EPA Administrator Train to Senator Jennings Randolph, chairman, Senate Public Works Committee, February 3, 1975.

(5) Coal Switching. This amendment proposed converting power plants and other major fuel-burning industrial plants from scarce oil and natural gas to coal by 1980. This change would permit greater use of coal, the nation's most abundant energy source, and reduce the rate of growth in U.S. dependence on imported oil. It would also begin to divert already scarce natural gas from industrial uses to home heating. But the proposed amendment would not allow conversion to coal if the primary health standard were violated in the process.

A companion to the Coal Switching Amendment would have authorized EPA to suspend until 1980 the emission standards and fuel limitations for plants ordered to switch to coal provided that health-based air quality standards were met.

(6) The Environmental Impact Statement Exemption. Because time was so short and legal sufficiency was needed if a plant went to the often-substantial expense of converting to coal, this amendment requested that power plants and some industrial plants switching to coal be exempt for one year from filing an environmental impact statement as required under the National Environmental Policy Act.

(7) Waivers for Research and Development Testing. This amendment would have waived air quality standards for plants engaged in the testing of new pollution control devices that promised to advance the state of the art. Because most of the risk for innovative technology is shouldered by the company experimenting with new pollution control devices, there is a tendency for new source performance standards to act as a disincentive for further technological development.

Congress, as it turned out, acted on very few of the Nixon-Ford proposed amendments relating to relief from stationary source emission standards. The Energy Supply and Environmental Coordination Act of 1974 gave EPA authority to suspend emission limits for power plants and other major industrial users of fuel, but this authority was surrounded by restrictions and conditions. The issue of significant deterioration was left unresolved and there was still some question about intermittent control. Significant revisions of the law seemed to be needed and, above all, a new approach required. The record indicated that policy makers should avoid unrealistic deadlines and unproven technology and, instead, should clarify EPA's authority to give specific extensions to specific facilities, on a case-by-case basis, through the mechanism of enforcement orders.

110

6
Solid Waste – Will the Free Market Solve the Problem?

Introduction

The Nixon administration did its best to restrict the federal government's role in solid waste management. Initially many of President Nixon's advisers, including the author, were uneasy about this, but Nixon was reluctant to press for federal regulation of solid waste disposal except in the area of toxic waste materials. It seemed to him that state and local governments were better equipped than the federal government to handle the problem and that emerging technologies and higher material costs would eventually lead to commercially viable recycling operations, a far more efficient approach than government regulation.[1] Proposals for a tax credit to make recycling more profitable, for a federal tax or bounty on abandoned automobiles, and for a mandatory deposit system for refillable bottles and cans were all studied and eventually abandoned. With the benefit of hindsight, the author believes Nixon was probably correct in deciding to keep the federal role in municipal trash and garbage disposal to a minimum. But the jury is still out. By the end of March 1973 high scrap metal and other material prices, costly pollution controls, and expensive land were beginning to make recycling competitive with land fill or incineration of solid waste materials. "The result is," CEQ's *Fifth Annual Report* concluded, "that market forces are now activated which promise simultaneously to reduce the problem of disposing of solid wastes and to provide needed resources in the form of energy as well as reuseable

---

[1] Comment by John Ehrlichman to the author.

raw materials." [2] However, as we shall see, the comfortable conclusion that the solid waste problem can be solved without any adjustment in the free market system is suspect.

Municipal Waste—Alternative Approaches

Resource Recovery Act of 1970. The Solid Waste Disposal Act of 1965 expired in 1970.[3] In his first environmental message to Congress, Nixon recommended that the act be extended, but with emphasis on recycling: "One way to meet the problem of solid waste is simply to surrender to it: to continue pouring more and more public money into collection and disposal of whatever happens to be privately produced and discarded. This is the old way; it amounts to a public subsidy of waste pollution." [4] Instead, Nixon requested more research on techniques to recycle material and to use biodegradable packaging.

Congress responded with the Resource Recovery Act of 1970, which authorized funds for demonstration grants for recycling systems and for studies of methods to encourage resource recovery. The act also authorized planning grants to interstate, state, intermunicipal, and municipal units or councils of government for up to 75 percent of the cost of planning a coordinated solid waste program. The administration's bill had provided essentially the same planning authority except that the federal share was to have been not more than 50 percent. Congress also provided grants to interstate, state, intermunicipal, and municipal agencies for up to 75 percent of the costs of "demonstrating" resource recovery systems or of "constructing" new or improved solid waste disposal facilities, if such facilities would result in advancing the state of the art. The congressional bill required EPA to recommend guidelines for solid waste systems compatible with public health and welfare, air and water quality standards, and land use practices. These guidelines would be binding on federal agencies and contractors involved in operating solid waste disposal systems.

Nixon nearly vetoed the Resource Recovery Act, almost solely on budgetary grounds. Congress had authorized a fourteenfold increase

---

[2] CEQ, *Fifth Annual Report,* p. 131.

[3] P.L. 89-272 (79 Stat. 997), October 20, 1965.

[4] *Public Papers of the Presidents, Nixon, 1970,* Special Message to Congress on Environmental Quality, p. 104.

in funding over a two-year period—$239 million for FY 1973 compared to the $17 million requested in the administration's FY 1971 budget. The bill was seen as a first step toward an all-out program that would shift responsibility for solid waste disposal construction from the local to the federal government, just as sewage construction funding gradually had been shifted from a state and local responsibility to a federal one. Furthermore, the bill's high authorization levels might create strong expectations of full funding, which might in turn lead localities to slow or stop their efforts to work out their own solid waste construction financing in the hope that they could get some of the new demonstration money or that a full-scale construction grant program would be enacted soon.[5] But what concerned the President most of all was that Congress had not worked out provisions for private or federal incentives to encourage the recycling of solid waste materials. But neither had the administration. So Nixon signed the bill, even though he had misgivings about its budget impact and feared it might eventually lead to federal financing of trash and garbage disposal. Also, looking to political reality, Nixon realized he had no chance to sustain a veto.

The sterility of both the congressional and administration approaches to solid waste disposal stirred the administration to look for new solutions to the problem. Of particular interest were the market mechanisms underlying the private solid waste disposal business. If they could be understood better, then a judgment could be made whether federal incentives for recycling would be useful.

Tax Incentives to Boost Recycling. In the fall of 1971, as CEQ prepared for the presidential environment message planned for February 1972, municipal solid waste loomed as an increasingly large environmental and economic problem. Waste loads were about 125 million tons annually and were growing at the rate of about 4 percent per year. Combined public and private costs of solid waste management were roughly $2.6 billion annually (excluding depreciation and interest)—about $22 per person—and they were rising. Of this cost, approximately $500 million went for disposal and the remainder for collection and transportation.[6] About 6 percent of all solid waste was

---

[5] These fears proved groundless. Congress subsequently limited federal funding to demonstration programs and did not advocate a full-scale federal construction program.

[6] EPA, Second Report to Congress, *Resource Recovery and Source Reduction* (Washington, D.C.: U.S. Government Printing Office, 1974), p. 7.

handled by incinerators, many of which could not meet air quality standards; the rest was disposed of in land fills, 90 percent of which were open dumps presenting mounting problems of air and ground-water pollution, aesthetic blight, and rodents. Recycling offered great potential for reducing the environmental effects and slowing the rapid increase in costs.

Largely through the work of two CEQ staff members, Eric Zausner, formerly with the Bureau of Solid Waste Management of HEW,[7] and Alvin Alm, formerly a Bureau of the Budget examiner for water pollution and water resources development programs, a proposal was floated within the administration for a tax credit equal to 15 percent of the value of recycled materials sold. The credit would be awarded to the firms that actually used secondary materials—for example, the steel mill, or the pulp and paper plant. Windfalls to those already recycling would be kept to a minimum by excluding forms of recycling that were already economic. The proposal's cost was estimated at about $40 million in revenues foregone for the first full year of implementation, a cost that was justified in terms of anticipated benefits from the resulting reductions in air pollution and other environmental damage.

OMB questioned the proposal, while Treasury strongly opposed it. During the interagency discussions, Treasury proposed that if there had to be some kind of recycling initiative, a direct cash subsidy would be preferable to a tax credit. A subsidy, Treasury argued, could be more precisely tailored to cost differences, so that larger subsidies could be paid in areas close to virgin materials in order to make recycling profitable. Moreover, a subsidy would be subject to the annual budget process, would therefore be more visible politically than a tax credit, and could be more easily withdrawn if, at some time in the future, recycling should become economically attractive and no longer in need of federal stimulation. Ways and Means Committee members, like Treasury officials, generally opposed tax credits, regarding them as a way to avoid a self-imposed commitment to hold the line on budgetary spending ceilings. Finally, just as in the case of the effluent fee strategy for water pollution abatement (see Chapter 4), the Public Works committees of the House and Senate might oppose a tax strategy for solid waste management so as not to lose jurisdiction over this area to the House Ways and Means Committee and the Senate Finance Committee.

---

[7] Mr. Zausner later served as deputy assistant secretary of interior and then deputy administrator of the Federal Energy Administration.

Arguments in favor of the tax credit proposal were made by others in the administration, notably by CEQ, the Department of Commerce, and the Domestic Council staff. They saw the tax credit as an efficient self-executing market mechanism that would avoid the build-up of federal bureaucracy between private firms and municipal governments.

Treasury Secretary Connally rejected both the tax credit and the cash subsidy idea, fearing that, in either case, windfalls could develop when recycling became profitable as a result of natural market forces. Ultimately Nixon sided with Connally. His decision was based on the following factors.[8]

(1) Tax credits or subsidies are poor tools for bringing about specific kinds of economic behavior. Material use decisions should be made by persons who are experts on the industries and their problems, not by federal accountants and revenue agents.

(2) Incentive provisions, such as a tax credit to encourage recycling, serve as crutches for the affected industries, generally are not reviewed regularly with respect to their efficiency, and too often, therefore, remain in the tax code long after their reason for being has disappeared.

(3) A tax credit to encourage recycling would lead to pressures for similar treatment of a multitude of other "motherhood" issues. Each variation in the tax credit would produce definitional problems and the proliferation of variations would create an administrative jungle for the Internal Revenue Service.

The idea of a tax credit or subsidy to make marginal recycling operations profitable died with the Nixon administration and was not revived by President Ford.

When the solid waste act came up for renewal in June 1973, the administration took the view that federal involvement should be limited to regulating the disposal of hazardous solid waste. This policy was reflected in the proposal to cut the budget request for waste disposal from $30 million in FY 1973 to only $5.8 million in FY 1974.[9] The administration judged private industry and local government to be better equipped to handle the job than the federal government—particularly since federal demonstration grants were already advancing the state

[8] Primarily from conversations with Alvin Alm, John Ehrlichman, and Eric Zausner.

[9] Later Congress increased the FY 1974 solid waste budget to $8.8 million, still a far cry from the $239 million FY 1973 level that Congress had originally authorized.

of the art in solid waste disposal technology. Moreover, recycling of materials was becoming increasingly attractive economically as the cost of virgin materials rose in response to booming demand and high pollution control costs. In addition, the rising costs of land disposal sites and incineration operations were making recycling more feasible for disposing of solid waste, and the rising cost of energy was expected to stimulate the use of solid wastes as an alternative energy source. Also scrap and metal prices rose to the point where recycling metals became a booming business. Junked autos, worthless a few years before, were bringing up to $50 per car; copper scrap prices rose 100 percent, making recovery efforts profitable; lead batteries were being retrieved as the price of battery lead rose fourfold. EPA's *Resource Recovery and Source Reduction Report* to Congress in 1974 summed up the status at the time.

> Studies indicate that fiscal incentives to stimulate the demand for recycled materials are not necessary at this time. For many recycled materials, demand is currently high, prices are up and supply shortages have occurred—[however] there are considerable uncertainties in this volatile market area, and the demand situation should be carefully analysed and monitored in the future.[10]

As it turned out, the high prices that characterized almost all secondary material markets at that time reflected more the short-term capacity constraints on virgin material production than any long-term trend. Secondary materials prices collapsed in 1974 as rapidly as they had risen. A conspicuous example was waste paper. Beginning in March 1974, waste paper prices began to fall, dropping from $60 per ton to $5 by mid-1975.[11] According to an EPA analyst, "it was a rather sobering experience because the 'great crash of 1974' came just at the time the idea was catching on that a turn around in the historical decline in paper recycling was finally occurring."[12]

Disposal Charges. Recycling is unlikely to become economically viable until the principle is embraced that pollution control costs should be

---

[10] EPA Second Report to Congress, *Resource Recovery and Source Reduction,* pp. xii-xiii.

[11] CEQ, *Sixth Annual Report,* p. 93.

[12] Fred Smith, "Waste Paper Recycling: Review of Recent Market Demand and Supply," *Pulp and Paper,* September 1975, p. 148.

handled like any other expense and not subsidized. In other words, whatever level of environmental quality is decided upon, the cost of obtaining that quality should be reflected in the costs of those goods and services that cause pollution, either "upstream" in the production or "downstream" in the consumption and eventual disposal of products. Specifically, prices should reflect the full production and disposal costs of products. One proposal is to levy a disposal charge (really an excise tax) on products that enter the municipal waste stream, with the charge reduced where secondary materials are used. The argument is that since the problem of solid waste results from the failure of the market to assess solid waste disposal costs correctly, the government should intervene to correct this problem by charging these costs to the products involved. Using this argument, it follows that recycled material should not be charged, since material recovered from the waste stream travels in a closed material-flow loop and therefore creates no solid waste problems.

Hearings were held on a bill incorporating these principles in the 93rd Congress.[13] However, at that time, resource recovery seemed less important than it had earlier because price levels for secondary materials were at their peak. The 94th Congress again investigated the disposal charge idea, but no proposal received administration endorsement. Despite the fact that the concept of internalizing the costs of pollution control gained general acceptance and regulatory approaches fell into disfavor, there remained many practical problems that made unlikely early adoption of solid waste disposal charges. In particular, there was concern over how much bureaucracy would be required to administer such a tax program and over whether a crude disposal charge system (the only kind likely to be feasible) would create sufficient benefits to justify disrupting the current market.

The CEQ's *Sixth Annual Report* stated the administration's position—or hope: "In the short run, the past year was a major setback for recyling and recovery, but the prospects for long-run progress are promising in view of the basic economic pressures associated with the costs of virgin materials, energy, and land." [14]

---

[13] *Resource Conservation and Recycling Hearings on S. 1879, the Solid Waste Source Reduction and Recycling Incentives Act of 1973,* before the Senate Subcommittee on Environment of the Committee on Commerce, 93rd Congress, 1st session (Washington, D.C.: U.S. Government Printing Office, June 11, 22 and July 18, 19, 20, 26, 1973), Part I.

[14] CEQ, *Sixth Annual Report,* p. 94.

The Problem of Abandoned Automobiles

In preparing for his first environmental message to Congress (February 1970), President Nixon gave considerable personal attention to the problem of abandoned cars, one of the most conspicuous solid waste disposal problems. He wanted to propose a bounty payment or some other incentive for recycling abandoned automobiles. But instead, because his advisers had considerable misgivings about the proposal, his message only asked CEQ to develop a recommendation "to promote the prompt scrapping of all junk automobiles." [15]

According to a rough estimate, the annual abandonment rate of automobiles in 1972 ranged from 700,000 to 1 million vehicles.[16] Yet, there did not seem to be a convincing case for federal stimulation of the automobile recycling market. On the contrary, there was considerable evidence that private market mechanisms were addressing the problem. One major breakthrough was the automobile shredder. Shredding automobiles and magnetically separating the ferrous component from the rubber, plastic, and other materials resulted in a higher quality scrap for which there was considerable demand. As steel prices rose, the number of car shredders increased dramatically. In 1972, according to the Institute of Scrap Iron and Steel, over 100 automobile shredders were operating in the United States, a growth of more than 45 percent since 1969, when there had been only 69 shredder plants.[17]

To encourage car recycling the administration considered three strategies: deposits, bounties, and free disposal sites. In each case it was concluded that the strategy was ineffective, that federal activity would do little to solve the problem, and that it was probably preferable to let the marketplace prevail.

Deposits and bounty systems are alternative ways of creating economic incentives to ensure that automobiles are not abandoned; either concept would typically be funded by a tax on the sale of new automobiles or by fees collected from present owners. Under a deposit system, a set dollar amount or deposit would be included in the selling price of the automobile. The system would work much like existing deposit schemes for soft drink and beer containers: all cans would

---

[15] *Public Papers of the Presidents, Nixon, 1970,* Special Message to Congress on Environmental Quality, p. 105.
[16] EPA Second Report to Congress, *Resource Recovery and Source Reduction,* pp. 74-75.
[17] Ibid., p. 69.

carry a deposit that would be passed along from owner to owner until finally a government agency would reimburse the final owner, automobile wrecker, or scrap processor. Under the bounty system, a monetary reward would be provided to some individual involved in the final stage of the car's life—the collector of the abandoned automobile, the junkyard dealer, the shredder operator, or the scrap dealer. Both proposals are somewhat inequitable in the sense that a cost or administrative burden is placed on the millions of car owners who properly dispose of their cars in order to avoid the problems created by those few who abandon their cars. The bounty system might possibly be restricted so that payments were made only for cars that had actually been abandoned, but this would require complex and costly arrangements for determining the status of each car before paying the bounty. The third alternative, free disposal sites, would work for car owners motivated not to blight the landscape, but the cost of transporting the vehicle to the disposal site would still lead others to the discarding of cars.

The major difficulty with each of these proposals was that it would entail a costly program involving large numbers of federal employees, with no certainty that the abandoned automobile problem would be solved. CEQ concluded:

> The Council is not persuaded that the demand for auto scrap would be improved by such a system, nor that it would in fact influence the economics affecting abandonment. . . . Any attempt to solve the problem of abandoned cars, however, must consider the problem of fluctuating scrap demand, steel production technology, transportation rates for scrap, export scrap markets, availability of shredding equipment and characteristics of the automobile parts market. Otherwise, assuming abandonment could be reversed, hulks would only continue to pile up in the junkyard.[18]

As reported by EPA, several states had car removal systems in 1974.[19] Maryland offered an $8 bounty to automobile wreckers and scrap dealers, financed through a $1 fee on each car title transaction. Also, to discourage building up junkyard inventories, the state levied a $5 per vehicle tax on automobile wreckers for vehicles older than eight years held for over eighteen months. In Vermont, if a community

---

18 CEQ, *First Annual Report,* p. 116.
19 EPA Second Report to Congress, *Resource Recovery and Source Reduction,* p. 74.

collected a minimum of 200 cars at its own expense, the state subsidized their removal. In New York City, wreckers contracted to remove and store abandoned vehicles while an owner search was undertaken. In California, the state paid the cities to identify abandoned cars, while the city contracted for their disposal.

If scrap prices should decline from their 1976 levels or if reduced metal content (smaller cars, plastic bodies) should make the recovery of cars less profitable, measures to dispose of abandoned automobiles will again receive attention.

"Throwaway" Beverage Containers

The label "throwaway society" describes America when it comes to the nation's attitude toward disposable beverage containers. Beer and soft drink cans and bottles are a highly visible feature of the nation's roadside litter. In 1972 about 8.2 million tons of beer and soft drink bottles and cans were discarded in the United States (6 million tons of glass, 1.6 million tons of steel and .6 million tons of aluminum), an amount equivalent to roughly 8 percent of the total product waste generated by business and commercial establishments. Furthermore, the use of nonrefillable containers was increasing. From 1959 to 1972, the quantity of beer and soft drinks consumed in the United States increased 33 percent per capita and the production of beer and soft drink containers increased from 15.4 billion to 55.7 billion. The estimate for 1980 was 80 billion containers. Beverage containers were the fastest growing part of municipal waste, with a growth rate of about 8 percent per year. Over 2 billion beverage containers wound up as litter every year.[20]

The Nixon administration studied three methods for dealing with the throwaway can and bottle problem: (1) a tax on bottles and cans to finance litter cleanup, (2) an outright ban on the manufacture and sale of nonreturnable bottles, and (3) a mandatory deposit system, such as the one proposed by Senator Mark Hatfield, Republican of Oregon, modeled after an Oregon law.

---

[20] John Quarles, deputy administrator of EPA, *Hearings on Non-Returnable Beverage Container Prohibition Act*, before the Senate Subcommittee on Environment of the Committee on Commerce, 93rd Congress, 2nd session (Washington, D.C.: U.S. Government Printing Office, May 7, 1974), p. 143; hereafter referred to as the *Quarles Testimony, May 7, 1974.*

Litter tax. Under this strategy, the federal government would impose a small tax varying from minimal levels to perhaps five cents per container, imposed at the first point of sale from the manufacturer to the wholesaler or retailer. If small, such a tax would not be likely to reduce the amount of littering but it would raise substantial funds that could be used for litter clean-up, broader pollution control, or even general purposes.[21] The strategy would not improve environmental quality (air and water pollution) except in the sense of scenic improvement.

Ban on nonreturnable containers. An outright 100 percent ban on nonrefillable containers would completely eliminate the beverage can industry ($1.5 billion in shipments in 1971) as well as the contracting canning industry.[22] The environmental benefits and energy savings would be considerable, but the economic losses would be even more severe than those that would result from the mandatory deposit system.

Mandatory deposit system. Under this strategy, the retailer charges a deposit—say, five cents—for every beverage container sold and refunds the deposit whenever an empty container is turned in; the distributor is required to reimburse the retailer for his expenditures. The states of Oregon and Vermont and the cities of Berkeley (California), Bowie (Maryland), and Oberlin (Ohio) all have mandatory deposit laws. The environmental and energy benefits of a nationwide mandatory deposit system would be substantial. EPA estimated the system would bring a 60-to-95 percent decrease in the number of beverage containers discarded as litter.[23] It also estimated that, if the 8.8 million tons of beverage containers used in 1972 were subject to a five-cent mandatory deposit, and if that law resulted in the use of fifteen-trip refillable containers exclusively, then the reduction in solid waste would be about 6 million tons.[24] Finally, based on a 90 percent returnable container market in which each container made ten trips, EPA estimated energy savings equivalent to 92,000 barrels of oil per day.[25]

[21] EPA estimated that, at five cents per container, the tax would have raised $278 million in 1972. See EPA Second Report to Congress, *Resource Recovery and Source Reduction,* p. 85.

[22] Ibid.

[23] *Quarles Testimony, May 7, 1974,* p. 144.

[24] EPA Second Report to Congress, *Resource Recovery and Source Reduction,* p. 84.

[25] *Quarles Testimony, May 7, 1974,* p. 144.

The economic effects of a mandatory deposit system were potentially severe enough to hold back the administration from endorsing this strategy. EPA estimated a loss of about 60,500 highly skilled jobs, chiefly in the container manufacturing industry, and the creation of 60,800 new but less skilled lower-paying jobs, primarily in the retail and product distribution sectors of the economy.[26] Moreover, tax revenues would decline because of the legislated obsolescence of much beverage-canning and container-handling equipment. EPA estimated that the loss in tax revenues from decreased beer excise taxes and increased corporate write-off of obsolete equipment during the first year of transition would range from $271 to $803 million.[27]

The experts were not clear about the impact of a mandatory deposit system upon industry sales—which had recorded an annual growth rate of about 6 percent. EPA forecast a small decrease in the cost of beer and soft drink containers because the lower-priced refillable containers would slightly more than offset increased handling costs and the cost of equipment changes in the brewing and soft drink industries. A study by the Midwest Research Institute estimated a 4-to-8 percent decline in sales.[28] However, experience with the mandatory deposit system in Oregon showed no loss in sales.[29]

EPA went on record as favoring a nationwide mandatory deposit system,[30] provided that implementation of the measure was phased in over a number of years so as to minimize economic and employment impacts. For example, assuming a 90 percent refillable bottle market, a national mandatory deposit system enforced all at once would affect about 57,000 employees. However, if the system were phased in gradually over ten years, only an estimated 16,000 employees, or less than 3,000 per year, would be affected.

But neither President Nixon nor President Ford felt comfortable with the talk of only slight employment dislocation. If the system were adopted and if estimates proved to be accurate, the 60,500 workers whose jobs were lost would take little solace in dispassionate analysis from Washington proving that 60,800 new jobs would be created,

---

[26] EPA Third Report to Congress, *Resource Recovery and Waste Reduction* (Washington, D.C.: U.S. Government Printing Office, 1975), p. 30.

[27] *Quarles Testimony, May 7, 1974*, p. 145.

[28] Midwest Research Institute, *The National Economic Impact of a Ban on Nonrefillable Beverage Containers*, U.S. Brewers Association, June 1971, p. 55.

[29] CEQ, *Sixth Annual Report*, pp. 96-97.

[30] *Quarles Testimony, May 7, 1974*, p. 146.

but not for them. Also, the details of phasing in a mandatory system were not worked out. So, in a time when the economy was weak, Nixon and Ford were content to let the proposal lie inactive. In June 1976, the Senate voted down (sixty to twenty-six) an amendment by Senator Mark Hatfield that would have levied a five-cent deposit on all soda and beer containers and banned the sale of beverage containers with removable ("pop-top") parts.[31]

---

[31] *Congressional Quarterly,* vol. 34, no. 28 (July 10, 1976), pp. 1819-1820.

7

Pesticides, Predator Control, and Toxic Substances

Introduction

In the fall of 1969, the task force preparing recommendations for the President's first environmental message to Congress soon discovered that the 1947 pesticide law, the Federal Insecticide, Fungicide, and Rodenticide Act (FIFRA),[1] required inordinately cumbersome and time-consuming procedures and provided no authority for dealing with pesticide use. Under the law labels had to contain information specifying the proper uses of the pesticide, but there was no way to ensure that the label would be read or obeyed. It was clear that significant environmental damage was occurring because of indiscriminate use of pesticides. The law needed revision.

Over the years increasing amounts of chemicals had been spread over the land by farmers and urban dwellers trying to control insects, ticks, mites, pest birds, rats, fungi, unwanted fish, plant diseases, and weeds. Prior to World War II, most insecticides were organic compounds that are found in nature and are not persistent—for example, nicotine sulfate, pyrethrins, and rotenone. But beginning in the early 1940s new compounds were brought on the market. First, there were the chlorinated hydrocarbons like DDT, dieldrin, aldrin, and endrin, followed in the late 1940s by the organo-phosphates like malathion and parathion and in the early 1950s by the carbamates like Zectran and Sevin. Herbicides also came along in the 1940s and early 1950s, bringing into common use products like 2,4-D and 2,4,5-T, Dalphon, and Diquat.

---

[1] Ch. 125 (61 Stat. 163), June 25, 1947.

In the 1960s, stimulated by Rachel Carson's *Silent Spring*, the public became concerned that persistent chemicals were remaining in the air, soil, and water for unusually long periods of time, were being dispersed widely around the world, and were concentrating in living organisms. Detrimental effects were confirmed in some bird and fish species and were strongly suspected in some mammals—including humans. Some pesticides, particularly the chlorinated hydrocarbon compounds, concentrated in body fat. Movement of chemicals through food chains, through the atmosphere, and through run-off water was demonstrated, and serious chronic effects in organisms were being identified. For example, fish behavior may be altered so that spawning is ineffective, bird eggs are not laid, shellfish disappear or show retarded growth. The next generation may be born with the pesticide load of their parents, or offspring die when the yolk of the egg is fully absorbed and the chemicals become active in the bloodstream. Pesticides, especially persistent chlorinated hydrocarbon compounds, seemed deeply implicated in the poor survival of the osprey, the bald eagle and peregrine falcon, the pelican, New York lake trout, and Sebago salmon in Maine. Changes due to pesticide residues were reported in the liver enzyme functions of mammals, and carcinogenic effects were reported in laboratory mice. DDT residues in human body fat and human milk are well documented, but the effects are not known.

By the fall of 1969 the President's environmental task force received estimates that about 8,000 manufacturers mixed 900 basic chemicals into approximately 60,000 pesticides registered for use. About 800 million pounds were being produced annually, valued at over $1 billion, and although the use of DDT was declining, the use of other persistent chemicals was still increasing. In the United States it was estimated that one acre in twelve was treated with an average of four pounds of some sort of pesticide, mostly by farmers, but also by foresters, by urban pest control operations and by vegetable and flower gardeners in cities and suburbs.

The Federal Environmental Pesticide Control Act

In spite of the obvious need for reform, the task force was unable to pull together corrective legislation in time for the February 1970 environmental message to Congress. As with so many other parts of the environment problem, too many agencies were in the act. Although authority to control pesticides resided in the Department of Agriculture, both HEW and the Fish and Wildlife Service at the Interior Department studied the health aspects of pesticides. In spite of the best efforts of the Office of Science and Technology and later of the President's environmental task force, it took almost a full year of study by the CEQ staff working with HEW, Interior, and Agriculture before a bill, the Federal Environmental Pesticide Control Act, was finally agreed upon. It was outlined in the President's 1971 environmental message to Congress.[2]

As originally proposed by CEQ, the bill would have repealed FIFRA and granted broad authority to the administrator of EPA to restrict the availability and use of those pesticides that pose "imminent" hazards to human health and the environment. Under FIFRA the Department of Agriculture was responsible for registering approved pesticides and could cancel or suspend the registration if any were found injurious. (Suspension removed a pesticide from the market while its case was being heard; cancellation allowed the product to remain on the market during the appeal period.) In addition, Agriculture was responsible for seeing to it that pesticide labels prescribed safe methods of use. However, under FIFRA, incredibly, no authority existed to enforce the instructions on the labels, and the cancellation system was so slow and cumbersome that products remained on the market for years pending the outcome of appeals. But the most fundamental problem with FIFRA was that it put officials who were responsible for increased agricultural productivity, rather than HEW's health-oriented scientists or Interior's environment-oriented experts, in charge of enforcing the act. It was not surprising that the enforcement agency, the Pesticide Regulation Division of the Department of Agriculture, did almost no enforcing. A classic conflict of interest existed, with both the regulator and the regulated in one and the same Department of Agriculture.

The key battle over how to resolve this conflict of interest had already been fought back in 1970 when Nixon, in proposing the formation of EPA, had decided to move the pesticide regulation program from the Agricultural Research Service to EPA. This decision had been put into effect over the objections of Secretary of Agriculture Clifford Hardin, who had denied the conflict of interest and had argued that

---

[2] *Public Papers of the Presidents, Nixon, 1971,* Special Message to Congress Proposing the 1971 Environmental Program, February 8, pp. 130-31.

the location of responsibility for increased crop productivity and pesticide regulation in one department was desirable.

Under the administration's 1971 bill, all pesticides sold in the United States would have to be registered by the administrator of EPA and classified for use according to the hazards they presented, as follows: (1) for general use—available for use subject only to the general provisions of the bill and state and local restrictions; (2) for restricted use—available for use only by or under the direct supervision of an "approved pesticide applicator"; (3) for use by permit only—available only with the written approval of an "approved pest management consultant." State licensing systems would have to comply with approved standards operating under EPA surveillance. (This provision was later eliminated by Congress.) In addition, the new bill would stop the sale of a pesticide if it were found to be an imminent hazard to human health, grant authority to register and inspect pesticide factories, and undertake pesticide research and monitoring.

The pesticide application provisions were the key to the bill. Under FIFRA there had been an enforcement gap, since the only practical way to control the direct use of pesticides was through complex and protracted cancellation hearings.

Over CEQ Chairman Train's objections, presidential assistant Ehrlichman and the author received Nixon's approval to try a strategy of amending FIFRA (rather than repealing it) so that the Agriculture committees of the two houses of Congress and not the environmental committees (Interstate and Foreign Commerce in the House and Commerce in the Senate) would hold primary jurisdiction. After two years of experience with environmental legislation it was clear that the environmental committees would increase the cost of the legislation so much or make its provisions so unbalanced in favor of the environmental concerns that the bill would be a likely candidate for veto. The risk in the strategy was that if the bill went to the Agriculture committees it might come out so oriented toward crop productivity and the use of pesticides that the environmentalists would find it "too weak" and be able to beat it on the floor. Representative Page Belcher (Republican of Oklahoma), minority leader of the House Agriculture Committee, convinced the author he could guide a bill through that committee that would be tough enough to prevail on the floor, even after some planned (and modest) concessions to the environmentalists were made following Senate Commerce Committee hearings.

The President chose this strategy, Belcher was as good as his word, and the strategy worked. The Agriculture committees of the House and Senate favored almost identical bills. Then, in the Senate, after the Commerce Committee had made several adjustments that were accepted by the Agriculture Committee, these two committees jointly referred the bill to the floor, where it promptly passed, 71 to 0.[3] In the House, the bill passed with a heavy 288-to-91 majority,[4] the environmentalist groups reckoning the House might kill the measure if they insisted on stronger provisions. With both sets of conferees favoring a moderate bill and wanting to avoid the charge of being "anti-farmer," the bill sailed through the conference committee in the best tradition of the "art of the possible." The President signed it on October 21, 1972.[5]

There were certain provisions that caused some concern. The bill provided for the indemnification of persons who suffered financial losses in cases where the EPA administrator ruled that a pesticide presented an imminent hazard and cancelled its registration. This indemnification would occur unless EPA found that the person, knowing that the pesticide did not meet registration requirements (which would be very difficult to prove), had continued to produce it without notifying EPA of the deficiency. This provision, some argued, could significantly inhibit the administrator of EPA from utilizing his emergency authority in the interests of public health and safety: the administrator should not have to consider the cost of indemnification when making such decisions. Also, some contended (see the discussion on toxic substance legislation that follows) that when a regulatory agency grants approval for marketing, it should not be in the position of having guaranteed that product's safety: the responsibility for potentially dangerous products should remain with the manufacturers. EPA argued that, although the provision was undesirable, the potential ramifications of the indemnification provision were not as bad as they might appear. First, indemnities under the bill were allowed only for a pesticide that was suspended for being an imminent hazard and finally cancelled, and not for pesticides that were cancelled without having been first suspended. Second, the expanded regulatory authority might, in the long run, reduce the need to suspend a pesticide.

---

[3] *Congressional Record,* vol. 118, part 24 (September 26, 1972), p. S 32263.

[4] *Congressional Record,* vol. 117, part 31 (November 9, 1971), p. H 40068.

[5] Federal Environmental Pesticide Control Act of 1972, P.L. 92-516 (86 Stat. 973), signed October 21, 1972.

Another undesirable provision added by Congress required that, if so requested by the manufacturer of a cancelled pesticide that had first been suspended, the administrator of EPA would have to take delivery of stocks of the pesticide at convenient locations for safe disposal. EPA and others opposed this provision for the same reason that they were uneasy about the indemnification provision. However, both the indemnification and the disposal provisions were known to the administration before House passage of the bill and President Nixon at that time agreed not to oppose them. This was the price, Congressman Belcher advised the President, that would have to be paid to gain farm-bloc support for the bill. Both men stuck to their bargain. As a matter of fact, over the years neither the indemnification nor the disposal provision has resulted in significant costs and neither seems to have affected EPA's decisions on cancellation of various pesticides.

In retrospect, the 1972 law embodied a good compromise. But even four years later polarization over the pesticide issue continued between the two iron triangles—the farmers, the Department of Agriculture, and the House and Senate Agriculture committees, on the one hand, and the environmentalists, EPA, and their respective congressional committees, on the other. Just as the environmentalists had accused the Department of Agriculture in the early 1970s of a bias in favor of using pesticides to increase productivity at the expense of ecological considerations, so by the mid-1970s the balance had shifted, and farmers, gaining a sympathetic ear from congressmen, were complaining that EPA had gone so far in restricting the use of pesticides that productivity would decline.

In the House Agriculture Committee, former Agriculture Committee Chairman W. R. Poage, Democrat of Texas, offered an amendment that would have required the concurrence of the secretary of agriculture whenever EPA took action to curb a pesticide's use (a virtual veto power over EPA's pesticide decisions). The amendment was defeated in committee by a narrow margin. However, Congress, sensing the changing public mood, passed a bill in November 1975 with the following major provisions: [6]

(1) It extended FIFRA for eighteen months rather than the two years recommended by the administration and the Senate, after compromising with House critics who wanted to "keep EPA on a short

[6] P.L. 94-140 (89 Stat. 751), November 28, 1975.

130

leash" by authorizing only a one-year extension of FIFRA before putting EPA under further congressional scrutiny.[7]

(2) It gave the Department of Agriculture more public visibility (although not veto power) by ruling that EPA must advise the secretary of agriculture at least sixty days before taking action with respect to the classification, suspension, or cancellation of a pesticide. The Department of Agriculture would have thirty days to comment and EPA must make Agriculture's comments public in the *Federal Register*. If the department did not act within thirty days, EPA could act. However, if suspension of a pesticide were necessary to prevent an imminent hazard to human health, EPA's administrator could waive the requirement for notice to and consultation with the secretary of agriculture.

(3) It gave the Department of Agriculture authority to comment on both proposed and final pesticide regulations and required EPA to publish the comments in the *Federal Register* and to notify the House and Senate Agriculture committees.

(4) It required EPA to assess the economic impact (the other side of the coin from an environmental-impact statement) on commodity prices, retail food prices, agricultural production, and the agricultural economy in general before acting to cancel, suspend, or change the classification of a pesticide.

(5) It provided authority for states to certify private (noncommercial) parties to apply dangerous restricted-use pesticides without requiring a test to see if they were competent to do so. Commercial pesticide applicators were not affected by this amendment, but the new law allowed states to require examinations if they chose to do so. Also, while the administrator of EPA could not require a private applicator to take an examination, he could require a certification form affirming that the applicator had completed an EPA approved training program.

Thus between 1972 and 1975 the pesticide regulation law twice was overhauled, first with major surgery favoring the environmentalists and later with slight adjustments tilted toward the farmer. Congress, clearly sensitive to the issue and anxious to keep oversight authority, extended the life of the statute only until March 1977, when the battle will again no doubt be joined.

The painful process of eliminating pesticides from agricultural use, beginning with DDT, is a story of much bitterness and conflict between two committed groups with honest differences in viewpoint.

---

[7] *Congressional Quarterly,* vol. 33, no. 47 (November 22, 1975), p. 2551.

Action on DDT

Among pesticides DDT seems to have a symbolism all of its own. Its inventor made it famous by winning the Nobel prize for its use in suppressing malaria. For a time the unquestioned leader of pesticides, particularly for cotton production, it came to be used less because of public concern about its effects and because some insects became immune to it. By the early 1970s, about 675,000 tons of DDT had been applied domestically. The peak year in the United States was 1959 when nearly 80 million pounds were applied. Thereafter, usage steadily declined to about 13 million pounds in 1971, most of it applied to cotton.[8] Following the administration's decision to phase out DDT as of December 31, 1972, only small stocks were kept on hand for emergency U.S. use, but over 56 million pounds were still manufactured for export in 1974.[9] The chemical industry fought hard to defend DDT, more because it was a symbol of all pesticide products than because of DDT itself, which no longer was a significant profit maker in the chemical industry. "DDT . . . enjoys a special reverence as the father of modern insecticides," wrote Harrison Wellford in *Nixon and the Environment.* "In defending it, the industry sees itself as defending the concept of progress against a plague of Luddites who would dismantle the scaffolding of organic chemistry which, in their view, supports the technology of agribusiness." [10]

The administration's first move on the DDT problem was to appoint a panel of eminent scientists in 1969. Their report recommended phasing out some chlorinated hydrocarbon pesticides (like DDT) and concluded, "The field of pesticide toxicology exemplified the absurdity of a situation in which 200 million Americans are undergoing life-long exposure, yet our knowledge of what is happening to them is at best fragmentary." [11] Following this report and relay of its findings to a cabinet meeting with Nixon, Secretary of Agriculture Hardin and Secretary of HEW Finch held a press conference to an-

[8] EPA news release, "DDT Ban Takes Effect," December 31, 1972.

[9] In 1974 the U.S. exported 56,376,060 pounds of DDT worth $18,785,492. See the *Pesticide Review 1974,* Department of Agriculture, Agricultural Stabilization and Conservation Service, Washington, D.C., 1975.

[10] Harrison Wellford, *Nixon and the Environment* (New York, N.Y.: Taurus Communication, 1972), p. 153.

[11] *Report of the Secretary's Commission on Pesticides and Their Relationship to Environmental Health* (Washington, D.C.: U.S. Government Printing Office, December 1969), p. 236.

nounce the cancellation of DDT for use on tobacco, or shade trees, in households, and, with certain exceptions, in aquatic areas.[12] In June 1970, Interior Secretary Hickel banned the use of DDT and fifteen other pesticides on all public lands managed by Interior.[13] And in August 1970, the Department of Agriculture cancelled federal registrations of DDT products for use on many classes of livestock, lumber, buildings, forest trees, and over fifty food crops.[14] However, manufacturers began the long appeal process under FIFRA procedures, and this process had not run its course by the time EPA Administrator William Ruckelshaus announced a final decision of a near-total ban on DDT nearly two years later—in June 1972.

Meanwhile, during the period when the administration was taking limited action on DDT, legal efforts to outlaw DDT were well under way. On October 1, 1969, the Environmental Defense Fund (EDF) petitioned Secretary of Agriculture Hardin to ban all uses of DDT and, when he refused, EDF went to court. On January 7, 1971, the United States District Court for the District of Columbia ordered EPA, which was by then responsible for pesticide regulation, to cancel all remaining uses of DDT, and on March 18, 1972, the court further directed the administrator of EPA to consider the stronger action of suspending the use of DDT, that is, stopping DDT sales altogether while the case was being heard. On March 18, Administrator Ruckelshaus announced he would cancel the use of DDT and hold public hearings rather than suspend its use outright. The hearings took more than a year.

Although there was a wide range of informed scientific opinion on the range and severity of DDT's side effects, every blue ribbon scientific committee that had been impaneled to advise the executive branch on the DDT question in a past decade had recommended a phase-out of crop uses for this pesticide because, at a minimum, the side effects caused by the persistence of DDT were a cause for concern. On the one hand, Ruckelshaus could find considerable evidence, based on the hearing record, that DDT had been shown to have adverse effects up the food chain, causing concentration in certain mammals; that DDT in

[12] Office of the White House Press Secretary, transcript of a press conference by HEW Secretary Robert Finch and Agriculture Secretary Clifford Hardin, November 20, 1969.

[13] Interior press release, "Secretary Hickel Bans Use of 16 Pesticides on Any Interior Lands or Programs," June 18, 1970.

[14] Department of Agriculture press release, "USDA Cancels Additional Uses of DDT," August 28, 1970.

high dosages had adverse health effects in laboratory animals; and that it was persistent in the environment (meaning that most people had about ten parts per million in their body tissues). The arguments on the other side, put forward largely by the manufacturers and the agronomists, were that nobody had ever proved direct adverse effect on man, that there was no alternative control agent for certain strains of pests, and that methyl parathion, the chief substitute for DDT for most crops, was highly toxic and a hazard to human health.

Ruckelshaus had three options: (1) deny cancellation, retaining the status quo, (2) suspend all domestic uses, or (3) phase out the domestic uses. No matter which he chose, litigation would almost certainly follow. The choice was between agribusiness, farm organizations, and the traditionally perceived needs of the American farmer on the one hand and the public health and environmental groups on the other—and both sides had strong vocal support. Ruckelshaus once told the author that listening to the experts could be very confusing. "One fellow will tell you DDT is so dangerous you shouldn't get closer to it than the next county, and the next witness will tell you it's safe enough to have on your cereal for breakfast."

On June 14, one day before the deadline stipulated in the court order, Ruckelshaus announced his decision at the United Nations Conference on the Human Environment in Stockholm. (The decision was also announced at EPA headquarters in Washington the same day.) He chose to phase-out almost all domestic uses of DDT by December 31, 1972. "The evidence of the record showing storage in man and magnification in the food chain is a warning to the prudent that man may be exposing himself to a substance that may ultimately have serious effects on his health," [15] Ruckelshaus wrote in his forty-page decision. He permitted the six-month phase-out in order to allow for an orderly transition to substitute pesticides, primarily methyl parathion, which constituted a short-term danger to untrained operators. Time was needed to train operators and to get farmers past the immediate growing season (chiefly cotton, soybeans, and peanuts). Public health and quarantine uses, as well as exports to other countries, were not halted. Also, EPA allowed continued use of DDT in three minor cases where no alternative pesticide was known to be effective—green peppers, onions, and sweet potatoes in storage—if it could be demonstrated that

---

[15] EPA Consolidated DDT Hearings, Opinion and Order of the Administrator, *Federal Register,* vol. 37, no. 131 (July 7, 1972), p. 13373.

not using DDT would result in a shortage of the product and that these particular uses did not constitute an environmental risk.

The reaction to the decision was immediate and at times bitter. The Environmental Defense Fund appealed the ruling, asking that the ban take effect immediately instead of on December 31, 1972, and that even minor uses of DDT should be banned. The manufacturers did not anticipate any immediate economic harm to their business, but nevertheless, a legal appeal prepared in anticipation of the ban was filed within minutes of Ruckelshaus's decision.[16] National Farmers Union President Tony Dechant called the near-total ban unexpected and unjustified. The cotton industry said, "you take an essential weapon like this out of the farmer's arsenal and it can be ruinous. We were surprised and dismayed." [17] An ABC television news report from Batchelor, Louisiana, indicated, among other things, that a cotton farmer's work for an entire season could be erased by insects. DDT substitutes, said the reporter, "are said to be far more toxic to humans than DDT and cost too much." On TV a farmer bitterly commented, "The only thing DDT is hard on is insects." [18]

In announcing a near-total ban to be effective December 31, 1972, the administration took a calculated risk that by that time Congress would have acted on the administration's new pesticide legislation— "since the present law," Ruckelshaus stated in his announcement, "is completely inadequate to allow me to regulate the use of pesticides for beneficial uses on a restricted basis." [19] Under the proposed administration bill, DDT could be used if EPA issued a permit and if an approved pest management consultant applied the pesticide.

A few years later, the wisdom of Ruckelshaus's stopping short of ordering a total ban on DDT—so that it would be available for emergency purposes—became apparent. In the Pacific Northwest the Tussock moth, in its caterpillar stage, was eating the needles of the valuable Douglas fir and other fir trees, defoliating or killing them. From time to time, the Tussock moth population increases radically, as

---

[16] On December 13, 1973, the D.C. District Court, 489 F2d 1247, upheld Ruckelshaus's original decision of June 1972 in Environmental Defense Fund v. EPA et al. Chemical companies participating in the action included Carolina Chemical, Cohoma Chemical, Olin Corporation, W. R. Grace Company and Octagon Process, Incorporated.

[17] CBS-TV Evening Network News, June 14, 1972.

[18] ABC-TV Evening Network News, June 14, 1972.

[19] EPA press release, "Bans General Use of DDT," June 14, 1972.

it did in 1972, when approximately 196,000 acres of evergreen forests in eastern Oregon and Washington were defoliated in varying degrees. In 1973 the states of Oregon and Washington and the United States Forest Service asked EPA's permission to use DDT on an "if needed" basis. EPA denied the permit because its scientists thought that a natural virus would be present in the egg in sufficient quantities to collapse the moth population. Contrary to EPA's expectation, however, the natural virus did not achieve larval kills sufficient to control the total Tussock moth population. In 1973 an additional 600,000 acres were defoliated. So in 1974, after the demonstrated failure of the virus to provide control, and because neither a biological control program nor the use of other less effective and more costly pesticides (Dylox or Zectran) could be effectively mounted in time, EPA Administrator Train concluded "that the potential for a serious emergency this summer [1974] is present, and that DDT is the most practical control available." [20]

Action on Other Pesticides

The administration also took action, though not as much as the environmentalists wanted, on the controversial herbicide 2,4,5-T. In April 1970, following a cabinet-level meeting of the Environmental Quality Council, Secretaries Hardin, Hickel and Finch ordered the suspension of all uses of 2,4,5-T in homes and gardens, in recreation areas, and in areas where water contamination could occur.[21] But in May 1971, an EPA scientific advisory board recommended that 2,4,5-T be cleared for unrestricted use. However, Ruckelshaus refused to clear the herbicide, except for use on rice, rangeland, and rights-of-way, and the fate of 2,4,5-T was still in doubt. In June 1974, EPA postponed hearings on both 2,4,5-T and its common contaminant known as tetra-chlorodibenzo-para-dioxin (TCDD) because of lack of data on their health effects. It cited difficulties with a new method for detecting TCDD and uncertainties concerning the persistence of 2,4,5-T as the primary obstacles to full evaluation of the herbicides. EPA also noted that both 2,4,5-T and its contaminant TCDD have been shown to produce birth defects after being fed to pregnant mice. But other

---

[20] EPA press release, "EPA Gives Authorization to Forest Service for Contingency Use of DDT against Tussock Moth," February 26, 1974.

[21] Department of Agriculture press release, "Home Use of 2,4,5-T Suspended," April 15, 1970.

studies showed that residues of 2,4,5-T on crops and in water disappeared quickly, thus removing the opportunity for human exposure. As a result, John Quarles, deputy administrator of EPA, concluded that the restricted use of 2,4,5-T "should not result in detectable residues of herbicides if it is used according to label instructions. Thus the health implications of these uses are believed to be minimal." [22]

Almost as controversial was EPA's decision on aldrin and dieldrin, two closely related, persistent pesticides belonging to the same chemical family as DDT. Aldrin breaks down into dieldrin after application, but dieldrin is also marketed separately. Aldrin is used primarily to control soil insects in corn,[23] citrus, and a variety of other crops like pineapples and onions, and for seed treatments. Dieldrin provides insect control on citrus. On October 1, 1974, EPA Administrator Train suspended production of aldrin and dieldrin, stopping the Shell Chemical Company, the nation's only manufacturer of the chemicals, from producing some 10 million pounds scheduled for 1975. However, he allowed the continued sale and use of stocks of aldrin and dieldrin made prior to August 2, 1974: "permitting the use of this relatively small amount of aldrin and dieldrin will be safer environmentally than attempting to retrieve the products, transporting them and then somehow disposing of the consolidated and remaining supplies." [24] Train had concluded that aldrin-dieldrin posed a high risk of cancer in man and that residues of aldrin-dieldrin were present in virtually every member of the U.S. population.

On December 24, 1975, Train suspended most uses of the pesticides heptachlor and chlordane, widely used for pest control in home lawns, gardens, and cornfields (the suspension order for use on corn was effective August 1, 1976).[25]

Thus, in a few years' time, production of five major pesticides—DDT, aldrin, dieldrin, heptachlor, and chlordane—was halted. Environmental groups insisted this was just a tiny fraction of the thousands of registered pesticides. But farmers rely primarily on only about

[22] EPA press release, "EPA Withdraws Formal Hearing on Herbicide 2,4,5-T Due to Lack of Data," June 24, 1974.

[23] About 90 percent of the aldrin is used on approximately 9 percent of the nation's corn crop.

[24] EPA press release, "Train Suspends Production of Aldrin-Dieldrin Pesticides," October 1, 1974.

[25] EPA press release, "Train Stops Manufacture of Heptachlor and Chlordane, Cites Imminent Cancer Risk," July 30, 1975.

twenty major pesticides; stopping the production of five of them could, in many farmers' view, constitute a serious threat to production. Whereas alternative pesticides were available, some argued, the quantities were often too small to be effective should an emergency arise. So far the dire predictions about crop failures as a result of EPA bans on pesticide manufacture have not materialized. Many farmers and pesticide specialists have their fingers crossed, hoping an emergency will not arise.

Integrated Pest Management Control

Anticipating the general restriction in the use of pesticides and the likely possibility that Ruckelshaus would suspend DDT, the staffs of CEQ, EPA, and the Department of Agriculture began working on an integrated pest-management package that was eventually announced in February 1972, as part of the President's third environmental message to Congress.[26] Integrated pest management means the use of biological, cultural, and other pest control techniques, which are of paramount importance where chemical pesticides have been restricted. The techniques are an essential ingredient, along with effective pesticide regulation, in reducing chemical contamination of the environment and in maintaining high crop productivity. The program consisted of five activities:

(1) expanding the Department of Agriculture's scout control program for several commodities and developing a program of crop protection, including monitoring of pest and beneficial insect levels, with a maximum number of inputs, in order to achieve quality production;

(2) expanding federal support for pest control research and development at EPA, the National Science Foundation, and the Department of Agriculture;

(3) increasing the field-testing of promising new methods of pest detection and control;

(4) establishing, through the Occupational Safety and Health Administration (OSHA) of the Department of Labor, safety standards for field workers to guard against pesticide poisoning from occupational exposure; and

---

[26] *Public Papers of the Presidents, Nixon, 1972,* Special Message to Congress Outlining the 1972 Environmental Program, February 8, pp. 178-80.

(5) training and certifying of crop protection specialists (integrated pest management consultants) by states and universities.

Later, the Department of Agriculture and EPA designed a program especially for farmers in fourteen states who, following the DDT ban, had to use organo-phosphate pesticides such as parathion, instead of DDT, on cotton. The organic phosphorous compounds that replaced DDT degrade rapidly and do not accumulate in the environment over a long period of time. However, in the short term, acute toxicity increases possible hazard to the user and field worker, if the compounds are not applied properly.

Predators

While the conflict between environmentalist and developer is a twentieth century phenomenon, that between sheep herder and predator has gone on for thousands of years. *Plutarch's Lives* records a bounty of five drachmas, or the price of an ox, for one male wolf. In 1630, shortly after the first settlers arrived in America, the first predator bounty law was passed in Massachusetts.[27] The federal government has been in the business of predator control since 1915, when Congress first appropriated $125,000 for this purpose, and in FY 1976 the predator control budget was $6.3 million. An act of March 2, 1931, directed to the eradication and control of predatory animals, states the philosophy of the time, that the people "conduct campaigns for the destruction or control of [predatory] animals." [28] But through the years attitudes toward predatory animals changed. As President Nixon wrote in his 1972 environmental message, "The old notion that 'the only good predator is a dead one' is no longer acceptable as we understand that even the animals and birds which sometimes prey on domesticated animals have their own value in maintaining the balance of nature." [29] What most concerned people was the indiscriminate use of poisons to kill predatory animals. For example, in May 1971, the Department of Interior announced that about twenty-five bald and golden eagles had

[27] University of Michigan, Institute of Environmental Quality, *Predator Control— 1971,* Report to the Council on Environmental Quality and the Department of Interior, January 1972, p. 1.

[28] Ch. 370 (46 Stat. 1468), March 2, 1931.

[29] *Public Papers of the Presidents, Nixon, 1972,* Special Message to Congress Outlining the 1972 Environmental Program, pp. 182-83.

been poisoned by Wyoming ranchers in one incident.[30] The eagles died after feeding on antelope carcasses treated with thallium poison that ranchers had used as bait to kill coyotes. Several investigations had taken place over the years. In 1964, the Advisory Committee Report to Interior Secretary Stewart Udall concluded that far more predators were being killed than required for effective protection of livestock, agricultural crops, wildlife, and human health.[31] The report proposed a new philosophy—that all animals should be protected and that all forms of wildlife should be husbanded, with predator control limited strictly to those species and, where possible, to only those individual animals that were killing livestock and to only those locations where danger existed or damage had taken place.

In 1971, CEQ and the Department of Interior contracted for another predator control study, which concluded:

> It is clear that the basic machinery of the federal cooperative-supervised program contains a high degree of built-in resistance to change. Not only are many of the several hundred field agents the same former "trappers" but the cooperative funding by federal, state and county agencies, and by livestock associations and even individual ranchers maintains a continuity of purpose in promoting the private interest of livestock growers, especially in the western rangeland states. The substantial monetary contribution by the livestock industry serves as a gyroscope to keep the bureaucratic machinery pointed towards the familiar goal of general reduction of predator populations with little attention to the effects of this on native wildlife fauna. Guidelines and good intentions will no longer suffice. The federal-state predator control program must be effectively changed.[32]

The report went on to recommend a prohibition against the use of poisons in predatory animal destruction, an expanded research program to determine the economics and ecology of predator losses, and the establishment of cooperative trapper extension programs to focus on individual offending predators.

If one has ever seen what a coyote can do to a lamb, it is no wonder that the administration approached with considerable caution

---

[30] Nathaniel Reed, assistant secretary of interior, press conference, May 27, 1971.

[31] S. Leopold, "Predator and Rodent Control in the United States," *Transactions of the Twenty-Ninth North American Wildlife and Natural Resource Conference* (Baltimore, Maryland: Monumental Printing Company, 1964), pp. 27-49.

[32] University of Michigan, Institute on Environmental Quality, *Predator Control— 1971*, p. 2.

the idea of banning the use of poisons for killing predators on the public lands. Sheep herders, ranchers, and farmers would be adamantly opposed and reluctant to forgive the government for meddling in their efforts to protect their livestock. Their claim would be that there is no effective alternative to poisons—that the traditional remedies of hunting and trapping would not do an effective job. Long after the environmentalists had applauded Nixon's action and forgotten it, the sheep herder, rancher, and farmers would still remember, as they counted each animal killed by a predator. In spite of this, President Nixon issued an executive order on February 8, 1972, banning the use of poisons against predators on all public lands except in emergency situations.[33] He also asked for legislation to transfer predator control functions to the states, to provide federal funding on a cost-sharing basis to states not using poisons for predator control, and to fund research into alternative methods of predator control that would be environmentally sound. The bill passed the House in July 1972,[34] but it was held up in the Senate committee.

In 1973 the administration proposed a new bill that closely resembled the House-passed bill, but Congress took no action. Instead, a controversy erupted over Nixon's executive order and EPA's later action ordering an immediate halt to the interstate shipment of pesticides used to control predatory animals.[35] Woolgrowers in particular put persistent pressure on western congressmen and senators to get Nixon to rescind his order. Twenty-one senators representing western woolgrowing states wrote Secretary Morton in December 1973 and accused him of ignoring the coyote threat to the sheep industry. Woolgrowers' cars displayed bumper-stickers bitterly proclaiming: "Eat American Lamb—Ten Million Coyotes Can't Be Wrong." In March 1974, President Nixon met with agricultural leaders and Congressman W. R. Poage, Democrat of Texas, then chairman of the House Agriculture Committee, who claimed that the executive order was ruining the sheep industry and asked Nixon to cancel it. But the President made no concessions because there was no solid evidence that sheep losses had increased since poisons had been banned for predator control. Instead the administration streamlined the procedures required under the emer-

---

[33] Executive Order 11643.

[34] H.R. 13152 with amendments.

[35] EPA press release, "EPA Stops Shipment of Predator-Control Pesticides," March 10, 1972. The pesticides in question were thallium sulfate, strychnine, cyanide, and 1080 (sodium monofluoroacetate).

gency provisions of the executive order to request officially an exemption to use poisons.

Ironically, in spite of complaints about the procedures, Assistant Secretary of Interior Nathaniel Reed stated that Interior had received only five official requests for the emergency use of poisons since the executive order was issued.[36] Doubtless more requests were made informally. Reed also testified that, in a cooperative program between Idaho ranchers and the Department of Interior, 11,980 lambs were put onto the summer range in nine bands by three operators. At market time, 11,327 lambs were shipped. Of the 653 missing lambs, 135 were confirmed predator kills—1.15 percent of the total number of lambs. One hundred lambs were known to be lost to other causes, and 418 were missing. If half of the latter were lost to predators the total predator loss would be only 2.86 percent. Reed also reported that a study of ten sheep herds in the Logan, Utah, area in the spring of 1973 put spring lamb losses to predators at 1.5 percent of the total number of lambs, while losses due to disease, starvation, abandonment, weather, parasites, and other causes amounted to 8 percent of the total.[37] Comparison of coyote population indices for 1972 and 1973 (the first full year following Nixon's executive order) indicated lower populations in three states, significantly higher populations in five states, and no significant change in nine states.[38] Research suggested that, under the present control program, about 20 percent of ranchers might sustain heavy losses and the remaining 80 percent might have a loss ranging from 1 to 4 percent. There is a serious question if more intensive control by any method can reduce the usual 1 to 4 percent stock losses without uneconomical expenditures.

EPA permitted the use of cyanide in an M-44 device for experimental purposes on private lands and, on May 28, 1974, it granted the Fish and Wildlife Service an experimental-use permit for the M-44 device to protect sheep and goats from depredation. The M-44, a spring-loaded cyanide-ejecting tube which is placed in the ground, kills a coyote almost instantly when the coyote tugs at scented bait, triggering a puff of cyanide into its mouth. There is little hazard to human beings,

---

[36] Nathaniel Reed, assistant secretary of interior, *Hearings on Predators,* testimony before the House Committee on Agriculture, 93rd Congress, 1st session (Washington, D.C.: U.S. Government Printing Office, September 18, 1973), p. 12.

[37] Ibid., p. 13.

[38] Robert Roughton, *Predator Survey of the Western United States* (Washington, D.C.: Department of Interior, U.S. Fish and Wildlife Service, 1974), p. 8, figure 2.

and the poison either decomposes or is metabolized immediately so that it does not persist in the environment or enter the food chain.

The same pressures were applied to President Ford that had been applied to Nixon. Ford met with woolgrowers and western congressmen and senators in April 1975. In July, he decided to amend Nixon's original executive order on predator control by allowing a one-year experimental program for the use of sodium cyanide and, on May 28, 1976, approved the operational use of sodium cyanide on federal lands and in federal programs. Since the poison breaks down once it kills the coyote, other kinds of wildlife would not die after feeding on the coyote carcass. On the other hand, Ford's decision would no doubt encourage efforts by livestock interests to attempt to erode the Nixon executive order still further by pressuring for resumed use of 1080 and strychnine.

Toxic Substances

PCBs and other known toxic chemicals might have been kept from being introduced into the environment had there been a federal law to control their commercial use. The same is true for detergents. Seeking a substitute for phosphates in detergents, which were thought to contribute to eutrophication of lakes and streams, the soap industry turned to the chemical NTA (nitrilotiacetic acid), a nonphosphate cleaning agent. NTA was then manufactured in large quantities with the enthusiastic support of environmental groups and the government. The author and representatives from EPA, CEQ, and the Commerce Department were in the middle of negotiations with industry to phase in NTA production as a replacement for phosphates in detergents when Dr. Jesse Steinfeld, the surgeon general of the United States, phoned the author to say that HEW scientists had just confirmed that large dosages of NTA caused birth deformities in laboratory mice. Based on this information, industry agreed to a voluntary ban on NTA production until further evidence of the health effects of NTA could be pinned down.[39]

Cases like this demonstrated the lack of legal authority to halt the manufacture and distribution of toxic chemicals, and they convinced the administration that some sort of federal regulatory authority was desirable. The bill finally proposed in Nixon's second environmental message

---

[39] William Ruckelshaus, administrator of EPA, and Dr. Jesse Steinfeld, surgeon general of the United States, press conference, December 18, 1970.

to Congress in February 1971 gave authority to the EPA administrator to restrict or stop the use or distribution of chemicals as necessary to protect health or the environment.[40] If the chemical substance created an environmental hazard, then the administrator could ask the courts to stop or curtail its use or distribution immediately. Also EPA would have authority to issue standards for various product categories of potentially toxic substances.

Originally, as CEQ drafted the bill, it had a prenotice requirement, stating that the manufacturer, before marketing a new chemical substance, must notify EPA of (1) the chemical identity and molecular structure of the substance, (2) the intended use, (3) the estimated amount of the substance that would be produced annually, (4) the environmental and health tests conducted on the substance and the results, and (5) the key products, if any, expected to result from production of the substance. In addition, within 120 days after receiving all the data under the prenotice requirement, the initial CEQ draft bill provided that EPA could require the manufacturer to conduct additional tests. This was known as the postnotice testing requirement. If EPA did not communicate with the manufacturer within 120 days after the prenotice requirement had been fulfilled, then the product could be manufactured.

After a tug of war between CEQ and the Department of Commerce, Nixon ultimately ruled out both the prenotice and postnotice testing requirements. With the pressure in Congress to practice "one-upsmanship" with the administration on environmental legislation, there was a good chance that, if the White House endorsed the prenotice and postnotice requirements, Congress would add a preclearance requirement, specifying that no new chemical could be sold until the manufacturer had performed every test that EPA required and satisfied EPA that there was no hazard. Not only would this have tended to stifle new products, but it would have put EPA in a very difficult position. Either EPA would have to be supercautious with preclearances, and perhaps needlessly stifle product innovation, or EPA would risk being blamed if a problem not considered at the time of the preclearance were to develop later. Even without the preclearance requirement, EPA, in order to prevent the sale of a product that later proved to be a problem, might be tempted to use the threat of its injunctive powers to pressure

[40] *Public Papers of the Presidents, Nixon, 1971,* Special Message to Congress Proposing the 1971 Environmental Program, p. 132.

a manufacturer into conducting all possible tests, no matter how marginal in value.

Another argument that Nixon subscribed to was the possibility of setting a precedent for expanding the prenotice and postnotice testing requirements to other safety laws—for example, consumer product safety (lawn mowers, washing machines, et cetera) and occupational safety (machine tools, hand tools, et cetera). These powers seemed unnecessary since safety in these fields could be ensured by mandatory performance safety standards coupled with injunctive powers to reach the cases not covered by performance standards.

Finally, with legislation authorizing regulatory or injunctive power to cut off production, as well as criminal penalties if adequate testing safeguards were not performed, it was difficult for Nixon to believe that the manufacturer would defy EPA and refuse to do further testing if EPA made a good case for it.

Primarily because of the tough issue of premarket testing, the toxic substance bill remained before Congress for more than five years without final action. In November 1975, the administration endorsed the concept of premarket notification of advanced testing, but only for a list of toxic substances that posed unreasonable risks to man and the environment, rather than for all new chemicals.[41] This still left the thorny question of developing carefully drawn criteria for those chemicals to which the prenotification provision of the bill would apply.

After almost a year of further deliberation, Congress passed a bill acceptable to President Ford which covered all new chemical substances produced in commercial quantities, as well as significant new uses of chemical substances, and subjected them to premarket notification of up to ninety days. Any chemical substance may be exempt from the premarket notification procedures if the administrator of EPA decides it does not present an unreasonable risk to health or the environment. Congress also limited the authority of the EPA administrator by requiring a court order to remove an existing substance from the market or to prevent marketing during the premarket notification period. The administration felt these combinations of authority and limitation would ensure protection of the health and environment without impeding technological innovation or imposing unnecessary regulatory costs.

---

[41] See letter of November 13, 1975, from James Lynn, director of OMB, to Congressman John McCollister, ranking minority member of the Subcommittee on Consumer Protection and Finance of the House Committee on Interstate and Foreign Commerce.

8

The Use of Land

Back in 1967, Dennis O'Harrow observed, "I see a great national program mounted against water pollution. I hear a hue and cry against air pollution. . . . But I see no comparable concern over pollution of our land . . . which is really the scarcest of the three basic resources of human life." [1]

But a few years later, as the bulldozers relentlessly chewed up trees and farmlands, turning rural scenery around our cities into monotonous suburbs, pressure for land-use planning began to mount. By the year 2000, our urban areas could require an additional 18 million acres alone to meet housing, economic, and social needs. By 1990, our needs in land for rapid transit, freeways, expressways, and major new airports will almost triple; they will certainly triple by the end of the century.

Yet, in retrospect, it seems strange that the Nixon administration would have taken up the cause of coastal zone management and land-use legislation. Certainly the move rubbed Nixon's natural conservative constituency the wrong way, and there were never any votes in it—as the narrow and bitterly contested defeat of land-use legislation in June 1974 proved. Moreover, it was out of character for a Republican administration to assert the radical proposal of giving federal funds to the states and encouraging them to override, in some cases, local zoning decisions. Here was a conservative President, elected primarily by white middle-class suburbia, asking Congress for federal grants to help

---
[1] Dennis O'Harrow, *Soil, Water and Suburbia*, report of the proceedings of a conference sponsored by the U.S. Department of Agriculture and the U.S. Department of Housing and Urban Development, June 15-16, 1967 (Washington, D.C.: U.S. Government Printing Office, March 1968), p. 106.

147

the states reassert control over land development decisions with greater than local impact. Among the most sensitive of these, of course, are state decisions to override local sentiment in the choice of sites for low-income housing when the benefits to a broader community outweigh, in the state's opinion, any detriment to the smaller community.

Still, the administration could not ignore the sprawling and uncontrolled development occurring across the land. Fred Bosselman and David Callies described the growing pressures in their land-use study for CEQ:

> This country is in the midst of a revolution in the way we regulate the use of the land. It is a peaceful revolution, conducted entirely within the law. It is a quiet revolution and its supporters include the conservatives and the liberals. It is a disorganized revolution with no central cadre of leaders, but it is a revolution nonetheless.[2]

In approaching the question, the new administration began with the traditional concept that a property owner has the right to treat land like a commodity, fully his and fully marketable. Indeed, the Fifth Amendment to the Constitution ensures that private property shall not be taken for public use without just compensation. Yet state and federal land-use regulations inevitably restrict the uses to which property can be put and, in doing so, often decrease land values. This fact alone does not mean that these controls are unconstitutional or that compensation is necessarily required when the controls result in reduced property values. Indeed, existing federal law has considerable effect on land use and land values. For example, the National Environmental Policy Act of 1969,[3] in requiring the use of environmental-impact statements, set in motion a process that can result in federal decisions to mitigate land-use impacts. Such decisions are particularly apt to be made over the siting of energy facilities. The Clean Air Amendments of 1970,[4] in granting powers to control air quality, also granted certain powers over land-use decisions since they control the location of power plants, industrial sites, transportation corridors, and so on. Similarly, federal powers to protect water quality can affect land use by affecting the location of flood control and reservoir structures and of low density

---

[2] Fred Bosselman and David Callies, *The Quiet Revolution in Land-Use Control* (Washington, D.C.: U.S. Government Printing Office, December 1971), p. 1. (Prepared under contract with CEQ.)

[3] P.L. 91-190 (83 Stat. 852), January 1, 1970.

[4] P.L. 91-604 (84 Stat. 1676), December 31, 1970.

148

or undeveloped buffer zones along rivers, lakes, and ocean front property. Even federal pesticide or noise-abatement laws might have some effect on land-use decisions. More direct than the land-use controls springing from federal pollution regulations, however, are those that arise under the commerce clause of the Constitution in connection with the siting of key facilities related to interstate commerce. As Philip Soper has pointed out,

> Proposals for national land-use legislation that rely on such key facility concepts—defined to include major airports and highway interchanges—and proposed power plant siting legislation, furnish examples of the kind of land-use decisions over which the Federal Government could theoretically exercise control on the basis of the effect of siting decisions on interstate commerce.[5]

Finally, in making decisions to locate large facilities on public lands, the federal government often affects land use and values on adjacent private land.

In theory, states are able to exercise much greater powers than the federal government over land use. The power to zone emanates from the constitutional police power of the states. Over the years, however, the states have delegated zoning authority to the counties and cities and, as a result, find it difficult, given a few recalcitrant local communities, to protect a large ecologically fragile area that extends through several local jurisdictions. The failure of the states to use their zoning powers has resulted, until relatively recently, in little or no statewide land-use planning or linkage of this planning to pollution-abatement regulations.

However, as the public became increasingly aware of the abuse of the land, there were greater numbers of suits demanding a change in the balance between the traditional rights of property owners and the public's right to environmental protection. The law seemed to distinguish between the actual taking of land, an act that required compensation, and regulation, an act that did not require compensation since it did not require direct physical interference with private property. Yet the latter tended to reduce property value. Judicial theories for determining when land-use regulations imply compensation to property owners have not been consistently applied. In spite of apparent agreement that compensation is required when regulation goes "too far"

[5] Philip Soper, *Federal Environmental Law, The Constitutional Framework of Environmental Law* (St. Paul, Minnesota: West Publishing Company, 1974), p. 39.

(exactly how far in quantitative terms is not clear), no rational distinction between regulation and taking has been precisely formulated.

In the absence of a set formula, several theories have been applied. The *physical invasion theory* holds that where physical control over private property results in transfer of title, then eminent domain powers have been utilized and compensation is required. Yet government can stop short of obtaining title to the property by passing legislation that limits the uses to which private property can be put even without acquiring title. The *nuisance abatement theory* says that if the uses of private property are harmful or perceived to be adverse to the interests of the general public, then compensation is not required if the government legislates restrictions to the particular nuisance. The *balancing theory* suggests that the amount of compensation should be decided by weighing or balancing the public benefit against the inconvenience to the property owner. Finally, the *diminution of value theory*, which the judiciary most often relies on in land-use cases today, holds that a substantial diminution in the value of private property due to government action is cause for compensation. Yet the theory provides no clear guide on how much economic harm constitutes substantial devaluation.

Given these legal uncertainties, the incoming Nixon administration was slow to move on national land-use legislation. Soon, however, it found itself supporting coastal-zone-management legislation, which involved principles identical to those involved in land-use legislation.

Coastal-Zone Management

In January 1969, the new administration was handed the newly published report by the Commission on Marine Science, Engineering and Resources which recommended legislation authorizing federal grants to establish state coastal-zone authorities to manage coastal waters and adjacent lands.[6] Russell Train, then undersecretary of interior, chaired an interagency task force that endorsed the concept of coastal-zone-management legislation. The report expressed the conviction that national interests are involved in coastal-zone management and that therefore this was a legitimate area for federal legislation. Coastal

[6] Commission on Marine Science, Engineering and Resources, *Our Nation and the Sea* (Washington, D.C.: U.S. Government Printing Office, January 1969), p. 57.

150

zones are unique, the report said, and their preservation is in the interests of all citizens, not just the people of the coastal states. Estuarine areas are especially valuable as habitat and transitional areas for fish and wildlife, which travel beyond state boundaries. Estuaries and marshlands are vital to the life support of two-thirds of the nation's commercial and sports fish harvest. Some members of the administration, including the author, argued that coastal-zone areas, although ecologically fragile, are no different from environmentally unique zones in the inland states.

As drafted, the coastal-zone legislation drafted by the administration applied to thirty states,[7] including the states bordering the Great Lakes. Why not expand the concept of land protection to all fifty states, to inland as well as coastal areas? But the time was not ripe. Determining which environmental areas aside from coasts deserved protection was problematic, and at that time the effects of statewide land-use laws already in force had not been studied in any detail. Furthermore, there was the possibility that a national land-use law might be interpreted as an intrusion into state affairs. Thus, the decision was made to hold back on land-use policy and to endorse coastal-zone management first.

This was also politically attractive. The clamor for protection of coastal zones was at the time much greater than the demand for national land-use regulation, for several reasons. Both population and industry were highly concentrated in coastal zones and recreational needs were expanding more rapidly in coastal areas than in inland areas. As affluence increased, second homes were being built on coastal properties, including both single dwellings and condominiums, that often encroached on prize wetland and beach areas. Finally, a highly organized professional group of marine biologists and oceanographers could bring pressure to bear on key committees and on congressmen representing districts in coastal states. Because the Interior committees of the House and Senate were dominated by members from rural areas, no comparable pressure was exerted in favor of controlling suburban growth through land-use legislation.

The decision to introduce coastal-zone-management legislation first, and at a later date to introduce land-use legislation, caused a considerable problem. If land-use legislation had passed Congress before coastal-zone-management legislation, the President would prob-

---

7 Thirty states plus Puerto Rico, the Virgin Islands, Guam, and American Samoa.

ably have vetoed the latter bill on the basis that the land-use legislation was national in scope, and therefore included coasts. But coastal-zone management moved rapidly through Congress, while land use stalled.

In November 1969, Secretary of the Interior Hickel transmitted the administration's coastal-zone-management legislation to the House and Senate Public Works committees. At that time, since the National Oceanic and Atmospheric Administration (NOAA) did not yet exist, the administration's bill gave the Department of Interior the lead responsibility for coastal-zone regulation, on the basis that it had more land-use expertise than any other agency. At the same time, the Senate Commerce Committee was holding hearings on a similar bill, whose grant program would be administered by the Marine Resources and Engineering Development Council. After NOAA came into existence, the committee supported NOAA as the lead agency for coastal-zone management.

In January 1970, Senator Henry Jackson, (Democrat, Washington), introduced S. 3354, a national land-use bill to be administered by the Water Resources Council. Jackson had an informal understanding with Senator Ernest F. Hollings, (Democrat, South Carolina), who chaired the Senate subcommittee on oceans of the Commerce Committee, that they would support each others' bills and avoid a jurisdictional dispute, even though potential duplication and overlap might occur. In 1971, when the administration introduced a land-use bill, its witnesses consistently supported placing coastal-zone legislation under the Department of Interior. But the House Merchant Marine and Fisheries Committee, because it had oversight over NOAA, reported out a bill in 1972 placing the coastal-zone-management program under NOAA, in the Department of Commerce. On the House floor, the administration supported an amendment to place jurisdiction under the Interior Department, and this amendment was adopted, 261 to 112.[8] However, the conference committee, composed entirely of members of the House and Senate committees with jurisdiction over NOAA, recommended NOAA as the lead agency and the conference report was adopted by a voice vote in both houses.[9]

The President almost vetoed the coastal-zone-management bill. EPA and the Interior Department opposed it while OMB and CEQ

---

[8] *Congressional Record*, vol. 118, part 20 (August 2, 1972), pp. H 26492-93.
[9] *Congressional Quarterly Almanac*, vol. 28 (1973), pp. 973-74.

favored it. The bill provided for two-thirds federal funding to states for development and administration of management programs for coastal waters and adjacent shorelines, and it provided a 50 percent cost sharing for state acquisition of estuarine sanctuaries. The secretary of commerce, through NOAA, would administer the program and the secretary of the interior was given veto power if he felt the coastal-zone-management program was inconsistent with state land-use programs adopted under subsequent legislation.

Arguments presented against signing the bill were:

(1) Coastal-zone planning was merely a facet of land-use planning, not a separate entity, and authority over land-use planning would therefore be divided between two executive departments, Commerce and Interior. Even if the proposed Department of Natural Resources were established, the situation might not be alleviated. The language in the bill gave the secretary of interior veto power over the coastal-zone-management program should land-use legislation later become law, but it also clearly implied that the two programs would continue to exist. It was likely that jurisdictional interests would keep the coastal-zone-management program going even if NOAA were placed in a Department of Natural Resources.

(2) The bill would be heavily "land-planning oriented" (despite claims that it was "water oriented"), yet NOAA, with no expertise or responsibility in land management, would administer the program.

(3) The bill provided for more substantive review at the federal level of the merits of state plans than the administration liked, and could be regarded as a rather heavy-handed federal intrusion into state planning programs.[10]

(4) In late October 1972, when the bill had to be either signed or vetoed, land-use legislation was doing well in the Congress and prospects were good that a land-use bill would be on the President's desk in 1973. The Senate had already passed a land-use bill and the House had ordered a bill reported. Some members of the administration felt that if the coastal-zone-management bill became law, opponents of land use would ask to delay passage of comprehensive land-use legislation on the grounds that Congress should wait and see how the coastal-zone-management program was working.

---

[10] But by January 1975, President Ford proposed legislation that went so far as to include federal override of state plans for siting energy facilities if the plans were thought by the federal government to be substantively deficient.

(5) Since the federal government already had ample authority to purchase lands, the administration opposed the 50 percent cost sharing for acquisition of estuarine sanctuaries.

(6) Finally, there were no sanctions or penalties in the bill for states' failures to develop coastal management plans once federal funds had been granted. In other words, all the carrots were there and no stick.

In the end, Nixon decided to sign the bill.[11] There was an acknowledged, overriding problem in the coastal zones because of uncontrolled development. The bill encouraged coastal states to assume responsibility for controlling development. Being water-oriented, the bill sought to lessen the conflict between land-use and coastal-zone management by giving the secretary of the interior veto power over any portion of coastal-zone-management planning that could adversely affect good land-use planning of inland areas, should land-use legislation eventually become law. Also, the prospect that Congress might act on a Department of Natural Resources proposal at least meant that states could look forward to dealing with a single department, even though it was likely that the two grant programs, accomplishing about the same objectives, would continue to exist. Nixon concluded that the overriding need to control land-use planning in ecologically fragile coastal zones should not be delayed even though he preferred a national land-use approach. Also, arguments against the bill may well have been lost on the public, which would have considered them technical and quibbling. Because there was such strong public support for protection and control of the coastal zone, a presidential veto would undoubtedly be misunderstood—and it was just a week before the presidential election. Politics aside, the issue closely divided the administration, and there would be little opportunity to explain a veto in the face of strong public opinion favoring environmental protection in coastal areas: Why take a chance?

But because Nixon had promised during the 1972 presidential campaign to cut federal spending to $250 billion, every possible corner was cut to reduce expenditures. No FY 1973 supplemental was sent to Congress after the bill passed and the program was zero-funded in FY 1974. Later, after considerable pressure from Senator Hollings in particular, as well as from the author, who hoped to get Hollings's

---

[11] The Coastal Zone Management Act of 1972, P.L. 92-583 (86 Stat. 1280), October 27, 1972.

cooperation on land use, superports, and Department of Natural Resources legislation, the administration sent up a FY 1974 supplemental for $5 million, which Congress increased to $12 million.[12]

Land Use

Meanwhile, land-use legislation moved on a much slower legislative track. Senator Jackson had introduced a land-use bill in January 1970 (S. 3354), and in April, Ehrlichman, Train, and the author met with Jackson and the Senate Interior and Insular Affairs Committee's minority leader, Senator Gordon Allott (Republican, Colorado). The administration had already introduced its coastal-zone-management legislation and Ehrlichman agreed to work closely with Senator Jackson on land use, speaking authoritatively on the issues since he had been a practicing land-use lawyer in Seattle before joining the administration. However, Ehrlichman did not commit the administration to specific legislation; staff work simply had not progressed that far. By August 1970, in his message transmitting CEQ's first annual report, President Nixon said, "I believe we must work toward development of a National Land-Use Policy to be carried out by an effective partnership of federal, state and local governments, together, and, where appropriate, with new regional institutional arrangements." [13] This seemed like a firm presidential commitment to land-use legislation, but behind the scene, as CEQ's staff drafted the bill,[14] considerable disagreement was expressed by OMB as to whether there should be a land-use bill at all. The CEQ draft was based upon the selective, extraterritoriality theory of the Model Land Development Code developed by the American Law Institute.[15] The real issue was to decide which authority—federal, state, or local—should hold power over land-use decisions and how the

---

[12] The act authorized $9 million per year for FY 1973-1977 for planning grants, $30 million per year for FY 1974-1977 for administrative grants, $6 million in FY 1974 for estuarine sanctuaries if matched by state acquisition funds and $3 million annually for FY 1973-1977 for administration of the program by NOAA.

[13] *Public Papers of the Presidents, Nixon, 1970,* Message to the Congress Transmitting the First Annual Report of the Council on Environmental Quality, August 10, p. 659.

[14] William Reilly, later president of the Conservation Foundation, and Boyd Gibbons drafted the Nixon bill for CEQ.

[15] American Law Institute, *A Model Land Development Code,* Tentative Draft No. 3 (Philadelphia, Pa.: American Law Institute, April 22, 1971).

land-use decision process should be sorted out between state-local and federal-state interests. The central thesis of the model code was that, if land-use decisions affect the interests of more than one local government in a state, then the state has jurisdiction over such decisions. Focusing on such decisions, the model code recommended that each state develop a statewide planning process for land-use control in areas of critical importance to the state and large enough so that several localities would be affected by the land-use controls ultimately established. The authors of the model code estimated that decisions affecting such areas might constitute 10 percent of all land-use decisions in any one state; the other 90 percent of the decisions, they estimated, were of purely local concern and therefore ought to remain under local government control.

As finally drafted, the administration's land-use bill provided $20 million a year for five years in aid to the states for the purpose of building institutions with the proper professional competence to develop land-use programs and to assume the land-use regulatory authority over areas of critical ecological concern—wetlands and flood plains; lands around key facilities, such as major airports and highway interchanges; lands surrounding new communities; and lands and developments of regional benefit.

OMB had genuine objections to the bill. (1) It was not clear what the federal guidelines for state land use would be, and although they did not have to be spelled out in the legislation, they would have to be specified in the regulations that would be drawn up after the bill became law. (2) The $20 million did not seem to be enough money annually for fifty states, but on the other hand, there was no clear idea of how large a professional staff would be needed by a creditable state land-use planning agency. (3) Federal coordination of the federal government's own construction and development plans was a most difficult task and there was concern about how federal construction projects would mesh with state land-use plans. (4) There seemed to be no assurance that a state land-use program, once approved by the federal government, would be carried out—in other words, even with sanctions written into the bill there was no assurance of good performance, only good planning. (5) The federal government, in an uncoordinated way, already controlled many land-use decisions through federal construction and siting decisions for major facilities (power plants, highway interchanges, jet ports, and so on) and through its air, water, and other pollution-abatement regulations. In addition, the new National Environmental Policy Act required the federal government to give greater consideration to environmental concerns than it ever had before. Therefore it could be argued that if federal decisions impacting development and land-use practices in the states were better coordinated, there would be much less need for land-use legislation. (6) In the year 1971, both land-use and special revenue-sharing proposals were sent to Congress. Special revenue sharing was the heart of Nixon's New Federalism. It would do away with large numbers of narrow special-interest grants—that is, categorical grants—and instead would package the funds in broad-purpose categories, leaving decisions as to precisely how the funds should be spent to state and local governments. Yet while it adopted this philosophical approach on special revenue sharing, the administration was proposing in its land-use legislation still another categorical grant. (7) Finally, Nixon knew that he might alienate his natural conservative constituency, who would assume or suspect, in spite of the administration's repeated denials, that land-use legislation conflicted with the constitutional right of the states to make their own zoning decisions. Conservatives felt that eventually the federal government would become a sort of board of zoning appeals, arbitrating local land-use disputes.

In November, Ehrlichman and the author met with Train and CEQ staff members Alvin Alm and Boyd Gibbons. They decided to support the bill, though it would be subject to further refinements. In spite of the administration's concern about the inconsistency between its policies on special revenue sharing and land use, Ehrlichman felt that land-use regulation was new and needed the "cutting edge" of federal leadership. Although the heart of Nixon's New Federalism was the elimination of multiple narrow-purpose federal grants and the allocation to local and state officials of decisions as to how federal funds should be spent, the administration was still ready to advocate a new special-purpose grant for land-use programs to get the concept off the ground.

On February 3, 1971, as pressure mounted and as Nixon prepared to deliver his environmental message to Congress in a few days, Train, Alm, Gibbons, Don Rice, associate director of OMB, and the author met in Ehrlichman's office. Everybody in the room strongly favored the land-use bill except Rice, who ended his strong opposition to the idea only when Ehrlichman made it clear that he already had Nixon's

157

approval. The purpose of the meeting was only to iron out the details of the legislation. Had Nixon personally involved himself with the land-use issue, he would have sensed the heat and emotion that this bill stirred among his own staff. Instead, he simply deferred to Ehrlichman's expertise in land use, and Ehrlichman advised that this was a good piece of legislation. Thus, as we shall see, when the critical moment came over three years later and the land-use legislation approached a final vote in the House, Nixon might have been better prepared to resist the pressure of conservatives to kill the bill.

At the February 3 meeting, it was decided to abandon the sanctions provision. If any state failed to develop adequate procedures for producing a land-use plan, this provision would have reduced the state's share of federal highway, outdoor recreation, and airport funds by increments of 7 percent each year up to a maximum reduction of 21 percent.

Train, Alm, Gibbons, and the author wanted to retain the sanctions. Beyond the tactical problems of getting the legislation through Congress was a concern about the fundamental political issue of how to get the states to assume the political power and responsibility for land use that were constitutionally theirs but that, for historical reasons, had come to be exercised at the local level. Sanctions seemed to be an effective means of controlling development. The politically painful loss of these funds (airport and highway money, for which the developers were eager, and parkland funds, sought by the environmentalists) for failure to develop adequate procedures for producing a land-use plan seemed a means of prompting the states to act and of tempering the rivalry between developers and preservationists. But no one had much hope that the sanctions provision would pass. It had originally been included largely for tactical reasons: certain lobby groups would feel they had accomplished something by removing the sanctions and then letting the bill through.

In addition to the possibility that sanctions might hinder passage of the bill, Ehrlichman had another reason for opposing them. The revenue-sharing bill did not include the Highway Trust Fund, but many categorical transportation grants were folded into special revenue-sharing legislation before Congress. Ehrlichman felt that it would be inconsistent to exempt the trust fund from revenue sharing and yet to restrict the use of the fund by earmarking part of it as a sanction in the land-use bill.

One last battle took place within the administration on whether HUD or Interior should be the lead department. In the beginning, when William Reilly and Boyd Gibbons at CEQ were drafting the administration's land-use bill, they received almost no help from Interior. For years, the old-line conservation groups and their bureaucratic counterparts at Interior, the Fish and Wildlife Service, the National Parks Service, the Bureau of Outdoor Recreation, and to a lesser extent, the Bureau of Land Management, had talked vaguely about land-use planning. But at best they had based their discussions on traditional central-planning concepts, while land-use planning meant, first and foremost, producing a map. When Secretary Hickel heard that CEQ was drafting land-use legislation he put his own staff to work drafting a bill. The Interior Department never really got past the traditional great-outdoorsman concept that land use meant parks and beautiful scenery and that if you wanted to preserve anything you had to buy it. Nevertheless, HUD saw that its planning "turf" might be eroded if Interior got the land-use lead, so Secretary Romney "saddled up" for the jurisdictional joust with Interior. After a long meeting between Secretary Morton of the Interior Department (by then Hickel had been fired) and Secretary Romney, with HUD Assistant Secretary Sam Jackson, Russell Train, and the author, Romney reluctantly agreed to drop his bid for HUD's administration of the land-use bill. Although HUD was heavily involved in urban planning programs, the department had had little experience with nonurban land-use questions, including the use of federal lands. Besides, HUD seemed too pro-development to administer what was essentially an environmentally oriented bill.

Much of 1971 was spent trying to harmonize Senator Jackson's bill and the administration's proposal. The original Jackson bill called on the states to establish a system of comprehensive land-use plans, while the administration bill, based on the theory of the Model Land Development Code proposed by the American Law Institute,[16] asked the states to develop plans only for environmentally "critical" areas and for specific large-scale development projects of regional benefit.

The difference in approach between the two bills was much greater than it might have appeared at first glance. Jackson held the traditional master-plan concept which holds that eventually everything can be planned and that, once in place, it somehow freezes there and is done with. Nixon's bill—conservative, but more sophisticated and wary of

[16] Ibid.

159

the central planners' traditional approach—would create a dynamic planning process that would lead to decision making. As a White House staffer put it, "The point is, we want the states to have selective controls, and Jackson wants maps."

Meanwhile, by December 1971, Bosselman and Callies, under contract with CEQ, had completed an intensive study of various state land-use laws, indicating how such complex issues were being addressed.[17] The report showed that several states' approaches were similar to the administration's rather than to Jackson's. The study focused on how states dealt with land-use issues of statewide concern, affecting areas larger than a single jurisdiction—such issues as those dealt with by Massachusetts's land-use laws covering coastal and inland wetlands, Wisconsin's laws concerning shoreline and flood-plain protection, or California's Bay Conservation and Development Commission, which protects San Francisco Bay. The report also indicated how states, besides concentrating on the protection of ecologically fragile areas, were attempting to control the runaway growth that often follows a decision to locate a major facility, such as a highway interchange or a major airport. Both Vermont's and Maine's land-use laws addressed the problem of controlling large-scale development; and the Twin Cities, in Minnesota, had enacted land-use controls around their airport.

The Bosselman/Callies report provided useful background material for the negotiations with Congress, which were carried out on Jackson's side primarily by Steven P. Quarles. To his credit, setting aside all partisan considerations, Quarles came to favor the administration's approach. "We came to the realization that our bill was less sophisticated than the administration's. We eventually saw that the states wouldn't realistically be able to set up comprehensive programs."[18] Jackson had originally used an interagency approach, enlarging the Water Resources Council to administer the program, but eventually agreed that those who administered the bill should not be promoting specific interests, as the Water Resources Council does. He decided that a grant program could not be properly run by an interagency council, and in the end agreed with the administration's recommendation to put the program in the Interior Department. The administration, in turn, compromised and agreed to a new Office of

[17] Bosselman and Callies, *The Quiet Revolution*, p. 327.
[18] James Noone, "Senate, House Differ in Approaches to Reform of Nation's Land-Use Laws," *National Journal*, July 22, 1972, p. 1193.

Land-Use Administration within Interior and a National Advisory Board on Land-Use Policy, really an interagency committee that would represent agencies administering programs with significant land-use impact.

In February 1972, Nixon reversed his position on sanctions and amended the land-use bill to include sanctions for states that did not establish acceptable land-use programs within three years.[19] Under his proposal, 7 percent of the funds allocated under certain sections of the Airport and Airways Development Act,[20] the Federal Aid Highway Acts,[21] including the Highway Trust Fund [22] and the Land and Water Conservation Fund [23] could be withheld. The reason for the switch was that Nixon had decided to take on the onerous political chore of advocating the use of highway trust funds for mass transit needs; this made the highway construction special interest groups so unhappy that sanctions in the land-use bill, which could theoretically restrict the use of highway trust funds, seemed a trifling matter.

On September 19, 1972, the Senate passed a land-use bill that would probably be acceptable to the administration. The House bill was not acceptable to the administration, primarily for tactical reasons. The House bill, championed by Congressman Wayne Aspinall, treated both private- and public-land issues in a single bill. The administration felt that the public-land issues were so complex that they should be treated in one bill, or perhaps even several, that would cover the recommendations of the Public Land Law Review Commission.[24] The Aspinall bill also required a review by all federal agencies that managed public lands, which might lead to multiple-use designations of land that had previously been set aside as national forests or national wildlife refuges. Environmentalists interpreted the bill as an attempt to relax conservation standards on public lands. Although the administration did not view the bill with alarm, many environmentalists did, and the administration knew that it would be hard to move the bill without their

---

[19] *Public Papers of the Presidents, Nixon, 1972*, Special Message to Congress Outlining the 1972 Environmental Program, February 8, p. 181.

[20] P.L. 91-258 (84 Stat. 227), May 21, 1970.

[21] P.L. 85-76 (72 Stat. 885), as amended August 27, 1958.

[22] Jackson's bill did not draw on the Highway Trust Fund in its sanctions.

[23] P.L. 88-578 (78 Stat. 897).

[24] A Report to the President and to the Congress by the Public Land Law Review Commission, *One Third of Our Nation's Land* (Washington, D.C.: U.S. Government Printing Office, 1971).

support. Finally, the House and Senate bills were so different they might easily stalemate in conference. On August 7, 1972, the House Interior Committee voted out a bill,[25] but it remained in the Rules Committee through the conclusion of the 92nd Congress.

In the new 93rd Congress, on January 9, 1973, Jackson introduced S. 268, the same bill that had passed the previous September.[26] The administration bill, revised to include some of the language of S. 268, was introduced by request by Senators Jackson and Paul J. Fannin (Republican, Arizona) on February 20.[27] After six days of hearings and eleven mark-up sessions, the Senate Interior Committee voted out a bill, 10 to 3, on June 7.[28] After two days of floor debate the bill passed the Senate, 64 to 21, on June 21, 1973.[29]

The House moved much more slowly, but on September 13, 1973, the House Interior subcommittee on the environment reported out a bill to the full committee. It was termed a "synthesis" of the key portions of the administration bill and the Senate bill; many of the complicated public-land aspects of Aspinall's original bill had been dropped. In the full committee, Congressman Sam Steiger (Republican, Arizona) introduced H.R. 11325. This bill, which had been drafted with the help of the United States Chamber of Commerce, was a shortened version of the subcommittee bill, but it omitted provisions requiring the states to establish methods for regulating ecologically fragile areas and areas of significant development. The committee supported the original subcommittee bill with some changes, including amendments suggested by the administration, and Congress recessed for the Christmas holidays.

In his state of the union message, on January 30, 1974,[30] President Nixon again called for early enactment of land-use legislation. But on February 6, Congressman Steiger and a group of twenty-one House Republicans met with Nixon to discuss pending bills, including land use. Steiger told the President that the administration's bill would encroach on the states' zoning powers and on individual property rights. In fact, neither the administration bill nor the House committee bill did this. According to Congressman Steiger, "The President told his staff in my

---

[25] *Congressional Quarterly Almanac*, vol. 28 (1973), p. 829.

[26] *Congressional Record*, vol. 119, part 1 (January 9, 1973), pp. S 654-663.

[27] *Congressional Record*, vol. 119, part 4 (February 20, 1973), p. S 4586.

[28] *Congressional Quarterly Almanac*, vol. 29 (1974), p. 661.

[29] *Congressional Record*, vol. 19, part 16 (June 21, 1973), p. S 20631.

[30] Office of the White House Press Secretary, State of the Union, January 30, 1974.

presence to look into what I told him about the bill, and to work on changing it if what I told him was correct." [31]

But on February 26, 1974, House Minority Leader John Rhodes (Republican, Arizona) told the House Rules Committee that he and the administration no longer supported the House committee bill. He added that the administration favored Steiger's bill (H.R. 11325) but that the administration was not prepared to say that the committee bill was completely repugnant. The administration would support the committee bill, Rhodes said, if the substitute H.R. 11325 was not agreed to. The combination of the apparent backing off by the administration from a hard commitment to the committee bill and the strong conservative bent of the Rules Committee proved fatal for land-use legislation. The Rules Committee indefinitely postponed floor consideration of the committee bill (H.R. 10294) by a vote of 9 to 4, with six Democrats and three Republicans voting to postpone and three Democrats and one Republican voting against postponement.[32]

Secretary of the Interior Morton was instructed by the White House staff to work with Congressman Rhodes to come up with a new bill that would, as Assistant Press Secretary Gerald Warren put it on February 28, "maximize the responsibilities of the States and local governments and minimize the role of the Federal Government." [33]

But Representative Rhodes's staff developed an entirely new bill, H.R. 13790, dubbed the "Rhodes/Steiger bill." Although Rhodes seemed genuinely to favor the bill, Steiger and many other conservatives wanted no bill at all. The essential feature of the administration's land-use bill was the requirement that states develop a mechanism to review and if necessary reverse local land-use decisions which had an impact on land outside the local jurisdiction. This feature was lacking in the Rhodes/Steiger bill, which provided no state oversight of local planning decisions. The bill was virtually a "no strings attached" categorical grant of $200 million in federal funds over five years with no federal review of the state planning process.

During March, with the momentum for land-use legislation faltering, the opposition pressed for more hearings. Congressman Morris Udall (Democrat, Arizona) held three more days of hearings

[31] James Noone, "Land-Use Bill Derailed after White House Ends Support," *National Journal*, March 9, 1974, p. 368.

[32] *Congressional Quarterly Almanac*, vol. 30 (1974), p. 790.

[33] See daily press briefing transcript, Office of the White House Press Secretary, February 28, 1974.

in April. On May 14 the House Rules Committee reversed its earlier 9-to-4 vote to postpone action on the committee bill indefinitely and voted 8 to 7 to send the bill to the floor of the House.[34] That same day, any question about the President's view was clarified when Kenneth R. Cole, assistant to the President for domestic affairs, wrote Rhodes, "the President has asked me to reply to your request that we review the land-use legislation currently before the House of Representatives. . . . After a careful examination of the different land use proposals pending before the Congress, the administration supports the Rhodes-Steiger Land Use Planning Act." [35]

Floor debate on H.R. 10294, the committee bill, which had had administration support until the White House switch, and on the Rhodes/Steiger substitute was scheduled for June 11. But Steiger sent letters to his colleagues asking them to oppose granting a rule—in other words, to kill land use. Just the day before, Secretary Morton, "soldiering" for the administration, had asked for support for the Rhodes/Steiger bill. When the committee's bill came to the floor, the issue was whether a rule permitting debate should be accepted by the full House. Congressman Udall, in a last minute attempt to garner support, offered amendments to ensure that there was nothing in his bill that could be construed as a threat to states' rights or private property rights.[36] He also agreed to accept an amendment by Congressman James G. Martin (Republican, North Carolina) clarifying the role of local governments in developing and implementing state land-use programs.[37] But after an hour of debate the House voted 211 to 204 to refuse to accept the rule, and land-use legislation was dead.[38]

President Nixon may have, as charged by some Democrats, abandoned land-use legislation to please the conservative wing of his party and solidify his position before the impending Watergate impeachment vote. In the author's opinion, this is highly unlikely. The President would not have been so naive as to think that by dropping land use, or even by taking a series of actions to please conservatives, he could influence votes on the impeachment issue. It is more likely that Nixon had never felt any genuine commitment to land use but had gone along

[34] *Congressional Quarterly Almanac*, vol. 30 (1974), p. 790.
[35] Letter from Kenneth R. Cole, Jr., assistant to the President for domestic affairs, to Congressman John J. Rhodes, May 14, 1974.
[36] *Congressional Record*, vol. 120, part 10 (June 11, 1974), p. H 5028.
[37] Ibid.
[38] Ibid., pp. H 5041-42.

Table 10
ANALYSIS BY PARTY AND REGION OF CONGRESSIONAL VOTE REJECTING THE RULE ON LAND-USE LEGISLATION

Against Land Use		For Land Use	
Republicans	136	Republicans	46
Southern Democrats	54	Southern Democrats	25
Northern Democrats	21	Northern Democrats	133
Total	211	Total	204

Source: *Congressional Quarterly Almanac,* vol. 30 (1974), p. 790.

with Ehrlichman, whom he had trusted to make sure that the administration's land-use proposal did not infringe on states' zoning rights or on the rights of private property owners. When Nixon heard charges from conservative lawmakers that the bill did in fact threaten constitutional rights, Ehrlichman was gone, and the President had no one to turn to whom he implicitly trusted on the matter. Of course, it is by no means clear that, even if Nixon had remained firm in his support of land-use legislation, the outcome would have been any different. In the author's opinion about twenty more Republicans would have supported the President on the issue if his leadership had been strong—more than enough to reverse the outcome in the House. As land-use legislation came closer to the floor of the House, support for it eroded. Organizations like the forest product manufacturers and livestock and other farm lobby groups, which had previously been either silent or in favor of the bill, strongly denounced it. The influential Chamber of Commerce stepped up its opposition, as did the John Birch Society and the Liberty Lobby. The conservative wing of the Democratic party joined the Republicans, and this always formidable coalition carried the day.

According to a *Congressional Quarterly Almanac* analysis, opposition to land-use legislation came from a conservative coalition of Republicans and rural members. The heavy southern Democratic opposition to the rule suggests that states rights remained the predominant issue in the South (see Table 10).

With Nixon gone, President Ford picked up the land-use question and Secretary Morton pressed him to ask Congress again for land-use legislation. Ford aired the subject in a long cabinet meeting and found lukewarm support or hostility to the idea everywhere except at Interior, EPA, and CEQ. Finally, he decided that there would be no new spending programs, at least for the time being, that were not energy-related. But in fact, with the economy faltering, Ford had no intention of championing land-use legislation, which, critics would charge, might limit jobs and economic growth.

Federal Laws Affecting Land Use. Also of substantive concern to the President was the possibility of duplication and overlap under all the existing federal laws and regulations that in one way or another already affected land-use planning decisions. Their effects seemed profound. Let us turn to a consideration of some of these laws and regulations.

The Clean Air Act. Section 110 of the act, which outlines the requirements for state implementation plans to meet the national ambient air quality standards, includes two sources of statutory authorization to employ land-use controls to achieve air pollution control. First, the state air implementation plans must include "emission limitations, schedules, and timetables for compliance with such limitations, and such *other measures* as may be necessary to insure attainment and maintenance of such primary or secondary standard, including, but not limited to, *land-use* and *transportation controls.*" [39] The provision authorizing the preconstruction review of new stationary sources of air pollution (like power plants and industrial smokestacks) could be construed as a land-use measure because the state air implementation plan required "a procedure . . . for review, prior to construction or modification, of the location of new sources . . . [of air pollution which] shall provide for adequate authority to prevent the construction or modification of any new source to which a [federal] standard of performance . . . [for pollutant emissions] will apply at any location which the State determines will prevent the attainment or maintenance . . . of a national ambient air quality primary or secondary standard. . . ." [40] It would seem from the above that the preconstruction review process, although specifically designed to protect air quality, implies land-use decisions.

EPA regulations also encourage states to "identify alternative control strategies, as well as costs and benefits of each alternative, for attainment and maintenance of the national standards." [41] Thus states

---

[39] 42 U.S.C., section 1857c-5(a) (2) (B). (Italics added.)
[40] Ibid. (4).
[41] 40 C.F.R., section 51.10(a).

are encouraged to consider the economic impact of specific land-use programs in developing their final strategy to meet national air quality standards. EPA regulations further affect land-use planning by regulating indirect sources of air pollution, such as airports, shopping centers, and stadiums. These siting decisions can increase traffic and therefore auto emissions, and they can create pressure for development in adjacent areas. These complex source regulations have a significant impact on state land-use plans. Recognizing the close relationship between air pollution and land-use controls, EPA regulations urge an integrated planning process so that "indirect source review will eventually be incorporated into comprehensive State and *local land-use planning processes* so that social, economic, and air quality factors can be considered in an integrated manner." [42]

The range of land-use controls that EPA may impose in reviewing a state's transportation-control plan to achieve ambient air quality standards is very broad. It includes limiting automobile traffic by restricting off-street parking and construction of new parking facilities and conceivably could extend to more traditional land-use controls in the nature of zoning ordinances. Recent court decisions have upheld EPA's authority to design transportation plans where state plans have failed to achieve the required auto-emission reductions.[43] But the change in land-use patterns resulting from the air pollution specifications for the design of transportation plans could conceivably lead to an emphasis on mass transit that would promote "cluster development" readily serviceable by mass transit and halt the spread of "strip development" pattern that has been encouraged by uninhibited automobile use. In fact, "strip development" became so widespread in this country that former presidential adviser Patrick Moynihan quipped that the country already had a national growth policy operating under the guise of the federal highway program.

The whole controversial question of reducing automobile use and concentration in order to meet ambient air quality standards is obviously land-use related. Congress has removed EPA's authority to impose parking taxes without the concurrence of the local authorities, and the administration has proposed up to two five-year extensions of transportation-control plans where the results of even best-effort

---

[42] 39 Federal Register 25291, 25293.
[43] South Terminal Corp. v. EPA, No. 73-1366 (C.A. 1, September 27, 1974); Pennsylvania v. EPA, No. 73-2121 (C.A. 3, June 28, 1974).

measures still do not meet air quality standards. And Congress may amend the Clean Air Act on the controversial issue of EPA's authority to implement regulations for the design of major construction facilities that attract concentrations of automobiles. Congress seems to be inclined to delay implementation of either indirect-source or transportation-control plans in the hope that improved auto emission controls over the next few years will render the issue moot.

EPA's air-quality-nondeterioration regulations are potentially a powerful means of land-use control. These regulations were proposed in response to a court order requiring the prevention of air quality deterioration in areas (principally in the pristine Rocky Mountain and western desert areas) where air quality exceeds national ambient air quality standards.[44] Under EPA's regulation each state must classify its entire area according to these possible grades of air quality; because they affect growth patterns, these air quality zones in effect establish land-use controls (see Chapter 5).[45]

In summary, EPA has considerable control over land-use decisions by virtue of the authority given it by Congress to design and enforce an air quality implementation plan for any state that has failed to produce a plan considered satisfactory by EPA.

The Federal Water Pollution Control Act Amendments of 1972. Land-use planning is clearly implied by this act. Like the Clean Air Act, it gives the federal government substantial powers to develop land-use plans. Section 101(b) instructs the states to "plan the development and use . . . of *land* and water resources." Section 201 requires the development of waste management treatment plans, and Section 208 requires areawide waste-water-management plans. Both sections extend the plan to include water pollution resulting from nonpoint sources like construction, mining, or farming, and specifically list land-use measures to control water quality at nonpoint pollution sources. Also, Section 303(e) requires each state to develop a continuing planning process which must incorporate, among other things, waste-management plans. Finally, the multibillion dollar public works program building new sewers and treatment plants is playing as major a role in land-use decisions in the 1970s as the federal highway program did in the 1960s.

---

[44] Sierra Club v. Ruckelshaus, 344 F. Supp. 253 (D.D.C. 1972), affirmed by a divided court, 412 U.S. 541 (1973).
[45] 39 Federal Register 30999.

The Rivers and Harbors Act of 1899.[46] Section 10 of this act restricts dredging and filling, which might alter a navigable body of water, and the building of manmade obstructions (piers, breakwaters, jetties, and so on) except where authorized through the U.S. Army Corps of (Civil) Engineers by the secretary of the army. Although Section 10 explicitly concerns navigable waters, the courts have liberally interpreted "navigability" to apply to all lands contiguous to commercially useful bodies of water, including tidal marshlands. Thus, Section 10 authorizes a great deal of federal land-use control.

The Coastal Zone Management Act of 1972. This act, as we have seen, is in fact a federal land-use grant program for the coastal and Great Lakes states.

Programs administered by HUD that affect land use. Under Section 701 of the Housing Act,[47] and under Title IV of the Housing and Community Development Act of 1974,[48] the secretary of HUD may make grants to state, regional, or local agencies, not only for comprehensive planning purposes, but also for the implementation of planning programs. To obtain a grant the applicant must set forth in his plan a *"land-use* element," including "(a) studies, criteria, and procedures necessary for guiding major growth decisions and (b) general plans with respect to the pattern and intensity of *land use* for residential, commercial and other objectives." [49] The grants are an incentive for land-use planning by state, regional, and local bodies. Some degree of federal control is indirectly ensured in that the grants made by the secretary of HUD can be withdrawn if reasonable progress is not made in comprehensive planning. The secretary, however, does not control the content of plans but is only entitled to determine whether or not planning is in fact being done.

Another HUD program influencing land-use controls is Title I of the Housing and Community Development Act of 1974,[50] which operates somewhat like special revenue sharing by packaging existing programs for community development into a single program of community development grants. Funds can be used for a variety of

---

[46] Ch. 425 (30 Stat. 1151), March 3, 1899.

[47] 40 U.S.C., section 461.

[48] P.L. 93-383 (88 Stat. 686), August 22, 1974.

[49] 39 Federal Register 43378.

[50] P.L. 93-383 (88 Stat. 686), August 22, 1974.

purposes (elimination of blighted areas, preservation of property, improvement in the use of land, and so on) necessary to develop a comprehensive plan or implementation of the plan.

HUD's "Community Development Corporation" [51] provides financial assistance to private developers and state land-development agencies. Comprehensive planning is clearly required before federal financial guarantees are forthcoming. The act seeks to coordinate the land-use plans of state and local planning bodies with the actions of private developers.

Finally, still another HUD program, Model Cities,[52] makes grants for planning, developing, and implementing comprehensive city demonstration programs, of which land-use planning is necessarily a major part.

Power of eminent domain. Land-use controls can be exercised through the power of eminent domain, that is, a taking for a public purpose, and, as we have seen, there has been a tendency in the courts to interpret "public purposes" liberally in order to carry out federal projects.

The public lands. Many public land-management policies have an indirect impact on land-use controls. For example, the imposition of grazing fees and the granting of grazing permits determine the extent of grazing on public lands. The checkerboard pattern of federal land ownership means that the federal government can, if it wishes, prevent private landowners from having access across federal lands; this is another form of land-use control. The federal government can also control the terms of surface mining and reclamation practices on public lands and see that they conform to good land-use practice. Thus, a great deal can be accomplished to promote sound land-use practices on the public lands without additional federal land-use legislation.

After reviewing the bewildering array of federal authorities that already had some control over land use, President Ford decided to delay proposing land-use legislation. He wanted to hold the line on spending. He also wanted more time to review all the federal programs and identify those that should be eliminated or changed. In addition, their administration needed to be coordinated and rationalized. In the

---

[51] 42 U.S.C., section 4511 et seq.
[52] 42 U.S.C., section 3301 et seq.

author's opinion, any land-use legislation would probably be bitterly contested. The emotion that land use invokes was evident on July 15, 1975, in what the *Congressional Quarterly* called "one of the most emotional lobbying campaigns in recent years," [53] when the House Interior Committee narrowly voted, 19 to 23, against reporting out a land-use bill.

Energy Facilities Siting. Land-use problems over the years have arisen in connection with the siting of large energy facilities such as electrical generating plants and refineries. In 1970, the Office of Science and Technology published a report that emphasized the need for longer-range planning by the producers of electric power.[54] Such producers should not only project their future needs, the report said, but also should identify specific power-plant sites and deal with environmental concerns well in advance of construction deadlines. Nixon adopted the recommendations made in this report and in his 1971 environmental message to Congress proposed power-plant-siting legislation which would require utilities to identify needed power-plant-supply facilities ten years prior to construction.[55] Under this proposal, five years before construction, utilities would be required to identify the power-plant sites and general transmission routes they had under consideration; two years before construction they would be required to apply for permits for specific sites, transmission-line routes, and other required facilities, and public hearings would be held. Though numerous hearings were held the legislation never reached the floor of either house.

In his January 1974 energy message to Congress, Nixon proposed to modify his original power-plant-siting proposal, calling it an energy-facility-siting bill. The bill was never submitted because of interagency conflict, principally over the relationship between a federal energy-facilities-siting bill and land-use legislation and over the question of the federal government's right to override a state's siting plan it thought inadequate.

Before these differences could be resolved, Nixon resigned, and President Ford began to review the issue. The bill he proposed went

---

[53] *Congressional Quarterly*, vol. 33 (July 19, 1975), p. 1520.

[54] Office of Science and Technology, "Electric Power and the Environment" (Washington, D.C.: U.S. Government Printing Office, August 1970), p. 71.

[55] *Public Papers of the Presidents, Nixon, 1971*, Special Message to Congress Proposing the 1971 Environmental Program, February 8, pp. 137-138.

much further than the Nixon bill. In addition to being offered federal planning and management grants, the states would be required to prepare energy-facility-siting programs within national guidelines established by the Federal Energy Administration (FEA). These programs, which would be subject to FEA's approval, would have to be set forth in considerable detail, and would have to include short- and long-term proposals for the siting of power plants and refineries. Any state that did not prepare an acceptable program would be required to carry out an alternative energy-facility-siting program promulgated by FEA. The proposed legislation would invalidate all state and local statutes and ordinances, including local zoning laws, inconsistent with the federal program.

The bill raised two basic issues: (1) the need for separate energy facility legislation, and (2) the need for a federal override. While energy facility siting is a land-use problem and could be handled under future land-use legislation or the Coastal Zone Management Act, in the coastal states the President felt that the need to control power-plant siting was so pressing that separate legislation, which would avoid the delay that any land-use bill would encounter, was justified. In addition, the concepts underlying coastal-zone and land-use legislation were inimical to the federal override granted to FEA under the Ford proposal and therefore should be treated in separate bills.

Ford, like Nixon, was concerned about preserving state zoning rights in the land-use bill. Nevertheless, he decided in favor of a federal override in the energy-facilities-siting legislation. Ford felt that, while states want adequate energy supplies, they are apt to shy away from the responsibility of siting often unattractive and growth-inducing refineries and electrical generating plants. Furthermore the concept of federal override had already been established in the air- and water-pollution-control laws. Ford decided that the importance of the problem justified an attempt to overcome the admittedly strong opposition to the federal override on the matter of energy facility siting. In the author's opinion it is not likely that the override will remain in any bill that might emerge from Congress. If Congress acts at all on this bill, it will probably produce legislation that gives grants to the states and leaves the override in the closet—all "carrot" and no "stick."

Incentives to Preserve Coastal Wetlands. Special tax-incentive legislation was proposed by President Nixon in 1972 to preserve coastal wetland areas by generally reducing federal income-tax benefits related to investments and improvements in those areas. Nixon outlined the problem the legislation was designed to correct. Wetlands "contain some of the most beautiful areas left on this continent," he wrote. "These same lands, however, are often some of the most sought-after for development. As a consequence, wetland acreage has been declining, as more and more areas are drained and filled for residential, commercial and industrial projects." [56]

Nixon's legislative proposal provided for (1) limited federal tax depreciation on new structures on identified coastal wetlands, (2) full recapture upon resale of improvements, (3) denial of the one-year write-off available to farmers for soil and water conservation expenditures where they affect coastal wetlands, and (4) capitalization of interest and taxes during construction. Although Congress did not act on the proposal, it remains, in the author's opinion, as sound today as it was when it was drafted. It provides incentives not to develop ecologically valuable wetlands that are so extensive that their purchase with public funds would be economically, and probably politically, impossible. The proposal also tends to correct the bias toward environmental degradation that springs from the federal tax benefits generally available to developers.

Strip Mining

Probably no single issue concerning the use of our land has so polarized the environmentalists and those whose primary concern is the provision of an adequate energy supply than the strip mining of coal. From an environmental perspective there is ample cause for concern. Over 2 million acres of land have already been stripped, chiefly in Appalachia, the rich coal lands of the Midwest, and the high northern plain country of Montana, Wyoming, and North and South Dakota. Furthermore, land is now being stripped at the rate of about 1,700 acres per week, or an area approximately the size of Manhattan every three months. Yet President Ford was advised that strip-mine legislation such as that he twice vetoed could restrict coal production during the first full year of its implementation by an estimated 40 to 162 million tons, which

[56] *Public Papers of the Presidents, Nixon, 1972,* Special Message to Congress Outlining the 1972 Environmental Program, February 8, pp. 181-182.

would have to be made up by oil imports of 450,000 to 1.8 million barrels per day, costing the consumer as much as $5.6 billion.[57]

Given the devastation of our landscape on the one hand, and the need for adequate supplies of coal on the other, it would seem reasonable that Congress and the executive branch might be able to agree on legislation that would adequately regulate strip-mining practices, including surface reclamation, and at the same time would result in as little economic impact as possible in terms of coal-production losses, job elimination, and consumer costs. But progress toward this goal has been remarkably slow and marked by bitter controversy.

Congress first recognized the environmental damages caused by strip mining in March 1965, when it enacted the Appalachian Regional Development Act.[58] Section 205(c) directed the secretary of the interior to survey and study strip mining and make recommendations to the President. In July 1967, the Interior Department's report recommended that federal strip-mining standards and reclamation requirements be established but that "regulation and enforcement should be explicit responsibilities of the State." [59] At the same time the recommendations moved a little closer to outright federal control: "In the absence of satisfactory State regulations to control current and future surface-mining operations, or a failure of enforcement, Federal standards and reclamation requirements upon the surface mining industry should be imposed until such time as the State is prepared to assume its responsibilities." [60] Only very general standards were mentioned in the report, however, and the Johnson administration never forwarded specific strip-mine legislation to Congress.

When the Nixon administration addressed the problem, CEQ and the Domestic Council staff received considerable help from the Appalachian Regional Commission in drafting legislation, but the Department of Interior, whose bureaucracy worked closely with the mining industry, was of little assistance. At that time twenty-two states had

---

[57] These calculations are based on the assumption that 4.14 barrels of oil equal one ton of coal; that 100 percent of the lost coal is replaced by imported oil (a reasonable assumption, with domestic oil and natural gas production declining); that coal is replaced by oil at the price of $11.60 per barrel; and that coal prices rise from $12 to $18 per ton.

[58] P.L. 89-4 (79 Stat. 5), March 9, 1965.

[59] U.S. Department of the Interior, *Surface Mining and Our Environment*, July 1967, p. 124.

[60] Ibid., p. 105.

laws regulating strip mining. According to a CEQ study, these state laws, with few exceptions, were weak and loosely enforced. The staffs of CEQ and OMB, Ehrlichman, and the author were unanimous in recommending federal regulation of strip mining to the President. The first bill submitted by the Nixon administration proposed regulation of both surface and underground mining.[61] It created national standards that would place the mining industry on the same footing in each state. It gave the states the opportunity to develop regulations to be submitted for approval by the secretary of the interior; any state that failed to develop an acceptable program within two years after the bill's enactment would be required to accept regulations promulgated by the secretary.

President Nixon asked Congress to act on strip-mining legislation in each of his environmental messages, but it was not until December 1974, after Ford became President, that Congress passed a strip-mining bill. This Ford pocket-vetoed at the end of the 93rd Congress. In February 1975, Ford sent a new strip-mining bill to Congress [62] identifying the critical points in the vetoed bill that he wanted changed. Ford's bill focused on the need to reduce coal-production losses and to make the estimates of such losses more precise than they had been in the vetoed version. But Congress made only minor changes in the bill and Ford vetoed it again on May 20, 1975. In spite of the bill's passing 333 to 86 in the House [63] and 84 to 13 in the Senate,[64] Ford was able, on June 10, to sustain his veto, 278 to 143, in the House,[65] three votes short of the two-thirds needed to override the President. The key to sustaining the veto was the strong shift in House sentiment toward concern over the economy and job security and away from the environment. When congressmen went home for the Memorial Day recess just before the strip-mining veto override vote, their constituents no doubt voiced their concern over jobs and rising prices, including fuel bills. The President focused on this point in his veto message [66] and the

61 *Public Papers of the Presidents, Nixon, 1971*, Special Message to Congress Proposing the 1971 Environmental Program, February 8, p. 138.

62 Letter of February 6, 1975, from President Ford to the Speaker of the House of Representatives.

63 *Congressional Record*, vol. 121, no. 44 (March 18, 1975), p. H 1908.

64 *Congressional Record*, vol. 121, no. 40 (March 12, 1975), p. S 3730.

65 *Congressional Record*, vol. 121, no. 90 (June 10, 1975), p. H 5205.

66 Office of the White House Press Secretary, Memorandum of Disapproval of H.R. 25, May 20, 1975.

administration witnesses [67] successfully defended, in the author's opinion, their estimates of the job losses, production cutbacks, and price increases likely to occur if the bill became law. One cannot really make an objective judgment of the merits of the bill without reviewing in some detail these estimates and the assumptions that underlie them.

Impacts of the Strip-Mining Bill. The Bureau of Mines [68] estimated that coal tonnage losses under the bill would be 40 to 162 million tons of coal during the first full year of implementation, as follows: small mines, 22 to 52 million tons; steep slopes, siltation and aquifer protection provisions, 7 to 44 million tons; and ban on mining alluvial valley floors, 11 to 66 million tons.

Large though they were, these estimates had to be considered conservative since they did not take into account several factors that would have large but unquantifiable impacts. These included: (1) the bill's requirement that various kinds of land be designated as unsuitable for mining; (2) surface-owner-consent provisions that would have modified existing law by transferring coal rights from the federal government to the surface owner, with the result that there was no way of estimating how much coal would actually be available for mining; and (3) the courts' interpretation of various ambiguous terms in the bill, which could have additional adverse impact on production by prohibiting or restricting mining even beyond the apparent intent of the bill's drafters. Congress rejected an administration provision in the bill explicitly granting authority to the secretary of the interior to define these ambiguous terms; such authority would have enabled the secretary to clarify the regulatory process and thus reduce litigation delays.

Small Mines' Losses. The administration estimated tonnage losses from small mines at 22 to 52 million tons of coal. This estimate was based on the assumption that very small mines, producing less than 50,000 tons per year, principally in the Appalachian area, would have very limited financial ability to satisfy the detailed provisions of the bill

---

[67] Frank Zarb, administrator, FEA; John Hill, deputy administrator, FEA; Eric Zausner, deputy administrator, FEA; Thomas Falkie, director, U.S. Bureau of Mines; Raymond Peck, Jr., Office of the General Counsel, Department of Commerce; and Rogers Morton, secretary of interior, *Hearings on the President's Veto of H.R. 25*, before the House Committee on Interior and Insular Affairs, Subcommittee on Energy and the Environment and Subcommittee on Mines and Mining (Washington, D.C.: U.S. Government Printing Office, June 3, 1975).
[68] Thomas Falkie, director, U.S. Bureau of Mines, in ibid., pp. 133-141.

relating to bonding and permit applications. The requirements set forth under these provisions included detailed geologic maps and cross-section test borings, acquisition of hydrologic data, and the assessment of the impact of mining on the hydrologic balance—requirements likely to exceed the sophistication as well as the financial means of many small companies. The Bureau of Mines estimated that given these difficult requirements, from about 40 to 100 percent of all small-mine production would be lost—from 22 to 52 million tons of the total production projected if no bill were enacted. (For the purposes of these calculations, small mines are defined as those producing less than 50,000 tons per year.) None of this production could be replaced from other sources.

Tonnage Losses from Steep-Slope Restrictions, Siltation, and Aquifer Protection. The steep-slope, siltation, and aquifer provisions in the bill were expected to cause tonnage losses estimated by the Bureau of Mines at between 7 and 44 million tons, which can be broken down as follows: steep slope, 7 to 25 million tons; aquifer protection, 0 to 9 million tons; and siltation protection, 0 to 10 million tons. In estimating potential production losses caused by the bill's steep-slope restrictions, the Bureau of Mines examined the total amount of surface production derived from slopes over twenty degrees, as calculated and updated from the CEQ report of 1973 prepared for the Senate Interior Committee.[69] The Bureau of Mines' best engineering estimates were that 6 to 23 percent of the estimated steep-slope production would be lost during the first full year of complete implementation of the bill's provisions, some loss of production being suffered by nearly every steep-slope operation. Provisions in the bill to protect aquifers could reduce planned production, in areas where aquifers received their water source, by at worst up to about 9 million tons, if court or regulatory authorities were adverse. On the other hand, if regulatory authorities or the courts allowed mining to continue as planned, there would be no production loss. The bill prohibited increased stream siltation, a requirement extremely difficult if not impossible to meet. The mining operators' inability to construct the diversion features and settling ponds required by the bill could result in an estimated production loss of 10 million tons. If the

---

[69] CEQ, *Coal Surface Mining and Reclamation: An Environmental and Economic Assessment of Alternatives*, a report printed for use of the Senate Committee on Interior and Insular Affairs (Washington, D.C.: U.S. Government Printing Office, March 1973).

siltation inhibition requirements were favorably interpreted by the regulating authorities or the courts, no losses in production need occur, but the costs of production would still increase substantially.

Tonnage Losses from Protection of Alluvial Valley Floors. One particularly troublesome provision of the bill established an absolute requirement to preserve the hydrological integrity of alluvial valley floors and prevented any off-site hydrological disturbance. This provision was naturally attractive to western ranch and farming interests as well as to environmental groups. But both requirements, in the administration's opinion, were impossible to meet and unnecessary for reasonable environmental protection; both would preclude most mining activities. In the administration's bill this provision was modified, balancing the needs for environmental protection and for coal production: the modified version required that disturbance of hydrological integrity be prevented to the maximum extent practicable. But Congress remained adamant.

The administration estimated losses resulting from the bill's provisions relating to protection of alluvial valley floors at 11 to 66 million tons. To arrive at its maximum-loss figure, the Bureau of Mines, after a mine-by-mine inventory of 1974 surface-mine production west of the 100 degree meridian, estimated that about 45 million tons of the 1974 production was mined either from alluvial valley floors as defined by the bill or in areas that could adversely affect the hydrological integrity of alluvial valley floors. Beyond this, many undeveloped rangelands could be considered potential farm or ranchlands and therefore could be excluded from mining—depending on the will of the courts and the regulatory authorities interpreting the intent of the legislation.

The minimum-loss estimate was arrived at by an inventory of actual mining operations and the application to them of three factors defined in the bill: (1) areas currently being farmed or ranched, (2) the amount of undeveloped rangeland, and (3) potential farm and ranch lands. The 11-million-ton estimated production loss assumed the most favorable interpretation of the bill.[70]

---

[70] The *New York Times* commentary (June 4, 1975, p. 20) on the administration witnesses' congressional testimony justifying Ford's veto erroneously reported that Congressman John Melcher (Democrat, Montana) "drew from the technicians a concession that a number of nine large Western strip mines listed by Interior Department as likely to be curtailed or closed by the bill's hydrological provisions would not, in fact, be affected," since they were not on alluvial valley floors. Actually, administration witnesses never claimed that the mines were on

Job Losses. In 1977, if no new legislation is passed, strip mining should produce 330 million tons of coal and employ about 40,000 miners. According to the administration [71] using a national average of 36 tons of coal stripped per man-day and an indirect employment multiplier of 1.8 (for every job lost in the mining industry, 0.8 jobs are lost in the economy), the strip-mining bill represented the following potential for job loss:

Annual Production Losses Implied
by Strip-Mining Bill

	Minimum estimate: 40 million tons	Maximum estimate: 162 million tons
Direct job losses	4,938	19,700
Indirect job losses	3,950	15,760
Total job losses (rounded off)	9,000	36,000

The impact of unemployment would be highest in Appalachia, chiefly because of the large number of small mines there that could be closed down by the steep-slope restrictions. The direct job loss estimates were calculated by applying the national productivity average of 36 tons per man-day to the minimum (40 million tons) and maximum (162 million tons) annual tonnage losses estimated for the country as a whole. The figure thus obtained was then multiplied by the number of working days per year in the industry to arrive at the estimated loss of 4,938 to 19,700 jobs.

The indirect job loss estimate of 3,950 to 15,760 was determined using a 1.8 multiplier. This number, commonly accepted for determining the indirect effects of coal mining, was developed by

---

alluvial valley floors, but instead that the bill's language stated that a permit to strip mine would not be approved unless the applicant could demonstrate that mining "would not have substantial adverse effect on alluvial valley floors" (H.R. 25, section 51065). This language left room for doubt as to how the regulator or the courts might interpret what constituted a "substantial adverse effect" or how the absence of a "substantial adverse effect" could be affirmatively demonstrated with any geological or legal precision.

[71] Office of the White House Press Secretary, fact sheet accompanying President Ford's memorandum of disapproval of H.R. 25, May 20, 1975, and Zarb's testimony at the *Hearings on the President's Veto of H.R. 25*, p. 17.

W. H. Miernyk,[72] an authority on input-output methods from the University of West Virginia.[73]

Proponents of the bill argued that the administration's estimates of job losses were inflated and that new jobs would be created in underground mining and in the land reclamation to be financed through a provision of the legislation. This provision would place an excise tax [74] on each ton of mined coal to create a trust fund for use in reclaiming publicly and privately owned abandoned mined lands. These arguments do not hold up, in the author's opinion.

In the first place, if the bill had been enacted, job loss would have hit the small mines of Appalachia most severely. These were the lowest productivity mines. A considerable time lag would also be caused by the need to retrain surface miners for underground mining. Some underground coal mining jobs would be created, but as a CEQ report on surface mining points out, the number of those jobs would increase slowly.[75] It takes three to five years to bring a new underground coal mine into production. Shortages of trained manpower and equipment are already significant and production is now operating at peak capacity.[76]

---

[72] William Miernyk, "The Interindustry Structure of the American Coal Industry Projected Until 1970," William Miernyk and Associates, Morgantown, West Virginia, October 1967.

[73] However, following FEA Administrator Frank Zarb's congressional testimony, the Associated Press (no. 52, June 5, 1975) reported that "the Ford administration misrepresented his [Dr. Miernyk's] research in claiming that the vetoed strip mining bill would cause heavy unemployment." Miernyk was quoted as saying that "the bill would actually have little effect on unemployment in the coal fields despite administration allegations that it would put 36,000 out of work." John Hill, FEA deputy administrator, reacting to the story, phoned Miernyk, to find out that in fact Miernyk and the administration were in agreement. Both agreed that over the long run there would be no net job losses if more labor intensive underground mining replaced strip mining. The point that the Associated Press story missed was that the administration was talking about short-term job losses. As Hill pointed out in a clarifying FEA press release ("FEA Substantiates Strip Mining Testimony," June 6, 1975) "FEA's estimates of 5,000 to 20,000 potential direct job losses were for 1977 only—the first year that the bill would have been activated. FEA used those figures to direct unemployment that could not be offset the first year and multiplied them by 1.8 to obtain the indirect unemployment impacts of the bill (which Dr. Miernyk agrees is an appropriate use of his multiplier). The indirect effects of 4,000 to 16,000 were added to the 5,000–20,000 to get the full range of 9,000–36,000 potential jobs that would not be available in regional areas as a result of the surface mining bill."

[74] Fifteen cents per ton on underground coal and thirty-five cents per ton on strip-mined coal.

[75] CEQ, *Coal Surface Mining and Reclamation*, pp. 58-59.

[76] At the time President Ford vetoed the bill, 1977 estimated coal production was 685 million tons, already 65 million tons below the 750-million-ton forecast in the Project Independence studies in the fall of 1974.

Land reclamation financed by an excise tax on coal would create some jobs, but fewer than would be lost by an overall decrease in coal production. As FEA Administrator Frank Zarb testified before Congress following Ford's veto,

> to the extent that reclamation activities funded by H.R. 25 would create jobs, they would do so only at the expense of other jobs and any actual offset would be illusory. The reclamation fee would withdraw significant funds from the economy and reduce employment elsewhere accordingly. To the extent that expenditures of these funds lagged there would be direct recessionary impact.[77]

The Consumer Effect. The tonnage losses estimated by the administration if the strip-mine bill had become law were expected to increase the spot market price of coal to $40 per ton—the oil equivalent level. At that time the spot market price was $22 to $28 per ton and therefore the increases caused by the bill were estimated at about $12 to $18 per ton.[78] The United States was a net importer of about one-third of its daily oil consumption and replacement oil would have to be imported. The increased demand for oil would have been substantial if 40 million to 162 million tons of coal per year were to be replaced with residual oil, assuming that electric utilities and industrial levels were maintained. Using a conversion factor of 4.14 barrels of residual oil per ton of coal, if 40 to 162 million tons of coal were to be replaced by residual oil the increased amount of oil necessary would be .45 to 1.84 million barrels a day.

At the time President Ford vetoed the bill, the average price of imported residual fuel oil was about $11.60 per barrel and the average price of coal (spot and long-term contracts combined) was about $20 per ton. The 1975 demand was estimated at 663 million tons of coal. Assuming that approximately 20 percent of the annual demand, or 132.6 million tons, would be purchased in the spot market, the increase in the annual fuel bill due to the replacement of coal by oil was calculated in two ways. A low estimate was calculated as follows: [79]

---

[77] Frank Zarb, administrator, FEA, in *Hearings on the President's Veto of H.R. 25*, p. 17.
[78] Ibid.
[79] Office of the White House Press Secretary, fact sheet accompanying President Ford's memorandum of disapproval of H.R. 25, May 20, 1975.

.45 million barrels per day $\times$ 365 $\times$ \$4.83 [80] = \$.79 billion per year. A high estimate was calculated this way:

1.84 million barrels per day $\times$ 365 $\times$ \$4.83 = \$3.24 billion per year.

The administration [81] also calculated that if the President had signed the strip-mining legislation, increased energy costs would have been \$2.38 billion to \$5.63 billion out of a total GNP of approximately \$1,500 billion.

The consumer price index increases were estimated as follows: [82]

low estimate: $\dfrac{\$2.38 \text{ billion}}{\$1,500 \text{ billion}} \times 100 = 0.16$ percent

high estimate: $\dfrac{\$5.63 \text{ billion}}{\$1,500 \text{ billion}} \times 100 = 0.38$ percent

With approximately 70 million households in the United States, the increased costs per household were estimated as follows: [83]

low estimate: $\dfrac{\$2.38 \text{ billion}}{70 \text{ million}} = \$34$ per household

high estimate: $\dfrac{\$5.63 \text{ billion}}{70 \text{ million}} = \$80$ per household

Finally, dollar outflows to pay for increased oil imports would rise—\$1.9 billion to \$7.8 billion, based on an average price of \$11.60 per barrel for residual oil.[84]

Thus it seemed to the author that the President had ample reasons to veto the bill:

(1) Tonnage losses resulting from the bill were estimated at 6 to 24 percent of the anticipated 1977 national production of 685 million tons of coal. Contrary to claims by proponents of the bill, these tonnage estimates were probably conservative because the losses that would be caused by several factors (court challenges, the surface

---

[80] \$4.83 is the estimated increase in the cost of using residual fuel instead of coal. The average increase in fuel costs due to the use of oil is the difference between the average price of coal and the BTU equivalent price of residual oil, adjusted for fuel use costs or \$40 per ton less \$20 per ton. Using the conversion factor of 4.14, this is calculated as $\dfrac{20}{4.14} = \$4.83$ per barrel of residual oil used.

[81] Office of the White House Press Secretary, fact sheet of May 20, 1975.

[82] Ibid.

[83] Ibid.

[84] Frank Zarb, administrator, FEA, *Hearings on the President's Veto of H.R. 25*, p. 14.

owner option not to lease, and so on) could not be quantified. Also, several terms used in the bill such as "significant," "substantial," and "potential," were ambiguous from an enforcement and engineering viewpoint and made it impossible to calculate precise minimum tonnage estimates. Neither the states nor the federal government, moreover, would have had the flexibility necessary to resolve the ambiguities and minimize potential losses. The broad citizen-suit provisions in the bill made the courts the final arbiters of the statute's language and, in view of the extreme controversy over strip mining, the President's advisers were forced to assume that extensive use would be made of this mechanism. Given the recent court record in other environmental areas, it seemed likely that the most restrictive possible interpretation would indeed result.

(2) At the very time when the administration was trying to reduce dependency on oil imports, the loss of coal production estimated by the requirements of the bill would increase oil imports from 450,000 to 1.8 million barrels per day in 1977, involving dollar outflows of $1.9 billion to $7.8 billion.

(3) The strip-mining bill would cost the consumers about $2.4 to $5.6 billion and the average household from $34 to $80 more per year in electricity bills.

(4) Job losses, both direct and indirect, estimated at 9,000 to 36,000, would take several years to be offset even partially, thanks to the lower productivity caused by the tighter restrictions.

(5) Finally, Congress, at the time President Ford vetoed the bill, had done nothing significantly to reduce consumption or increase production in order to offset the loss of coal production caused by the bill.

The administration's narrow three-vote victory sustaining the President's veto should not, however, be interpreted as a mandate to draft a strip-mining bill with weak standards. The problem with the vetoed bill was that the imprecision of its language produced widely varying estimates of its impact on coal production, jobs, consumer costs, and so on. In fact, the administration's own bill, submitted by President Ford on February 6, 1975, provided for estimated tonnage losses of 33 to 80 million tons and direct and indirect job losses of 7,000 to 18,000. Its language was much more precise than that of the vetoed bill, and much more accurate estimates of tonnage losses were expected from the administration.

A compromise should be reached that will achieve a sound solution to a problem that has waited far too long for our attention. Such a solution must effectively balance the need to develop our abundant coal resources against the need to guarantee environmental protection while sustaining a strong economy.

In July 1975,[85] the Senate passed a coal-leasing bill affecting federal lands and attached to it the strip-mining bill vetoed by Ford. But on November 12, 1975, the House Interior Committee, by a narrow 21-to-20 vote,[86] rejected an amendment by Representative John Melcher (Democrat, Montana) to attach the vetoed strip-mining bill to the House version of the federal coal-leasing bill. In February 1976, by a vote of 28 to 11, the House Interior and Insular Affairs Committee passed a bill, only slightly different from the ones Ford had vetoed, which was designed to attract further support,[87] and Melcher filed a discharge petition hoping to attract enough votes to bypass the Rules Committee.[88] But the House Rules Committee voted to sidetrack the bill rather than clear it for a floor vote. In August the House Interior Committee passed another slightly changed version of the bills Ford had twice vetoed, but on September 15 the House Rules Committee voted 9 to 6 to block the bill for the second time in one year.[89] Meanwhile Interior had published its final regulations governing strip mining on public lands.[90]

[85] *Congressional Quarterly*, vol. 33, no. 31 (August 2, 1975), p. 1661.

[86] *Congressional Quarterly*, vol. 33, no. 46 (November 15, 1975), p. 2449.

[87] *Congressional Quarterly*, vol. 34, no. 9 (February 28, 1976), pp. 469-470.

[88] *Congressional Quarterly*, vol. 34, no. 13 (March 27, 1976), pp. 705-706.

[89] *Congressional Quarterly*, vol. 34, no. 38 (September 18, 1976), p. 2503.

[90] Department of Interior Press Release, "Surface Mining Regulations Provide Protection and Production," May 11, 1976.

9

The Legacy of Parks

Seated in the gallery of the House of Representatives on January 22, 1970, listening to President Nixon's first state of the union address, the author was pleased to hear the President expounding on the need for park and recreation lands. "As our cities and suburbs relentlessly expand, those priceless open spaces needed for recreation and accessible to people are swallowed up—often forever. Unless we preserve these spaces while they are still available, we will have none to preserve." Nixon added, "Therefore, I shall propose new financing methods for purchasing open space and parklands now, before they are lost to us." [1] The trouble was, there was no agreement within his administration on what these "new financing methods" might be.

The confusion had started in the fall of 1969 when Secretary of the Interior Walter Hickel had made a strong impression on the President discussing the problem of acquiring many authorized but unfinanced federal recreation lands. Hickel had reported that the cost of acquiring these lands was escalating every day. He wanted to buy all the parkland he could, as soon as he could, before the costs rose even higher. Why should one generation of taxpayers, he asked the President, have to pay the costs of buying parks now that will be used for generations to come? Hickel went on to recommend that the costs be paid over the years, as they are when a home is mortgaged or a car bought on the installment plan. Later, in his memoirs, Hickel touched on the same problem, calling it "A Great Deception":

> A citizen, hearing the announcement that such-and-such
> national park has been authorized, believes it has thereby

---

[1] *Public Papers of the Presidents, Nixon, 1970*, Annual Message to Congress on the State of the Union, January 22, p. 13.

been acquired. Often only the concept of the park has been authorized. No money has been appropriated to pay for it. . . . I believe that when it comes to protecting the American people and protecting America's open spaces, authorizations should be tied to appropriations, or else long-term real estate contracts should be signed, a down payment made and the balance paid over a period of ten or twenty years.[2]

The President, impressed by Hickel's reasoning, directed Ehrlichman and Budget Director Robert Mayo to see if they could work out a new financing plan. As it turned out, they could not, because any variation of Hickel's proposal would increase the government's indebtedness to the taxpayer over the years. But the announcement of new methods of financing park acquisition was written into the State of the Union speech (without the knowledge of this author) by the President himself at Camp David in the hope that something would be worked out. By using the phrase "new financing methods," the President put pressure on his staff to come up with a plan, and quickly, since his first environmental message to Congress was only a few weeks off. In that message the new methods of financing park acquisition would have to be explained.

The new financing method that Nixon's staff devised was the policy of giving federal land away to local governments, that is, financing "in kind," in real property, rather than in dollars. In Nixon's words, "I propose that we adopt a new philosophy for use of the Federally-owned lands, treating them as a precious resource—like money itself—which should be made to serve the highest possible public good."[3] The program worked, and worked exceedingly well, despite the bureaucratic title of its administrative body, the Property Review Board. The key to its success was sensible enough. Under the Federal Property and Administrative Services Act of 1949,[4] the General Services Administration (GSA) could make available to state and local governments surplus federal properties. The federal government had a track record of giving up little if anything in the way of real estate, and GSA had always lacked the clout to make the various departments release their unneeded property. But Nixon forced the bureaucracy to shed

---

[2] Walter Hickel, *Who Owns America?* (Englewood Cliffs, N.J.: Prentice-Hall, Inc., 1971), p. 119.

[3] *Public Papers of the Presidents, Nixon, 1970*, Special Message to the Congress on Environmental Quality, February 10, p. 105.

[4] Ch. 288 (63 Stat. 377), June 30, 1949.

its real estate by appointing a high-level board and backing it with his interest and authority. The Property Review Board was chaired by Bryce Harlow,[5] counsellor to the President, and its members included the chairman of the Council of Economic Advisers, Paul McCracken; Robert Mayo, director of the Bureau of the Budget; Russell Train, chairman of the CEQ; Robert Kunzig, administrator of GSA; and John Ehrlichman.

Nixon, in his environmental message to Congress, pointedly gave the Property Review Board members their marching orders: "Special emphasis will be placed on identifying properties that could appropriately be converted to parks and recreation areas. . . ." In other words, when in doubt, create a park. And they did. By September 1976, the Nixon and Ford administrations had converted 82,232 acres in fifty states, the District of Columbia, Puerto Rico, Guam, and the Virgin Islands, at a fair market value of nearly $241 million, into 642 parks, the majority of them in or very close to cities, really bringing parks to the people.[6] And at last the program got a better name. Raymond Price, Nixon's chief speech writer, suggested to the President that, as President Eisenhower had left a legacy of interstate highways by proposing the Highway Trust Fund, President Nixon, through this program, could leave a "Legacy of Parks."

Nixon had seen first-hand some of the prime real estate owned by the federal government that the public was unable to use. Walking beside the Pacific at San Clemente, he could see the magnificent surfing beach at the adjacent Marine Corps Training Center at Camp Pendleton, which included eighteen miles of choice California coastline. He decided that the first major action of the Property Review Board would be to turn over six miles of the Camp Pendleton beach to the State of California. He made the announcement himself.

> I say that it probably wouldn't have happened unless I'd taken a walk on the beach two years ago at San Clemente and walked an extra mile, and saw the great possibilities and decided that the time had come for Presidential initiative, which has overridden, I must say, very deep and understandable opposition in some segments of Congress, only because

---

5 Subsequent chairmen of the Property Review Board (later called the Federal Property Council) were Arnold Weber, associate director of OMB, and Donald Rumsfeld and Anne Armstrong, both counsellors to the President.
6 Personal communication, Department of Interior, September 1976.

Members of Congress, at times, were reflecting the views of the bureaus.[7]

The bureaucratic infighting sparked by the new parks policy was often intense. One reason was that federal departments tend to acquire new real estate rather than to find out whether or not there is already federal land that can be made available simply by transferring it from one agency to another, sometimes within the same department. There is also a bureaucratic tendency to hang on to property rather than give it up to public use. Time and again the Property Review Board, tentatively recommending that the holding agency release some piece of property for transfer to a local government for parkland use, provoked a violent reaction from the holding agency, including calls from a cabinet member to the President or the chairman of the Property Review Board. Nixon usually resolved such conflicts on the basis of option papers laying out the facts. These would be followed, if transfers were approved, by direct written orders from the President to the appropriate cabinet officer directing the disposal of property.

Since the Defense Department owned far more urban property desirable for transfer out of federal ownership than any other department,[8] the toughest battles were fought with the Pentagon. Often compromise solutions were reached. One of these involved Fort DeRussy, seventy-one acres of lush beach-front property in Honolulu, Hawaii. The land was worth about $75 million. The military had planned to let a contract to build on this property a fifteen-story hotel for the use of Vietnam personnel on leave and, after the war, for the use of retired military families. Initially, the Property Review Board decided that the property along the beach should be converted into a public park for the city of Honolulu and the back part of the property, away from the beach, sold, the funds to be used to buy other parklands. After the board's decision, Darrell Trent, executive director of the

---

[7] Office of the White House Press Secretary, Remarks of the President upon Ordering Portions of Camp Pendleton Property Released for Public Use, March 31, 1971. Nixon was referring to the House and Senate Armed Services committees, whose members, like the Marines in another corner of the iron triangle, did not want Camp Pendleton's beaches turned over to the public.

[8] Federal property is the largest federal asset, with market value that, to the author's knowledge, has never been realistically calculated. Federal property includes about 760 million acres in fifty states, Guam, the Virgin Islands, the Trust Territories, American Samoa, Puerto Rico, and in 129 foreign countries. There are about 55 million prime acres of significant current value of which 1.6 million are in urban areas. By far the most valuable lands are owned by the Department of Defense, which holds 92 percent of federal urban property.

Property Review Board, and Daniel Kingsley, commissioner of property management and disposal services at GSA, flew to Honolulu to discover that not only was the military preventing the use of the public beach (contrary to Honolulu custom), but also it intended to build its fifteen-story hotel parallel to the beach. Those using the hotel would all have a spectacular view of the ocean and Diamond Head, but the public's view would be blocked. The military had planned all this in spite of the fact that it is a basic land-use practice at resort beaches the world over, including Honolulu, to build hotels perpendicular to the beach so that a minimum amount of concrete obstructs the public's view of the beach area. Trent phoned Bryce Harlow in the White House, who stopped the Department of Defense from letting the contract for the construction of the hotel until the matter could be evaluated further. In the end the hotel was built in the rear of the property and perpendicular to the beach, thereby opening the entire area to the general public. President Nixon might have eliminated the hotel project altogether; however, he was strongly advised against this by his congressional relations staff, who perceived a need for the support of conservative members of the House and Senate Armed Services committees on other "fish to fry."

Some of the properties turned over to state or local government under the Legacy of Parks program will become outstanding recreational areas; others will be simply cleaned-up downtown lots with a few picnic tables. In Fountain Valley, in populous Orange County, California, for example, 507 acres of a 633-acre marine helicopter landing field, worth about $15 million, is being developed into a recreational complex with picnic tables, barbecue pits, hiking and bike trails, a model airplane field, and a Little League baseball diamond. In Fairfax County, Virginia, with a population of over half a million, 1,262 acres of navy property is being converted into a nature conservation and equestrian complex, including a stable, two show rings, a cross-country course for horses, and nature and riding trails. And one of the largest areas to be handed over to the public under the program, a 2,040-acre portion of the Energy Research and Development Administration's Argonne National Laboratory in populous Du Page County southwest of Chicago, will be used for boating, fishing, hiking-nature-bridle trails, and for environmental education.

Besides issuing an executive order setting up the Property Review Board, Nixon, in his environmental message to Congress in 1970, proposed legislation designed to expedite the disposal of federal lands.

He proposed a statute, passed by Congress on October 22, 1970,[9] which allowed the federal government to convey surplus real property to state and local governments for park and recreational use at up to 100 percent discount. This enabled local governments to obtain land at no charge and to use their resources for financing recreational facilities or for obtaining federal-state matching grants from the Land and Water Conservation Fund. Another statute proposed by President Nixon and enacted by Congress on June 16, 1972,[10] required federal agencies to pay rent for space assigned by GSA, beginning in FY 1975. In theory, this should have been an incentive for agencies to dispose of unneeded property rather than pay the rents. The program would probably have been much more successful than it has been if a companion piece of legislation had become law. This would have established a fund to relocate government installations and facilitate the disposal of underutilized federal property. Unfortunately, the second proposal died, and as a result many properties that could have been put to much more beneficial public use remained in federal hands because departments were unwilling to pay the high cost of relocation out of their own appropriations. GSA is still seeking legislation to establish a relocation fund for this purpose.

The need for prime federal recreation acreage near or in big cities prompted President Nixon to take another initiative by proposing the creation of large national recreation areas in New York and San Francisco harbors. For several years the Department of the Interior had been proposing to combine three recreational units in New York harbor on land that was 95 percent publicly owned by either New York City, the State of New York, or the federal government. The Gateway National Recreation Area, as the proposal was called, consisted of about 23,000 acres, including ten miles of ocean front in New York harbor. The Jamaica Bay unit, including the Jamaica Bay Wildlife Refuge, contained about 14,000 acres, and despite the inroads of civilization, Jamaica Bay remained an ecologically viable wetlands area. The Breezy Point unit at the southern tip of Long Island included four miles of ocean beach, some existing city and state parks, the army post at Fort Tilden, and the beach property in front of a residential community known as the Breezy Point Cooperative. The final unit of the proposed Gateway National Recreation Area included Sandy Hook,

---

[9] P.L. 91-485 (84 Stat. 1084), October 22, 1970.
[10] P.L. 92-312 (86 Stat. 218), June 16, 1972.

New Jersey, which was almost totally in federal ownership. This unit included six miles of beach on the Atlantic Ocean and two more miles of beach on Sandy Hook Bay.

The project was feasible only because federal lands could be made available to reduce acquisition costs. Even so, the costs were enormous, estimated at $137 million; the federal lands, consisting of 2,900 acres, were worth an estimated $161 million. But President Nixon thought the project was well worth the expenditure, since it would serve about 20 million people. He made this point when speaking to the press on May 10, 1971, shortly after helicptering over New York harbor and proposing the Gateway National Recreation Area to Congress:

> I remember as a young boy what a great thrill it was for me to go to Yosemite, the Grand Canyon and the other great parks in the West.
>
> When I moved to New York I remember a conversation that I had with an elevator operator in our building. He was about my age and he had grown up in New York. And he spoke of his love of the outdoors and particularly of the hope that some day he might be able to visit some of those parks or parks like them that I had grown up with in the West.
>
> The point of these remarks simply is to bring home the fact that millions of Americans today do go to the great national parks that are all over this country, and particularly in the Western part of the United States.
>
> But here in the New York area, for example, 20 million people live. I would say that perhaps less than a million have ever had the opportunity to go to some of those parks, and less than half of the 20 million people that live in this area have automobiles. So what we need to do is to bring to the 20 million people who live in this area those recreational opportunities that they otherwise could not have.[11]

The Gateway National Recreation Area, P.L. 92-592 (86 Stat. 1308), was signed by President Nixon, October 27, 1972. A similar Nixon proposal led to the creation of the Golden Gate National Recreation Area serving the 4.5 million residents of the San Francisco-Oakland, California, metropolitan community. First proposed in Nixon's environmental message to Congress in February 1972,[12] the Golden Gate

---

11 Office of the White House Press Secretary, Remarks of the President Following a Helicopter Tour of the Proposed Gateway East Recreation Area, May 10, 1971.

12 *Public Papers of the Presidents, Nixon, 1972*, Special Message to Congress Outlining the 1972 Environmental Program, February 8, p. 184.

National Recreation Area includes 24,000 acres of federal, state, county, and private land in Marin County, San Francisco Bay, and the Pacific Ocean, including a twenty-two mile stretch from the Golden Gate Bridge northward to the southern boundary of the Point Reyes National Seashore.[13] About 3,600 acres of this land are owned by the federal government, 11,300 acres by the State of California, and nearly 200 acres by the counties. Acquisition costs for the 8,000 acres that are privately owned were estimated at about $27.6 million. Development costs were estimated at about $58 million.

Options for an Enlarged Recreation Program

The very success of the Legacy of Parks program, and especially the decision to purchase the National Recreation Areas in New York and San Francisco harbors, raised serious questions about the nature of the process by which parklands are authorized by Congress. This process is political rather than analytical.

With the establishment of Yellowstone Park over 100 years ago, Congress enunciated and institutionalized a land-use ethic recognizing that the scenic, scientific, and natural wonders of our nation have a value for all the people and should be preserved and held in trust by the government for the enjoyment of present and future generations. Within a few years, this concept was applied to historic as well as natural resources. Given these guidelines, a clear distinction could be drawn between resources that fell under federal responsibility and those that did not: If the property were of national significance by virtue of its unique historical or natural characteristics, then the federal government, not a state or local government, had the responsibility to acquire,

---

[13] Point Reyes National Seashore is a spectacular example of how speculation can drive up the land prices once parkland has been authorized by Congress. The acquisition of Point Reyes was first authorized by Congress in 1962 for $14 million (P.L. 87-657 [76 Stat. 538], September 13, 1962). Later in 1966, the authorization was increased by $5,135,000 to $19,135,000 (P.L. 89-666 [80 Stat. 919], October 15, 1966), yet by November 1969, Nixon had to propose increasing the authorization by another $38,365,000 to cover the additional increase in land values. (See Office of the White House Press Secretary, transcript of a press briefing announcing Nixon's decision with Senator George Murphy, Republican, California, Congressmen Wayne Aspinall, Democrat, Colorado, and Don Clausen, Republican, California, November 18, 1969.) By the fall of 1976 Point Reyes had been completely purchased except for 27.5 acres in condemnation proceedings and about 6 of 440 additional acres authorized in 1974 (P.L. 93-550 [88 Stat. 1744], December 26, 1974). The entire area covers 65,291 acres.

192

develop, and maintain the area. But today Congress increasingly shows a tendency to incorporate properties into the national park system that are without unique natural or historic value. As a result, the integrity of the national park system is being threatened.

In theory, the qualifications for inclusion in the national park system—which, since the establishment of Yellowstone in 1872, has grown to include about 300 entities—are set forth in guidelines that cover three general categories: natural, historical, and recreational. In the natural and historical areas, the emphasis is on preservation of nationally significant resources. Although somewhat vague, the criteria are generally adhered to. For example, the areas of natural significance include sites of unique scenic grandeur (such as Yosemite) and outstanding geological formations that illustrate geological processes and natural phenomena (such as the Grand Canyon and the geysers of Yellowstone). There is a growing consensus that the national park system, as far as areas of unique natural beauty are concerned, has become nearly complete with the congressional authorization in October 1974 to begin acquiring Big Cypress National Preserve in Florida [14] and the Big Thicket National Preserve in Texas.[15] Just two areas widely regarded as deserving preservation remain to be added to the system, parts of the Sawtooth Range in Idaho and the proposed Prairie National Park in the Flint Hills of Kansas and Oklahoma.

The guidelines for federal acquisition of areas of national historical significance are also reasonably firm. They provide, for example, for the acquisition of structures associated importantly with the lives of famous Americans (such as Lincoln's birthplace in Kentucky, Ford's Theater in Washington, D.C., and Carl Sandberg's home in North Carolina) and of structures or sites that represent unique periods of national importance in American history (such as Fort Laramie, Wyoming, and Jamestown, Virginia). But even here, elaborate and fuzzy distinctions among numerous historical categories have sprung up. The national park system now differentiates between National Historic Parks, National Monuments, National Military Parks, National Memorial Parks, National Battlefields, National Battlefield Parks, National Battlefield Sites, National Historic Sites, National Memorials, and National Cemeteries. How it does so could be the subject of a book in itself.

---

14 P.L. 93-440 (88 Stat. 1257), October 11, 1974.
15 P.L. 93-439 (88 Stat. 1254), October 11, 1974.

It is in the National Recreation Area (NRA) category that the guideline system really breaks down. NRAs should be (1) spacious areas, (2) located and designed to achieve a comparatively high recreation-camping capacity, (3) attractive enough to achieve interstate patronage and, to a limited extent, patronage outside the normal service area, and (4) areas where outdoor recreation is recognized as the primary resource. But "beauty is in the eye of the beholder," and when his reelection is at stake, what congressman from California, for example, is going to say that the Santa Monica Mountains are not of outstanding national significance or will not draw visitors from across the nation?

NRAs first came into existence during the 1960s, many of them inspired by the recreational possibilities of irrigation and hydropower reservoirs in the West like Lake Mead NRA in Nevada, the Grand Coulee Dam and Ross Lake NRAs in Washington, and the Glen Canyon NRA in Utah and Arizona. By the 1970s, political pressure was mounting to create NRAs in urban areas too, where land costs are enormous. Nixon's proposed Gateway NRA in New York harbor and the Golden Gate NRA in San Francisco Bay were but the tip of the iceberg. When Secretary of the Interior Morton and the author were talking with President Nixon about the Gateway and Golden Gate decision, they pointed out to him that the Bureau of Outdoor Recreation and the National Park Service had almost a dozen more similar urban NRAs on the drawing board, which would cost an additional several billion dollars.[16] President Nixon paused with conservative concern to ponder the federal government's stepping headlong into the urban park business and then said, "I'll take two. You fellows take the political heat on the rest." [17] But the administration did not "take the heat" all that successfully. During his Christmas-New Year's work-and-ski vacation at Vail, Colorado, President Ford signed into law a bill establishing yet another urban park, the Cuyahoga Valley NRA, at an estimated land acquisition cost of $34,500,000.[18] The Cuyahoga River Valley is a flood plain between Cleveland and Akron, Ohio, backed by heavily wooded valley walls and ravines. The valley is inhabited by

---

[16] NRAs in the planning stages covered the metropolitan areas of Washington, D.C., Los Angeles, St. Louis, Houston, Atlanta, Denver, Minneapolis/St. Paul, Chicago/Milwaukee, Detroit/Toledo, Cleveland/Akron, Memphis, and Hartford/Springfield.

[17] Author's recollection of Nixon's comment.

[18] P.L. 93-555 (88 Stat. 1784), December 27, 1974.

a variety of plant and wildlife and still retains its rural character. But it hardly qualifies as an outstanding natural area, and it is not likely to attract a large number of visitors from out of state, though the federal imprimatur may lure people—the prophecy may be self-fulfilling. Also, the Interior Department's Bureau of Outdoor Recreation was already in the process of helping Ohio in the acquisition of 6,212 acres in the Cuyahoga Valley for outdoor recreation and open space purposes through the state-grant portion of the Land and Water Conservation Fund. As planned, this joint federal, state, and local project would entail the acquisition of 14,500 acres at a cost of about $35 million, half of which would be paid by the federal government. However, there was a serious question whether the acquisition schedule could keep ahead of the pressures for development in the area. Proponents of the bill argued that the Cuyahoga NRA was a logical extension of the program to buy the Gateway NRA in New York and the Golden Gate NRA in San Francisco. But it could also be argued that these two parks should be viewed as pilot projects, from which local governments could derive ideas and operating experience, and that the responsibility for urban parks should rest with state and local governments.

The dilemma is still with us. It raises fundamental questions about how far the federal role in recreation should extend and about the future of the Land and Water Conservation Fund. This fund was signed into law by President Johnson on September 3, 1964.[19] Since then it has been a very significant factor in financing recreation, providing almost $2 billion for the purchase of land and the promotion of recreational development. In recent years, annual appropriations from the fund have equalled the authorized ceiling of $300 million. The fund is financed from outer-continental-shelf oil and gas receipts and other miscellaneous revenues. Forty percent of the annual appropriation, or $120 million, is set aside for purely federal acquisitions for the National Park Service, the U.S. Forest Service, the Fish and Wildlife Service, and the Bureau of Land Management.[20] The remaining 60 percent of the fund, or $180 million annually, is transferred to state and local

---

[19] This was a historic day for conservationists. In a Rose Garden ceremony, President Johnson signed both the Land and Water Conservation Fund, P.L. 88-578 (78 Stat. 897) and the Wilderness Bill, P.L. 88-577 (78 Stat. 890). See *Public Papers of the Presidents, Johnson, 1964*, September 3, pp. 1033-34.

[20] The purchases include lands purchased within lakeshore, seashore, river, and trail systems as well as within the traditional National Park and Forest Service systems.

governments in the form of matching grants for nonfederal park acquisition and development.

In 1968, the financing of the fund was altered.[21] Instead of merely providing for the deposit of recreational user fees in the fund, the law established a new source of funds at an annual income level of $200 million for FY 1969–FY 1973, namely the outer-continental-shelf oil and gas leasing program.

In February 1970, Nixon proposed increasing the Land and Water Conservation Fund from $200 million to $300 million annually for FY 1971–FY 1989, still to be provided by outer-continental-shelf oil and gas leasing receipts.[22] This proposal became law.[23] The President also tried unsuccessfully to change the state grant apportionment formula in the fund to favor heavily populated states, in another attempt to create parks where the people are.[24] But the Interior and Insular Affairs committees, dominated by members from western states with low populations, would have none of it.

Over the years, the pressure to increase the size of the fund has been enormous. It was exacerbated by three costly park authorizations in 1974: Big Cypress, Big Thicket, and Cuyahoga. In each of these cases Congress, to avoid the problem of escalating land prices that arises when parks are acquired over a long period of time, specified in the statutes that the acquisition of land for the parks must be "substantially complete" within six years of enactment. The backlog of acquisitions that have been authorized by Congress but still have not been paid for has become enormous: it is now estimated at more than $2.9 billion (see Table 11).

Additional pressures for purchases are created by rising land values and construction costs. Congress continues to propose expensive National Recreation Areas, just as Nixon and Ford had been warned it would. Proposed city parks along the Potomac and Anacostia rivers in Washington, D.C., would cost $35 million.[25] The Chattahoochee NRA in Atlanta, long on the drawing boards of the National Park Service, would cost $40 million plus another $22 million in develop-

---

[21] P.L. 90-401 (828 Stat. 354-355), July 15, 1968.

[22] *Public Papers of the Presidents, Nixon, 1970,* Special Message to Congress on Environmental Quality, February 10, p. 105.

[23] P.L. 91-485 (84 Stat. 1083), October 22, 1970.

[24] *Public Papers of the Presidents, Nixon, 1971,* Special Message to Congress Proposing the 1971 Environmental Program, February 8, p. 136.

[25] H.R. 3102, 94th Congress.

Table 11

ESTIMATED BACKLOG IN ACQUISITION OF FEDERAL
RECREATION AREAS, OCTOBER 1976

(in millions of dollars)

Acquisitions specifically authorized by Congress for	
National Park Service	$ 342.5
Forest Service	313.0
Fish and Wildlife Service	28.1
Bureau of Land Management	4.4
	688.0
Inholdings[a] to be acquired by	
Forest Service (Department of Agriculture)	1,156.1
National Park Service (Department of Interior)	72.0
Bureau of Land Management (Department of Interior)	20.0
	1,248.1
Funds needed to complete purchases authorized by the Fish and Wildlife Service for	
Protection of endangered species	242.5
Recreation additions	47.5
Natural areas	21.0
	311.0
Estimated cost of acquisitions authorized under pending or proposed legislation, and of proposed ceiling increases and boundary changes on existing properties	615.7
Estimated relocation costs and court awards in excess of appraisal estimates	62.3
	678.0
	2,925.1

[a] Inholdings are isolated, privately owned parcels of land within or next to larger federally owned blocks of land.

Source: Department of Interior, Bureau of Outdoor Recreation, Land and Water Conservation Fund, FY 1977 Five-Year Acquisition Plan, submitted by agencies and adjusted October 1976 for FY 1977 appropriations and recent congressional action.

ment costs.[26] The record breaker in terms of expense is the proposed Santa Monica Mountains and Seashore NRA in California, which would run upwards of $300 million.[27]

During the 94th Congress, the Senate passed legislation that increased the fund from $300 million to $1 billion annually, effective in FY 1976,[28] and the House passed a bill to increase the fund to $450 million in FY 1978, $625 million in FY 1979, and $800 million in FY 1980.[29] After compromising in conference, the President signed a bill in September 1976, increasing the authorization levels to $600 million in FY 1978; $780 million in FY 1979; and $900 million annually from FY 1980 to FY 1989. The new law also created a Historic Preservation Fund for five years, funded as follows: FY 1977—$24.4 million; FY 1978–1979—$100 million annually; FY 1980–1981—$150 million annually.[30] If the full authorized amounts are in fact appropriated over the years, then the law would make available more than $10.8 million in state and federal outdoor recreation and historic preservation money through FY 1989.

A month earlier on August 29 at a stop in Yellowstone National Park, President Ford, himself a former park ranger, announced his own proposal for a $1.5 billion Bicentennial Land Heritage Program. Ford's proposal included:

- $141 million to buy lands for parks, wildlife refuges, and historic site lands;
- $700 million to develop new and existing parklands and refuges;
- $459 million for more staff and upgrading of the national parks and wildlife refuge systems;
- $200 million to fix up existing city parks in disrepair to be appropriated as part of HUD's community development block grant program.

---

[26] S. 661 and H.R. 3078, 94th Congress.

[27] S. 759 and S. 1640. The latter bill authorizes only $50 million, which in the author's opinion is likely to be only a first installment to avoid facing up to ultimate costs, which will be in the $300 million range. The $50 million in theory will be used largely to purchase strategic areas that will retard development, protect ecologically fragile areas, and provide recreational opportunities.

[28] *Congressional Record*, vol. 121, no. 158 (October 29, 1975), pp. S 18901-S 18917.

[29] *Congressional Record*, vol. 122, no. 65 (May 5, 1976), p. H 3955.

[30] P.L. 94-422 (90 Stat. 1313), September 28, 1976.

There seems little doubt of the need. Over 11,000 recreation units, from small-corner "tot lots" to 20,000-acre wildlife recreation areas, have been established from the fund. Visits to state parks increased at the rate of 5 percent annually in the 1960s, reaching 474 million in 1970.[31] About 50 million of these were by overnight visitors. The 1973 National Recreation Plan of the Bureau of Outdoor Recreation projected a 10-to-15 percent increase in demand between 1972 and 1978. Factors contributing to recreational growth include increased incomes, shorter work weeks, longer vacation periods because of diversified and flexible work schedules, and earlier retirement.[32]

The existence of the fund itself helped generate statewide recreational planning. Prior to enactment of the Land and Water Conservation Fund, only four states had any kind of statewide outdoor recreation plan, but now all fifty states maintain plans and timetables for future recreation acquisition and development programs. Over 75 percent of the nation's 3,167 counties have at least one Land and Water Conservation Fund project. State and local recreational bonds have grown steadily from about $1.2 billion in 1968 to $1.4 billion in 1972 and an estimated $1.6 billion in 1976.[33]

To demonstrate further the need for increased funding, the Bureau of Outdoor Recreation, in June 1974, did an informal survey requesting estimates of state and local capital expenditures on recreation through 1989. Admittedly, their estimates are a "wish list"; state, like federal, employees like to see their fiefdoms grow and prosper. Nonetheless, their capital recreation estimates total a staggering $45.6 billion, which translates into a federal matching share of almost $23 billion. If the Land and Water Conservation Fund's annual appropriations for the state matching portion had remained at the level of $180 million through 1989, when the fund expires, then only $2.7 billion, or 12 percent, of the federal portion of the perceived need of $45.6 billion could be met.

Instead of simply increasing the amount of money in the Land and Water Conservation Fund, Congress should, in the author's view,

31 *State Park Statistics, 1970* (Arlington, Va.: National Recreation and Parks Association, 1970).
32 Department of the Interior, Bureau of Outdoor Recreation, Nationwide Outdoor Recreation Plan, *Outdoor Recreation—A Legacy for America,* November 1973, pp. 10-11.
33 Department of Interior, Bureau of Outdoor Recreation, Land and Water Conservation Fund, FY 1977, mimeographed, May 1, 1975, p. 28, figure 5.

transform the state-grant portion of the fund into a special revenue-sharing package. Over a five-year period, this package could complete the acquisitions that clearly meet the federal criteria and then phase out the federal portion of the Land and Water Conservation Fund, transferring its funds to the state share. There would be annual appropriations for the revenue-sharing state funds and for individual appropriations from the general treasury fund as the occasion arose for future federal acquisitions. To reduce further the overhead in grant administration, the Land and Water Conservation Fund and the Historic Preservation Grant Program could be merged. The states could use their share of the funds for recreation or historic preservation at their own discretion, and the Congress could authorize funds for historic areas of true national significance on a case-by-case basis.

The revenue-sharing aspect of this plan would be popular with local officials and would mean that the funds could be distributed to the widest possible number of communities. At the same time, the federal overhead cost of dispersing grants would be eliminated. One potentially troublesome point is that statewide recreation planning might be deemphasized. Revenue-sharing funds could be fragmented into such small amounts that major projects for the benefit of all the state might have difficulty in acquiring funds. However, common sense and cooperation between the governor's office and the mayor's office and the county executives could easily prevent this from happening.

The plan would tend to force both Congress and the executive branch to determine the limits of federal responsibility for park acquisition and development. Expansion of the state share of the fund through revenue sharing reaffirms a policy of expanding state and local government responsibility. Operation and maintenance costs for parks not of national significance, that do not attract a significant number of national visitors, would be borne, as they properly should be, by state and local government. The number of units in the national park system should stabilize, and finally the Bureau of Outdoor Recreation should cease to exist. The bureau was instituted to administer a grant program and to provide recreational consulting service to state and local governments. It has done its job so well that every state now has a recreation agency and a statewide outdoor recreation plan—and the reason for the bureau's continued existence is not apparent. Let all the funds go directly to state and local governments, which will know how to manage their own recreational needs after a decade of help from Washington.[34]

Wilderness

The original Wilderness Act of 1964 [35] set aside four wilderness areas, with a total acreage of 9.1 million, in the National Forests. These were the initial component of the wilderness system. The executive branch was charged with studying all roadless areas of at least 5,000 acres within the National Parks and National Wildlife Refuge systems and in the National Forests and with recommending to Congress the creation of further wilderness areas. The job was supposed to be completed in ten years, and it was.

When Nixon became President almost half of that time had already expired but only 0.7 million acres, covering six areas, had been proposed by the Johnson administration for inclusion in the wilderness system. This was out of a potential of approximately 20 million acres (excluding Alaska) that appeared to be eligible for classification as wilderness. But by the time Nixon left office, seventy-five areas comprising 13.6 million acres had been proposed to Congress, including sixteen areas comprising 184,000 acres of eastern forest land. By December 1974, ten years and two months after the Wilderness Act had become law, President Ford completed the task of proposing wilderness areas in roadless areas of 5,000 acres or more in National Parks, Wildlife Refuges and National Forests by recommending that thirty-seven additional areas totaling 6.5 million acres be classified as wilderness. By the time the objective of the Wilderness Act was completed, 130 wilderness-area proposals had been sent to Congress (forty-five in National Parks, sixty-six in Wildlife Refuges, and nineteen in National Forests), yet Congress had acted on only forty-two proposals (four in National Parks, twenty-six in Wildlife Refuges, and twelve in National Forests). The reason for the reluctance of Congress to declare wilderness areas is that the mineral, timber, and grazing interests are

---

[34] As discussed in Chapter 3, the "iron triangle" principle would strongly oppose this option. The Interior and Insular Affairs committees would have little to do, the Bureau of Outdoor Recreation would cease to exist, and the special interest groups in Washington that lobby for higher park budgets would have few people to talk to that shared their specialized interest. They would have to focus their lobbying effort on the governors, county executives, mayors, and state legislators, in other words, those elected officials likely to be "closer to the people" than their congressmen and senators in Washington.

[35] P.L. 88-577 (78 Stat. 890), September 3, 1965.

strongly represented in both the Agriculture and the Interior committees of Congress. Their members often strongly resent seeing portions of the public lands allocated for recreation use.

A legislative initiative during this period was adding eastern wilderness areas to the system. The designation of wilderness areas within the National Forests east of the 100 degree meridian was proposed by Nixon in his State of the Union Message on Natural Resources and Environment of February 15, 1973.[36] The administration's proposal would have amended the Wilderness Act of 1964 by broadening the admission criteria to allow restored wild areas to be added to the National Wilderness Preservation System, east of the 100 degree meridian only. It would have designated sixteen areas (184,000 acres) as wilderness and thirty-seven areas (336,000) for wilderness study. The proposal would have withdrawn such wilderness in the East from appropriation or disposition under the mining and mineral-leasing laws, eliminated commercial grazing, and allowed condemnation of privately owned lands. On January 3, 1975, President Ford signed the final version of this bill, which designated sixteen essentially restored areas (207,000 acres) in thirteen states as wilderness (twelve of the sixteen that the administration had studied and recommended for designation, and four others), and seventeen areas (125,000 acres) in nine states for wilderness study under a broad interpretation of the Wilderness Act.[37] Condemnation is provided for, but mining and grazing remain subject to the provisions of the Wilderness Act and are not prohibited. The study areas are ones which the Department of Agriculture might have reviewed on its own initiative, but Congress wanted to make sure the studies were carried out. This legislation is a strong beginning towards enlarging the wilderness system in the eastern National Forests beyond the three relatively small areas— totaling 26,000 acres—that were placed in the system by passage of the original Wilderness Act.

The National Wild and Scenic Rivers System

In 1962, the Department of Interior and the Department of Agriculture, extending the thinking that led to the passage of the Wilderness Act,

---

[36] Office of the White House Press Secretary, President's State of the Union Message on Natural Resources and Environment, February 15, 1973.
[37] P.L. 93-622 (88 Stat. 2096), January 3, 1975.

began a joint effort to set up a national system of protected free-flowing rivers. Initially about 650 rivers seemed worthy of consideration. But as better guidelines were established,[38] the Bureau of Outdoor Recreation and the Forest Service reduced the list to sixty-seven rivers. With the completion of more detailed studies, twenty-two rivers were found to deserve protection or preservation in a free-flowing condition. Legislation was drafted and became law in October 1968. The Wild and Scenic Rivers Act [39] placed all or parts of eight rivers [40] into the system, designated twenty-seven other rivers for study, and authorized $17 million. In May 1974, Congress responded to an administration request by authorizing an additional $37.6 million to complete the acquisition of the eight rivers originally designated Wild and Scenic Rivers.[41] In January 1975, Congress amended the act by adding twenty-nine more rivers to be studied for possible inclusion in the system.[42] By the fall of 1976 the following eleven additional rivers had been added to the system: the Allagash Wilderness Waterway in Maine; [43] the Lower St. Croix River, Minnesota and Wisconsin; [44] the Chattanooga, flowing through North and South Carolina and Georgia; [45] the Little Miami [46] and the Little Beaver in Ohio; [47] the Snake, flowing through Idaho and Oregon; [48] the Rapid River of Idaho; [49] the New

---

[38] Department of Interior and Department of Agriculture, "Guidelines for Evaluation, Wild, Scenic and Recreational River Areas Proposed for Inclusion in the National Wild and Scenic River System under Section 2, P.L. 90-542," mimeographed, February 1970.

[39] P.L. 90-542 (82 Stat. 906), October 2, 1968.

[40] The eight rivers were called "instant rivers" because they were designated as National Wild and Scenic Rivers under the statute without any further study. They are: The Middle Fork of the Clearwater in Idaho, Eleven Point in Missouri, Feather in California, Rio Grande in New Mexico, Rogue in Oregon, Saint Croix in Minnesota and Wisconsin, the Middle Fork of the Salmon in Idaho, and the Wolf in Wisconsin.

[41] P.L. 93-279 (88 Stat. 122), May 10, 1974.

[42] P.L. 93-621 (88 Stat. 2094), January 3, 1975.

[43] Secretarial designation, July 19, 1970.

[44] Twenty-seven miles under P.L. 92-560 (88 Stat. 1174), October 25, 1972 and twenty-five miles by secretarial designation, June 17, 1976.

[45] P.L. 92-279 (88 Stat. 122), May 10, 1974.

[46] Secretarial designation, August 20, 1973.

[47] Secretarial designation, October 23, 1975.

[48] P.L. 94-199 (89 Stat. 1117), December 31, 1975.

[49] Ibid.

River in North Carolina; [50] the Missouri [51] and the Flathead [52] in Montana; and the Obed River in Tennessee.[53]

Also, two rivers—34.5 miles of the Snake in Washington, Oregon, and Idaho,[54] and 50 miles of the Housatonic River in Connecticut [55]—have been added for study. Two rivers—the Upper Iowa in Iowa and the Suwannee flowing through Florida and Georgia—have been recommended for preservation through action by the states. Three rivers—the Allegheny and the Clarion in Pennsylvania, and the Maumee in Indiana and Ohio—have been found not to qualify. The remaining studies are in various stages of completion.

Finally, in Alaska, Interior has proposed adding twenty new units with a total of 2,753 miles of river to the National Wild and Scenic River System.[56]

Alaskan Parks, Refuges, Forests, and Wild and Scenic Rivers

Under Section 17(d)(2) of the Alaska Native Claims Act signed by President Nixon on December 18, 1972,[57] the secretary of the interior was to recommend to Congress within two years Alaskan lands for classification into each of the four systems (National Parks, National Wildlife Refuges, National Forests, and National Wild and Scenic Rivers). This was a spectacular opportunity to set aside recreation areas for the use of future generations. Secretary Morton proposed to Congress doubling the size of both the National Parks and National Wildlife Refuge systems by the addition of 32.26 million acres of new National Parks and 31.59 million acres of new National Wildlife Refuges. Morton also recommended adding 18.8 million acres to the National Forests and twenty new units to the National Wild and Scenic Rivers System.[58] Cries of anguish from development-minded

---

[50] Secretarial designation, April 13, 1976.

[51] P.L. 94-486 (90 Stat. 2327), October 12, 1976.

[52] Ibid.

[53] Ibid.

[54] P.L. 94-199 (89 Stat. 1117), December 31, 1975.

[55] P.L. 94-486 (90 Stat. 2327), October 12, 1976.

[56] Department of Interior press release, "Secretary Morton Proposes Doubling Areas of Parks, Wildlife Systems and Boosting National Forest and Wild Rivers Systems in Alaska," December 18, 1973.

[57] P.L. 92-203 (85 Stat. 688), December 18, 1971.

[58] Department of Interior press release, "Secretary Morton Proposes Doubling Parks," December 18, 1973.

Alaskans that too much land was being set aside were joined by equally bitter protests from conservation groups complaining that not enough land was being withdrawn, which suggested to some that Morton had achieved the proper balance in his decision.

The World Heritage Trust

Another initiative was in the international field. The United States acted as host for the Second World Conference on Parks at Grand Teton National Park in Wyoming in the summer of 1972. In his environmental message to Congress in 1971, President Nixon had directed the secretary of the interior, the chairman of the Council on Environmental Quality, and the secretary of state to develop a World Heritage Trust initiative—an idea first proposed by Russell Train when he was president of the Conservation Foundation. Nixon noted that there were over 1,200 parks in ninety-three nations and that "certain areas are of such unique world-wide value that they should be treated as part of a heritage of all mankind and accorded special recognition as part of a World Heritage Trust. . . . and [the United States] would make available technical and other assistance where appropriate to assist in their protection and management." [59]

At the Seventeenth UNESCO Conference in Paris on November 16, 1972, a "Convention Concerning the Protection of the World Cultural and Natural Heritage" was adopted. In October 1973, the Senate voted 95 to 0 to accept the convention, which Nixon signed on November 13, and the United States became the first nation to ratify the World Heritage Convention. The convention became effective on December 17, 1975, three months after twenty nations had voted ratification.

---

[59] *Public Papers of the Presidents, Nixon, 1971,* Special Message to Congress Proposing the 1971 Environmental Program, February 8, p. 140.

10

Modernizing Energy and Mineral-Leasing Policy on the Public Lands

The environmental revolution that burst on the nation's capital in the late 1960s and early 1970s was followed in the fall of 1973 by the Arab oil boycott. Congress and the executive branch were ill prepared to modernize federal leasing policy on the public lands to ensure an adequate supply of energy and minerals, while at the same time taking environmental values into full account.

Unrestricted development of natural resources was the national policy for 150 years, until Teddy Roosevelt's trustbusters and Warren Harding's Teapot Dome ended forever the "giveaway" of energy and mineral resources on the public lands. Indeed, the reaction against the wasteful practices of this early period was still so strong in Washington in the 1960s that too few understood the danger of creating shortages through an excessively restrictive leasing policy.

Thus by the 1970s, it was clear that the development of coal, oil, natural gas, and mineral resources on the public lands and of two promising new energy sources, oil extracted from shale and electricity produced from geothermal steam, had to be accelerated. What is more, it was time to change the anachronistic policy of letting the nation's naval petroleum reserves lie dormant and undeveloped on the theory that they would be available in time of war, since any war would probably be over before the first well could be drilled. And these objectives had to be accomplished while preserving environmental values. At the same time a policy had to be developed guaranteeing that, even at an accelerated rate of leasing, competitive bids would produce a fair-market-value return to the public. Finally, the policy must ensure that the development of resources held under lease would proceed promptly, thus preventing the speculative private holding of excessive mineral and energy reserves and the possibility that private firms might accumulate windfall profits at the public's expense when higher prices prevailed.

Coal-Leasing Policy

Until the early 1970s, the Department of Interior's coal-leasing policy was simply a reactive one, responding to industries' applications on a case-by-case basis. Acreage under lease on the public lands had ballooned from approximately 80,000 acres in 1945 to about 778,000 acres in 1970, yet coal production had declined from a wartime high of 10 million tons in 1945 to only 7.4 million tons in 1970. Less than 10 percent of the total coal acreage leased was being mined.[1] Overall, coal prices were falling and federal coal leases were cheap, which encouraged lessees to hold leases without mining coal, speculating that prices would rise. Also, with little market for western coal, large capital expenditures were risky. But by 1973, the trend had reversed dramatically. Because of the impact of the Arab embargo and the effect of the implementation of the Clean Air Act Amendments of 1970, demand for low-sulfur western coal sharply increased and coal prices shot upward, following oil and gas prices. By the end of 1974, 800,000 acres of federal coal lands containing about 16 billion tons of recoverable coal reserves were being held under 533 leases. Coal production on the public lands had increased to approximately 24 million tons a year (up from 13 million tons in 1973).

In May 1971, when it became apparent that the Department of Interior was leasing far more land than the actual production of coal should have warranted and that leasing procedures were not environmentally adequate, Secretary Morton placed a moratorium on coal leasing that lasted until February 1973. By that time Morton was caught between the conflicting pressures of a Senate resolution calling for an indefinite moratorium on coal leasing on the public lands and the sudden rise in the demand for western low-sulfur coal. On February 17, 1973, Morton announced a continuation of the leasing moratorium, but with short-term leasing criteria designed to supply established operators

---

[1] Department of Interior, Bureau of Land Management, "Holdings and Development of Federal Coal Leases," mimeographed, November 1970.

with sufficient reserves to continue operations and supply existing markets.[2]

It was at about this time that the Interior Department really began to work out a coherent leasing policy, one not made public until January 1976. The process of policy development featured several major steps. One was the Northern Great Plains Resources Program, a very large cooperative effort involving the Interior and Agriculture departments, the Environmental Protection Agency, and the northern Great Plains states of Montana, Nebraska, North and South Dakota, and Wyoming. The study took almost three years, covered sixty-three counties, and projected the development of the area's coal resources at hypothetical rates for twenty-five years. Possible environmental, economic, social, and cultural consequences resulting from low, intermediate, and high rates of coal development were estimated over time frames ending in 1980, 1985, and 2000. The study area, chiefly the Powder River and Williston basins, contains about 160 billion tons of coal located less than 1,000 feet below the surface in beds 5 to 200 feet thick. This is the nation's future center of surface mining coal production, representing about 60 percent of the country's surface-minable coal. The northern Great Plains coal could eventually replace a significant portion of the high-sulfur midwestern coal. Also, electric power generated at mine sites in the northern Great Plains area could be transmitted to distant load centers on the power grids. But in spite of these economic benefits and the enormous opportunity for jobs (under the assumption of a high rate of coal development, the population of the principal impact area would increase from 434,000 to 939,000 between 1970 and 2000), the study also warned that "successful reclamation of mined land in the arid and semi-arid Northern Great Plains is as yet unassured."[3] Nor did everyone view the large projected increases in jobs as a blessing. Employment projections showed increases ranging from 28 percent to 148 percent between 1970 and 2000, depending on whether the coal development rate was high or low. This contrasted with a population growth rate in the area of only 1 percent during the 1960s. During the early construction phase, the report emphasized, with a sudden population increase, institutional and community housing,

---

[2] Department of Interior press release, "Secretary Morton Announces New Coal Leasing Policy," February 17, 1973.

[3] Department of Interior, "Effects of Coal Development in the Northern Great Plains, a Review of Major Issues and Consequences at Different Rates of Development," mimeographed, May 1975, p. 2.

medical care, education, and water supplies would be severely strained.

In addition to the northern Great Plains study a second factor in developing a new coal-leasing policy was the design by the Bureau of Land Management of the Energy Minerals Activity Recommendation System (EMARS). The purpose of EMARS was to define the extent to which federal coal must satisfy domestic needs, first by providing a multiple land-use management process that would identify areas of highest quality coal and of high environmental rehabilitation potential, then by "matching" these areas against other resources (for example, ranching, farming, and recreation potential) to create a land-use plan. Nominations from industry and the public, both for and against coal leasing, would be requested to aid in selecting proposed lease tracts within areas classified by the land-use plan as suitable for coal leasing. This system of combining resource and environmental data would make it possible to provide the secretary of the interior with a rational basis for deciding where, when, and how much coal should be offered for lease.

The third step in the process of developing a coal-leasing policy was to revise the strip-mining regulations to conform to the highest justifiable environmental standards. These regulations were first published as proposed rules on January 30, 1975, and subsequently revised; they were again proposed on September 3, 1975, and issued as final regulations in May 1976. It was President Ford's intention to regulate strip mining in such a way as to achieve a balance between coal production and environmentally sound reclamation practices. In the absence of a federal strip-mining law, the regulations would have the force of law on the public lands. They applied to the public lands the principles incorporated in the administration's proposed strip-mining bill.

Another element in the leasing system was the calculation of the value of the coal deposits which were being considered for lease. The U.S. Geological Survey was developing improved methods for tract evaluation so that no lease would be sold competitively for less than its fair-market value. Tract evaluation also helped in arriving at a judgment on whether the value of the coal itself was great enough to warrant taking whatever environmental risks were present in mining it.

Finally, the Department of Interior prepared an exhaustive programmatic environmental-impact statement, evaluating the cumulative impact of the entire national coal-leasing program. The purpose of this study, which was first issued in draft form for public comment in May

1974,[4] and in final form in September 1975,[5] has been frequently misunderstood. It was intended to be a general analysis of the environmental impact of major leasing alternatives for all federal lands, including lands outside the northern Great Plains area, and it served this purpose adequately. It was never designed to satisfy the need for the site-specific environmental-impact statements that should be required for general competitive sales. In spite of this intent, environmental groups sued,[6] contesting the adequacy of the final programmatic coal-leasing-impact statement. They wanted the Interior Department to expand the statement and republish it in draft form before issuing a final statement.

In the light of the experience and knowledge gained in the course of the northern Great Plains study, the creation of the EMARS system, and the preparation of programmatic, regional, and site-specific leasing environmental-impact statements, it became clear that any new coal-leasing policy should have four objectives: (1) to provide a proper balance between the use of coal and environmental protection, (2) to prevent energy costs from rising because of a coal-leasing policy that is too restrictive, (3) to prevent private holdings of excessive reserves of federal coal, and (4) to obtain a fair-market value in the competitive sale of coal leases for the benefit of the taxpayer.

There may have been too little planning in the past, but it would be just as serious an error to attempt to do too much planning, no matter how strongly it is urged. It is a delusion to think that the development of a resource can be so finely controlled as to achieve the optimum of each of the four objectives listed above. Too many factors are unpredictable. For example, if leasing is too restrictive unnecessary delay will cause energy prices to rise. One cannot predict exactly where or how much acreage should be leased or how much tonnage should be mined, and a policy has to be enunciated before one knows whether the leasing rate is too fast or too slow. There is the crucial matter of deciding specifically which areas should not be strip-mined because of unacceptable environmental cost. This cannot be decided in the abstract, but only on a case-by-case basis, after careful study of all of the necessary data.

---

[4] Department of Interior press release, "Interior Releases Environmental Statement on New Coal Leasing Program," May 7, 1974.

[5] Department of Interior, *Final Environmental Impact Statement: Proposed Federal Coal Leasing Program* (Washington, D.C.: U.S. Government Printing Office, September 1975).

[6] Natural Resources Defense Council, Environmental Defense Fund, Inc., Northern Plains Resource Council and Powder River Basin Resource Council v. Kleppe, U.S. District Court of the District of Columbia, October 21, 1975.

A federal coal-leasing policy must rest on four precepts:

(1) *Only those deposits that are needed for development should be leased.* Those areas should be chosen for lease whose market value exceeds the cost, including the environmental cost, of production. No other standard of selection could serve the public interest so well, because leasing only those deposits whose value exceeds costs will result in a proper rate of leasing, neither too fast nor too slow. This is a more reliable means of arriving at the proper leasing rate than the forecasts of bureaucratic central planners in Washington, which are notoriously subject to error.

On the other hand, care must be taken to ensure strong competition. Here there is some cause for concern. For example, given the checkerboard pattern of ownership that exists on much of the choice coal land of the West, a coal company might own private land adjacent to federal coal lands and therefore, when bidding for a federal lease, be the only company that could form an efficient mining unit. Other bidders would have to buy out the private company or enter into a joint venture, and either alternative might be prohibitively costly. As a result, all companies might put in low "token" bids, except the company owning the adjacent private coal land, which would bid low itself, and obtain the lease for well below its potential value.

Another factor that can drive bidding down is the uncertainty of surface ownership where the subsurface coal is owned by the federal government. Bidders may be unsure of the amount they will ultimately have to pay to the surface owners for the right to disrupt the ground to get at the coal. Then, too, one company might have already bought the surface rights (coal companies are now stepping up their purchasing of surface rights in anticipation of renewed federal leasing) and enjoy a competitive advantage. In each of these situations federal revenues from leasing could suffer.

To ensure strong competition, the Department of Interior should consider first identifying a number of tracts in a region to be put up for bid, but, in the end, instead of awarding leases to all high bidders who have met the usual tests for fair-market value, award leases only to those companies offering the highest price per ton until the desired amount of coal is leased. The remaining high bids could be rejected. Here again, care must be taken not to pursue an artificially restrictive coal-leasing policy and end up with too little coal to meet national needs and with the price paid by the consumer higher than necessary. In fact, for the next few years, to be sure of meeting the country's vastly expanded need for coal, the government should award somewhat above the level anticipated to fill production needs.

(2) *It is in the public interest to lease low-cost coal, or national energy costs will rise unnecessarily.* On the other hand, federal coal leased long ago that has no value as a low-cost source should not be produced. A coal policy should be designed to encourage relinquishment of these leases and to prevent undue speculation. Large amounts of western coal are now under federal lease, but this does not mean, as many have concluded, that further leasing is not required. Existing leases may not be located where they now can be mined most economically. Coal ownership in the West follows a checkerboard pattern that is a vestige of the grant system of the nineteenth century, designed to encourage the westward extension of the railroads. Blocks of private coal holdings are not sufficiently contiguous to form logical and economical mining units. Some private mining operations are on private lands surrounded by federal lands and are unable to expand in order to fulfill long-term contractual commitments to utilities without being allowed to lease on the contiguous federal lands. As a result, utilities, no longer having assurances that a coal vein can supply a specific grade of coal for decades, cannot rationally justify the capital expenditures necessary for the construction of furnaces designed to burn the specific grade of coal from a particular source. Transportation costs are a large part of the cost of coal, and the constantly changing geographic pattern of demand for energy can mean that a coal deposit valueless a few years ago will be a valuable low-cost source of supply next year.

(3) *The holding of excessive reserves must be remedied.* Regulations must be designed to discourage excessive holdings without disrupting the operation of leases whose reserves and production are in reasonable proportion to each other. In May 1974, a report on federal coal leasing, *Leased and Lost,* by the Council on Economic Priorities, concluded that a considerable number of federal leases were being held at low cost on a speculative basis and that only 52 of 474 federal lease holders studied in seven western states actually were producing coal.[7] The Department of Interior's final programmatic environmental-impact statement concluded that, of the approximately 16 billion tons of federal

7 Council on Economic Priorities, *Leased and Lost, A Study of Public and Indian Coal Leasing in the West,* Economic Priorities Report, vol. 5, no. 2 (May 1974), p. 4.

coal under lease, "excluding leased reserves that are either uneconomic to develop or environmentally unsuitable, approximately half of the recoverable leased reserves have not been committed to future development." [8] Many leases were not in production and there were no near-term plans to produce from them. Other leased tracts produced at rates that were low in proportion to the size of their reserves. In May 1976, the Department of Interior issued final "diligence" regulations designed to increase the pace of development of these leases.[9] These regulations defined the terms "diligent development" and "continuous operations" and set up procedures for combining federal and private coal operations into logical mining units, as well as requiring the payment of advance royalties. Diligent development requires that a lessee, by the end of ten years from the date of the regulations, produce at least one-fortieth of his reserve or his lease would be subject to cancellation. Continuous operation would require the production of at least 1 percent of the reserve per year after the payment of advance royalties had ceased.

Many urged that production royalty rates be increased on existing leases, but this would have violated the contractual terms between the government and the lease holder. The period of most rapid leasing was between 1965 and 1967, under Interior Secretary Udall. Under the terms of the Mineral Leasing Act of 1920,[10] these lease terms cannot be revised for a twenty-year period, or in most cases until the mid-1980s. However, at the time of each twenty-year revision, the opportunity to place these old leases on the same terms as new leases will be available to the secretary. Indeed, the Interior Department, in its final diligence regulations, required that advance payment of royalties be imposed on the lessee at the time of the issuance or renewal of the lease, together with production royalty rates of 8 percent or more of the value of the coal at the mine mouth, but never less than 5 percent. The major financial incentive in Interior's regulations to prevent the acquisition or holding of excessive quantities of federal coal reserves was to set for each lease a schedule for payment of advance royalties year by year, so that the leased deposit would be mined out in forty years from the date of the lease. Advance royalties at the production royalty rate would start in the sixth lease year and rise in each successive year, remaining at their

---

[8] Department of Interior, *Final Environmental Impact Statement*, p. 1-5.

[9] Department of Interior press release, "Diligent Development Coal Regulations Final," May 26, 1976.

[10] Ch. 85 (41 Stat. 437), February 25, 1920.

maximum level from the tenth year onward. The lessee would be required to pay the advance royalty or the production royalty, whichever was greater. In other words, the lessee would be required to pay royalties in advance to the extent that he fell behind the forty-year schedule. This provision seemed prudent, making it financially less attractive to hold federal coal reserves simply in anticipation of higher prices and encouraging purchasers of leases to buy mining rights only to the amount of coal they actually expected to produce. The forty-year schedule selected as a basis for calculating advance royalty payments was about as short a time as could reasonably be required without forcing lessees to operate uneconomically or preventing them from negotiating long-term contracts for delivery of coal to users.

In an effort further to reduce the amount of acreage under lease, the Interior Department stopped granting prospecting permits in February 1973. As it was, more than 190 applications for noncompetitive leases were on hand.[11] A holder of such a permit was entitled, under the terms of the Mineral Leasing Act of 1920, to be offered a noncompetitive lease if he demonstrated the presence of coal in "commercial quantities." These applications could have resulted in the issuance of noncompetitive leases for 490,000 acres of public land covering about 9.3 billion tons of recoverable coal reserves. The legal issue that had to be resolved was whether the backlog of potential noncompetitive leases would eventually have to be granted by the secretary of the interior. In the absence of a change in the law, the secretary of the interior has no choice but to offer a noncompetitive lease to an applicant who has, in the judgment of the secretary, demonstrated the existence of coal in "commercial quantities." In May 1976, the department issued rules defining "commercial quantities." The rules set "marketability"— or the prudent man test, as used in the 1872 Mining Law—as the test for determining whether such leases would be eligible for approval.[12] The marketability test includes showing that all the costs of operation, such as the cost of environmental protection under the lease and all applicable laws, would not exceed expected revenues. The secretary of interior has broad discretion in the establishment of lease terms and is

---

[11] Noncompetitive leases are often called preference right leases, but this term is incorrect, because the permittee who shows the necessary discovery has an absolute right to a lease and not a mere preference right if the secretary of interior determines to issue a lease.

[12] Department of Interior press release, "Interior Defines Test for Federal Preference Right Lease Application," May 7, 1976.

required, under the National Environmental Policy Act, to impose strict environmental protection standards. Only if the applicant can show marketability under such conditions is he entitled to a noncompetitive coal lease.

(4) *Adequate environmental analysis must be performed under the National Environmental Policy Act (NEPA).* The Department of Interior must judge whether a leasing action is a major federal action having a significant effect on the quality of the human environment and, if so, it must write an environmental-impact statement. But in most cases the significance of leasing goes beyond the issuance of an individual lease or even a group of leases or the approval of one or a few mining plans. Federal leasing frequently sets the course of development for a sizeable geographic area on both federal and nonfederal "checkerboard" lands, because the geological distribution of the coal formations, along with the efficiency of pooling transportation and other facilities, in most cases leads to grouping or clustering of development projects. Where this is the case, the environmental-impact statement should cover the whole area of cluster development. Controversy, however, arises over determining the limits of the area to be covered by the environmental-impact statement. In other words, what are the geographical limits of (1) the area of primary impact, that is, the area of coal development including mines, power plants, and so on, and (2) the area of secondary impact, that is, the area affected by community development, changes in air and water quality, and so forth, caused by the coal development?

Through court action, environmentalists have put the Interior Department's coal-leasing policy in a "damned if you do and damned if you don't" position. On the one hand the department produced, in its programmatic environmental-impact statement on the overall national implications of leasing coal, a study that was bound to be vague on details. This is true of almost any central-planning study that tries to analyze a problem with nonquantifiable long-term implications. Environmental groups have sued the Department of Interior, charging that its final programmatic coal-leasing environmental statement is inadequate.[13] On the other hand, in the case of *Sierra Club* v. *Morton,* on July 16, 1975, the U.S. Court of Appeals upheld its January 3, 1975, injunction against the mining plans of four companies[14] and the granting

---

[13] Natural Resources Defense Council et al. v. Kleppe et al.
[14] The affected strip-mining operators are Atlantic Richfield, Carter, Kerr McGee, and Wyodak.

of federal rights-of-way for the construction of a railroad spur in the Eastern Powder River Coal Basin of Wyoming (a two-county area) until the Department of the Interior had decided whether or not to prepare an environmental-impact statement covering the entire sixty-three county, three-state area of the northern Great Plains. In the author's opinion this action served no purpose except to long delay a decision to authorize coal development. The decision by the court showed an unjustified faith in central planning and implied that the federal government should have an overall development plan for this multistate region. The Interior Department appealed to the Supreme Court arguing that NEPA does not require the Department of Interior to prepare an environmental-impact statement for the entire northern Great Plains region, since there is no proposal for major federal action with respect to the region. The Sierra Club's contention that the relationships between all proposed coal-related projects in the region required one comprehensive impact statement was held to be incorrect. In some cases, a comprehensive impact statement may be necessary for an agency to meet its duty under NEPA. When several proposals for actions are pending, however, determination of the extent and effect of cumulative environmental impacts is assigned to the special competency of the appropriate agency. Absent a showing of arbitrary action, the Court assumes that the agency has exercised this discretion appropriately.

Thus, four key elements must be present in any coherent planning system for coal leasing: multiple land-use plans, nominations, environmental analysis, and tract evaluation. Some say such a system is merely a process without specific content and that long-term decisions should be made now on what to lease and what not to lease, after environmental-impact studies of varying geographic scope have been completed. This thinking, in the author's view, is based on the delusion that the central planner has the foresight to make long-term decisions as to exactly what should be leased. Instead, what is needed is a process ensuring that careful comparisons of values and costs will be made, case by case, taking into account all of the information available and circumstances surrounding each leasing decision.

Congress recognized these basic elements of a coal-leasing process when it passed the federal Coal Leasing Amendments, which became law on August 4, 1976. The Department of Interior did not fully support the measure, and it became law over the President's veto. The changes it brought in the department's coal-leasing process were not

217

significant. Basically, the new law required that: no lease will be issued unless a comprehensive land-use plan is completed; leasing will be by competitive bidding only; leases not producing in commercial quantities after ten years will be terminated; royalties will be for 12½ percent, but they can be lower for underground mining; and no bid will be accepted which is less than fair-market value. The act also repeals provisions for prospecting permits; requires leases to be developed within forty years; authorizes a comprehensive exploration program (codifying and extending the department's existing program); and, prior to lease issuance, compels the secretary to consider impacts on the environment, on public services, and on agricultural and other economic activities.

Coal is such a key element in U.S. energy policy that leasing should certainly be accelerated. The energy strategy of the Ford administration has been to raise the price of oil in order to reduce consumption and dependence on oil imports, while at the same time expanding domestic energy supplies—oil, gas, nuclear, and coal. The nation needs to increase its coal production by 80 to 100 percent by 1985, and possibly even more, if the anticipated increases in oil production in Alaska and the outer continental shelf and the development of nuclear energy fail to materialize. Of this large and needed increase in coal production, one-fourth to one-third will come from low-sulfur western coal, and a sizeable portion will be federal coal. If the coal-leasing policy outlined above is implemented, it could lead to a reduction in the total amount of coal under federal lease by imposing diligence requirements and advance royalties that might cause more old leases to be relinquished than new leases sold.

Mineral Leasing

Mineral leasing started in the California gold rush of 1849. In a legalistic sense, the gold rush was a massive trespass on the public lands. At the time, there were no federal laws authorizing the extraction of minerals from public land, but, in a graphic example of grassroots democracy, the California mining camps put together their own mining codes, modeled after the Spanish colonial mining laws, which provided that a person could hold and work a mineral deposit after filing papers and paying a royalty to the Spanish Crown. The California miners set up mining districts and agreed that each district would stand behind any claimant who staked a claim and filed notice with the district. Con-

218

veniently for their own self-interest, however, they dropped any requirement of a royalty to the federal government. Soon the California experience was carried into other areas as the nation's mineral search widened in the 1850s and 1860s. Having neglected the issue since the California gold rush, Congress had no alternative but to accept local custom. This it did by providing a special preemption, that is, the right to purchase public lands ahead of any scheduled competive sales. The Mining Law of 1872 [15] provided that any claimant, upon proof of the discovery of a valuable mineral deposit on public lands, could purchase title to the lands for a nominal sum. Written at a time when incentives to settle and develop the western public lands were considered good public policy, the Mining Law of 1872 conferred what is regarded by many today as an unnecessary privilege for hard-rock mining claimants. Without any rental or royalty and without regard for any other uses to which the land he claimed might be put, the mining claimant was granted an option on the use of the land and the ultimate right to purchase it at an unrealistically low price.

In 1971, in an attempt to modernize the mining laws, the administration sent Congress two draft bills, the Mineral Leasing Act of 1971 and the Mining Law of 1971.[16] When Congress failed to act, the original bills were combined into the proposed Mineral Leasing Act of 1973. Nixon's environmental message to Congress in 1973 pointed out the most glaring fault of the archaic mining law. "Under a statute now over a century old, public land must be transferred to private ownership at the request of any person who discovers minerals on it. We thus have no effective control over mining on these properties. Because the public lands belong to all Americans, this 1872 Mining Act should be repealed and be replaced with new legislation which I shall send to Congress." [17]

The basic objective of the original Mining Law of 1872 was to encourage prospecting and mineral development by offering the right to a patent to land where valuable minerals were discovered. But where mining was in conflict with other uses of the public land, the secretary of the interior had only two choices: withdraw the land altogether from mining, or allow mining irrespective of its effect on the environment. Congress reacted over the years with two major reforms. In the Mineral

---

[15] Ch. 152 (17 Stat. 91), May 10, 1872.

[16] See letters to the speaker of the House and the president of the Senate from Interior Secretary Morton, dated October 12, 1971, transmitting both bills.

[17] Office of the White House Press Secretary, President's Environmental and Natural Resources State of the Union Message, February 15, 1973.

Leasing Act of 1920, certain minerals, mainly the fossil fuels—oil, gas, and coal—and certain bedded minerals like potash, phosphate, sodium, and sulfur were placed under a leasing system. In 1955, Congress amended the Materials Act of 1947 [18] to provide for the disposal by competitive bidding of common building materials such as sand, stone, and gravel, except where it was impractical to obtain competition.

The reform proposed by the administration in 1973 would have provided policy direction and implementing authority to make multiple land-use decisions ensuring that, if mining took place, the environment would also be protected and that a fair-market value would be received for minerals mined on the public lands. These objectives were applied to all minerals covered by the Mining Law of 1872, the Mineral Leasing Act of 1920, and their related statutes. The bill prohibited commercial prospecting on public lands unless the prospector obtained a prospecting license. A prospecting license would not allow any significant disturbance of the surface and would give the Department of Interior some notice of and control over prospecting on the public land. A subsequent exploration and development permit would allow development and mining and would require the payment of rent and royalties on the extracted minerals as well as imposing conditions to protect the environment if minerals were found. And to correct one of the most heavily criticized aspects of the leasing system, the Nixon administration bill required that, where public lands were believed to contain commercially valuable mineral deposits, the secretary should require permits to be based on competitive bidding. Competitive bidding would be required where two or more permit applications were filed on the same land on the same day, and all those minerals (oil, gas, coal, phosphates, and so on) covered by the Mineral Leasing Act of 1920 would be leased only by competitive bidding.

The decision to advocate a system of leasing and competitive bidding for minerals resulted in considerable infighting. Predictably, those in the Department of Interior with responsibility for mineral development, as well as the mining interests, strongly advocated the traditional "finders-keepers" code of the old prospector. They claimed that a significant number of the hard rock mineral discoveries were made by individual prospectors, with the incentive of "hitting it rich," who claimed land and then turned to large mining companies, selling out and/or

---

[18] P.L. 80-291 (61 Stat. 681), July 31, 1947, as amended by P.L. 84-167 (69 Stat. 367), July 23, 1955.

taking a percentage of future production. On the other side were the staff of the Office of Management and Budget, the Domestic Council, and the environmental elements of the Interior Department, who advocated additional environmental protection and argued that ample incentive for prospecting already existed. They claimed that a fair-market-value return to the public, which, after all, owned the land, could best be achieved through competitive-bid leasing. The author took this position while he was on the White House staff and later at the Department of Interior. Opposition to this position was strong, both within the Department of Interior and in Congress, and the issue remains unresolved.

Rather than deal with so large a reform package, Congress focused on revising the Mineral Leasing Act of 1920 only as it applied to the politically visible subject of coal leasing. The complicated and time-consuming business of repealing the Mining Law of 1872, the Mineral Leasing Act of 1920, and other related laws, and creating a single comprehensive statute for the disposal of minerals on the federal lands still need the attention of Congress.

Oil Shale

The oil shale story started a long time ago—in fact, about 60 million years ago—when a large inland sea formed in what is now western Colorado, eastern Utah, and southwestern Wyoming. As the sea shrank, it formed two shallow lakes and huge amounts of organic material were deposited on the lake bottoms, interbedded with silts and sands washed in from the surrounding uplands. This material might have formed commercial oil deposits if it had been heated under pressure and had migrated into reservoir rocks. But this never happened. Instead, the organic material trapped in the lake bottoms remained in a solid state, locked into the close-grained formation so securely as to become an integral part of it.

This is the root of the great difficulty with oil shale: how to get at it. It involves mining the native rock, crushing it, heating it to distill off the liquid and gaseous fractions, and disposing of the residue, which is almost as heavy and half again as bulky as the original volume extracted. The environmental problems are severe and the costs enormous, but the amount of oil potentially recoverable is staggering. The in-place resource is estimated at about 1.8 trillion barrels. From the highest-grade deposits (over 30 gallons of oil per ton of oil shale), some 139 billion barrels of oil may eventually be recovered.[19] A single square mile in the richest part of the Green River formation in Colorado could contain 2 to 3 billion barrels of oil, almost enough to run the country for six months. Using oil shale alone, the country could be self-sufficient in oil well beyond the year 2000. Yet this promise remains unfulfilled after more than half a century of frustrating efforts to bring the oil to market, because shale oil has never been able to compete economically with crude oil. This is true overseas as well. In Scotland an oil shale industry competed against coal for a hundred years, until the abundance of low-priced Persian Gulf oil closed it down in 1963. For a few years in the 1920s, the United States had one company in the oil shale industry, the Catlin Shale Products Company, selling fuels, wax, and lubricants around Elko, Nevada.

In the early part of the nineteenth century, there was some interest in the marine oil shales in Tennessee and Kentucky, but this was dissipated by Colonel E. L. Drake's discovery in 1859 that oil could be much more cheaply produced from wells. Not until the field work during the summers of 1913 to 1915 were any serious scientific appraisals made of the oil shales of Colorado and the surrounding areas. Dean Winchester of the U.S. Geological Survey inspected the Green River formation and concluded that it contained at least 20 billion barrels of oil.[20] At the time, this figure was about three times the known reserves of the entire country. In 1917 in his annual report, the director of the Geological Survey noted, "it seems probable not only that oil will be distilled from the shales of the Green River group long after the principal oil fields of the world have been exhausted but also that the total amount that will be obtained from this source may exceed the world's total production of natural petroleum."[21]

Such optimism set off a rash of newspaper stories,[22] and *National Geographic* published an account that was positively lyrical: "No man who owns a motor car will fail to rejoice that the United States Geologi-

---

[19] Department of Interior, "Oil Shale Status Report," mimeographed, April 18, 1975, p. 1.

[20] Dean Winchester, "Oil Shale in Northwestern Colorado and Adjacent Areas," *U.S. Geological Survey Bulletin 641-F* (Washington, D.C.: U.S. Government Printing Office, 1916), p. 140.

[21] "Thirty-Eighth Report of the United States Geological Survey," *Annual Report of the Department of Interior* (Washington, D.C.: U.S. Government Printing Office, 1918), p. 403.

[22] For an excellent history of U.S. shale oil development see Chris Wells, *The Elusive Bonanza* (New York, N.Y.: E. P. Dutton and Company, Inc., 1970).

cal Survey is pointing the way to supplies of gasoline which can meet any demand that even his children's children for generations to come may make of them." [23] The publicity produced no shale oil, only thousands of staked claims. In all, about one-sixth of the entire Green River formation in Colorado, Utah, and Wyoming was claim-staked over a period of three or four years. The hills swarmed with prospectors and more than 200 shale oil corporations were formed.[24] Many were paper stock promotions, but others struggled boldly against the uncompromising realities of physics, economics, and geography for a few years before finally expiring. None of the companies remain in operation, but a few claimants still retain rights obtained by work on their holdings.

The Mineral Leasing Act of 1920 ended the claim-stake rush by excluding oil shale and other nonmetalliferous materials like crude oil, natural gas, coal, phosphate, and so on from the provision of the Mining Law of 1872. The 1920 act specified that these minerals could be obtained only through a leasing procedure that involved the payment of rentals, royalties, and bonuses. The Mineral Leasing Act of 1920 protected those mining claims that had been initiated validly prior to the effective date of the act and, as a result, thousands of claims eventually went to patent. Other thousands have been challenged successfully and invalidated, but thousands more remain unpatented, a cloud on the ownership of the oil-shale-rich lands of Colorado, Utah, and Wyoming.

But for many, the confusion over who owned what oil shale lands made little difference. The fear that the nation might run out of oil vanished in the mid-1920s with the advent of the reflection seismograph. With this new instrument, so much oil was discovered in Texas,[25] Oklahoma, and California over the next twenty years that oil companies, concerned about maintaining some semblance of order in the market for their too-plentiful products, were understandably not interested in investing money in oil shale that would further increase the supply. World War II temporarily did away with oil surplus and sparked renewed interest among oil companies in at least acquiring oil shale acreage as a long-term hedge against the time when reserves of petroleum might begin to decline. In the 1940s and early 1950s, a number of oil companies, most

---

[23] Guy Mitchell, "Billions of Barrels Locked Up in Rocks," *National Geographic Magazine*, vol. 33, no. 2 (February 1918), p. 201.

[24] Wells, *Elusive Bonanza*, p. 28.

[25] In 1930, the discovery of the 6 billion barrel East Texas oil field caused such a glut on the market that crude oil prices fell as low as ten cents a barrel. East Texas was the largest known oil field in North America until the 1968 discovery of Prudhoe Bay in Northern Alaska, with 9.6 billion barrels of proven reserve.

of them short on crude supply, acquired substantial holdings in the Piceance Basin of Colorado—by far the richest of the basins in which the Green River shales were deposited. But for most companies, the oil shale acreage acquisitions were a hedge and nothing more. The Union Oil Company of California did make an honest attempt to develop a commercial process for extracting and producing shale oil but gave up in 1958 after spending about $12 million. By then there was again a domestic surplus of crude oil, exacerbated this time by a worldwide surplus from the incredibly prolific Persian Gulf area, which seemed to promise an almost endless supply.

The indifference of the oil companies to oil shale was matched by that of the federal government, which, in spite of the land rush of the 1917–1920 period, still owned about 85 percent of the oil shale acreage in the Green River country. But the U.S. Bureau of Mines, responding to renewed interest in oil shale during World War II, established a small experimental retorting facility an Anvil Points, Colorado, which operated from 1947 until 1956. The facility was leased to private companies under a research contract during the 1960s until it was closed down again in 1968. It was later under lease to a consortium of seventeen companies for further testing of retorting methods.

But leasing federal land for oil shale development was something else again. The Teapot Dome syndrome still deeply influenced the thinking of both Congress and the Department of Interior. On the other hand, the oil companies, with a few exceptions, shied away from the long-term financial commitment needed to make the technological breakthrough necessary before shale oil could compete economically with crude oil production. Chris Wells aptly described the situation:

> The federal government, specifically the Department of Interior, as guardian of the 85 percent share of the shale contained on public land, has always been considered the logical party to encourage development of the shale land. The oil industry, as the possessor of petroleum technology and the refining and marketing organization through which oil must eventually flow, has always been considered the logical party to develop the shale. Both, though, have acted not unlike the reluctant bride and bridegroom at a shot-gun wedding. In the face of the demands for action they have inched forward slowly, ever so slowly, toward the altar, but their hearts have not been in it.[26]

---

[26] Wells, *Elusive Bonanza*, pp. 31-32.

The courtship between the federal government and industry continued at a slow pace, with a few efforts to lease oil shale lands during the Lyndon Johnson years. Secretary of Interior Udall was sufficiently sensitive to the pressures of the Colorado, Utah, and Wyoming congressional delegations (eager to bring an oil shale industry to their states) to appoint an Oil Shale Advisory Board in June 1964.[27] But its members were hopelessly divided. The only conclusion that could safely be drawn from the report presented by the board in February 1965 [28] was that more study was needed—a conclusion that, some thought, eminently suited the secretary's purposes since he was sensitive to the "giveaway" charges and to the environmental concern over oil shale that was beginning to emerge.

In January 1967, Udall announced an oil shale development program that included: (1) clearing titles to contested oil shale lands; (2) a "blocking up" program so that owners of scattered tracts of shale land could exchange them for consolidated blocks of federal land of comparable value; (3) an investigation of the possibility of nuclear *in situ* retorting; (4) a proposed $100 million, ten-year, industry and federal research program; and (5) the heart of the development program, a system of "provisional developmental leases" under which companies would be invited to request leases for research and development work on small parcels of a 30,000-acre tract set aside for this purpose.[29]

But then the courtship between the oil companies and the Department of Interior slowed down and came to a predictable halt. Because of the financial uncertainties of the lease terms, the oil companies showed no interest and the program died. During the research phase, which could have lasted as long as ten years, the lessees would have had to divulge each year all the technological data they had acquired so that little or no proprietary competitive edge would have been gained by the oil company for its trouble. Much later, the secretary of interior would have decided whether the shale production process developed by the lessee was commercially feasible and whether or not he would issue a commercial lease. To make a forecast of long-term cash flow and potential profits virtually impossible, the Department of Interior had stipulated

---

27 Department of Interior press release, "Oil Shale Advisory Board Established," June 30, 1964.
28 "Interim Report of the Oil Shale Advisory Board to the Secretary of the Interior," Resources for the Future, Washington, D.C., February 1965, unpublished.
29 Department of Interior press release, "Five-Point Oil Shale Development Program Announced," January 27, 1967.

Table 12
AVERAGE PRICE OF CRUDE OIL IN THE
UNITED STATES, 1950–1976

Year	Dollars per Barrel	Year	Dollars per Barrel
1950	2.51	1971	3.39
1953	2.68	1972	3.39
1956	2.79	1973	3.89
1960	2.88	1974	6.74 [a]
1964	2.88	1975	8.00 [b]
1968	2.94	1976	7.66 [c]
1970	3.18		

[a] The July 1974 price for new oil was $9.95/bbl.
[b] The July 1975 price for new oil was $12.30/bbl.
[c] The estimated average domestic crude oil price for 1975 was about $8.00 per barrel, but Title V of the Energy Policy and Conservation Act (P.L. 94-163 [89 Stat. 871], December 22, 1975) requires the President to adjust the price of various categories of domestic crude so that the average domestic price does not exceed $7.66/bbl.
Source: U.S. Bureau of Mines, personal communication.

that the size of the development lease could be smaller or larger than the original research lease and that the royalties could be fixed at some point, to be determined later, between 10 and 50 percent of net income from operations.

But the pressure to lease continued: 1968 was an election year and the development-minded congressional delegations of Colorado, Utah, and Wyoming threatened to make Udall's lack of action on oil shale an issue in the presidential campaign. Also, shale oil was starting to look more attractive economically, if only slightly so, because of the gentle rise in the price of domestic crude oil (see Table 12). Also, the Middle East War of 1967 had given the nation and the oil men a fresh sense of urgency about self-sufficiency in energy. Finally, on September 10, 1968, Udall announced the details of a formal invitation to bid on December 20 on "test leases" located on three tracts of land under a system of sealed competitive bids, with a one-eighth royalty.[30] The purpose of the program was to test the market, to see if there really was a company able and ready to proceed with oil shale development imme-

---

[30] Department of Interior press release, "Udall Invites Bids on Three Oil Shale Test Leases," September 10, 1968.

diately. The program was a fiasco. The Department of Interior put up three tracts for lease and stated that it expected cash bonuses to exceed $30 million for Tract One, $20 million for Tract Two, and $25 million for Tract Three. In fact, high bids were received of $249,000 for Tract One, and $250,000 for Tract Two. Both bids were made by the Oil Shale Corporation. The third tract received no bids at all.[31]

The program failed for several reasons. Probably most important, the price of crude oil was still relatively low. The giant northern Alaska Prudhoe Bay field had just been discovered, the recently leased Santa Barbara Channel was proving productive, and additional leasing was being planned for the outer continental shelf. The oil companies were again concerned about overproduction and lower prices, which meant that shale oil, with all its technological uncertainties, might not be competitive with crude oil. Another obvious reason for the failure of the program was the short time between the announcement of the lease terms and the bidding deadline. Industry had only about three months from the announcement of the program to evaluate the tracts, review the leasing terms, and arrange financing before committing themselves. Furthermore, there had been little consultation between the government and industry before the program was announced. The bidders had had no opportunity to participate in the selection of the tracts to be leased and had been allowed to drill only a single geological core per tract in evaluating them.

During 1969 and 1970, the new administration began redesigning the program and in May 1970 it proposed a "prototype" program that contemplated a package of twenty-year leases to be offered on the basis of sealed, competitive bonus bids with a fixed royalty rate.[32] Bidders would be permitted to nominate tracts on which they were interested in bidding, with a year allowed for core drilling and nomination and an additional year allowed for appraisal of the tracts by the Interior Department. After two years, the Department of Interior would offer tracts for bidding, two from each of the three oil shale states. The department hoped that the companies would experiment with underground, open pit, and *in situ* mining technologies. A massive environmental-impact state-

---

[31] Department of Interior press release, "Interior Rejects Bids Submitted in Oil Shale Test Lease Sale December 20," December 27, 1968.

[32] Hollis Dole, assistant secretary of interior, *Hearings on Oil Shale Development,* before the Subcommittee on Minerals, Materials and Fuels of the Committee on Interior and Insular Affairs, United States Senate, 91st Congress, 1st sess. (Washington, D.C.: U.S. Government Printing Office, May 21, 1970), pp. 23-27.

ment would have to be prepared before any decision could be made to proceed.

The courtship between the department and the oil companies quickened again in the wake of events that made forecasts of rising crude oil prices more plausible: the Santa Barbara blowout had slowed the pace of offshore leasing, and Prudhoe Bay oil was being delayed in reaching the market because of the time needed to meet rigorous environmental control standards in construction of the Alaska pipeline. The price of oil began to rise (see Table 12) and, although few people if any realized that the price of newly discovered domestic oil would go over $10 per barrel following the OPEC boycott, still, for the first time shale oil started to look competitive with crude oil. In June 1971, in President Nixon's first energy message to Congress, he endorsed an oil shale program that provided for environmental controls:

> I am requesting the Secretary of the Interior to expedite development of an oil shale leasing program including the preparation of an environmental impact statement. If after reviewing this statement and comments he finds that environmental concerns can be satisfied, he shall then proceed with the detailed planning. This work will also involve the states of Wyoming, Colorado, and Utah, and the first lease would be scheduled for next year.[33]

But it was not until the winter and spring of 1974 that the lease sales actually took place. It took about three years to complete a 3,200-page, six-volume environmental-impact statement.[34]

Even with stringent controls, the environmental problems accompanying the prototype oil shale development scheme gave the administration considerable concern. If the land were mined by open pit, nearly all of the surface of an approximately 5,000-acre tract would be turned into open pits and overburden storage and disposal piles for twenty years or more. In fact, shale and overburden disposal piles might occupy as much as 10,000 more acres. Although the land would be reclaimed eventually, it could not be returned to its original contour, nor was it likely that the original type of vegetation could be restored. To a much lesser extent, the same environmental problems would arise from under-

---

[33] *Public Papers of the Presidents, Nixon, 1971,* Special Message to the Congress on Energy, June 4, p. 709.

[34] Department of Interior, *Final Environmental Impact Statement for the Prototype Oil Shale Leasing Program* (Washington, D.C.: U.S. Government Printing Office, August 23, 1973).

ground oil shale mining, since only part of the spent shale could be disposed of underground. Over time, surface waters would erode and leach the spent shale piles even though they would eventually be reclaimed with vegetation. As a result, silt and salts would find their way into nearby drainages (as they do now) and would eventually increase the mineral loading of the Colorado River system.

The mining of the two Colorado tracts also presented potential ground-water pollution problems. Beneath the oil-rich upper Mahogany zone in the Piceance Basin of Colorado is a "leached zone" of fractured shale containing up to 25 million acre-feet of water. In some places this water is of high quality (less than 1,000 ppm dissolved solids), but in others its level of dissolved solids increases to a maximum of 60,000 ppm. Below the "leached zone" are about 750 feet of shales rich in nahcolite (sodium bicarbonate) and dawsonite (dihydroxy sodium aluminum carbonate, a source of alumina). In order to mine these minerals, the saline "leached zone" must be penetrated, which means pumping out large amounts of ground water that would gradually become saline. This change in flow patterns might result in pollution of ground waters, seepage of reinjected saline waters into surface waters, or leaching of spent shale from ground water.

Air pollution was also a concern. The whole shale region has excellent air quality. Oil shale processing and refining would produce hydrogen sulfide, sulfur dioxide, and nitrogen oxides. In order to mitigate air pollution effective technology for disposing of these gases would have to be developed. Unless there is a technological breakthrough, the 1980 sulfur dioxide standard for Colorado will limit production to about 200,000 barrels of shale oil per day. Oil shale mining would also have considerable impact on the local fauna, including mule deer, and elk. The deer population would slowly be deprived of its habitat and, at a time when hunting pressure and road kills were increasing, a rich recreational resource would slowly be depleted.

The prototype program for the production of 250,000 barrels per day of shale oil (200,000 barrels per day from underground and open-pit mining and 50,000 barrels per day from *in situ* production) considered in the final environmental-impact statement was expected to produce 13,000 new jobs and to bring 34,000 people to a region that now has a population of 119,000. In ten years an investment of nearly $1 billion would be needed to implement the prototype program, but the program would generate local tax revenues of about $33 million, state revenues of $22 million, and federal revenues of $135 million annually. The prototype 250,000-barrels-per-day shale oil program would require about 13,000 acres for development, including urban expansion. The mature 1-million-barrels-per-day shale oil industry, the statement projected, would double the population and use about 80,000 acres for shale oil mining and urban development. This acreage represents only about 0.5 to 1 percent of the oil shale lands in the three-state area.

Because of environmental problems, considerable thought was given to not leasing in Colorado Tract A, the richest of all the tracts, since this area would have to be open-pit mined, while the other Colorado tracts and the two Utah tracts would be underground mined and the two Wyoming tracts would use the *in situ* mining method. In the end, Secretary of the Interior Morton decided to offer for lease all six tracts [35] because he hoped to see all mining technologies applied to oil shale development, including open-pit mining. Furthermore, since oil shale mining seemed at the time to be only marginally profitable, he did not want to exclude the most economically attractive site from the leasing program.

Some form of federal subsidy for the leasing program was also considered. There were a number of reasons for doubting the competitiveness of shale oil with other forms of energy. The costs of shale oil production were uncertain and any estimate might turn out to be low if, for example, ground-water management proved to be a major problem. Even if the production-cost estimates were accurate, shale oil was computed to be competitive only if crude oil prices rose rapidly, and at the time there was no strong reason to suspect that the price would rise sharply. As it happened, the OPEC cartel action was only a few months away. Crude oil prices had been remarkably stable, as Table 12 shows, for a long period. From the Interior Department's analysis it was clear that to achieve a rate of return of 15 percent or more, which was believed to be necessary to encourage oil shale development, crude prices would need to rise substantially or shale oil production costs would need to drop more than expected. The department could not foresee that, within two years, the price of newly discovered domestic crude would almost triple and construction costs, which historically rose by 4 to 6 percent each year, would shoot up, increasing by 30 percent in 1974 alone.

[35] Department of Interior press release, "Secretary Morton Announces Prototype Oil Shale Lease Sales," November 28, 1973.

Eight subsidy alternatives were reviewed and ranked against the no-subsidy prototype leasing program as follows:

(1) Price contract—a contract for government purchase of a specific quantity of shale oil at a fixed price.

(2) Price floor—federal guarantee of a minimum price for a specific quantity of shale oil produced.

(3) Loan—a federally guaranteed low-interest loan for part of the capital requirement for shale oil production under the lease.

(4) Accelerated depreciation—permission for rapid write-off of capital assets.

(5) Increased depletion allowance—rise in depletion allowance above the standard rate for shale oil.

(6) Interest tax credit—a rise in rate of credit against taxes for new investment.

(7) Royalty reduction—a downward adjustment of the royalties stated in the lease terms.

(8) Specific subsidy—payment to the lessee of a dollar sum per barrel of shale oil produced.

These eight subsidy alternatives were ranked on the basis of five judgment criteria: (1) reduction of risk of crude oil price fluctuation, which was considered to be the major risk involved in the lease; (2) financial incentives to develop all stages of the development process; (3) cost to the Treasury; (4) feasibility under present law; and (5) feasibility without major redesign of the program. The administration concluded that if a subsidy program were to be implemented, the best subsidy alternative, all things considered, was a purchase contract: this would eliminate the risk of fluctuating crude oil prices and maintain production incentives, although it was somewhat more difficult to implement than royalty reductions or an accelerated depreciation alternative. The next best alternative was thought to be the price floor, which reduces, although it does not eliminate, price risk. If the crude oil price falls below the price floor, there is, of course, no impact on the lessees' profits. Profits fluctuate if the price of oil varies above the price floor, but the amount of risk has been reduced. The two alternatives that were easiest to implement—royalty reduction and depreciation acceleration—either increased or left unchanged the crude oil price risk and therefore seemed less desirable than the purchase-contract or price-floor alternatives. The

231

remaining alternatives were judged inferior on grounds of effectiveness or feasibility of implementation or both.

In the end, Secretary Morton decided against any subsidy. First, it was not at all that clear that a subsidy was needed; the unexpectedly high bid prices paid by the lessees suggested that it was not. Also, the program would be delayed considerably if congressional approval for a subsidy program had to be sought, and there was no assurance that Congress would approve it. Finally, the old political charge of giving away the nation's mineral resources would undoubtedly descend on the secretary's shoulders.

Between January and June 1974, the six leases were offered for bidding, and bonus bids worth a total of $448,796,800 were accepted.[36] The program had finally gotten off to a successful start after years of ineffectual interest in shale oil development. The bids were much higher than anticipated—in fact, five to ten times higher—probably because of the impact of the Arab embargo and OPEC cartel action on the bidders, who had to project the price of crude oil in 1980, when shale oil would come into production, and beyond.

A number of changes had taken place between 1968 and 1974 to improve the chances of success for the oil shale prototype leasing program. First, unlike the Udall program, the Morton program gave the oil companies ample time to evaluate the leasing offer. The companies had a chance not only to nominate the tracts that they believed would be most suitable for the technology they had chosen to use, but also to conduct extensive core drilling. Although the costs of holding and producing the leases were higher in 1974 than they had been in 1968, the requirement that the developer guarantee the entire bonus, even in the case of early lease relinquishment, was removed and credits for early development were incorporated. Also, the performance bond and provisions against unexpected costs allowed companies to calculate their operating costs much more closely.

The change that had taken place in the depletion allowance through the Tax Reform Act of 1969 [37] was another factor that helped make

---

[36] Results of the six lease sale opportunities were as follows: January 8, 1974: Colorado Tract A—$210,305,000 offered by Standard Oil of Indiana and Gulf; January 12, 1974: Colorado Tract B—$117,788,000 offered by Atlantic Richfield, Tosco, Ashland and Shell; March 12, 1974: Utah Tract A—$75,596,000 offered by Phillips and Sun; April 9, 1974: Utah Tract B—$45,107,200 offered by the White Corporation (Phillips, Sun and Sohio); May 14 and June 11, 1974: no bids received on Wyoming Tracts A and B.

[37] P.L. 91-172 (83 Stat. 487), December 30, 1969.

the 1974 prototype lease sale successful. An allowance of 15 percent on raw oil shale remained, but the depletion allowance on crude oil dropped from 27.5 percent to 22 percent, thus making shale oil slightly more competitive with crude.

The absence of bids on the Wyoming prototype tracts, which had been offered for lease in order to test industry's interest in *in situ* oil shale development, impressed upon the Department of Interior and the newly formed Energy Research and Development Administration (ERDA) the need to design and bring to the point of commercial viability alternative methods for *in situ* recovery of shale oil.

In situ processing of oil shale will offer many potential advantages over open-pit or conventional underground mining if the technological difficulties can be overcome. Its great attraction is that it allows the shale to be processed almost entirely underground. *In situ* processing uses a borehole technique and fractures the oil shale underground. Then heat is applied to retort the shale. A variation, the modified *in situ* method, is different in that some mining is done to create a chamber in which the oil shale is fragmented and retorted.

In situ oil shale development requires about half as much water as open-pit or conventional underground mining, uses about two-thirds fewer people, and brings to the surface a maximum of one-third of the spent shale, and in some cases virtually none. Finally, of the 1.8 trillion barrels of estimated shale oil reserves, about 1.2 trillion barrels are low grade (less than twenty gallons of oil per ton of oil shale) which will never be recovered by conventional mining techniques, given current estimates of future crude oil prices.

In March 1975, the Interior Department and ERDA announced plans that could result in *in situ* lease sales and an accelerated *in situ* research program.[38] However, the lease sale was delayed while an environmental-impact statement was being completed. The Department of Interior would ask industry to nominate oil shale tracts for possible development using *in situ* methods. If, after the completion of the environmental-impact statement, it was decided to go ahead with the program, tracts in Colorado and Utah would be leased.

In situ oil shale development is still in the experimental stage; its capability has not been actually demonstrated and its potential contribution is difficult to judge. The reaction of the prospective bidders will

---

[38] Department of Interior press release, "Interior, ERDA Disclose Plans to Accelerate Oil Shale Development," March 19, 1975.

perhaps be the best indication of what may be expected in the way of *in situ* oil shale development.

Indeed, the future of oil shale development is still very much in doubt. The successful bidders under the prototype leasing program have delayed construction on both the Colorado and the Utah tracts. A shock wave went through the industry when Atlantic Richfield, which had started work on a 50,000 barrel-per-day plant on private land on the edge of the Piceance Basin, suddenly suspended operations. Its cost estimates had risen from $250–$300 million in 1973, to $400–$450 million in early 1974, and to $850–$900 million in September 1974, just before the decision to close down. This last figure indicated a capital cost per daily barrel of production of about $18,000. This level of investment put the capital costs alone at something over $7 per barrel of oil produced. Once again, in the spring and summer of 1975, the question of a federal subsidy was raised within the administration.

In fact, the idea of a government authority that would lend financial assistance to a wide range of energy projects, including oil shale development, was hotly debated within the Energy Research Council. Originally, it had been the brain child of the Critical Choices study group set up by Nelson Rockefeller before he became vice-president. President Ford finally sided with Rockefeller and against his more conservative advisers, and in the fall of 1975 the administration drafted a bill for an Energy Independence Authority,[39] a government corporation designed to provide loans, loan guarantees, price guarantees, and other forms of federal assistance (up to $100 billion, $25 billion in equity and $75 billion in debt) to private energy-sector projects. The program was designed to promote, through financial assistance, the development of energy technologies in fields like oil shale extraction, synthetic fuels made from coal, and solar and geothermal energy. Research in such fields requires long lead times and has been held up by the vicissitudes of worldwide oil prices. Also some projects, like the development of uranium enrichment plants, the administration felt, were simply too large and economically risky to be financed by the private sector alone. The administration was

---

[39] The idea of an Energy Independence Authority was first unveiled in a speech delivered by President Ford on September 28, 1975, in San Francisco. For details of the proposal see the bill with a letter transmitted to Congress by President Ford, a fact sheet, and the transcript of a press conference by FEA Administrator Frank Zarb, OMB Director James Lynn, William Seidman, assistant to the President for economic affairs, and Deputy ERDA Administrator Robert Fri, all released by the White House press secretary, October 10, 1975.

also concerned about the fact that electrical utilities were cancelling plans to build needed nuclear and coal-fired plants: with limited profits they could not meet the capital requirements of such projects, and the delays caused by their dealings with the regulatory agencies were frustrating.

But the administration proposal seemed dead even before the fifty-four page draft bill reached Congress. Liberals expressed concern that the Energy Independence Authority would not be accountable to Congress and hardly relished giving financial relief to energy companies, many of which had shown spectacular earnings in recent years. Nor did many lawmakers want to see one segment of the economy subsidized at the expense of another. Conservatives joined the liberals in expressing concern about allocating up to $100 billion, most of which would be dispensed without congressional review. Finally, many congressmen agreed with some of Ford's advisers that the program would result in federal interference and distortion of the free market system.

In December 1975, the House dealt a blow to both the Ford administration and the energy leaders in the Senate. By a vote of 263 to 140 it approved an amendment by Congressman Ken Hechler, Democrat of West Virginia, striking a $6-billion loan guarantee authority for synthetic fuels from the conference version of H.R. 3474, a bill authorizing $5 billion in energy research funds for ERDA. By a vote of 283 to 117, the House also rejected the Senate version of another bill authorizing the use of public lands without charge (a form of subsidy) for *in situ* oil shale research and development projects, with the familiar charge that the senators were giving away the public lands.[40] The Senate relented on both issues in conference and approved the House version of the bill.[41] This outcome killed off any chance for the 94th Congress to subsidize oil shale development through free use of the public lands or through loan guarantees.

Using an interagency task force, the administration prepared a report in 1975, on a synthetic-fuels-commercialization program,[42] which presented detailed and extensive analysis and recommended federal economic incentives for oil shale development. Although printed

---

[40] *Congressional Record*, vol. 121, no. 183 (December 11, 1975), p. H12421 and pp. H12423-24.

[41] *Congressional Record*, vol. 121, no. 188 (December 18, 1975), pp. S22778-79.

[42] Report submitted by the Synthetic Fuels Interagency Task Force to the President's Energy Resources Council, Recommendations for a Synthetic Fuels Commercialization Program, 3 vols. (Washington, D.C.: U.S. Government Printing Office, November 1975).

in November 1975, the report had not been available to most members of Congress in time for the key House debate in December 1975. One can only speculate that the availability of this report might have changed the outcome.

In December 1975, following Congress's action, Atlantic Richfield and the Oil Shale Company dropped out of their partnership with Shell and Ashland on Colorado oil shale Tract B, which they had jointly obtained with a high bid of $117.8 million in February 1974.[43] The companies cited rising construction costs and Congress's rejection of a loan-guarantee program for synthetic fuels which would have shared the risk and eased the financial burden of constructing oil shale conversion plants. By the fall of 1976 the remaining operators on the Colorado and Utah tracts had requested that the secretary of interior defer payment of annual bonus and rental. Unless the economics of oil shale becomes more attractive, the leases may not be mined.

Finally, on September 28, 1976, a coalition of fiscal conservatives and environmentalists in the 94th Congress, with a generous dose of anti-oil sentiment, rejected by the closest of margins—193 to 192—the rule to consider a synthetic fuels bill. The bill would have authorized $3.5 billion in federal loan guarantees and $500 million in price supports of synthetic fuels.[44]

Naval Petroleum Reserves

The naval petroleum reserves of the United States have been the focus of litigation, scandal, honest concern, and bureaucratic parochialism between the navy and the Department of Interior for more than fifty years. These much discussed reserves, however, have yet to make a contribution of any significance to national security, the economy, or the country's energy supply.

The term "giveaway" has haunted the Department of Interior since the days of the Teapot Dome scandal. In fact, however, the "giveaway" program that dominated U.S. natural-resources policy for the better part of a hundred and fifty years was in many ways a huge success. With the promise of mineral and oil wealth for incentive, between 1860 and 1900

---

[43] *Wall Street Journal*, December 22, 1975, p. 5, and *Oil and Gas Journal*, vol. 73, no. 52 (December 29, 1975), p. 198.

[44] *Congressional Quarterly*, vol. 34, no. 39 (September 25, 1976), p. 2672.

more than a million families settled the Great Plains, six railroad systems were built from the Mississippi to the Pacific, farms flourished, cities sprang up, and miners and oilmen made the nation virtually self-sufficient in energy and minerals.

But along with the successes the policy created problems. One of the most acute sprang from the discovery and development of oil fields in California. Until the Mineral Leasing Act of 1920, oil and gas were locatable minerals, specifically provided for under the Petroleum Placer Act of 1897[45]—which was enacted just about the time that petroleum exploration was getting well under way in California. All a prospector had to do was to stake out a twenty-acre claim and if he discovered oil on it and spent $500 improving it, he could patent the land and the minerals it contained for $2.50 an acre. He was, moreover, protected against entry on his claim by third parties as long as he was making an honest effort to discover petroleum.

The oil fields discovered in Southern California turned out to be of enormous size, and the discoveries of such super-giants as Coalinga, Kern River, Midway, and Sunset between 1896 and 1900 brought thousands of oil seekers to the San Joaquin Valley in a frantic rush of claim-staking. Even worse, once a discovery was made, the relentless operation of the "rule of capture" decreed by the courts drove the producer to drill and pump as many wells as he could put down on his property to prevent drainage by his neighbors. The result was a horrendous waste of oil and gas, both in physical and economic terms. This arrangement did violence to the notions of both equity and conservation. The government was giving away resources worth billions of dollars to people whose expenditures of labor and money on their claims were negligible compared with the benefits they derived, and who were letting vast quantities of their discovered resources go to waste.

On February 24, 1908, Dr. George Otis Smith, director of the U.S. Geological Survey, was moved to complain about this state of affairs in a letter to the secretary of the interior. Smith recommended that the filing of claims to oil lands in California be suspended. He wrote: "The present rate at which oil lands in California are being patented by private parties will make it impossible for the people of the United States to continue ownership of oil lands there more than a few months. After that, the Government will be obliged to repurchase the very oil

---

[45] Ch. 216 (29 Stat. 526), February 11, 1897.

that it has practically given away."[46] Smith enclosed a newspaper article citing the advantages of fuel oil over coal for ships in general and naval ships in particular. He noted that coal was virtually nonexistent on the West Coast and that the demand for oil there was outstripping the supply. With the conservatism typical of early geological survey estimates, he calculated that "those areas in which the probabilities are greatest for striking commercial deposits of oil have nearly all been prospected with a drill and either proven or condemned. . . . All the larger oil companies realize not only that the supply of the proven fields is limited, but that the area over which prospecting is liable to result favorably is also restricted."[47]

Nothing came of Smith's letter, so the following year, on September 17, he tried again, this time with a new pitch to a new secretary. Although he included a copy of his earlier letter, his main argument was for restricting entry to prevent the waste of scarce resources. This time he specifically mentioned the increasing use of fuel oil by the navy and concluded that "there would appear to be an immediate necessity for assuring the conservation of a proper supply of petroleum for the Government's own use."[48] This time Smith had better luck. Secretary Richard A. Ballinger addressed a letter the same day (September 17, 1909) to President Taft making the navy's prospective fuel oil requirements the central point of his appeal for legislation to provide for an adequate supply of petroleum to meet the government's needs. "This legislation," wrote Ballinger, "should give authority to fix the terms of disposition of public oil lands so as to provide for the future demands of the Navy and should also authorize the permanent reservation of such areas as the Executive, after full investigation, may find necessary for this Federal purpose."[49]

Within ten days Secretary Ballinger had authority from the President to withdraw 3 million acres of western lands from entry pending legislation. The withdrawal order was issued on September 27, 1909, and listed 3,041,000 acres of land in California and Wyoming, denying further entry to these tracts by newcomers but protecting all previously located

---

[46] Reginald Ragland, *A History of the Naval Petroleum Reserves and the Development of the Present National Policy Respecting Them* (privately published, Los Angeles, California, 1944), p. 18. Copy available, Department of Interior Library Catalogue number VC 276 A47 R2.

[47] Ibid., p. 19.

[48] Ibid., p. 23.

[49] Ibid., p. 26.

claims. Included in the lists were claimants who were diligently pursuing work leading to the discovery of oil, even if they had made no discovery to date.

The withdrawal order was immediately attacked in the courts, but it was upheld several years later by the Supreme Court. Meanwhile, Congress passed legislation. The Pickett Act [50] gave statutory support to the withdrawals that had been made earlier and formed the basis for future withdrawals of public land by the executive. Like the withdrawal order of September 27, 1909, the Pickett Act protected the claims of all holders who at the time of enactment were "in diligent prosecution of work leading to the discovery of oil and gas." Pursuant to the Pickett Act the Department of Interior issued a series of orders, all dated July 2, 1910, setting aside approximately 4.5 million acres, constituted as eight numbered petroleum reserves (but not *naval* petroleum reserves), located in Arizona, California, Colorado, Louisiana, New Mexico, Oregon, Utah, and Wyoming. These were *temporary* orders, designed not to keep the oil in the ground, but merely to stop the practice of giving away the public oil lands. From the time these orders were issued until the enactment of the Mineral Leasing Act of 1920, the federal government in effect had no policy with respect to the disposition of its oil lands. It was during this period that the first three naval petroleum reserves (NPRs) were created.

There was, apparently, considerable discussion of the navy's switch from coal to oil and the implications of this switch for strategic fuel requirements during the period between 1909 and 1912. The debate culminated in a recommendation on May 5, 1912, by the chief of the navy's Bureau of Steam Engineering to the secretary of the navy that necessary steps be taken to establish a reserve of public oil-bearing lands in California to provide fuel for the navy.[51] This recommendation was seconded on June 26 by the Navy General Board, which recommended to the secretary that "permanent reservation be made for future Naval fuel oil supply of adequate territory in both the Pacific Coast and Gulf oil fields."[52]

The secretary of the navy in turn communicated the substance of these recommendations to the secretary of the interior, requesting his assistance in securing the reservation of oil-bearing public lands in Cali-

---

[50] Ch. 421 (36 Stat. 847), June 25, 1910.
[51] Ragland, *History of the Naval Petroleum Reserves,* p. 38.
[52] Ibid.

fornia sufficient to ensure a supply of 500 million barrels of oil. The secretary of the interior thereupon instructed the director of the U.S. Geological Survey to recommend acreage for inclusion in a naval petroleum reserve. On August 8, 1912, Smith, still director of the Geological Survey, made his recommendation that 38,069 acres in the Elk Hills area of Kern County, California, be identified for the exclusive use and benefit of the navy.[53] This area became NPR #1 by order of President Taft on September 2, 1912.[54] As the months went by Smith began to have second thoughts about the volume of oil that might be contained in NPR #1, and on December 6, 1912, he wrote to the secretary of the interior recommending the designation of an additional 29,541 acres in the nearby Buena Vista Hills as a naval petroleum reserve.[55] This became NPR #2 by President Taft's order on December 13.[56] NPR #3, located northeast of Casper, Wyoming, was created by President Wilson on April 30, 1915,[57] at the request of Secretary of the Navy Josephus Daniels. By the Act of June 4, 1920, Congress placed the naval petroleum reserves expressly under the authority of the secretary of the navy.[58]

Setting aside naval petroleum reserves on paper was one thing. Constituting them as viable productive entities turned out to be quite another. All bona fide prior claims upon acreage within the designated NPRs were protected both by the withdrawal orders and the Pickett Act, and the navy found itself with quite a number of bedfellows in its two newly acquired reserves in California. There were not only the private location claims of prospectors under the Petroleum Placer Act, but also some claims of farm homesteaders and other nonmineral entrymen. Two sections of each township on the public lands were dedicated to the states in aid of public schools, and both NPRs #1 and #2 were checkerboarded with lands granted to the Southern Pacific Railroad Company in aid of construction. In the case of NPR #2, the federal government owned less than one-third of the acreage enclosed by its boundaries. Because the private holders were busily extracting all the oil they could under the Rule of Capture, the navy had no choice but

---

[53] Ibid., p. 39.

[54] Ibid., pp. 39-40.

[55] Ibid., pp. 40-41.

[56] Ibid., pp. 41-42.

[57] Ibid., pp. 46-47.

[58] Actually the so-called Act of June 4, 1920 was only a section of the act making appropriations for the naval service for the fiscal year ending June 30, 1921, Ch. 228 (41 Stat. 813-814), June 4, 1920.

to lease its own acreage for production to avoid drainage from the surrounding properties. NPR #2 thus never served as a "reserve for the future needs of the U.S. Navy," and the field is now in the stripper stage after having given up 600 million barrels of oil.

The navy had better luck with Elk Hills. Although exploration during 1910 and 1911 had revealed the presence of some oil and gas, the amounts discovered had been disappointing. It was not until 1919 that significant amounts of oil and gas were found in the Elk Hills by the Standard Oil Company of California, which had succeeded to the land-grant patents originally held by the Southern Pacific Railroad. The federal government was, moreover, able to upset the State of California's title to the two sections of school lands that were included in the reserve, as well as title to ten sections originally patented to the Southern Pacific Railroad, on the grounds that the grants were void because the company knew of their mineral content at the time it made its selections. A number of subsequent court tests, adjustments, and accessions left the federal government with ownership of about 80 percent of the acreage contained in the present boundaries of the reserve. The Standard Oil Company of California owns the remaining 20 percent.

The delay in the discovery of oil and gas, the government's extensive holdings, and the absence of a large number of other owners within the reserve made it possible for the navy to fairly successfully prevent the Elk Hills field from being depleted. As it happened, production had first been established on one of the "school" sections granted to the State of California, then patented to the Standard Oil Company of California, and ultimately acquired by the federal government after the nullification of the original grant. When the federal government shut down production on this section, some 5 million barrels of oil had been withdrawn by the previous claimants. Another more serious threat appeared on February 12, 1920, when Standard found oil on another "school" section in the adjoining township. This section lay outside the boundaries that had been established for the reserve.[59] Development proceeded rapidly, and just before his retirement, Secretary Daniels asked for bids for the drilling of twenty-two offset wells on a section inside the reserve immediately adjoining the one being developed by Standard to prevent drainage of oil underlying the reserve. The bids

---

[59] This section plus six others and parts of four more were incorporated into NPR #1 by executive orders of President Franklin Roosevelt on October 15 and November 13, 1942.

were not received until Harding had become President and the administration of the NPRs had been transferred to the Interior Department by his order.[60] In the course of the next eighteen months nine leases were made of NPR #1 lands by Secretary of Interior Fall, initially for the announced purpose of preventing drainage, but culminating, on December 11, 1922, in the leasing of the entire remaining government lands in NPR #1 to the Pan American Petroleum Company in consideration for Pan American's building and stocking fuel facilities for the navy at Pearl Harbor. A more relevant consideration that came to light a few months later was a suitcase full of money amounting to $100,000, which was conveyed to Secretary Fall from E. L. Doheny, chief executive officer of Pan American.

This and concurrent high jinks by which Fall, on April 7, 1922, leased the entire NPR #3 in Wyoming noncompetitively to the Mammoth Oil Company, an affiliate of Harry Sinclair's oil empire, undoubtedly did more to ensure the sanctity and integrity of the navy's petroleum reserves than any other single event that has occurred in their long history. The scandal broke early in 1923. The opposition politicians thundered and muckraking journalists had a field day. The avenging wrath of an outraged nation fell upon all who had had any connection with naval petroleum reserves, the wicked and the just alike. Everybody ran for cover, including the Standard Oil Company of California, whose pursuit of its discoveries on its own lands outside NPR #1 had started the whole thing. Standard's operation thereafter became a model of circumspection and restraint, and a "gentleman's agreement" with the government restricting production on the privately held portions of the Elk Hills field developed. This ripened into a formal contract in 1944 under which Standard unitized its properties with those of the navy. Under the Unit Plan Contract, Standard operated the NPR field for the navy subject to the navy's decision as to how much oil will be produced. The field was exploited to satisfy wartime oil requirements between

---

[60] Harding's Executive Order 3473 of May 31, 1921, was later voided by the lower federal court (United States v. Pan American Petroleum Company et al., U.S. District Court, May 28, 1925), to the extent that the executive order purported to confer on the secretary of interior authority that Congress had lodged with the secretary of the navy. But the executive order played a key role in the later history of the NPRs, chiefly because Secretary of Interior Fall relied on Harding's executive order for authority to lease naval petroleum reserves—the action that led to the Elk Hills-Teapot Dome scandal. Following the scandal, the administration of the NPRs was restored to the navy on March 17, 1925, by Executive Order 4614.

June 1944 and September 1945, when Congress revoked authority for production. After a phasing-out period, production was reduced to the minimum necessary for testing and maintaining the wells (about 2,000 to 3,000 barrels per day for the entire field). The maximum production level achieved during the war period was between 60,000 and 65,000 barrels a day.[61]

Since World War II and until new legislation authorizing production became law in 1976,[62] the Elk Hills field remained inactive. The old law[63] governing its operation specifies that the field will be operated only for (1) the protection, conservation, maintenance and testing of the reserves, or (2) the production of petroleum whenever and to the extent that the secretary of the navy, with the approval of the President, finds that it is needed for the national defense and the production is authorized by a joint resolution of the Congress. During the long period when there was a petroleum surplus on the West Coast, there was virtually no pressure to add to the supply by opening Elk Hills. The Nixon administration did, however, support such an attempt between 1969 and 1973 in an effort to buy its way out of thirty-five leases in Santa Barbara Channel which it felt constrained to suspend to placate the environmentalists in the aftermath of the Santa Barbara blowout (see Chapter 11).

By late 1973, the nation was in the grip of an oil shortage to which was added the rapid deterioration of the natural gas supply in Southern California. President Nixon asked Congress[64] for authority to produce oil from Elk Hills, indicating that production could reach 160,000 barrels per day in sixty days. Nixon also proposed that proceeds from the sale or exchange of navy Elk Hills oil be used to fund exploration of NPR #4 in Alaska.

The House Armed Services Committee chairman, F. Edward Hebert, Democrat of Louisiana, gave this new legislation no more

---

[61] U.S. Navy, "History of Naval Petroleum and Oil Shale Reserves," Washington, D.C., mimeographed, October 1, 1973, pp. 8-9.

[62] Under the Naval Petroleum Reserves Production Act of 1976, P.L. 94-258 (90 Stat. 303), signed by President Ford on April 5, 1976, naval petroleum reserve production up to 350,000 barrels a day was authorized. Because both the Justice Department Antitrust Division and the Congress always had been concerned with the production of Elk Hills by Standard Oil of California, which owns the pipeline system from Elk Hills and would want to use the oil in its refineries, the law assures that production is available to small refineries as well.

[63] Ch. 262 (58 Stat. 280), June 17, 1944.

[64] Office of the White House Press Secretary, President's Energy Message to Congress, November 8, 1973.

cordial a reception than he had given to previous overtures of the administration, and the proposal died in his committee with the expiration of the 93rd Congress.[65] The Ford administration renewed Nixon's request for legislation in January 1975.[66] The Ford bill's chances for passage were marginally better than those of the Nixon bill because of Hebert's unfrocking as Armed Services Committee chairman by the young Democratic caucus elected in the fall of 1974. The proposal, very similar to the law passed by Congress in April 1976, called for extracting 160,000 barrels a day from the field, with production rising to 350,000 barrels a day over about a two-year period. The rise in production would be made possible by additional drilling and the installation of additional handling and transport facilities. The armed forces would receive first claim on the production, with any amounts of oil not taken by the military to be made available to civilian markets. As in Nixon's proposal, the proceeds from the sale of production would finance further exploration and field development in Elk Hills, plus an extensive exploratory program for NPR #4 on the North Slope of Alaska.

The President laid out an extensive development program for Elk Hills that involved the drilling of 784 wells over a four-year period. Under normal circumstances this would have been carried out by the Standard Oil Company of California, the contract operator of the field for the navy. In view of the acute shortage of rigs, skilled crews, and supervisory forces, this new assignment was more than Standard was prepared to assume, however, and Standard served notice of its desire to terminate its contract with the navy. The Resource Sciences Company was hired as Standard's successor as contract operator of the field. A barrage of harassment by California politicians, as well as other difficulties between the navy and Standard, no doubt contributed to the company's decision to withdraw. The most significant of the friction points was Standard's discovery in late 1973 of a new field (Tule Elk) on a section outside of, but adjoined on three sides by, the reserve. Exploration within the reserve has determined that the Tule Elk field does in fact extend into the reserve and thus comes under the terms of the Unit

---

[65] Former Secretary of Defense Melvin Laird, and later counsellor to the President, made a special pilgrimage to Georgia to see retired House Armed Services Committee Chairman Carl Vinson. Laird hoped he could get Vinson's help to change Hebert's mind, but the retired chairman evidently felt that Elk Hills oil was for Defense Department use only.

[66] Office of the White House Press Secretary, State of the Union Message, January 15, 1975.

Plan Contract. The navy obtained an injunction[67] preventing Standard from pumping the wells on its portion of the Tule Elk reservoir pending an agreement between the navy and Standard as to disposition of the new reservoir, as provided by the Unit Plan Contract. The indications are that the Tule Elk reservoir is a large one, on the order of 300 million barrels, and its inclusion in the Elk Hills NPR would lift the latter's total reserves to more than 1.3 billion barrels.

NPR #3 (Teapot Dome) consists of an area of about 9,500 acres in east-central Wyoming, next to the prolific Salt Creek field. It is ironic that its name should have become the by-word for the scandalous misappropriation of public resources, for the property has proved to be virtually worthless as a source of petroleum. In retrospect, it is possible to believe that justice would have been better served had the federal government quietly stood aside and let the Mammoth Oil Company bankrupt itself drilling dry holes on its fraudulently acquired lease. The maximum production ever achieved was 3,700 barrels a day at the time the Mammoth lease was taken over by the receivers appointed by the federal court. By the time the receivership was closed, production had declined to 600 barrels a day—barely enough, as one of the receivers noted, to fuel one battleship during an afternoon of active maneuvers. Like NPR #2, NPR #3 never came close to functioning as an effective naval petroleum reserve. Its present producing capacity is estimated to be 1,000 barrels a day, which might be boosted to 5,000 barrels a day with additional drilling.

NPR #4 is of a different vintage and genre from the first three. Created on February 27, 1923,[68] by President Harding, it comprises a vast area of some 37,000 square miles on the North Slope of Alaska. Because of its isolation, NPR #4 was spared all the difficulties over divided land ownership that plagued NPRs #1 and #2. Because nobody else wanted it, there was almost no protest over the withdrawal of an area the size of Indiana in the vague hope that someday oil might be found on it and that some way would be found to bring the oil to market. Shortly after the creation of NPR #4, the navy asked the Geological Survey to survey and map the reserved area and to determine the geological facts necessary for guiding the Navy Department in its administration of the property. A surface investigation was made be-

[67] United States v. Standard Oil Company of California, U.S. District Court, February 14, 1974.
[68] Executive Order 3797-A.

245

tween 1923 and 1926, but the remoteness of the region and the memory of the Elk Hills-Teapot Dome scandals combined to extinguish all further interest in NPR #4 until the strains of World War II on the nation's petroleum supply stimulated the navy to begin a program of exploration in 1944. Exploration was discontinued in 1953 when a market surplus once more prevailed in the forty-eight states.

Although the petroleum possibilities of NPR #4 were in no way fully evaluated in the 1920s, much was learned about the geology of the area. Three oil fields and six gas fields were discovered, and enough gas was found in the Barrow area to provide a continuing source of fuel for the government installations at Point Barrow as well as for a number of native villages. None of the discoveries was sizable enough to be considered commercial, although the Umiat field was estimated to contain some 55 million barrels of recoverable oil. In addition to the drilling program carried out by a private contractor, some 67,000 miles of seismic surveys, 26,000 miles of gravimetric surveys, and 75,000 miles of airborne magnetometer surveys were made, and geological mapping was conducted on 21,000 square miles by the U.S. Geological Survey.[69] Despite all of these studies, the extent of the petroleum resources underlying NPR #4 is not known; estimates range between 10 billion and 33 billion barrels of oil and 60 to 192 trillion cubic feet of natural gas. The Oil Task Force of Project Independence Blueprint credited NPR #4 with the potential of producing as much as 2 million barrels of oil a day.[70]

But from the beginning, the navy and its congressional committees have insisted that there is a positive benefit to the nation in preserving crude oil in the ground in readiness specifically for the navy's use in the event of war. The experience of World War II and the subsequent unification of the armed forces have broadened this concept to include the army and the air force. The insistence that the nation should maintain oil fields dedicated exclusively to the use of the fighting forces in wartime has frustrated all attempts to put these resources to more rational use.

One has to understand the navy's way of doing things to appreciate its position on its historic petroleum reserves. Even before there was an American navy, the Royal Navy of Great Britain had found it neces-

---

[69] U.S. Navy, "History of Naval Petroleum and Oil Shale Reserves," pp. 12-14.
[70] Federal Energy Administration, *Project Independence Report* (Washington, D.C.: U.S. Government Printing Office, November 1974), p. 82.

sary to reserve certain forests for its exclusive use for ships' timbers and masts. At the time, the best forests of England were being depleted by the ironmasters of Birmingham and Sheffield in their scramble for charcoal, and the navy had to secure a way of providing for its needs. The expansion of farms and the depletion of timber also concerned the new American navy. There seemed to be a certain wisdom in establishing a navy forest reserve close by the Atlantic Coast that would ensure a supply of good timber for the navy's use against the time when the forests of the Atlantic coastal plain would all be cut down by homesteaders. In the first act of the new government concerning the nation's forests, Congress in 1799 appropriated $200,000 for the purchase of timberlands for the exclusive use of the navy.[71] A stand of live oak on two islands off the Georgia coast became the first naval forest reserve. Later reserves of oak and cedar in Florida, Alabama, Mississippi, and Louisiana were acquired by the navy. With a declining measure of success (because of poachers and settlers), the government maintained timber reserves for the navy until after the end of the Civil War. In the meantime the navy acquired facilities for building its own ships and making its own rope, clothing, and guns. When the airplane became an item of military interest, the navy built an aircraft factory in Philadelphia, with a congressional mandate that 10 percent of all aircraft owned by the navy should be built there. The Naval Aircraft Factory was still laboring valiantly to discharge its mission as late as World War II, when it succeeded, through a monumental four-year effort, in turning out 164 flying boats copied from the design of the Consolidated PBY. One by one, however, these monuments to autarky have all fallen by the way, except for a modest amount of shipbuilding still done in navy yards. When nuclear power came to the navy, no one suggested the need for establishing naval uranium reserves to serve the nuclear fleet.

At the time when it became apparent that oil was going to be the fuel of the future fleet, however, it was still entirely natural that the navy should embrace the necessity for its very own oil fields. In 1910, the navy's use of oil for power was almost unique. The automobile was still a rich man's toy; airplanes were stick-and-wire curiosities; railroads, factories, homes, utilities, and commercial establishments burned coal almost exclusively. Oil supplied 6 percent of the nation's energy, and

---

[71] An Act Authorizing the Purchase of Timber for Naval Purposes, Ch. 16 (1 Stat. 622), February 25, 1799.

nobody thought any great amount of it would ever be found. The outlook was one of continuing, perhaps even worsening, scarcity of oil, and prudence demanded that supplies be set aside for purposes crucial to the nation's existence. It would not do for the United States Navy to forfeit the advantage it had in using liquid fuels for its combat ships.

As usual, the course of events was not what had been expected. Immense quantities of oil were found, not only in the United States but all over the world. Oil became the principal fuel of every modern industrial nation. Oil powered not only the navy's ships, but every other form of mechanized transport. The navy soon lost its unique position as the nation's prime consumer of petroleum products and became simply another claimant, among many millions, upon the resources of the nation's versatile, ubiquitous petroleum industry. In two world wars and numerous other shooting engagements, the navy's petroleum needs were dependably supplied by this industry, on whose output the armed forces could and did exercise a preemptive claim, to ensure that their needs would be met. But the rationale for a separate war reserve of crude petroleum, locked in the ground on the remote North Slope of Alaska, for the exclusive use of the navy or the armed forces, has long since disappeared. In the author's opinion, the proponents of this concept would perform a valuable service to the nation by doing the same.

In the fall of 1974, the Department of the Interior tried to do away with the naval reserve concept, with only partial success. It was always the tactical position under Nixon, and at first under Ford, that, although it would be immensely more efficient economically to lease NPR #4 in Alaska than to continue a limited navy exploration program, leasing NPR #4 was a hopeless course, given the inflexibility of the members of the Armed Services committees on this question. As a result, the Nixon administration, hoping to gain congressional approval to mitigate the near-term petroleum shortages by producing oil from Elk Hills, had never asked for the authority to develop NPR #4. The administration reasoned that asking the Armed Services committees to lease NPR #4 would so anger the members that there would be no action on the short-term problem of pumping Elk Hills. A bird in the hand, it thought, was worth two in the bush. But, as the administration assessed its chances of discovering major oil deposits before 1985, it realized that the largest potential lay on the outer continental shelf and in NPR #4. As we have seen, it was estimated that as much as 2 million barrels of oil per day might be produced from NPR #4.

Once he had been made "energy czar"—officially, chairman of the Energy Resource Council—Secretary Morton had the power to bring the navy to heel, or almost. The issue of the development of NPR #4 could be brought before the President in the proper forum of the council. Under the law, the secretary of the navy had the authority to explore and develop naval petroleum reserves but he could not produce oil from them unless three conditions were met: (1) the secretary of the navy found that production was required for the national defense, (2) his findings were approved by the President, and (3) petroleum production was authorized by a joint resolution of Congress. In 1973, following the Arab boycott, the secretary of the navy found that production was required and President Nixon approved it, but Congress failed to act. However, it did appropriate in FY 1974, 1975 and 1976 funds for the exploration of Elk Hills and NPR #4.

The Navy and Interior departments brought competing plans for the development of NPR #4 to the President. The navy's plan proposed to continue a federal exploration program, deferring a decision on whether and how to develop NPR #4 until the petroleum reserves had been delineated. The Interior Department's plan proposed legislation for commercial leasing, in the belief that production could be brought on line much more quickly by the private sector than through a government exploration program. The navy planned a seven-year exploration program with two wells and 2,500 line-miles of seismic work in FY 1975 and an additional 6,400 line-miles of seismic work and twenty-four wells over the next six years. The costs were estimated at about $45 million for seismic work and about $333 million for the twenty-six wells. A development plan would be drawn up only after it had been proved that the reserves were sufficiently large to support a commercial agreement that would provide a fair profit to the lease holder after he had recovered not only the cost of production but also the cost of leaving a substantial reserve in the ground. The income from each area developed would be applied to the cost of exploring additional areas. The navy estimated that within three years, but perhaps in as little as one and one-half years, sufficient proved reserves would have been discovered so that a commercial development plan could be established.

The Department of Interior, the Federal Energy Administration, and the Office of Management and Budget felt that the navy should pursue its exploration plan, because any exploration plan was better than none until Congress acted. Interior was also willing to let the navy run the commercial leasing program, hoping to placate the Armed Services committees and to demonstrate to the President that Interior's basic concern was not to build a bureaucratic empire but to find oil as quickly and efficiently as possible. This, however, would probably mean some duplication of capability for the navy, even if it contracted part of the leasing management program to Interior.

Three meetings between Interior Secretary Morton and Defense Secretary James Schlesinger failed to resolve the impasse. Their final meeting was held at the White House in the Roosevelt Room, across the hall from the Oval Office, in one last attempt at least to sharpen their arguments and reduce their differences to a minimum before presenting them to President Ford.

First of all, the Interior Department felt that the navy did not understand the underlying strategy of oil exploration. It was probable, Interior believed, that twenty-six exploratory wells, covering an expanse of such magnitude and drilled over a seven-year period, would be unable to delineate commercial production. As the North Sea and other exploration experiences had shown (see Chapter 11), numerous wells were often necessary before a discovery was made or its real commercial possibilities assessed. Given this probability, it became likely that Congress's eagerness to appropriate funds would languish as the explorations dragged on. Also, the navy program would establish its exploration strategy by committee consensus. The chances of finding oil and natural gas would be less than if the area were leased to several commercial companies exploring different tracts with different exploration strategies.

The Interior Department stressed that the costs to the federal government would be much lower if NPR #4 were leased for commercial exploration. The seven-year navy program would cost the taxpayers an estimated $378 million. The Interior Department estimated its preleasing costs for the environmental impact statements, resource fair-market evaluation, and other lease-management functions at only $25 million. It also estimated that bonus bids of about $11 billion would go to the federal government and, assuming $11 per barrel of oil and 2 million barrels of production per day at 16.66 percent royalty, that the royalty revenues would be about $1.3 billion annually beginning in 1985.

But the navy and many members of Congress argued that a commercial leasing program was a "giveaway." The federal government would receive "only" an estimated $20 to $30 billion in bids and royalties over the producing life of NPR #4, but estimated reserves of

30 billion barrels of oil worth at, say, $10 per barrel would eventually give the oil companies about $300 billion, as well as earnings on unknown quantities of natural gas. This appealing rationale, of course, was based on the assumption that the oil was there, when in fact nobody knew for sure. It also implied the policy that the taxpayers, not the oil companies, should assume the risk of the very significant exploration costs, a fact that advocates of a federally contracted exploration program never chose to emphasize. The overall exploration program to develop NPR #4 could cost anywhere from $7 to $15 billion. Even if Congress were willing to sustain appropriations over a ten-year period, this amount would be a significant contribution to an already large budget deficit. Finally, the navy plan did not focus on the cost of delivering oil from the North Slope of Alaska to the forty-eight state markets or, for that matter, even to their ships. The cost of the delivery system—a second 2-million-barrel-a-day pipeline parallel to the Alaska pipeline, coupled with a tanker delivery system to the West Coast—was estimated at $7 to $10 billion. The navy wanted spare capacity built into the line to be used in event of a national emergency. This would probably raise the cost to $12 billion. It was not only uneconomical to store excess petroleum capacity in a reserve so far from the nation's industrial markets and military centers, it also seemed militarily unsound to have the reserve at the end of a supply line thousands of miles from the heartland of the nation.

President Ford agreed that the most efficient approach would be commercial leasing. However, he accepted Secretary Schlesinger's political assessment that the Armed Services committees would not agree to that solution. He decided to take the matter one step at a time. In his January 1975 state of the union address [72] he asked Congress to grant authority to explore, develop, and most significantly, produce oil from NPR #4, and to give the President, as a first step, the discretion to determine the optimum approach. This left open the possibility that once a law was passed, the President would direct the navy to substitute a commercial leasing program for the federally operated exploration program with all its built-in shortcomings. The administration's legislation earmarked 15 to 20 percent of the production for military needs and strategic reserve. This share would be used to help finance a strategic storage system, and the balance of the receipts would go to the Treasury.

---

[72] Office of the White House Press Secretary, State of the Union, January 15, 1975.

Finally, in April 1976, Congress acted, or at least moved the ball down the field a few yards. In addition to creating a national strategic reserve partially to offset the impact of any emergency comparable to the Arab embargo of 1973 and 1974, Congress compromised on the jurisdictional dispute between the navy and the Armed Services committees on one side and the Interior Department and the Interior and Insular Affairs committees on the other. The navy retained control over NPR #1, Elk Hills, NPR #2, Buena Vista, and NPR #3, Teapot Dome, and the Department of Interior was designated the manager of NPR #4 on the North Slope of Alaska. The navy was authorized to produce oil from the three reserves under its jurisdiction at a maximum efficiency rate of about 350,000 barrels a day. That was not a large amount of oil, but under the circumstances the nation needed to be grateful for "every drop." On the key provision on NPR #4, however, the Interior Department, instead of being allowed to lease NPR #4 commercially, was directed to study the best method of producing and transporting NPR #4 oil (if in fact it exists in commercial quantities) and to report its findings to Congress before any further action could be taken.

In the author's opinion, for the reasons already cited, the Interior Department should recommend commercial leasing on NPR #4. However, since probably two years will already be lost by the time the Interior Department makes a recommendation (assuming it proposes leasing) and Congress decides to approve this recommendation (assuming it does), Congress was well advised to require under the new law that we start now on a feasibility study of means of transporting NPR #4 oil to the forty-eight states. Even if NPR #4 were leased now, production could not begin for a number of years. The lessees would undoubtedly begin serious work on a delivery system only when they were satisfied that the proven reserves were large enough to justify the capital costs, estimated at $7 to $10 billion, of building a pipeline, either across Canada or parallel to the Alaskan pipeline, and an ocean tanker delivery system to West Coast ports. A long delay is inevitable, but it can be minimized if a transportation feasibility study and environmental analysis are begun now—at public expense.

Congress has taken some much-needed action on the matter of petroleum reserves. Nevertheless, in the author's view, the strategy Congress has chosen for the development of NPR #4—perhaps the brightest petroleum exploration prospect, together with the offshore areas adjacent to Prudhoe Bay, in the entire United States—sets us on the slower road to petroleum self-sufficiency. If significant amounts of oil are in fact present at NPR #4 and the area is not commercially leased, there is a good chance, given the exploration record in other petroleum provinces of the world, that it might take a decade to make the key discovery, even if one assumes that Congress will hang in there for the long pull, appropriating huge sums of the public's money year after year without any sign of hitting oil. If, on the other hand, the federally contracted consensus-exploration strategy is lucky enough to find oil quickly, a hesitant Congress and a ponderous bureaucracy will collectively scratch their heads trying to decide what to do next, both institutions unable to cope with the high financial risks and quick decision making essential to a well-run privately operated petroleum development program.

Geothermal Energy

In 1847, about ninety miles north of San Francisco, explorer-surveyor William Elliott, hiking through what is now northwestern Sonoma County, was startled to see puffs of white steam coming from a hillside. He had discovered "The Geysers," which is today the only commercial geothermal development in the United States and the largest in the world.[73]

Geothermal energy is the natural heat of the earth. There are three kinds of geothermal systems: (1) "Hot spot" systems consist of either a vapor or a hot water system; steam or hot water moves through fractures in heated rock, appearing on the surface often in the form of geysers or fumaroles. Of the three types of geothermal system, this is the most promising for commercial development. (2) Geopressured brine systems, buried deep in the sediments along the Louisiana coast and off the Texas shore, consist of highly porous sands saturated with brines at high temperatures and pressures. The commercial development of these systems will probably not be undertaken for some years. (3) Hot dry rock systems are rocks heated by their proximity to a heat source such as a magma chamber. In their exploitation, wells are drilled and water introduced. The water flows down one well and through the rock, from which it picks up heat; as the water expands, it is forced up

---

[73] Pacific Gas and Electric's Geysers complex produces 502,000 kilowatts of electricity from eleven generators, slightly less than enough electricity to supply a city the size of San Francisco.

the second well. This type of system, too, will probably not produce commercial electric power for a long time.

The federal government has become involved in geothermal energy largely because there is so much potential for geothermal development on the public lands. About 98 million acres of land in the western states are thought to have some potential for geothermal development. Of this total, about 3 million acres have been classified by the Geological Survey as "known geothermal resources areas" (KGRAs),[74] and 55 percent of these are public lands. Of the remaining 95 million acres believed to have some potential, about 61 percent are public lands.[75]

In November 1966, President Johnson pocket vetoed a geothermal leasing bill. He gave six reasons for his decision.[76]

(1) The bill automatically granted "grandfather rights," meaning that holders of mineral or mining leases as of September 7, 1965, would be entitled to convert them into geothermal leases. In other words, there was no opportunity for competitive bidding to determine ownership.

(2) The maximum lease size permitted by the bill was 51,200 acres in any one state, which was much larger than a unit had to be to be economical. Johnson called this "monopolizing the geothermal resources of entire states."

(3) Royalties were payable only on steam "sold or utilized" but developers were not required to pay royalties on steam they wasted.

(4) The bill did not allow for adjustments in lease terms over time.

(5) The bill provided a perpetual lease to the developer as long as he produced steam in commercial quantities.

(6) The bill gave the developer twenty years to begin production, which was too long a period to encourage expeditious development of the resource. Instead, it encouraged speculation.

Harry McPherson, special counsel to President Johnson, in his memoirs quoted his memorandum to the President on the subject. He called this "a bad bill," adding, "I believe you should veto it. . . . Interior is for signing primarily because the bill does provide a way to get geothermal steam development going. In my opinion Interior has

[74] Department of Interior, Geological Survey, Office of the Area Geothermal Supervisor, "Monthly Geothermal Report," mimeographed, December 1975.

[75] Department of the Interior, "Final Environmental Statement for the Geothermal Leasing Program," mimeographed, vol. 1 (1973), p. II-16.

[76] Office of the White House Press Secretary, "Memorandum of Disapproval on S. 1674, The Geothermal Steam Act of 1966," November 14, 1966.

folded after being beaten down on every issue of consequence. This matter has been before Congress for four years. It can wait another year." [77]

In fact it would have to wait four years. In December 1970, a new geothermal leasing bill, sponsored, like the vetoed bill, by Senator Alan Bible, Democrat of Nevada, passed Congress just before the Christmas adjournment. OMB, supported by Treasury, adamantly opposed this bill, and Interior and the Council of Economic Advisers favored it—along with Ehrlichman and the author. President Nixon signed it on Christmas Eve 1970.[78] The key issues were:

(1) OMB objected only that KGRAs would be under a competitive bid system, since this meant that millions of acres could be leased on a first-come, first-served basis. But the President accepted the argument that an infant industry with an untried technology should be encouraged to develop through prospecting and "wildcatting."

(2) The Interior Department could not collect royalties on steam of more than 15 percent or less than 10 percent during the first thirty-five years of production or more than 22.5 percent during lease extensions. OMB in particular, knowing as little as it did about the extent and potential uses of geothermal resources, felt that the federal government should not limit the amount of the royalty it could charge. However, Nixon viewed the glass of water as half full, not half empty. Royalties should be reasonably low, he believed, to encourage industry in the early stages. With all the technological difficulties, the chances of a windfall profit seemed remote, and Nixon felt that strong incentives were needed.

(3) The "grandfather" rights provision was still bothersome, though it had been improved. Under the new bill a person wishing to convert a mineral lease or mining claim into a geothermal lease in a known geothermal resources area had to match the highest bid. There was concern that few people would be likely to go to the trouble of offering sealed bids if they knew a "grandfather" could meet their bids. Still, Congress had come a long way from the provision it had endorsed in the bill President Johnson vetoed, giving the "grandfather" the rights even without his meeting the highest bid. Under the new bill during

---

[77] Harry McPherson, *A Political Education* (Boston, Mass.: Little, Brown and Company, 1972), pp. 274 and 276.
[78] The Geothermal Steam Act of 1970, P.L. 91-581 (84 Stat. 1565), December 24, 1970.

Table 13

ESTIMATED POTENTIAL FOR GEOTHERMAL ELECTRIC POWER PRODUCTION IN 1985

(in megawatts)

Source of Estimate		Estimate for 1985
Walter J. Hickel		132,000
Geothermal Energy Coordination and Management Project, ERDA		30,000
Carel Otte, Union Oil, Chairman, Geothermal Industry Liaison Group		20,000
National Plan for Energy Research, Development and Demonstration, ERDA		10,000–15,000
National Petroleum Council	High Assumption	19,000
	Low Assumption	3,500
Project Independence	High Assumption	7,000–15,000
	Low Assumption	4,000– 6,000

Source: In order of appearance in table: Walter J. Hickel, *Geothermal Energy, A Special Report,* University of Alaska, 1972; Energy Research and Development Administration, *Second Interim Report, Geothermal Energy Coordination and Management Project,* January 31, 1975; Carel Otte, "Statement on Geothermal Energy," *Congressional Record,* vol. 121, no. 162 (November 4, 1975), p. S 19121; Energy Research and Development Administration, *National Plan for Energy Research Development and Demonstration: Creating Energy Choices for the Future,* vol. 2, July 1975; National Petroleum Council, *U.S. Energy Outlook,* 1972; Federal Energy Administration, *Project Independence,* November 1974.

1974 slightly over $1.6 million accrued from the lease of grandfather tracts. This was 2.2 times the bids offered by the "grandfathers," which indicated the values received in all these cases were reasonable, since several bidders participated in the sales.

(4) Congress had cut the maximum amount of land a lessee could hold in any one state from 51,200 to 20,480 acres. This tended to reduce the chances of a monopoly industry's emerging.

(5) Royalties covered not only steam or any form of heat energy "sold or utilized," but also, under the new bill, "steam susceptible to sale or utilization."

(6) The possibility of a national energy shortage was beginning to be understood, and whatever encouragement could be given to the development of alternate energy sources seemed to be sound policy.

Geothermal sources may make a minimal contribution to the nation's energy supply. But estimates of the 1985 production of geothermal electric power vary widely (see Table 13). The lowest estimates generally are based upon the assumption that existing technology will be used and relatively few fields developed. High figures, on the other hand, are based on the assumption that significant technological breakthroughs will be made. Should the high estimates prove to be accurate, geothermal energy will be making a significant contribution by 1985. ERDA's estimate of 30,000 megawatts, for example, corresponds to a saving of approximately 1 million barrels of oil per day.

To give financial encouragement to this infant energy industry Congress in 1974 authorized appropriations of $50 million in loan guarantees for the acquisition of geothermal resources and the development of facilities for both demonstration and commercial production of geothermal energy. The loan guarantees were limited to $25 million for any single loan, with a $50 million limit on any one borrower.[79] With the benefit of hindsight, it appears that the fair-market value is being received for leases of geothermal public lands. As of December 1975, bonuses ranged from $1.00 to $3,288 per acre. Competitive bidding in KGRAs fairly well ensures a fair-market-value return to the Treasury. For example, bids on two tracts at the Geysers KGRA in California were rejected and in a later sale the same two tracts were sold for $1,793,861 more than the highest bids rejected in the first round.[80] As of December 1975, 548 geothermal leases covering 983,645 acres of public land and four covering 286,180 acres of Indian land had been issued.[81] Two observation holes had been drilled and nine wells had been determined to be producible. Of these, five were suspended, three were drilling, and one was abandoned.

[79] Geothermal Energy Research, Development and Demonstration Act of 1974, P.L. 93-410 (88 Stat. 1079), September 3, 1974.

[80] Bids in Geyser Tracts #7 and #9 were rejected on sales held January 22, and accepted on May 29, 1974.

[81] Department of Interior, Geological Survey, Office of the Area Geothermal Supervisor, Monthly Geothermal Report, December 1975.

11

Offshore Oil, Superports, and the Environment

The History of Offshore Oil

As long ago as 1896, oil derricks were inching their way out along wooden-finger piers on the Pacific Coast as the Summerland field was being extended seaward. These wells, which stood in a few feet of water in the Santa Barbara Channel,[1] were technically "offshore." A number of other Southern California oil fields showed similar disregard for the coastline, including two of the nation's largest, Huntington Beach and Wilmington, whose jutting piers with tanks and derricks were a familiar sight to anyone living in the Los Angeles area in the 1920s.

But it was not until 1938 that the first free-standing well, drilled in twenty-six feet of water, was completed. By the end of 1946, nine wells had been drilled in near-shore shallow waters off Louisiana and Texas. The next year, a discovery was made twelve miles off the coast of Louisiana. This was the first well located out of sight of land and, even more significant, the first to use a mobile platform—a breakthrough in technology that was to be employed successfully to drill over 18,000 wells in U.S. waters.[2]

---

[1] In the Santa Barbara Channel, seven exploratory wells have been drilled in water more than 1,200 feet deep. Nearly all large U.S. oil companies are developing deepwater drilling technology. About 275,000 acres of the outer continental shelf (OCS) were under lease in U.S. waters deeper than 650 feet. Shell Oil planned two production platforms in more than 1,000 feet of water, developing the Cognac field in the Gulf of Mexico. A group led by Shell and Amoco drilled in 900 to 1,150 feet of water off Louisiana in 1975. A wildcat drilled off Gabon in 1974 in 2,150 feet of water is the current record holder. "Oilmen Tackle Technology, High Cost of Deep Waters," *Oil and Gas Journal,* April 7, 1975, p. 40.

[2] More than 18,000 wells have been drilled in U.S. waters of which more than 12,605 wells are located in waters under federal jurisdiction. See *Leasing and*

One hardly need ask the question, when drillers find oil in the ocean, can lawyers be far behind? The advent of offshore drilling set off bitter and long controversy between the states and the federal government over the ownership of the resources of the continental shelf.

As early as 1937 attempts were made to pass legislation asserting federal ownership of the seabeds beyond the low-water mark,[3] where California and later Louisiana and Texas had begun to lease rights for oil and gas exploration. As World War II was ending, the federal government brought suits against California, Louisiana, and Texas to establish title to the resources of the continental shelf adjacent to those states.[4] The suits were still pending in September 1945 when President Truman, proclaiming that the entire continental shelf was a federal responsibility,[5] issued an executive order placing the resources on the shelf under the secretary of the interior.[6] Notwithstanding the pending litigation and the Truman proclamation, the states continued their leasing. By the end of 1946 Louisiana had more than 675,000 acres under lease, and several companies were actively prospecting for petroleum.

The Supreme Court ruled on the California case in 1947, denying to California any entitlement to lands beyond the low-water mark and awarding full dominion to the federal government out to a distance of three geographic miles from the coastline.[7] Texas and Louisiana continued to lease until the Supreme Court enjoined them from doing so in 1950.[8] At about the same time the solicitor of the Department of Interior came to the conclusion that the Mineral Leasing Act of 1920 did not apply to the continental shelf, and therefore contained no authority permitting the Department of Interior to grant leases there.[9] Meanwhile, Congress was unable to muster support for legislation to confer this authority on the Department of Interior. By the end of 1950, leasing on the continental shelf was dead in the water.

This had about the same effect as tying down the safety valve on a

Management of Energy Resources on the Outer Continental Shelf, U.S. Geological INF-74-33 (Washington, D.C.: U.S. Government Printing Office, 1976), pp. 7 and 8.

[3] S.J. Res. 208, 75th Congress, 2nd sess. (1938).

[4] United States v. California, 332 U.S. 19 (1947); United States v. Texas, 339 U.S. 707 (1950); United States v. Louisiana, 339 U.S. 699 (1950).

[5] Proclamation No. 2667, September 28, 1945 (59 Stat. 884).

[6] Executive Order No. 9633.

[7] United States v. California, 332 U.S. 19 (1947); see also S. Res. No. 133, 83rd Congress, 1st sess. (1953).

[8] United States v. Texas; United States v. Louisiana.

[9] Solicitor's Opinion, M-34985, 60 I.D. 26 (1947).

boiler. The leases granted by Louisiana between 1945 and 1950 had resulted in the discovery of some immense fields. In fact, five of the nine largest fields that have ever been discovered off Louisiana were found during this period. But further exploitation of the promising new province had to await a political decision that would clear the log-jam preventing further leasing. The wait lasted three years and involved, among other things, a national referendum. The misnamed "tidelands" ownership issue became a major battleground in the presidential campaign of 1952, during which General Dwight D. Eisenhower pledged to restore to the coastal states the entitlements they had lost a few years before. The pledge was redeemed by the Submerged Lands Act of 1953.[10] This act established the seaward boundaries of the coastal states at three geographic miles from their coastlines, and gave each of the states bordering the Gulf of Mexico the opportunity to prove further entitlement out to three marine leagues, or nine miles, by proving that its boundary had extended beyond three miles from its coast when it came into the union, or that such a boundary was subsequently approved by Congress. After extended litigation, Florida (along the Gulf of Mexico side) and Texas were able to establish claim to the nine-mile limit.[11] Louisiana, Mississippi, and Alabama could not.[12]

The second landmark piece of legislation dealing with the continental shelf was the Outer Continental Shelf Lands Act, which became law in August 1953.[13] This act gave the federal government jurisdiction over the lands lying seaward of those awarded to the coastal states by the Submerged Lands Act. Because of its position relative to the state-held portion of the shelf, the federally controlled part of the seabed was designated the outer continental shelf (OCS). This term is a creation of law and has nothing to do with the topography of the ocean bottom. It merely denotes the part of the continental shelf that is administered and controlled by the federal government. The OCS Lands Act, which gave the secretary of the interior authority to lease the federal portion of the shelf, is the charter for all the federal leasing activity on the OCS that has taken place since the first sale in 1954.

The two statutes were hardly on the books before the dispute over their application erupted into litigation that continues to this moment.

---

[10] Ch. 65 (67 Stat. 29), May 22, 1953.
[11] United States v. Florida, 363 U.S. 121 (1960).
[12] United States v. Louisiana, 363 U.S. 1 (1960).
[13] Ch. 345 (67 Stat. 462), August 7, 1953.

It was charged that the Submerged Lands Act was unconstitutional—"an unwarranted and invalid attempt to abdicate the sovereignty of the United States to a few of the States" and a violation of the trust under which all lands beneath the marginal sea are held by the United States for the benefit of all the people, not just of those who reside in the adjacent states.[14] These challenges failed.

There were other disputes between the federal government and the states over just what constituted state coastlines. In many cases the coastlines were not fixed with certainty, and the question was further clouded by conflicting criteria for designating such coastal features as "historic bays" and inland waters, whose subsoil belonged to the coastal states under the Submerged Lands Act. The problem was nowhere so acute as it was in the Louisiana marshlands, where the land is so deeply indented with bays and bayous, and sinks into the sea so gradually, that it is impossible in some areas to tell by visual inspection where the shoreline is. This amphibious ambiguity produced an astonishing difference of opinion between the state of Louisiana and the federal government about the location of Louisiana's coastline. The state seized upon a "line" established off its coast by the U.S. Coast Guard for the purposes of defining the limits of inland waters for navigational purposes. In some instances this line was as much as forty miles offshore. In 1954, Louisiana enacted a law specifying that the so-called Coast Guard Line was the state's coastline and establishing the state boundary three leagues seaward of this line.[15] The federal government contended that the Louisiana boundary lay no more than three miles seaward of a constructed line along the shore named for once Under Secretary of the Interior Oscar Chapman. The area between the two claimed boundaries remained in dispute until 1969, when the Supreme Court rejected the Coast Guard Line as Louisiana's coastline for purposes of measuring the state's entitlement to submerged lands in the Gulf of Mexico.[16]

An earlier case, decided in 1960, had already voided the state's claim to any part of the seabed beyond three miles from its coastline, wherever that was.[17] The Chapman line was not, and was never intended to be, the legally established coastline of Louisiana. The Court thereupon referred the matter of determining the Louisiana coastline to a

---

[14] Arkansas v. McKay, Civil No. 53-3109 (D.D.C. 1953).
[15] Louisiana Act No. 33 of 1954; 49 La. R.S. 3.
[16] United States v. Louisiana, 394 U.S. 11 (1969).
[17] United States v. Louisiana, 363 U.S. 1 (1960).

special master. The special master filed his report with the Court in February 1975.[18] *Sic tempus transit.* On March 17, 1975, the Supreme Court adopted the special master's recommendation and ordered preparation of a decree establishing a base line.[19]

The significant aspect of this encounter between the state of Louisiana and the federal government, however, is not the protracted litigation or the related posturing and parrying of state and federal officials, but the fact that the parties could agree to disagree and thus permit the essential business of development to go forward. In 1956, the state of Louisiana and the Department of Interior entered into an interim agreement under which Interior would lease and manage the acreage in the disputed zones, with all income from these leases to go into an escrow fund pending a final disposition of the lands in dispute.[20] The interim agreement worked well, in no way interfering with petroleum operations on the continental shelf off Louisiana. It remained in effect, along with the escrow fund, and would so continue until final settlement of the Louisiana boundary issue could be made.

On March 17, 1975, the Supreme Court rendered its decision against a group of Atlantic coastal states that had asserted claims to the seabed extending in some instances as far as eighty miles into the Atlantic Ocean, based on their colonial charter grants from the English Crown.[21] This decision fixed the boundaries of these states at the traditional three miles from their coastlines, and removed a legalistic obstruction to federal leasing of the OCS in the Atlantic. Thus, step by slow step, the legal issues in the ownership of the OCS were being resolved.

Under Presidents Truman and Eisenhower the battle had been one of state versus federal ownership. Under Presidents Kennedy and Johnson OCS exploration had proceeded smoothly, but slowly. Only a small percentage of the potential OCS acreage had been leased by the mid-1960s. In the late Johnson years, and at a much accelerated pace under Nixon and Ford, development of the OCS was encouraged in an attempt to stem the flow of oil imports and move the nation toward petroleum self-sufficiency. But in January 1969, when Nixon came to the White House, no one could have foreseen what a volatile issue offshore oil development would become.

---

[18] Armstrong, Report of the Special Master, March 1974.
[19] United States v. Louisiana, 43 U.S.L.W. 4363.
[20] See generally Outer Continental Shelf Lands Act of 1953.
[21] United States v. Maine, 43 U.S.L.W. 4359 (March 17, 1975).

The Santa Barbara Blowout

On January 28, 1969, only eight days after Nixon took office, crude oil from a Union Oil Company well located in Santa Barbara Channel began to leak from the sea floor and collect in a large oil slick, which floated to the shore. Instantly it converted the beachfront into a disaster area, trapping thousands of sea birds in a gooey, black mess. Many of the birds died, but not before presenting the nation with some of the most pathetic sights ever beamed to the antennae of 80 million television sets. People were sickened by the sight of a lone bird floundering in the glop on the beach—terrified, helpless, and doomed.

The Santa Barbara incident was comparable to tossing a match into a gasoline tank: it exploded into the environmental revolution, and the press fanned the flames to keep the issue burning brightly. Writing three years later, James Keogh reviewed the negative treatment that Union Oil's president, Fred Hartley, had received from the press and called attention to the unfortunate tendency of the press to run in a pack: "The environment was one of those issues on which the good guys and the bad guys were stereotyped in lead and frozen on the screen. Reporters, writers, and editors went on automatic pilot when they saw the pattern: pollution, oil company boss, loves profits, hates birds." [22] First, the *New York Times* directly quoted Hartley: "I'm amazed at the publicity for the loss of a few birds." [23] That night, David Brinkley picked up the *Times*' quote and added: "A few more remarks like that and Mr. Hartley could never be confirmed as Secretary of Interior." [24] The next day, the *Wall Street Journal* headlined a story: "Union Oil Acts to Calm Uproar over Pollution, but Boss Doesn't Help. Hartley's Shrugging Off of Bird Losses Angers Californians." [25] The Sunday Review Section of the *New York Times* stated: "Alarm over the situation was hardly abated by the testimony of the President of Union Oil." [26]

---

[22] James Keogh, *President Nixon and the Press* (New York, N.Y.: Funk and Wagnalls, 1972), p. 88.

[23] *New York Times,* February 6, 1969, p. 19.

[24] NBC Evening News, February 6, 1969. Brinkley's quip referred to Hickel's difficulties obtaining Senate confirmation a few days earlier for the controversy he set off by his offhand remark, that he didn't support conservation merely for conservation's sake.

[25] *Wall Street Journal,* February 7, 1969, p. 1.

[26] *New York Times,* Sunday Review Section, February 9, 1969.

Then, as Keogh pointed out:

> On February 14th, the *Washington Post,* whose staff had read both the *Times* and the *Wall Street Journal* and had seen Brinkley, printed an angry editorial headlined "The Loss of a Few Birds." The editorial said the tendency to exonerate the industry had been strong until Hartley weighed in with his view of what it meant to unleash an oil slick the size of Rhode Island off the coast of California. The *Post* bitterly condemned Hartley for sheer insensitivity, blind, and arrogant.[27]

Finally, picking up the original *New York Times* quote of February 6, which Brinkley had featured the same night, the *Wall Street Journal* had used on February 9, and the *Washington Post* had editorialized about on February 14, *Time* magazine called Hartley a "blunt, short-tempered executive." [28]

The trouble is, Hartley never said what the *New York Times* quoted him as saying, nor what Brinkley, the *Washington Post,* and the *Wall Street Journal* used as the basis for their stories, nor what *Time* magazine attributed to him. Here is what Hartley actually said on February 5, at a hearing before the Senate Public Works Committee on air and water pollution:

> I think we have to look at these problems relatively. I am always tremendously impressed at the publicity that the death of birds received versus the loss of people in our country in this day and age. When I think of the folks that gave up their lives when they came down into the ocean [in an airliner crash] off Los Angeles some three weeks ago, and the fact that our society forgets about that within a 24-hour period, I think relative to that, the fact that we have had no loss of life from this incident [the Santa Barbara oil spill] is important.[29]

---

[27] Keogh, *President Nixon and the Press,* p. 87. As to the *Washington Post* remark about Rhode Island, the state encompasses a 1,214 square mile area. According to a Department of Interior press release of January 30, 1969, the oil slick "lay in patches within an area about three miles wide and fifteen miles long." But at one point the oil slick covered about 500 square miles (see Battelle Memorial Institute *Review of Santa Barbara Channel Oil Pollution Incident,* Water Pollution Control Research Series 15080EAG, Department of Interior, July 18, 1969, Chapter 4, p. 9).

[28] *Time* Magazine, February 14, 1969, p. 24.

[29] Fred Hartley, president, Union Oil Company of California, *Hearings on Bills to Amend the Federal Water Pollution Control Act, as Amended, and Related Matters Pertaining to the Prevention and Control of Water Pollution,* before the Subcommittee on Air and Water Pollution of the Committee on Public Works of the United States Senate, 91st Congress, 1st sess. (Washington, D.C.: U.S. Government Printing Office, February 5, 1969), p. 342.

Hartley went on to affirm that the oil spill was a serious problem and to outline the efforts being made by Union Oil to clean the beaches and save the birds.

But correction rarely catches up with error and, in this case, even if it had, it would not have altered the fact that a mass reaction set in against offshore drilling. Santa Barbara became a code word and a cry to battle against all forms of industrial pollution. But to make matters worse and to ensure additional concern over offshore oil exploration, the oil industry had a spectacular run of bad luck. Before the Santa Barbara incident, thousands of wells had been drilled off the coasts of Florida, Louisiana, Texas, California, Oregon, and Washington—with only a single instance of significant oil pollution.[30] Yet in the two years following Santa Barbara three more blowouts and one fire occurred and served to keep the public reminded of the perils of offshore oil production.[31]

The new administration reacted quickly to the Santa Barbara incident once it realized it was sitting on a time bomb that had been set one year and nine days earlier. On February 6, 1968, in Los Angeles, Department of Interior officials had received sealed bids totalling $602.7 million for exploration and development rights to seventy-one tracts totalling 363,181 acres in the Santa Barbara Channel. At the time this was the highest return to the government for any lease sale in the history of the continental shelf. The next day, Secretary Udall made specific reference to the Santa Barbara sale's special significance in the international picture.

> This is a most gratifying response to President Johnson's appeal for increased investment of capital resources within the dollar area in this period of concern over our balance of payment posture. The petroleum industry has demonstrated that it welcomes the opportunity to invest not only its money but its great talent in the development of our domestic resource base. The result of this sale also reflects some other lessons of recent history. It was conducted while the memory of the Middle East crisis is still fresh. Undoubtedly, much of the

---

[30] A blowout occurred on Ship Shoal (Block 29, operated by Amoco) on July 19 and was extinguished July 25, 1965. There were 1,688 barrels of oil lost.

[31] The blowouts were (1) Vermilion (Block 46, operated by Mobil), lasting from March 14 until May 16, 1969; (2) Ship Shoal (Block 72, operated by Mobil), lasting from March 16 until March 19, 1969, with 2,500 barrels of oil lost; and (3) Southern Timbalier (Block 26, operated by Shell), lasting from December 1, 1970 until April 17, 1971, with 53,000 barrels of oil lost. The fire was at Main Pass (Block 41, operated by Chevron) and lasted from February 10 until March 10, 1970, with 30,500 barrels of oil lost.

interest and resulting competition stems from a realization that new domestic reserves must be developed to assure uninterrupted supplies for our burgeoning energy market.[32]

Udall went on to highlight the financial success of the sale and to voice optimism about the oil and gas potential of the OCS. Ironically, he made no mention of the problem of oil spills or of steps that would be taken to protect the nearby beaches.

The Santa Barbara blowout occurred at 10:30 A.M. California time on January 28, 1969. Interior Secretary Hickel sent out a technical team from Washington on January 30 and made a personal inspection of the damage on February 2.[33] On February 3, he obtained a voluntary shutdown from the six oil companies operating in the area while a technical team of federal, state, and oil company representatives continued to assess the situation.[34] On February 7, Hickel telegraphed all the oil companies operating in the Santa Barbara Channel ordering a halt in operations. He had talked with President Nixon and Attorney General Mitchell and "both strongly concurred in the action being taken." [35] On February 11, Nixon and Hickel met and the President ordered his science adviser, Lee DuBridge, to put together an advisory team to recommend ways to restore the beaches and waters around Santa Barbara as rapidly as possible. Because there was disagreement within the Department of Interior over the adequacy of the federal regulations governing offshore drilling, as well as over the wisdom of the original Udall decision to allow leasing and drilling off Santa Barbara, Nixon, responding to Hickel's suggestion, asked DuBridge "to determine the adequacy of existing regulations for all wells licensed in past years now operating off the coast of the United States [and] to produce far more stringent and effective regulations that will give us better assurance than the Nation now has, that crises of this kind will not recur." [36]

---

[32] Department of Interior press release, "California Oil Lease Sale Proves Industry Interest in Domestic Investment, Udall Says," February 7, 1968.

[33] President Nixon visited the area later, on March 21, 1969, and resisted pleas by Santa Barbara Mayor Gerald Firestone and State Senator Robert Lagomarsino for a permanent shutdown of drilling activity in the Santa Barbara Channel.

[34] Department of Interior press release, "Secretary Hickel Announces Halt in Drilling Operations in Santa Barbara Channel," February 3, 1969.

[35] Department of Interior press release, "Secretary Hickel Orders Halt in All Santa Barbara Drilling and Production," February 7, 1969.

[36] Office of the White House Press Secretary, Statement by the President, February 11, 1969.

By February 18, Hickel had approved tighter drilling guidelines and announced that Department of Interior and oil company technicians would meet "to see if the industry itself will suggest ways for making our regulations more stringent and more compatible with today's needs and more advanced technology." [37] On February 22, at the recommendation of the DuBridge task force, Hickel ordered temporary pumping of all existing wells on Union's Platform A, where the oil seepage was occurring, to reduce pressure in the oil-bearing Repetto formation.[38] A month later a final set of regulations was published for oil drilling in all federal waters off the coast of California, and Hickel announced an "Ecological Preserve" or a 21,000 acre, two-mile-wide buffer zone between the Santa Barbara oil sanctuary and the seaward federal area under lease to the oil companies.[39]

By April, Secretary Hickel felt he had a good enough technical assessment of the situation to allow resumption of drilling and production on five of the Santa Barbara Channel leases that were somewhat removed from the area of the original blowout. At the same time he reaffirmed his shut-down order on sixty-seven other leases.[40] As the spring and summer passed, additional scientific assessments were in progress and reports on the effects of the oil spill on the marine environment began to be issued. One early report concluded that there had been no deaths of seals or sea lions attributable to the oil spill.[41] A later report, representing two years of extensive investigation, concluded

> that damage to the biota was not widespread, but was limited to several species, and that the area is recovering. In retrospect, it is not surprising that the studies after the Santa Barbara oil spill revealed such a small amount of damage. However, recurrent spills of this type at frequent intervals would probably result in large ecological changes. Likewise,

[37] Department of Interior press release, "Secretary Hickel Issues New Oil Drilling and Production Guidelines," February 18, 1969.

[38] Department of Interior press release, "Oil Dumping Safety Measure Begins in Santa Barbara Channel," February 22, 1969.

The task force consisted of eleven scientists named by DuBridge and was headed by Dr. John Calhoun, vice president of Texas A & M University.

[39] Department of Interior press release, "Statement by Secretary Hickel at a Press Conference," March 21, 1969.

[40] Department of Interior press release, April 1, 1969.

[41] Department of Interior report, "San Miguel Island: Marine Mammals as Related to Oil Spills in Santa Barbara Channel," June 27, 1969.

spills of refined oils present an entirely different problem and one that warrants far more concern.[42]

By late summer, the Department of Interior published entirely new OCS leasing and operating rules.[43] This was the first update of offshore drilling regulations since the department had begun its leasing program fifteen years before. The regulations were much more stringent but, more important, they were the first offshore drilling regulations that not only factored in environmental controls but also considered the possibility of prohibiting certain areas of the continental shelf from leasing if the environmental hazards were considered substantially high.

Meanwhile, crisis management of the Santa Barbara accident was coming to an end. The oil seepage had been reduced from an average of about 500 barrels per day right after the blowout to thirty barrels a day from March to June; by September technicians estimated the leakage at about ten barrels a day.[44]

As the immediate problems subsided, a sort of schizophrenia on Santa Barbara developed within the administration. The environmentalist sympathizers wanted the leases rescinded and a permanent ban placed on exploration and production. Those with an eye to energy shortages wanted to resume development. The oil companies had paid almost $204 million in bonus bids for the right to develop the thirty-five leases that were proposed to be rescinded. Add to that the potential loss in oil and gas production and the interest on funds tied up during the leasing moratorium, and it was conceivable that the federal liability could easily come to $500 million. There was also concern that if the federal government halted OCS development in the Santa Barbara Channel, there would be public pressure to halt offshore lease sales and drilling elsewhere. With plenty of imported oil available at the time, the immediate loss of oil production from the Santa Barbara leases seemed like a secondary matter, a completely opposite outlook from that which set in with the Arab boycott in late 1973 when every drop of oil counted. Hickel came up with a compromise that the President accepted, over the objections of OMB: Hickel neatly avoided the potential budget liability

[42] Compiled by Dale Straughan, *Biological and Oceanographical Survey of the Santa Barbara Channel Oil Spill 1969-1970, Volume 1, Biology and Bacteriology* (Alan Hancock Foundation, University of Southern California, 1971), p. 417.

[43] Department of Interior press release, "New Outer Continental Shelf Leasing, Operating Rules Adopted in Final Form by Secretary Hickel," August 22, 1969.

[44] Department of Interior news release, "Oil Seepage Reduced in Santa Barbara Channel," September 18, 1969.

by proposing compensation to the oil companies holding the rescinded leases, with the funds provided by revenues from oil production at the Elk Hills Naval Petroleum Reserve in California. President Nixon sent the proposed legislation to Congress in June 1970 with a declaration that financial value should not be the only, or even the chief, factor in land-use decisions.

> This recommendation [to rescind the leases] is based on the belief that immediate economic gains are not the only, or even the major, way of measuring the value of a geographic area. The ability of that area to sustain wildlife and its capacity to delight and inspire those who visit it for recreation can be far more important characteristics. This proposal recognizes that technology alone cannot bring national greatness, and that we must never pursue prosperity in a way that mortgages the nation's posterity.[45]

The legislation never went anywhere and was probably a mistake in the first place.[46] Members of the Armed Services committees of the House and Senate were adamantly opposed, viewing the proposal as a "raid" on the naval petroleum reserves (see Chapter 10 for more on this mentality). Members of the Interior committees were split between those who wanted to produce oil and those concerned over the risk of pollution. The legislation was submitted with slight modifications in 1971,[47] and again in 1973 as part of President Nixon's energy message in April. But in November 1973, with the Arab boycott in full effect, the administration formally asked Congress to hold up consideration of the proposed bill, giving as its reasons the energy crisis and the development of improved and safer drilling technology.[48] Even before the Arab boycott,

---

[45] *Public Papers of the Presidents, Nixon, 1970,* Special Message to Congress Urging Legislation to Avoid Further Pollution in the Santa Barbara Channel, June 11, p. 497.

[46] The mistake was primarily the author's, who, along with Ehrlichman, backed Hickel's proposal over the objection of OMB.

[47] The number of leases proposed to be rescinded was increased from twenty to thirty-five.

[48] Stephen Wakefield, assistant secretary of interior, *Hearings on Santa Barbara Channel on S. 1951 and S. 2339,* before the Subcommittee on Minerals and Fuels, Committee on Interior and Insular Affairs, United States Senate (Washington, D.C.: U.S. Government Printing Office, November 13, 1973), pp. 39-49.

The administration could not flatly support a resumption of drilling because the Department of Interior was in the midst of preparing an environmental-impact statement on the Santa Barbara Channel. If Secretary Morton had made a final decision to resume drilling without waiting for the final impact statement, the result more than likely would have been a suit from an environmental group charging him with failure to comply with NEPA.

there were deficiencies of 55,000 barrels a day in the Los Angeles and San Joaquin Valley, and the boycott increased the shortfall to 250,000 barrels a day. President Nixon, in his energy message to Congress of November 7, 1973, proposed a joint congressional resolution authorizing oil production from Elk Hills for general consumption.

Finally, the unresolved question of Hickel's legal authority to suspend operations in the Santa Barbara Channel came home to roost. On August 3, 1971, Gulf et al. filed a complaint in district court challenging the secretary of interior's authority to suspend operations on the Santa Barbara Channel leases pending consideration of the legislation by Congress.[49] On June 21, 1972, the district court held, in *Gulf* v. *Morton*,[50] that the secretary's act was not in the interest of conservation as required by the Outer Continental Shelf Lands Act. The decision was appealed and, on March 25, 1974, the Ninth Circuit Court modified its earlier opinion (of November 27, 1973) and found that the suspension of operations was in the interest of conservation, but that the reason for suspension terminated when Congress adjourned on October 18, 1972 without taking action on the legislation.[51] Then on May 8, 1974, the district court entered a judgment pursuant to the Ninth Circuit Court opinion which ordered the secretary of interior

> forthwith to take such action as is authorized under the Outer Continental Shelf Lands Act and the regulations thereunder. . . . promptly to act upon applications for drilling permits submitted by plaintiffs respecting such leases, and to take such further action in accordance with said Act and regulations as is necessary and proper to comply with the provisions of the leases.[52]

This order became final on July 8, 1974, and the Department of Interior immediately started approving oil company requests for exploratory drilling in the thirty-five-lease area. But Interior could not allow the installation of production platforms, because the only two platform requests pending—those for Union Oil Company's Platform C and Sun Oil Company's Platform Henry—were in litigation and because the environmental-impact statement on production platforms was clearly inadequate. So after a long delay the Department of Interior decided to prepare

---

[49] Gulf was joined in the suit by Mobil, Texaco and Union.

[50] 345 F. Supp. 685 (C.D. Cal. 1972).

[51] Gulf Oil Corporation v. Morton, 493 F.2d 141 (9th Cir. 1973).

[52] Gulf Oil Corporation v. Morton, Civ. No. 71-1669-FCW (C.D. Cal., May 8, 1974), p. 3.

a new environmental-impact statement covering exploration as well as production in the Santa Barbara Channel while continuing to approve exploration—but not production—under the original environmental-impact statement.

The Santa Barbara incident ended with Congress not acting on what was a poorly conceived piece of legislation. Because of the over-whelming popularity of the environmental issue, the administration had elected to abandon an area of potentially significant oil production. This decision seemed even less sound when domestic production began to decline in 1971 and when the Arab embargo of 1973–74 cut oil imports to a trickle. What the administration should have done, after tightening drilling regulations to make accidents much less likely, was to complete immediately an environmental-impact statement and, if the study showed the environmental costs to be acceptable, to allow leaseholders to resume exploration and production in the thirty-five-lease reserve area. Instead, an environmental-impact statement on the Santa Barbara Channel was not completed until the spring of 1976. Valuable time was lost gathering data for a decision by the secretary of interior.

Santa Barbara alerted the nation to the problem of oil pollution in its oceans and on its beaches. In spite of these fears, which fanned popular sentiment against OCS development, the administration began facing up to the need to develop the oil and natural gas potential of the OCS.

This was to involve decisions in four key policy areas: (1) the rate of expansion of the OCS program, (2) selection of the various leasing systems that might be used, (3) administrative reforms in the leasing program, and (4) ways of implementing environmental safeguards, for example, institution of an environmental OCS monitoring program, con-tinuing evaluations of on-shore impacts from OCS activity, and the designing of comprehensive legislation for oil-spill liability.

Rate of Expansion in OCS Leasing

Realizing the immense oil and gas potential in the OCS, the administra-tion gradually expanded the amount of acreage to be leased. From 1954, when the first OCS sale took place, until the end of 1968 only 6,513,621 acres had been leased (see Table 14), and none of the very attractive, potentially productive frontier areas of the Atlantic, off Alaska, or off Southern California (with the exception of Santa Barbara Chan-

Table 14

OCS ACREAGE LEASED, 1954–1976

Year		Acres Leased Annual	Acres Leased Cumulative
1954–1968		6,513,621	
1969		114,282	6,627,903
1970		596,040	7,223,943
1971		37,222	7,261,165
1972		826,195	8,087,360
1973		1,032,570	9,119,930
1974		1,762,158	10,882,088
1975		1,679,877	12,561,965
1976		1,274,809 [a]	13,836,774 [a]
February	Gulf of Mexico	161,286	
March	Northern Gulf of Alaska	409,057	
August	Mid-Atlantic	529,466	
November	Gulf of Mexico	175,000 [a]	

[a] Estimated, assuming the schedule is maintained.
Source: Personal communication to author from personnel in Bureau of Land Management, Department of Interior.

nel) had ever been explored. In his first energy message, President Nixon called on the secretary of interior "to increase the offerings of oil and gas leases" and to publish a five-year lease-sale schedule for the OCS.[53] But because of environmental litigation, the Interior Department was unable to increase the amount of OCS acreage leased.[54] In fact, leased acreage dropped to only 37,222 acres in 1971 and did not exceed 1 million acres annually until 1973 (see Table 14).

In the spring of 1973 the Department of Interior was leasing at the rate of only about 1 million acres per year. In fact, by that time a mere 8 million acres had been leased on the entire OCS since the begin-

---

[53] *Public Papers of the Presidents, Nixon, 1971,* Special Message to Congress on Energy Resources, June 4, p. 709.

[54] Natural Resource Defense Council v. Morton, 458 F.2d 827 (D.C. Cir. 1972). On January 13, 1971, the circuit court of Washington, D.C., ruled that the Interior Department's environmental-impact statement on a proposed lease sale for oil and natural gas in the Gulf of Mexico was legally inadequate. The court held that the environmental-impact statement was required to discuss the environmental effects of reasonable alternative courses of action, including courses of action not within the authority of the Department of Interior to adopt.

ning of the program in 1954, a small percentage of the potentially productive acreage. As Nixon said in April 1973, "at a time when we are being forced to obtain almost 30 percent of our oil from foreign sources, this level of development is not adequate." [55] He then ordered Secretary Morton to triple the acreage leased on the OCS for drilling of oil and natural gas by 1979. The fact sheet accompanying the message said:

> He also announced that leasing would begin in new frontier areas including beyond the 200 meter isobath, and beyond the Channel Islands in the Pacific if the environmental impact statements indicate it can be done safely. He directed CEQ, in cooperation with the National Academy of Sciences and other Government agencies to complete studies within one year on the environmental suitability of drilling on the Atlantic OCS and the Gulf of Alaska. By 1985, this accelerated OCS leasing schedule could increase annual production by approximately 1.5 billion barrels of oil (approximately 16 percent of our projected requirements) above what could be expected if the current lease schedule were maintained. [56]

But even a tripling of the leased acreage in the OCS seemed too little in the face of the October Mideast War, the ensuing Arab embargo, and administration forecasts for shortfalls of 2.7 million barrels of oil per day (compared to consumption of 18 million barrels per day). [57] So when Congress convened in January 1974, Nixon ordered the Interior Department to step up its OCS leasing program to 10 million acres in 1975 (about ten times the rate achieved in 1973). He also announced that no decision would be made on leasing in the frontier areas of the Gulf of Alaska and the Atlantic until CEQ completed its environmental study of those two areas. [58]

It was apparent at that time that all the attractive geological projects in the Gulf of Mexico could be leased that year and that it would be necessary to move into the frontier areas of Southern California, the Atlantic, and offshore Alaska. Estimates were that 10 million acres of leases (1) would aggregate about 10 to 15 billion barrels of undiscovered

[55] Office of the White House Press Secretary, Special Message to the Congress on Energy Resources, April 18, 1973.

[56] Office of the White House Press Secretary, President's Energy Message Fact Sheet, April 18, 1973.

[57] Transcript released by the White House January 19, 1974, of President Nixon's address on the national energy situation on network radio.

[58] Office of the White House Press Secretary, President Nixon's Energy Message to Congress, January 23, 1974.

recoverable oil and 35 to 75 trillion cubic feet of natural gas and (2) would yield about 2 to 3 million barrels of oil per day and 10 to 15 billion cubic feet of gas by 1985. This yield could amount to 15 percent of estimated U.S. oil consumption in 1985—a very significant addition to the domestic supply at a low cost compared to imported oil or other domestic energy sources.[59]

In October 1974, with CEQ's environmental study of the OCS frontier areas completed, President Ford reaffirmed Nixon's goal of leasing 10 million acres of the OCS annually in 1975.[60] But by November 13, when Ford and Secretary Morton met with the coastal state governors, the emphasis had shifted from a specific quota of 10 million acres in 1975 to beginning a leasing program in all frontier areas as soon as possible. The proposed schedule entailed six OCS sales per year from 1975 through 1978. President Ford said, "I might note that although the ten million acres has been a useful planning objective, we are not wedded to this particular goal. Our primary objective is to produce oil and gas where we can do so safely. But, in any case, we will insure that leases are not sold below fair market value." [61]

In summary, in the years from 1969 through 1974, Nixon and Ford developed an entirely new policy on OCS leasing. No longer would the federal government's primary goal be to restrict OCS leasing in order to bring high bids. Instead, policy would have a double objective: (1) to ensure a fair market value for the public and (2) to offer as many OCS leases as could be absorbed by the private sector so as to stimulate the private sector's ability to build rigs and platforms and to increase its capacity to explore.

The Case for Accelerated OCS Leasing. There were five major reasons for expanding the OCS leasing program.

---

[59] John Whitaker, under secretary of interior, *Hearings on Accelerated OCS Leasing,* before the Appropriations Subcommittee of the Interior and related agencies of the House of Representatives (Washington, D.C.: U.S. Government Printing Office, October 8, 1974), p. 62.

[60] Address by President Ford to a joint session of Congress, transcript released by the Office of the White House Press Secretary, October 8, 1974. Actually, during 1975, only 1,679,877 acres of the OCS were leased (see Table 14), because of the longer-than-anticipated startup time and delays from legal challenges and because, in the Southern California OCS sale in December 1975, industry bid on far fewer tracts than Interior had anticipated.

[61] Office of the White House Press Secretary, Text of Remarks by the President at a Meeting of Governors on Outer Continental Shelf Oil and Gas Development, November 13, 1974.

275

Large potential reserves. The prospects for large additional supplies of oil and gas from OCS development looked promising. In 1973, OCS oil production averaged 1,081,000 barrels daily—1,029,000 barrels from wells in the Gulf of Mexico and the remaining 52,000 barrels from offshore California; natural gas output totaled 8.9 billion cubic feet per day that year—all but 20 million cubic feet from the Gulf of Mexico. In twenty years the OCS had produced 3.3 billion barrels of oil and 20.7 billion cubic feet of natural gas.[62]

The U.S. outer continental shelf is an attractive exploration target if worldwide OCS activity is any indicator. There are over 780 oil and gas fields on the submerged continental margins of eighty countries. As of 1973, the volume of offshore oil and gas discovered worldwide amounted to 172.8 billion barrels of oil, about 26 percent of the world total, and 168.4 trillion cubic feet of natural gas.[63] Within the United States, the rates of onshore production and of onshore discoveries were declining (with the conspicuous exception of Northern Alaska) because each new discovery decreased the conventional places to drill. The only hope for reversing this trend was to increase the exploration pace in the OCS. Figure 1 shows how the U.S. exploration pace lagged well behind those of other nations and regions, both in square miles leased and in the proportion of submerged continental shelf land open to exploration.

Geological Survey estimates of offshore undiscovered recoverable crude oil and natural gas amount to 3 to 31 billion barrels of oil and 8 to 80 trillion cubic feet of gas in Alaska; 2 to 5 billion barrels of oil and 2 to 6 trillion cubic feet of gas off the Pacific coastal states; 3 to 8 billion barrels of oil and 18 to 91 trillion cubic feet of gas in the Gulf of Mexico; and 2 to 4 billion barrels of oil and 5 to 14 trillion cubic feet of gas in the offshore Atlantic.[64]

---

[62] John Whitaker, under secretary of interior, *Hearings on Outer Continental Shelf Oil and Gas Development,* before the Subcommittee on Minerals, Materials and Fuels of the Committee on Interior and Insular Affairs, United States Senate, 93rd Congress, 2nd session (Washington, D.C.: U.S. Government Printing Office, May 6, 1974), p. 180.

[63] Henry Berryhill, *The Worldwide Search for Petroleum Offshore—A Status Report for a Quarter Century 1947-72,* U.S. Geological Survey Circular 694 (1974), p. 1.

[64] Billy Miller, Harry Thomson, Gordon Dolton, Anny Coury, Thomas Hendricks, Frances Lennartz, Richard Powers, Edward Sable, and Katherine Varnes, "Geologic Estimates of Undiscovered Recoverable Oil and Gas Resources in the United States," U.S. Geological Survey Circular 725, Tables 4 and 5 (June 1975), pp. 28-31.

Figure 1

LEASED AREA COMPARED TO TOTAL SHELF AREA*

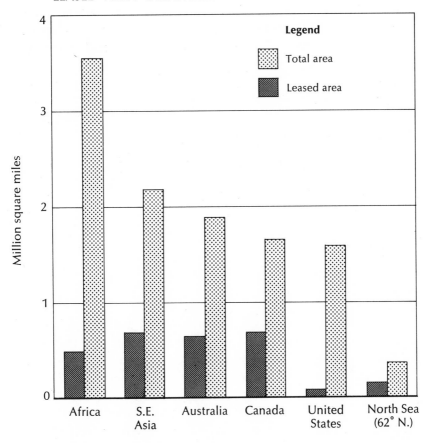

*Within 3,000 meter water-depth contour.

Source: Y. Bonillas, "New Reserves for U.S. Keyed to OCS," paper presented at the annual meeting of the Western Gas Processors and Oil Refiners Association, Anaheim, California; reprinted in the *Oil and Gas Journal,* October 14, 1974, p. 42.

Balance-of-payments drain. Imported oil cost the United States $7.8 billion in 1973. With the Arab embargo of 1973–74 the nation imported 6.4 million barrels a day in 1974 at an annual cost of $24.6 billion. Projections in the fall of 1974 estimated that U.S. imports could reach 10 million barrels a day in 1988, for a yearly total of $36.5 billion based on a price of $10 per barrel.[65]

[65] Whitaker, *Hearings on the Outer Continental Shelf Leasing Program,* p. 37.

The inflation factor. Another compelling reason for a vastly accelerated OCS leasing program was that the importation of large quantities of high-cost petroleum had inflationary effects. Sooner or later these imports would have to be paid for with the export of real domestic resources. The resulting increased export demand for U.S. products would tend to raise the domestic price of these products.

Cost savings from domestic oil. It was simply more economical to produce domestic oil than to buy high-cost imports. For example, excluding bonus and royalty payments and assuming production from large (500 million barrel) oil fields, OCS oil cost about $3.50 to $5.50 in the Atlantic and in the range of $4.50 to $7.00 per barrel in the Gulf of Alaska to produce and deliver, compared to about $11.50 per barrel, less any profit return to this country, for imported oil. On the other hand, if a barrel of OCS oil is produced, only $3.50 to $7.00 of goods and services is consumed in the process. The savings from producing OCS oil will be captured by the federal government, primarily in the form of bonus bids for tracts developed and in the form of taxes and royalties.

No practical alternative. The only practical way to expand energy resources was to accelerate the pace of OCS development. By the time of Nixon's first energy message to Congress in June 1971, it was clear that it would be about fifteen years before the nation could expect enough energy from alternative energy sources—coal gasification and liquefaction, oil shale, geothermal energy, nuclear fusion, the liquid metal fast breeder reactor, or solar energy—to reduce substantially projected increases in petroleum demand. These alternatives were more costly on a BTU basis than petroleum, and the technology for reducing their costs did not yet exist. Coal could be expected to be used more widely, primarily for electrical generation, but not to replace petroleum in enough applications to alter OCS development policy during the next decade.

The Case against Acceleration. Several factors were considered.

Lower bonus bids. OMB was concerned that an accelerated leasing program could lead to lower bonus bids and thus lower budget receipts. However, the Department of Interior argued that the large price-cost gap, which was producing the high bonus bids, was evidence of a serious misallocation of resources that could be rectified best by a policy of accelerated leasing. A reduction in the gap would mean that the policy was succeeding and would automatically reduce the leasing pace because fewer tracts would look profitable enough to attract bids.

The problem of fair market value. A compelling argument was that rapid leasing would result in less competition in lease sales and consequently in bids that did not represent fair market value for the tracts. Therefore, as lease sales went forward, it would be important to watch for a reduction in the ratio of high bids to the Geological Survey's pre-sale estimated values. If competition should become weak, this ratio would fall. Other signs of a lack of competition would be fewer bidders, a change in the composition of the bidding group, or less bidding by previously active firms. Any or all of these indicators could vary substantially from lease sale to lease sale for reasons unrelated to the degree of competition, so the trend over several sales would have to be studied.

Mounting backlog of leased but undeveloped tracts. There was also concern that rapid leasing might bring longer than normal delays between leasing a tract and exploring and developing it. This could be particularly true in Alaskan waters, where the working seasons are short, but also might occur in older leased areas as competition for drilling rigs increased. The federal government would prefer not to have numbers of unworked tracts in the oil companies' hands. On the other hand, it was argued, the more tracts that lessees hold the more likely they are to devote their earlier efforts to the best prospects. Moreover, if evidence of delays between leasing and development were to accumulate, the rapid leasing policy could be reviewed. In any event, the five-year development requirement in OCS leases limited the government's exposure to this risk.

The decision to go ahead. The administration therefore decided that the proper policy was to lease rapidly and to monitor the results carefully. The errors that might result (excluding for the moment the environmental concerns of marine pollution and potential onshore impact) seemed trivial compared to the obvious and serious energy problems the nation faced.

The main danger of too rapid leasing related to whether bonus bids paid by the oil companies to the federal government would adequately reflect the value of the resource, that is, "fair market value." On the other hand there could even come a time, if the nation were still exposed to unacceptable risks of import interruption and if the price-cost gap for oil and gas were still high, when it would be sound policy to continue rapid leasing even in the face of clear evidence that the returns to the federal government were inadequate. In other words, despite the costs, the government might choose to continue the policy for resource-allocation reasons alone. Although there were risks in leasing too rapidly, the administration concluded that greater risks lay on the side of planning to lease too slowly. It is administratively difficult to raise the planned leasing rate quickly, because baseline studies, environmental-impact statements, and resource assessments must precede lease sales, and they involve long lead times. However, once these preliminaries are geared to a high leasing rate, it is easy to slow down—simply by postponing sales.

Rig availability. The administration's analysis estimated that, even with optimistic assumptions, requirements for mobile platforms and for fixed platforms would exceed projected availability by 38 percent and 36 percent, respectively.[66] However, with early leasing and a sustained rate of leasing, manufacturers might expand capacity to close this gap. Also, increased leasing activity would tend to draw units of the world's mobile platform fleet, some of which had moved overseas when OCS leasing was severely curtailed in 1971,[67] to return to U.S. shores.

Other possibilities, should the free market fail to respond, would be a materials allocation program or government loan guarantees of offshore drilling rigs.[68] A final possibility would be to revise OCS leasing regulations to allow unitizing OCS leases. Under the unitization system, the exploration management of a tract would be unitized rather than being handled by several operators who subdivide the tract and carry

---

[66] Federal Energy Administration, *Project Independence Report* (Washington, D.C.: U.S. Government Printing Office, 1974), p. 243.

[67] The curtailment followed National Resources Defense Council v. Morton, which held the environmental-impact statement to be inadequate and delayed Gulf of Mexico leasing for about a year.

[68] Under the Merchant Marine Act of 1936, which authorized federal loan guarantees of seagoing equipment (Ch. 858 [49 Stat. 1985], June 29, 1936).

on independent drilling programs. In theory this would permit more acreage to be evaluated with fewer wells, leading to estimated equipment savings as high as 40 percent.[69]

Capital requirements. The oil and gas industry, as well as many congressmen and senators representing oil and natural gas producing states, argued that expanded OCS leasing would find the industry short of the needed capital and asked for a change in the bonus bidding system to eliminate the "front money problem." However, the *Project Independence Report* found no clear evidence that the industry would be short of capital to pursue expanded leasing aggressively. The report concluded that to achieve the maximum (and unlikely) goal of no imports by 1985 would require a cumulative total of $98 billion in capital investment (including plant, equipment, working capital, and land) between 1975 and 1985, and that this would not be a problem.[70]

Alternative OCS Leasing Systems

As OCS leasing was accelerated under the Nixon and Ford administrations, a number of proposals were entertained by Congress and by the administration (privately) to change the leasing procedure. A description of each system and major pro and con arguments are presented below.

The OCS Lands Act of 1953 allows leasing by competitive sealed bids on the basis of a cash bonus bid with a fixed royalty (not less than 12.5 percent) or on the basis of a bid royalty with a fixed bonus. Leases are for a five-year term. After extensive analysis the administration concluded that, as a legislative strategy, there were not sufficient benefits in proposing a change in this act because the new legislation could impose many undesirable features, such as built-in delays to leasing in the OCS, or even a federal exploration company. Therefore, no change was advocated in the leasing system. Instead, administrative reforms were made within the scope of the OCS Lands Act of 1953 to compensate for some of the perceived deficiencies in the traditional method of leasing OCS lands.

---

[69] Federal Energy Administration, *Project Independence Report,* pp. 257-258.
[70] Ibid., p. 289.

(1) Bonus bidding. Companies submit sealed bids proposing bonuses that would be paid to the federal government prior to exploration and development. Also, a fixed 16⅔ percent royalty on the discovered oil is paid to the federal government. Except for a few experiments with higher fixed royalties or royalty-bidding lease sales, bonus bidding is the only system that has been employed by the government. However, under the OCS Lands Act of 1953, bonus bidding could be carried out with royalty rates higher than 16⅔ percent, or with profit shares fixed at some arbitrary level. Bonus payments might also be divided into several non-contingent installments.

Arguments for:

—Large amounts of capital bid provide companies with an incentive to develop the lease rapidly because bonus payments on dry leases may be expensed immediately for tax purposes.

—No government action is required once leases are awarded, except oversight to ensure due diligence.

—It is the oil company, not the public, that assumes the full risk.

Arguments against:

—High bonus payments divert money that might better be spent for exploration and development.

—If the industry in general or smaller independents in particular are short on capital, then high front-money costs paid in bonus payments could decrease competition.

(2) Contingent bonus bidding. Companies would award leases on the basis of the highest bid bonus, but only a portion of the bid would be paid prior to exploration and development. The balance would be paid only if the company held the lease longer than five years. An alternative which amounts to the same thing is called bonus bidding with an oil pledge. This system would entail a bonus bid plus a fixed royalty, plus a fixed pledge set by the government and payable in cash or oil in fixed installments following a firm's commitment to explore a tract. Before each installment, the firm would have another chance to decide whether to continue paying the installment and exploring the tract or to relinquish the tract, together with all exploration and drilling data, to the government.

Arguments for:

—Front-end costs are decreased by deferring liabilities. Full liability is deferred until the lease has been completely explored, and then the oil pledge is amortized over a period of time.

—Companies have time to test before deciding to assume the pledge. If the lease is abandoned, the government could reoffer it with a lower oil pledge, thus encouraging the development of marginal tracts.

Arguments against:

—The same problems arise as in cash bonus bidding, but to a lesser extent. The government (the taxpayer) shares a greater part of the risk, since the oil company can abandon the lease and thereby avoid paying the total bonus.

—Reoffering leases delays production, causing a cost to the public.

—Contingent bonuses may encourage drilling holes simply to determine when to give up a lease and not to look for oil. For example, assume a company can drill a well next month on tract A or B. Tract A has a $20 million contingent payment due in one month and a 20 percent probability of finding $50 million in oil in one hole. Tract B has a $2 million contingent payment due in one month and a 50 percent probability of finding $30 million in oil in one hole. The company would drill tract A, even though the expected value of the oil is higher in tract B. In another example, assume the last contingent payment is $20 million and the oil company discovers oil worth $15 million before the payment is due. The company would not develop the lease. Thus, deferred bonus payments may lead to resource losses, although the government will eventually recapture some of these by reoffering the tract.

(3) Royalty bidding. Companies would bid the share of future production, in cash or in oil, they would be willing to pay the government, and a minimum fixed bonus would be set to eliminate nuisance bidders and undue speculation.

Arguments for:

—The front-money problem is reduced and funds are freed for exploration and development expenditures.

—The opportunity for independents with less capital to operate in the OCS is increased.

283

—If an unanticipated large discovery is made, the dollar return to the government from the royalty bid would greatly exceed the revenue from the bonus bid.

Arguments against:
—The risk that bidders may obtain tracts without intending to drill is greater.
—A high royalty bid may result in abandonment of potentially recoverable but marginally profitable reserves. As production declines and operating costs increase, there may be early abandonment of a field and loss of potential production because of failure to apply secondary recovery methods.
—The speed of development may be delayed since the firm has much less capital invested than it does with a bonus bid system. There is no bonus payment to expense for tax purposes once the lease has proved to be dry.
—The winning firm may have had a high royalty rate that turns out to exceed its ability to pay, thereby causing protracted litigation delays and/or a reoffering of the lease for sale. In either case there is a cost to the public associated with delaying production.
—Under royalty bidding the government (the taxpayer) assumes a greater share of the risk than the oil company.

(4) Sliding scale royalties. As under royalty bidding, companies would bid a share of future production, but a schedule would be established that reduced the royalty payment over time. By tying royalty payments to production (or, alternatively, to the field's total reserves), this method attempts to rectify the major problem with royalty bidding, the tendency toward early abandonment.

Arguments for:
—Maximum development of the tract's oil and gas resources is encouraged, including application of secondary recovery, by lowering the royalty to a minimum allowable rate in the later years of the reserve's life.
—Since the risk can be transferred to the production rate or to the estimated reserves, the bonus bid will tend to be lower and therefore create fewer front-money problems.

Argument against:

—It is difficult to estimate the field's recoverable reserve, and this estimate is most speculative in the early phases of development. Since the base royalty rate is achieved by competitive bidding it is possible that competitive pressure may bid up the base royalty rate so high that subsequent sliding royalty schedules, even though declining, might result in early abandonment of the field.

(5) Net profit bidding. Oil companies would bid on the percentage of the profit base (set above a minimum amount) that would be paid to the federal government.

Arguments for:

—Unlike a high royalty system, this system does not encourage early abandonment of a field or maximum production of a potentially marginal discovery.

—Elimination of the cash bonus probably decreases the front-money problem by transferring the lessee's front-end capital costs to exploration and production activities.

Arguments against:

—The administration of profit sharing is complicated, may require a federal bureaucracy, and increase the need for federal decision making.

—Establishing precise operating costs would be difficult.

(6) Work bid bonus leasing. Under this system, competition would be on the basis of cash bonus bids, but the funds would be held in escrow by the federal government to be drawn by the leaseholder in order to finance the exploration and development of the lease. Any costs in excess of the amount in escrow would be borne by the oil company, and any unused funds would revert to the government.

Arguments for:

—With no front money tied up simply to pay for the right to explore, companies are able to invest their funds directly in exploration and development. This increase in capital for exploration and development can be expected to increase the possibility of finding oil and natural gas.

—The system may increase competition in the bidding for OCS tracts by reducing risks and front-money problems for smaller companies.

Argument against:

—Exploration and production are likely to be inefficient because of the possibility that companies will overdrill their lease to avoid forfeiting the balance of their work development pledge to the government.

(7) Lottery systems. The government would set a bid level or entry fee for each tract and companies would enter into a lottery for each tract for which they would be willing to pay the bid level. A limit would be put on how many tracts one company could obtain.

Arguments for:

—Presumably the tract is leased at fair market value and no front money is extended for the right to lease.
—Competition will be increased.

Arguments against:

—This system presumes that the government can forecast fair market value, whereas a greater collective capability for doing so exists in the private sector. As a result, the size and number of bids, significant indicators of fair market value, would be lacking.
—There will be pressure for a large, expensive federal capability for assessing fair market value so that "giveaways" or "windfalls" can be avoided.

(8) Negotiation of the lease. Leases would be negotiated on the basis of net profit paid to the government and work commitments in exploration and development. This system is a variation of Britain's North Sea system under which the government privately negotiates the work program and examines the applicants' ability, resources, capital, et cetera, to perform the work program with diligence.

Arguments for:

—Front-money problems are eliminated.
—Capable firms are assured of operating with due diligence.
—Nuisance bids and speculators are avoided.

Arguments against:
—Larger firms with more proven capability and capital might be favored.
—There is more chance of real or apparent preferential treatment under negotiation than there is under competitive bidding.

(9) Special frontier leasing program. The Department of Interior privately considered a special frontier area leasing program. The idea was to separate exploration leases from development leases for a short time in order to increase rapidly knowledge of the oil and natural gas potential on the OCS. Under the scheme, the secretary of the interior would select about ten of the most promising tracts (based on Geological Survey, industry, and environmental information). These tracts would be awarded by competitive bidding, based on percentage profit from anticipated production. The leases would convey exploratory but not development rights and would have to be drilled in one year. Strong safety regulations would apply, all exploratory data would be made public, all discoveries would be shut-in, and no production could occur until a development lease sale had been held. At the same time the secretary would award about thirty tracts noncompetitively (not more than one per company), taking into account the objectives of ensuring environmental protection, dispersing exploration effort and, in general, producing an optimal exploration program. A preference-right lease would be granted to any company making a major discovery (determined by the secretary). But exercise of these rights would be delayed until an environmental-impact statement was completed and the secretary decided that development could take place on environmentally acceptable terms.

Arguments for:
—The program would make the best use of limited equipment and manpower.
—It might minimize environmental costs because development could be quickly concentrated in areas where oil and gas had been located.

Arguments against:
—New legislation was required, including the waiving of the National Environmental Policy Act requirement for an environmental-impact statement prior to exploratory drilling. It was

unlikely that Congress would take this action even though the environmental damage, in the Department of Interior's view, would be minimal.

—There would still be delays, because it takes about one year to prepare an environmental-impact statement after the exploratory lease is granted.

—The most serious drawback was the questionable premise that government and industry can collectively decide upon the best locations for a limited number of wells, ten or so, and that the most promising areas for OCS development be targeted by drilling those wells. Successful oil exploration depends, among other things, on different judgments by many experts. Without these differences it would be likely that whole areas of the OCS would be written off when in fact they contained major deposits of oil or natural gas. The existence of divergent exploration strategies is crucial to the rapid and efficient discovery of oil and natural gas resources.

The story of North Sea oil illustrates the point. A large natural gas discovery onshore in Holland in 1959[71] stimulated exploration in the British sector of the North Sea beginning in 1964. Large natural gas deposits were found there between 1965 and 1969. But the oil potential of the North Sea was still not rated highly, and the consensus was to focus the search on the British sector and on natural gas. Fortunately there were divergent views. Nine groups explored the Norwegian sector, drilling a discouraging twenty-nine dry holes by 1969. All but one group gave up—and it discovered oil in 1969.[72] Soon after, more oil was found in the Norwegian area and the first oil discoveries were made in the British sector. Two lessons seem relevant: (1) a large number of dry holes does not necessarily mean that an area will be unproductive, a lesson that is particularly applicable to the OCS where there are large areas with no prior discoveries; and (2) if a collective judgment had been made it is very probable that exploration would have been given up before oil was discovered. Today the North Sea is one of the world's major oil provinces, with 16 billion barrels of proven reserves and 40 billion barrels of potentially recoverable reserves.

---

[71] Bryan Cooper and T. Gaskell, *North Sea Oil—The Great Gamble* (Indianapolis, Indiana: The Bobbs-Merrill Company, Inc., 1966), pp. 32 and 132.

[72] *Oil and Gas Journal,* "Norway Claims Phillips Has a Big One," November 10, 1969, p. 130.

Several times in the history of oil exploration conventional wisdom has counselled stopping exploration programs, or never beginning them, in areas that ultimately proved productive. Libya was ignored for years because there were no seepages. At one time Arabia and Kuwait were considered poor prospects because of the absence of the Asmari limestone, the oil-bearing rocks in Iran where the original Middle East discoveries were made.[73] The large Reforma oil fields discovered in southern Mexico in 1972 had been drilled to shallower depths for years before deeper exploration was tried against the consensus of the conventional wisdom.[74]

(10) Government-financed exploration and/or development strategies. During 1974 and 1975, as the administration rapidly expanded leasing in the OCS, Congress became increasingly interested in some type of government exploration programs. Proposals ranged from limited stratigraphic drilling at government expense through actual government exploration, either limited or covering all phases of exploration, to formation of a Federal Oil and Gas Company ("FOGCO," its opponents dubbed it with ridicule) to compete with private corporations. The common theme of these proposals was to retain public control over the OCS area until more definitive estimates of its oil and natural gas reserves could be made.

Arguments for:
—The government would have better information on which to base a national energy strategy.
—The decision to develop individual areas could be withheld until better information was available about the extent of oil and natural gas deposits and the specific environmental problems, including onshore development.
—With the government rather than corporations financing the initial exploration the competition for leases would be increased, thus reducing the likelihood that a few large companies would own a majority of the leases, increasing the chances of getting fair market value for the leases, and eliminating the charge of a "giveaway."

---

[73] Cooper and Gaskell, *North Sea Oil—The Great Gamble,* pp. 32-33.
[74] "Mexican Find Emphasizes Need for Deeper Look," *Oil and Gas Journal,* November 18, 1974, p. 97.

Arguments against:

—Government exploration would tend to mean that a diversity of exploration strategies would be replaced with a single, bureaucratically formulated strategy which could delay and perhaps prevent oil and natural gas discoveries.

—Presumably, unless the government exploration program encountered early success, there would be political pressure to stop exploration for budgetary reasons. Overall, the success ratio of wildcat drilling is about one-to-ten. To limit a drilling program in area or in number of holes drilled shifts the odds in favor of a given area being unproductive. A competitive private enterprise approach involving varied exploration strategies and larger budgets generally permits more thorough exploration.

—If a limited federal exploration program did not discover oil quickly, there could be political pressure never to lease the area, presumably because of environmental concerns, and the area would be condemned as unproductive even though it had never been explored thoroughly.

—Once a government agency is born, it seldom is allowed to die. The civil servants have a vested interest in their jobs, the congressional subcommittee dealing with the agency wants to keep its authority and, in the case of a federal oil and gas exploration program, an entire constituency of petroleum and natural gas service industries would grow up to protect and perhaps control the agency. It is possible, for example, that if excess capacity developed, say, in drilling rigs, there is a risk of overdrilling.

—There would be significant problems in designing a public agency to explore for oil and natural gas. How would leases be allocated for government exploration and private exploration? What arrangements would be necessary to make government-explored land available for private exploration when the government had failed to discover oil? What would be the agency's objective? Presumably the objective would be to compete directly with private companies by providing a representative government exploration interest in each OCS area. There could be political pressure to extend or limit this interest, depending on the perceived political gain of economic development or preservation of the environment. In either case, these political judgments would inhibit efficient exploration strategies.

290

Summary of Leasing Alternatives. After reviewing the merits and shortcomings of the various methods of leasing, the administration reached some fundamental conclusions:

(1) A completely public exploratory program was ruled out. Its virtues—more effective control over decisions affecting the environment and onshore development and greater assurance that oil and natural gas leases would be sold at fair market value—seemed far outweighed by its pitfalls. A government program would be less likely to find oil and natural gas than private efforts and would probably be carried out much less efficiently. Moreover, the risk that it would stray from its ostensible goal of finding oil and natural gas could not be dismissed. In the short run, political influences would probably reduce the effectiveness of the program, and in the longer run the program might produce excessive drilling simply to satisfy vested interests.

(2) Federally sponsored stratigraphic drilling also was ruled out. Presumably stratigraphic drilling, with disclosure of the geologic data to all bidders, could reduce the information advantage of large companies, increase the competitiveness of OCS lease sales, and thereby provide greater assurance that the public received fair market value for the leases sold. But the program would tell the public little about the production potential of a given area and would contribute little to the development of a "national energy strategy." How could it, since a limited exploration program could not really evaluate the productivity of potential areas and therefore would not give the government greater knowledge and greater control over development and production decisions. Finally, federally sponsored stratigraphic drilling could lead, like the "nose of the camel under the tent," to a federal oil and gas company.[75]

(3) Finally, it was concluded that the OCS Lands Act of 1953 allowed the administration to make most of the desired reforms administratively without delays and without using methods that were likely to decrease efficiency and productivity.

Administration Reforms in Leasing Procedures

Most of the proposals to change the bidding procedure focused upon front money paid out in high bonus bids or upon the influence the

[75] S. 521, which passed the Senate in July 1975, contained an amendment by Senator Jackson (adopted by a 48-to-39 vote) providing for a federal OCS exploration program.

Table 15

COMPARISON OF COMPETITION: BONUS VERSUS
ROYALTY BIDS ON OCS SALE NO. 36

	Number of Tracts		
Type of Bid	Offered	Receiving bids	Bids per Tract
Bonus bids	287	149	2.2
Royalty bids	10	8	7.1

Source: Department of Interior, Office of OCS Program Evaluation, "An Analysis of the Royalty Bidding Experiment in OCS Sales #6," mimeographed, 1975, p. 2.

major oil companies had on OCS leasing and their unfair advantage over the independent oil companies. The administration took steps to ameliorate these problems within the limits of the existing law.

Royalty Bidding and Increased Fixed Royalty Experimental Lease Sales.
The administration designed a royalty bidding sale, which was administratively feasible under the law,[76] to see if front-end costs were a real problem and if it was on solid ground in favoring a change in the leasing system. For OCS sale No. 36 in the Gulf of Mexico in October 1974, ten tracts, one each on ten separate geologic structures, were offered for competitive bidding on the basis of a royalty rate plus a fixed bonus of $25 per acre. The balance of the tracts were sold on the conventional fixed-royalty, bonus-bid basis. In terms of the percentage of tracts receiving bids and the number of bids per tract, bidding turned out to be more competitive on royalty-bid tracts (see Table 15).

Analysis of the results also showed royalty-bid tracts received significantly more bids than bonus tracts with comparable Geological Survey resource evaluations. The statistical evidence was not so strong in the latter case as in the former because there was insufficient bidding

---

[76] The Outer Continental Shelf Lands Act (43 U.S.C. 1331-1343), Section 8(a), required that the bidding be at the secretary's discretion on one of two bases: (1) a cash bonus with a royalty fixed by the secretary in advance or (2) a royalty (not less than 12½ percent of the amount or value of the production saved, removed, or sold from the lease) with a fixed bonus.

on some structures. However, in no case was bidding found to be more competitive with bonus bidding than with royalty tracts.[77]

Analysis of this sale indicated that royalty bidding attracted more bidders, including new ones, and might also increase the ability of the independents to compete. To the extent that this results in a broader distribution of OCS revenues among companies, royalty bidding would have a positive impact on the structure of the oil industry. Also, bringing more companies into the auction probably decreases the chances that potentially valuable tracts will be ignored in the bidding—although one would expect this effect mainly on marginal tracts.

But the analysis also indicated that, under the royalty bidding system, competition might have undesirable effects. Royalty bidding seems to push the royalty rates to such high levels that there is a strong possibility of eroding the potential recovery from a tract. The analysis projected a decrease in the ultimate recovery from the reservoir and a marked increase in the probability that tracts would be abandoned after exploration drilling, with no production occurring. If maximum efficient recovery were a matter of reducing production rates to avoid premature suspension of production due to high royalty rates, the problem could be mitigated through provisions for royalty reductions downstream. However, the analysis indicated that this was not the case. Instead, the royalty bidder bet $25 per acre (the minimum per acre value set by the Department of Interior) plus anticipated exploration costs on finding his most optimistic projection of the resource potential for a given tract. If he found less, there was a good chance he would walk away from the lease and the government would have to offer it for resale to get any production at all.

The administration, therefore, concluded that the potential benefits from a reduction of the front-money problem and from the presumed greater competition were not worth the liabilities. In addition, there was a real question about the degree of seriousness of the front-money problem, because there were public benefits downstream after the exploration phase, at production time, thanks to substantial bonus bids. The fact that a major portion of the investment was at the front end increased the probability that production would take place even if the original estimated reserves proved to be too optimistic. As long as the estimated

---

[77] Data here and in the next two paragraphs are from Department of Interior, Office of OCS Program Evaluation, "An Analysis of Royalty Bidding Experiment in OCS Sales #36," mimeographed, 1975, pp. 18-19.

return on investment production was better than that on alternative investments, the lease holder would decide to produce on the lease.

In another experiment in Southern California, OCS sale No. 35 in December 1975, royalties were doubled from the traditional 16⅔ percent to 33⅓ percent on a few experimental tracts, each with an estimated high potential for commercial oil discovery. These tracts were selected because presumably the resource value was so high that there was little chance of early abandonment of the tracts even at the relatively high royalty rate of 33⅓ percent. This system, like royalty bidding, has the advantage of increasing competition but, unlike royalty bidding, reduces the probability of early abandonment. It tends to reduce the size of the bonus bid, thereby increasing the prospects that smaller companies will enter the lease sale competition. Because the royalty payments are contingency payments, the risk is reduced to the oil company but increased to the public. This also should tend to increase competition. The difficulty is that if the tract ultimately fails to have the predicted high resource value, early abandonment is likely to occur, but this is less likely than under royalty bidding. This system of lease sales showed promise and additional experiments were planned on future OCS sales to reduce the front-money problem and increase competition.

Competition was being enhanced administratively in two other ways without resorting to legislative change. One way was to ban joint bidding among major companies. In an OCS lease sale it is common for two or more companies to submit joint bids, in order to reduce exploration risks. Small oil companies with limited exploration budgets need joint bidding if they are to diversify their risks. Large firms, on the other hand, have such large exploration budgets that joint bidding is not required for diversification or, at best, only slightly reduces their risk.

In addition to diversifying risks, joint bidding may reduce lease sale competition so that the government receives lower bonus bids than it would if the same companies were forced to bid separately. Since the large companies do not need to bid jointly to diversify risk, they would be likely to bid separately for leases if joint bidding were not allowed. The result would be an increase in lease-sale competition. The Interior Department therefore decided to ban joint bidding on OCS leases among the major oil companies.[78] This ban was designed to

---

[78] Department of Interior press release, "Interior Bans Joint Bidding by Major Producers on Offshore Oil and Gas Tracts," September 26, 1975. Nine of 126 oil

encourage the smaller independent companies, thereby increasing competition, and to increase bonus bid prices without interfering with the desirable arrangement of joint bidding for diversification purposes by the independent oil companies.

A second way to enhance competition was early disclosure of geological and geophysical OCS data. It was widely believed that access to industry-collected-and-held geological and geophysical data would increase OCS development, helping the smaller companies particularly, and would make it easier for the government to assess resource value accurately. Traditionally, these data had been kept secret because of the high cost of acquisition and the belief that they provide a competitive advantage. The question was, what set of procedures would provide a maximum transfer of geological and geophysical data to the federal government and to the public without discouraging the industry's collection of the information?

Numerous options were reviewed, public hearings were held, and the Interior Department's final regulations were published June 1976.[79] They required that:

(1) all companies holding geological and geophysical data for any part of the OCS and wishing to be a qualified bidder for subsequent lease sales must file that data with the Geological Survey within three months;

(2) permits be obtained in the future in order to acquire all geological and geophysical data;

(3) all geological and geophysical data collected in exploring, developing, and producing on any leased tract be filed with the Geological Survey as soon as collected;

companies under the regulations were prohibited from bidding jointly with each other because they had an average daily production of more than 1.6 million barrels per day of crude, natural gas, and liquefied petroleum products over the six-month period of January 1 to June 30, 1975. The nine companies were Amoco, B-P Alaska, Chevron Oil Company, Exxon, Gulf, Mobil, Shell, Standard Oil Company of California, and Texaco. However, in December 1975, President Ford signed the Energy Policy and Conservation Act, P.L. 94-163 (89 Stat. 871), which exempted major companies from a ban on joint bidding "for lands located in frontier or other areas determined by the secretary to be extremely high risk lands or to present unusually high cost exploration or development problems." To conform with the law, the Department of Interior amended its regulations (Department of Interior press release, "Amendment to Joint Bidding Ban Announced by Interior," January 23, 1976).

[79] *Federal Register,* vol. 41, no. 22 (June 23, 1976), p. 25891.

(4) geological data be disclosed to the public in two years and geophysical data within ten years, or whenever a lease was relinquished, whichever period was less.

The benefits of these requirements were that they would provide that all geological and geophysical data, collected and to be collected in the future, be made available for government use. This would increase the government's capability to predict more accurately resource value and therefore to give better protection against a "giveaway" of the public lands. The requirements would also make data available for public and general industry use in the shortest possible time period, while providing each company with a short, but significant, period of time in which to use its proprietary data. Thus, competition should be significantly increased.

There was also a possible negative effect. The regulations might discourage future collection of data because of the short time period for proprietary use. This could result in less data available for government use and possibly fewer bonus bids. However, the administration did not expect these potentially harmful effects to be felt, because the profits from oil and gas discoveries were high enough to stimulate continued geophysical activity.

Environmental Safeguards

The chief concern about expanding the OCS leasing program was the potentially harmful effect it might have on the environment. In addition to the safeguard of requiring site-specific environmental-impact statements for each proposed lease sale, President Nixon ordered a moratorium on leasing frontier areas until a one-year environmental study, led by CEQ, could be completed on the Gulf of Alaska and the Atlantic.[80] The CEQ study took some qualitative impacts into account and ranked the frontier areas according to its best estimates of the overall risk to marine coastal and human environment that might result from OCS oil and natural gas development. In the Atlantic and Gulf of Alaska areas, the lowest risk areas were Eastern Georges Bank, Southern Baltimore Canyon, Western Georges Bank, Central Baltimore Canyon, Northern

---

[80] Office of the White House Press Secretary, Special Message to Congress by President Nixon, April 18, 1973.

296

Baltimore Canyon, and Southeast Georgia Embankment; the highest risk areas were Western Gulf of Alaska and Eastern Gulf of Alaska.[81]

The final report did not attempt to balance the environmental risks against the value and benefits of the oil and natural gas that might be discovered. The net financial value of oil and natural gas development is equivalent to the present value of the returns for oil and natural gas sales minus the total costs of production, including exploring, developing, and marketing. The Department of Interior attempted to calculate the net financial value and benefits of a typical 5,000 acre tract in Santa Barbara, Baltimore Canyon, Georges Bank, and the Gulf of Alaska (see Table 16). The present value per 5,000-acre tract of expected net revenue (see row 11) was approximately $41 million for Santa Barbara Channel, $31 million for Baltimore Canyon, $31 million for Georges Bank, and $27 million for the Gulf of Alaska. Table 16 assumes financial values based on the most promising 5,000-acre tracts. As gas production was not included in the financial values, the revenue figures are somewhat underestimated. However, if instead of using the most promising tracts, only average tracts within the geologic structures were used, and assuming production of only 800 barrels a day at Santa Barbara and 500 barrels per day in the other frontier areas, the net present value estimates would fall from $41 million to $39 million at Santa Barbara, from $31 to $11 million for Baltimore Canyon, from $31 million to $0.6 million for Georges Bank, and from $27 million to −$4.5 million for the Gulf of Alaska. However, using an average-value-per-5,000-acre-tract assumption rather than a most-promising-tracts assumption spreads the recoverable reserves over all the available acreage. The result is greatly to understate the net productivity of the most valuable tracts. The sensitivity of the estimates of net revenue to the assumptions about the rate of production and the level of undiscovered recoverable reserves cannot be understated. Thus, the use of the average tract assumption probably understated the financial values.

Environmental costs are also difficult to calculate. Table 17 attempts to estimate the costs of two major consequences of OCS development: (1) fishing losses resulting from exclusion of areas from fishing because of the presence of drilling platforms and (2) onshore damages computed from expected value of oil reaching beach areas.

---

[81] A Report to the President by the Council on Environmental Quality, *OCS Oil and Gas—An Environmental Assessment* (Washington, D.C.: U.S. Government Printing Office, April 1974), vol. 1, p. 6.

Table 16

EXTRACTION COSTS, PRODUCTION, REVENUE, AND VALUE TO POINT OF CUSTODY TRANSFER FOR BEST OIL PROSPECT FOR 5,000-ACRE TRACTS OF SELECTED OCS AREAS

Item Area	Santa Barbara	Baltimore Canyon	Georges Bank	Gulf of Alaska
1. Average number of exploratory wells to evaluate each tract	1.67	0.9	0.9	1.11
2. Average depth of exploratory wells (feet)	10,000	10,000	10,000	10,000
3. Number of producing wells	4.65	6.80	6.80	7.60
4. Depth of producing wells (feet)	7,000	9,000	9,000	9,000
5. Peak production per day (bbl)	1,000	1,000	1,000	1,500
6. Total extraction costs				
Current value	$ 12,109,188	$ 15,560,940	$ 20,229,222	$ 48,134,564
Present value equivalent	7,622,326	7,398,065	7,617,485	20,297,254
7. Total production (bbl)				
Current	18,756,456	24,187,770	24,187,770	39,474,750
Present equivalent	7,240,898	5,621,662	5,621,662	8,051,410
8. Real (present value) price per barrel (at custody transfer)	$7.10 to 1982, $6.12 after	$6.90	$6.90	$5.91
9. Total revenues				
Current value	$121,785,802	$166,895,613	$166,895,613	$233,295,773
Present value equivalent	48,253,221	38,789,470	38,789,470	47,583,832

10. Extraction costs per barrel				
Current value	$0.65	$0.64	$0.84	$1.22
Present value equivalent	1.05	1.32	1.71	2.52
11. Net value				
Current value	$109,676,614	$151,334,673	$146,666,391	$185,161,209
Present value equivalent	40,630,985	31,391,405	31,171,985	27,286,578
12. Net value per barrel				
Current value	$5.85	$6.26	$6.06	$4.69
Present value equivalent	5.61	5.58	5.19	3.39

Note: *Current value* indicates value of the oil at the time of production; *present value equivalent* indicates discounted value of the oil on future production.

Source: Department of Interior, Office of Minerals Policy Development, "Evaluation of OCS Areas by the Net Financial Benefits and Environmental Costs of Development," mimeographed, October 1974, p. II-3.

Table 17

SUMMARY OF ENVIRONMENTAL DAMAGES OF OCS
OIL AND GAS DEVELOPMENT FOR EACH 5,000-ACRE TRACT

Environment Consequence	Gulf of Alaska	Baltimore Canyon	Georges Bank	Santa Barbara
Area lost to commercial fishing (acres)	182	159	159	132
Expected volume of oil spilled (present value barrels)	4,090	607	607	782
Expected number of large spills (life of the field)	0.0542	0.0390	0.0390	0.0108
Expected volume of oil reaching beach (present value barrels, worst season)	3,988	121	304	782
Expected number of large spills reaching beaches (worst season)	0.0529	0.0078	0.0195	0.0021
Environmental damages ($):				
To commercial fishing	3,250	4,375	9,600	750
To coastal areas	1,236,120	37,505	94,228	242,389
Total	1,239,370	41,880	103,828	243,139

Source: Department of Interior, Office of Minerals Policy Development, "Evaluation of OCS Areas," p. III-17.

The net value of development equals the present value of oil sales less the total costs of production, exploring, producing, and marketing the oil. Costs of some kinds of environmental damages cannot be estimated. Oil spills and potential fishing losses are two of the major costs that can be quantified. The expected net values of developing a 5,000-acre tract in frontier areas is presented in Table 18, indicating that development would be worthwhile in each of the areas considered. The alternative of increasing oil imports was rated to be environmentally more hazardous than OCS development, based on the preliminary data at hand. The best source of data on the oil-spill rates of tankers is a Massachusetts Institute of Technology study contracted by the Council on Environmental Quality. Using a worldwide data base, the study

Table 18

FINANCIAL VALUES AND ESTIMATED ENVIRONMENTAL
DAMAGES FOR EACH 5,000-ACRE TRACT

(in thousands of dollars)

Item	Gulf of Alaska	Baltimore Canyon	Georges Bank	Santa Barbara
Financial value net of production costs[a]	27,287	31,391	31,172	40,631
Estimated environmental damages[b]	1,239	42	104	243
Financial value net of environmental damages	26,048	31,349	31,068	40,388

[a] Taken from Table 16, row 11, present value equivalent.
[b] Taken from Table 17.
Source: Department of Interior, Office of Minerals Policy Development, "Evaluation of OCS Areas," p. V-2.

estimated the average spill rate to be approximately sixteen barrels spilled for every 100,000 barrels transported (.016 percent).[82]

The Geological Survey has calculated spill rates by type of accident. The total OCS production spill rate is estimated at almost nine barrels of oil per 100,000 barrels produced (.0089 percent).[83] This figure compares favorably to the tanker spill rate of .016 percent, suggesting a net savings in oil spillage if oil is produced from the OCS rather than imported.

However, much more study is required and site-specific environmental-impact statements for each OCS region are essential to aid the decision-making process. Conditions are likely to vary considerably. For example, in the Northern Gulf of Alaska, severe environmental conditions (chiefly weather and seismic activity) combined with the need for a tanker delivery system lead to the conclusion that the oil-spill rate from pipeline accidents, platform fires, minor spillage, et cetera, could be as high as 12,650 barrels each year during the period of maximum production. In addition, along the tanker route between the

---

[82] Massachusetts Institute of Technology, "Analysis of Oil Spill Statistics," mimeographed, April 1974, p. 126.

[83] Department of Interior, "Final Environmental Impact Statement Proposed Increase in Acreage to be Offered for Oil and Gas Leasing on the Outer Continental Shelf," mimeographed, vol. 2 (July 1975), p. 47.

Gulf of Alaska and West Coast ports, up to an additional 32,000 barrels of oil might be spilled each year. These figures do not include an estimated 2,100 barrels spilled from one blowout that must be expected sometime during the life of production.[84]

Another environmental concern was the impact of offshore oil and natural gas development upon coastal areas. The problems of assessing this impact, of planning for it and of financing the needed public facilities—roads, schools, hospitals, et cetera—were being raised by governors, Congress, and the administration.

To increase the planning capability of the coastal states, the administration proposed that an additional $3 million be added to the amount of funds available for developing coastal-zone-management programs, raising the level from $7 to $10 million for FY 1975. The funds were to be spent on programs for those coastal states adjacent to OCS frontier development: California, Alaska, and the Atlantic coastal states. In a further attempt to increase cooperation and understanding between the federal government and the coastal states, the Department of Interior established an OCS advisory board consisting of state and federal officials to advise the secretary of interior.[85] Regulations were amended so that OCS lessees were required to provide affected coastal states with information on their proposed development plans, both offshore and onshore, and the states were given an opportunity to comment on the lease development plans.[86]

More fundamental was the question of sharing revenues from OCS leases with the states. The coastal states saw OCS leasing as an opportunity to obtain revenues from offshore oil even though federal court decisions had continued to hold that the OCS lands were public and belonged to the federal government (that is, all the people, not just the people of the coastal states).[87] There were three justifications for federal aid to the coastal states in connection with the OCS program: (1) to make a payment to the states in lieu of the taxes they would have collected had the OCS lands been put on the state tax rolls instead of kept within federal jurisdiction; (2) to compensate for actual

---

[84] Department of Interior, "Northern Gulf of Alaska Final Environmental Impact Statement," mimeographed, vol. 2 (November 1975), pp. 28-29.

[85] Department of Interior press release, "Outer Continental Shelf Advisory Board Established," October 2, 1975.

[86] Department of Interior press release, "Final Regulations Published to Involve Coastal States in OCS Development and Planning," November 5, 1975.

[87] Most recently United States v. Maine, 43 U.S.L.W. 4359 (March 17, 1975).

adverse impacts caused by OCS development; and (3) to provide an incentive which would encourage the states to cooperate with rather than hinder OCS development.

Congress considered the sharing of revenues on several occasions. In 1974 the Senate passed a bill allocating to the coastal states 10 percent of federal revenues from OCS oil and gas receipts, not to exceed $200 million annually with an immediate grant of $100 million from general Treasury funds.[88] As pressure mounted for some sort of federal initiative, the administration looked at several different ways of sharing revenue with coastal states adjacent to OCS development.

Alternative 1: Share a portion of the oil revenues, say 10 percent, with those coastal states directly affected by OCS development. The arguments for this alternative were that it linked revenue sharing with potential need or impact and provided an incentive for a state to look more favorably on OCS development. The arguments against it were that it ran counter to the court-established principle that OCS oil and natural gas belong to the nation as a whole and that it would be difficult to determine which states were affected and precisely how much, so that sharing would be fair. This could be a particular problem off the Atlantic OCS, where no one can know which states would be affected until oil and/or gas are discovered. Louisiana, for example, would receive a large amount of federal funds even though impacts there are relatively minimal compared to, say, Alaska.

Alternative 2: Earmark some portion of all OCS revenues for sharing with all of the fifty states through general revenue sharing. The arguments for this alternative were that it followed the principle that OCS oil and natural gas belong to all the nation, would give all states an incentive to encourage OCS development if the revenues should be significant, and would have a better chance to pass Congress, since all states would share in the potential revenues. The arguments on the other side were that it would provide no particular incentive to the coastal states to reduce opposition to development off their coasts and would complicate state and local budget planning if revenues should vary widely from year to year.

Alternative 3: Provide an incentive bonus to the coastal states based

---

[88] For a good background on this bill and the OCS issue in general, see *Congressional Quarterly Almanac,* vol. 30 (Washington, D.C.: Congressional Quarterly, Inc., 1974), pp. 806-811.

on the value of all OCS oil flowing ashore through each coastal state, and then earmark the difference between this bonus and a higher percentage of the revenues from OCS oil for a general revenue-sharing fund for all the states. The arguments in favor were that this plan would compensate the coastal states for onshore impact, would give an incentive to bring the oil ashore and build refineries there, and should reduce opposition to offshore development, except among strong environmental groups. On the other side, it was argued that the plan could complicate state and local budget planning because of annual variations in revenues, that it would reward coastal states even though the need for federal onshore impact aid was not demonstrated, and give benefits to the economy in onshore facilities that could be higher than environmental costs.

Alternative 4: Establish a Federal Energy Development Impact Assistance Fund, which would provide direct or guaranteed loans for infrastructure development, as well as planning grants to states experiencing population growth as a result of development of federal energy resources. In February 1976, Interior Secretary Kleppe forwarded this proposal with administration endorsement to Congress. There were three major arguments for the proposal: (1) Given the difficulty of designing impact aid programs because of great uncertainties about the location and size of future offshore oil fields and about specific plans for producing them, this proposal has the virtue of providing a mechanism for calculating specific needs and then providing the correct amount of federal assistance; it would eliminate the "shotgun" approach of making automatic grants or revenue sharing allotments to meet future unspecified needs. (2) In the long run, state and local corporate and personal income taxes on the new industries, services, and jobs created at the onshore facilities needed for exploration and development of offshore oil fields should bring in enough revenues to finance these needs and more. However, in the first few years, revenues might lag behind the cost of the facilities and services, and in some very remote rural areas, they might never catch up. In these cases federal aid should be timed to solve these front-end problems. (3) States would be more likely to meet the test of genuine need under this proposal than under the others, because relief would be in the form of loans to meet fiscal strains resulting from federal energy decisions, rather than outright grants or revenues from OCS oil and gas. Furthermore, loan forgiveness would be only to the extent that development activities failed to achieve projected levels of employment and population as a result of circumstances beyond the control of the state or locality.

As the administration reviewed the four alternatives in the summer of 1975, Congress, responding to pressures from the environmentalists and to what was a questionable need for onshore impact aid to coastal states, saw an opportunity to share OCS oil and gas receipts with coastal states. In July 1975, the Senate Commerce Committee (which had jurisdiction over federal coastal-zone-management programs) and the Senate Interior and Insular Affairs Committee (which had jurisdiction over OCS lands) reported out similar bills.[89] These bills were then amended on the floor to make their provisions for federal aid for energy-facility-siting-impact programs the same. As amended, the two bills authorized the Department of Commerce to provide $200 million annually over three years for grants and loans to coastal states to offset adverse impacts on the coastal zone resulting from energy-related development. In addition, they authorized $100 million annually for automatic grants to coastal states adjacent to OCS oil production or to states landing oil from the OCS. Both "adjacent" and "landing" states would receive the same treatment: namely, grants for production in excess of 100,000 barrels per day but not exceeding 1.5 million barrels per day, the grants to be on the basis of 20 cents per barrel in the first year, 15 cents the second, 10 cents in the third, and 8 cents in the fourth.

In the House and later in conference, the administration was successful in eliminating some of the costly provisions in the Senate bill and in July President Ford signed the Coastal Zone Management Act Amendments of 1976. The chief feature of the law was to provide financial assistance for coastal states in planning for and responding to the impacts of coastal energy activity. The law authorized $1.2 billion. Of this amount, $400 million was authorized over eight years ($50 million a year) for formula grants available to OCS-impacted states according to the following formula: OCS acreage initially leased (33.3 per cent); residents gaining new OCS-related employment (33.3 per cent); OCS oil and natural gas produced (16.7 percent); and OCS oil and gas first landed (16.7 percent). The remaining $800 million was

---

[89] S. 586, the Senate Commerce Committee bill, passed the Senate 73 to 15 on July 16; S. 521, the Senate Interior and Insular Affairs Committee bill, passed the Senate 67 to 19 on July 30, 1975.

authorized to be appropriated over the next ten years. It would provide planning grants to help states prepare for the impact of energy facilities; loans and guarantees to finance public facilities and services associated with coastal energy activity; repayment assistance for full or partial forgiveness of loans where adequate state tax revenues are not generated by energy-facility-related impacts; and environment grants to cover damage by energy activity if liability cannot be identified.

The companion bill, S. 521, in September 1976 was recommitted to conference by a House vote of 198–194.[90] If Congress had passed the bill it was likely that the President would have vetoed it for the following major reasons:

(1) The bill provided for cancellation of leases because of pollution hazards but allowed the secretary to take into consideration only environmental benefits, even when it might clearly be in the public interest to continue oil or natural gas production.

(2) Congress required that one-third of all OCS frontier acreage should be devoted to new, untested bidding systems. Interior had already been conducting experimental bidding systems and required far less acreage to test the effectiveness of new systems. With the large amounts of acreage involved, a needless reduction in revenues or a substantial loss of oil and gas might result if an experimental bidding system failed.

(3) If it is to explore the OCS, a company must be able to protect the proprietary information it collects and pays for, but the bill required that the states be given access to this data, thus tending to undermine the firm's competitive position.

(4) The bill required permits for on-structure stratigraphic drilling to be offered before leases are sold. This requirement erroneously implies that one test is enough to determine fair market value, but, if oil were discovered in the initial stratigraphic test, there would be intense pressure for further exploration by the government before a lease sale was held. As a result, the federal government would intrude further into a realm that should be preserved for industry, risking private capital rather than the taxpayer's money.

The above objections do not imply that revision of the Outer Continental Shelf Act of 1953 is undesirable. Some revisions are needed. More administrative flexibility in the lease terms would be useful, for

---

[90] *Congressional Quarterly,* vol. 34, no. 40 (October 2, 1976), p. 2729.

example, and so would authority to lease geologic structures larger than 5,760 acres. Also, the primary terms of a lease should be extended perhaps to ten years in the Arctic, where severe weather and ice conditions limit exploration seasons.

Environmental Assessment Monitoring. In March 1974, the secretary of interior established the Outer Continental Shelf Research Management Advisory Board to advise the Interior Department on the design and implementation of OCS environmental studies.[91] Membership originally included representatives of Mississippi, Alabama, Florida (in preparation for a Gulf Coast lease sale affecting these states), the Department of Interior, NOAA, and EPA but, as OCS work proceeded, it was expanded rapidly to include all the coastal states. The group was brought together to help achieve and refine these objectives: (1) to compile information needed to identify valuable competitive resources and natural hazards and to assess the environmental impacts of OCS development; (2) to develop a data base against which to monitor change attributable to development; (3) to develop contract stipulations and regulatory controls to minimize the undesirable environmental effects of OCS development; (4) to contribute to an understanding of the potential effects of offshore spills by sponsoring toxicity studies and other research; and (5) to assist in making better decisions on the sale and management of leases.

The principal purpose of the environmental program is to assess OCS areas before development in order to avoid damage to valuable competing resources (such as shrimp beds) and to identify hazards (such as fault zones) that must be avoided or handled by engineering innovation. A second purpose is to establish a data benchmark against which change in environmental conditions over a long period of time can be judged. Work starts with an information inventory of the OCS lease area, which is to say, acquisition of published and unpublished data that may be useful in characterizing the environment and identifying data gaps. Once the gaps in information have been identified, a data collection program is begun. Offshore benchmark surveys generally consist of three-dimensional grid samplings of the water column and bottom sediments, together with physical, oceanographic, geologic, and meteorologic measurements to help describe environmental conditions.

---

[91] *Federal Register,* vol. 39, no. 57 (March 22, 1974), p. 10919.

As OCS exploration begins, a joint government-lessee monitoring operation is set in motion to detect refuse from the operation (for example, drill cuttings) and environmental change related to the operation that might be mitigated by improved regulations. Once reserves have been discovered and likely land falls have been identified, the data collection program expands to related coastal areas. The special research studies, for example, on oil spill trajectories, socioeconomic impact modeling, and toxicity, proceed concurrently with inventory and monitoring. They help to identify probable land falls for OCS spills, to improve contingency plans for dealing with them, and to improve basic understanding of socioeconomic and ecological risks.

Benchmark studies were begun in the undeveloped eastern Gulf of Mexico off Mississippi, Florida, and Alabama just before this area of the OCS was leased in May 1974. Similar benchmark studies were started in the Gulf of Alaska in July 1974, in the Gulf of Mexico off south Texas in November 1974, and in the Mid-Atlantic OCS in January 1975.[92] The budget for such studies more than doubled between fiscal years 1975 and 1976 (see Table 19), and the program was rapidly expanded to provide more comprehensive environmental inventories, benchmark surveys, monitoring, and special studies for the frontier areas.

Oil Spill Liability. Increased transportation of petroleum products and stepped-up offshore drilling have raised the likelihood that there will be oil spill damage to fisheries and waterfront properties. As a result, both Congress and the states have in recent years passed laws increasing industry liability for damages and creating individual funds to compensate for damages. Among these laws are the federal Deepwater Ports Act and Trans Alaska Pipeline Act and the laws of Florida and Maine. Because of the rush to legislation, there are overlapping liability systems, duplicative compensation funds, and procedural uncertainties. Moreover, the ability of an injured party to receive full compensation for oil damages varies from state to state and for different federal funds.

In July 1975, the Ford administration sent Congress a bill to provide a single nationwide liability system for damages from all oil discharged from U.S. offshore operations and from ships operating in U.S. waters. The bill would establish a fund adequate to pay claims up to $20 million for a tanker oil spill and up to $50 million for spills related

---

[92] For details refer to the Outer Continental Shelf Research Management Advisory Board, Department of Interior, *Annual Report 1974* and *1975*.

Table 19

BUDGET FOR OCS ENVIRONMENTAL STUDIES
(in millions of dollars)

Program Element	FY 1975	FY 1976
Inventory	$ 0.6	$ 1.0
Benchmark surveys	17.4	38.3
Monitoring	2.2	7.0
Special studies	3.1	6.0
Total	$23.3	$52.3

Source: Personal communication from Department of Interior.

to onshore and offshore facilities such as pipelines and drilling rigs. A $200 million fund would be financed by (1) fees, not to exceed three cents per barrel, assessed on oil moving through terminals for import or export and on crude oil received at refineries and (2) receipts collected from civil and criminal fines paid by those responsible for oil spills.

By the fall of 1976 Congress had not ratified international conventions for preventing oil and other toxic materials from being discharged into international waters and for establishing an international fund to compensate for damages. The following was the status of other matters that had been pending before Congress:

(1) An international convention for prevention of pollution from ships (November 2, 1973). Not ratified and no bills pending.

(2) An international convention on civil liabilities for oil pollution damage (November 27, 1973). Not ratified, but addressed in H.R. 9294 and S. 2162.

(3) The establishment of an international fund for compensation for oil pollution damages (December 18, 1971). Not ratified, but addressed in H.R. 9294 and S. 2162.

(4) A protocol relating to intervention on the high seas in the cases of marine pollution by substances other than oil (November 2, 1973). Not ratified, but addressed in H.R. 11406 and S. 2549.

Superports

By 1972, as oil imports continued to rise following the peak in domestic crude production in 1971, and as the number of supertankers and superports increased in virtually all the major industrialized coastal nations except the United States, it became more and more obvious that the United States would have to address the superport issue. At that time about one quarter of the world's oil tanker capacity was in ships heavier than 175,000 deadweight tons.[93] None of these ships could enter U.S. ports. East and Gulf Coast ports were limited to forty-five-foot channels and the Los Angeles channel was about forty-eight feet; whereas the 200,000 deadweight tankers require a draft of about fifty-eight feet. There were about fifty superports around the world, but not one in U.S. waters.

President Nixon set up a task force (John Schaefer of the Domestic Council took the lead among the key White House staff) that included representatives of the Council of Economic Advisers, CEQ, EPA, the Army Corps of Engineers, the Maritime Administration, the Coast Guard, OMB, the Department of Interior, the Office of Emergency Preparedness, and NOAA. The major issues that had to be thrashed out were these:

(1) Are there economic benefits to the nation, net of environmental costs, from constructing superports?

(2) Is legislation necessary or is there sufficient legal authority for issuing a license for a superport beyond the three-mile limit?

(3) Should ports be financed wholly or partly with federal funds?

(4) What is the role of the federal and state authority in licensing a superport and what are the implications of this authority on decision making as it relates to onshore impact, including refinery siting?

(5) What bureaucratic machinery is necessary to provide one-window licensing by one agency, with adequate coordination with other responsible agencies.

The Economics of Superports. The task force concluded that under most circumstances the construction of a superport would produce substantial

---

[93] By the end of 1973, there were 388 supertankers of 200,000 deadweight tons in service worldwide and 493 under construction or under order. See Noel Mostert, *Supership* (New York: Alfred Knopf, 1974), p. 19.

Table 20

SAVINGS RESULTING FROM AN EAST COAST
U.S. MONOBUOY SUPERPORT

(cents per barrel)

Throughput[a]	Worst Case[b]	Best Case[c]
0.600	−4.0	3.3
0.800	−1.6	5.7
1.000	−0.2	7.2
1.135	0.4	7.8
1.200	1.0	8.4
1.572	3.2	10.5
2.000	5.3	12.7
2.500	6.6	14.0
3.200	7.4	14.8
5.106	8.1	15.5
6.600	9.1	16.5

a In millions of barrels per day.

b Tankers serving U.S. superports required to have double bottoms, while tankers serving foreign ports not so required.

c For the most part, tankers serving both U.S. and foreign ports required to have double bottoms.

Source: Department of Interior, Final Environmental Impact Statement, "Deepwater Ports," mimeographed, vol. 2 (April 1974), Table B7, p. B-44.

savings in the cost of oil and that the amount of savings per barrel would tend to increase as throughput rose. Analysis showed exceptions where there were low levels of throughput. At the same time, supertankers serving U.S. ports would be newly required to have double bottoms whereas tankers serving foreign ports would not. There are three technologies for building superports—monobuoy, a sea island, and an artificial island. Table 20 shows the savings that could be achieved by a monobuoy superport.

If there were full environmental safeguards at both foreign and U.S. ports, the estimated savings in the cost of oil would range from 3.3 cents per barrel for 0.6 million barrels a day to 16.5 cents per barrel for 6.6 million barrels a day throughput. On the Gulf Coast the task force estimated cost savings ranging from 2.7 cents per barrel for a 1.4 million barrel per day throughput to 18.2 cents per barrel for a 14.7 million barrel per day throughput.[94] However, much if not all of the cost saving from superports could be nullified if a U.S. flag were required for tankers docking at U.S. ports. U.S. costs for supertanker construction are much higher than costs elsewhere, and the tanker itself is by far the largest cost component of the superport system.

Also, the cost study concluded that a pipeline distribution system from the supertanker facility offshore is generally the least costly alternative and the greater the throughput, the greater the cost savings for the pipeline. The exception would be a Gulf Coast port handling less than 2 million barrels a day throughput, for which tug-barge distribution produces slightly lower costs—this because crude oil demand on the Gulf Coast is more dispersed than crude oil demand on other coasts. In general, the more concentrated the demand, as on the East Coast, the more cost effective is the pipeline distribution system. It may be noted that sea islands and artificial islands are generally not competitive with monobuoys except at protected East Coast sites like Raritan and Delaware bays, where the monobuoys will not require expensive breakwaters.

Environmental Considerations. The task force's major environmental findings may be briefly summarized. Vulnerability to environmental damage is reduced with distance from shore. The further offshore the site, the less the chance of oil spills reaching beaches and estuaries, and the longer the oil spill is at sea the less toxic it becomes. The greater the distance of the superport site from shore, the more likely that an oil slick would disperse seaward from wind and current forces and never reach shore.

Monobuoy construction, with buried pipeline, results in less environmental degradation than onshore terminal construction, which can require massive dredging and the added problem of dredge-spoil disposal at onshore sites, destruction of near and onshore habitats, saltwater intrusion into ground water, and an increase in the salinity of estuaries. A strong case was made that the amount of oil spilled was likely to be less with some U.S. superports than with none, where there would be a large number of smaller tankers operating. Table 21 gives

---

[94] Department of Interior, Final Environmental Impact Statement, "Deepwater Ports," mimeographed, vol. 2 (April 1974), pp. B-43 to B-45.

Table 21

ESTIMATES OF OIL SPILLS FOR TWO KINDS OF SUPERPORTS
OR WITH NO SUPERPORT

Item	Barrels of Oil Spilled Annually
No U.S. superports	3,500
U.S. superports: 100 percent transshipment by vessel	
Vessel accidents	6,935
Transfer operations	+4,015
	10,950
U.S. superports: 100 percent transshipment by pipeline	
Vessel accidents	730
Transfer operations	365
Per 10 miles of pipeline	+360
	1,455

Source: Department of Interior, "Deepwater Ports," vol. 1, p. IV-143.

estimates of the oil that would be spilled annually without environmental controls in U.S. coastal waters for every million barrels a day of throughput.

From these data, it seems clear that the use of U.S. superports with 100-percent transshipment by pipeline would cut in half the amount of oil spilled under the present system, which relies on small tankers and no superports. On the other hand, there would be a much larger amount of oil spilled with superports using 100-percent vessel transshipment (instead of pipeline transshipment) than under the no-superport alternative. Two steps in the vessel transport system are not present in the pipeline system: (1) loading oil into smaller vessels from the superport facility, thus risking more transfer spills, and (2) shipping the oil to shore on many smaller vessels, risking groundings and collisions.

The task force cost-effectiveness analysis indicated (1) that the single most cost-effective control to reduce oil spills is pipeline transshipment from the superport to shore; (2) that double bottoms on supertankers are highly cost effective, but double-bottom barges are not cost effective when compared to pipeline transshipment; (3) that siting the superport away from shore is more cost effective than onshore alternatives; and (4) that traffic controls are cost effective for all studied alternative sites and transshipment modes.

Onshore secondary environmental impact was analyzed at five most likely superport sites—Machias, Maine; northern and southern New Jersey; southern Louisiana, and the mid-Texas coast. In Machias, Maine, the analysis indicated that 650,000-barrels-per-day refinery capacity would result in a minimal long-term strain on the environment because of the area's unused land and water supply and its small population. Unquestionably, however, the character of the area would change, the chief problem being the influx of skilled workers for refinery construction. There would be significant environmental impact in the New Jersey area, particularly if one large superport were constructed to serve the entire middle Atlantic region. The impact would be mitigated if East Coast refinery development were limited to continuing the arrangement in which 75 percent of East Coast products are refined in the Gulf Coast or overseas. There would, however, probably be considerable pressure to add a massive superport and refinery complex to the refinery complex already in existence. Also there would be the economic advantage of refining products close to their market. A less environmentally degrading scenario would be to disperse the refining capacity and related industry by having offshore receiving facilities at several locations along the coast. Along the Louisiana and Texas coasts, secondary impact appears to be less severe than in some other areas even for very large superport transshipments. Both areas already support major refinery and petrochemical industries. Dispersion, as in the case of the mid-Atlantic area, would do much to mitigate secondary impact.

Onshore effects of superports should not be discounted. New refineries and petrochemical plants require large amounts of land and water and can cause air and water pollution. Secondary industries will grow up to support refinery and petrochemical plants and the increased population will bring additional pressure for industrial and residential housing, with accompanying pressure on the water supply and public services.

However, with strict environmental controls, with federal funds to assist in financing planning through the Coastal Zone Management Act, and with a detailed environmental-impact statement required for each superport permit, there should be ample opportunity to build in the required environmental controls.

Legal Issues. The task force concluded that no existing federal law specifically authorized the federal government to license construction of a superport beyond the three-mile limit. The Army Corps of Engineers has authority under 33 U.S.C. 401-415 to regulate construction, dredging and filling, and alteration of navigable rivers. Under subsection 4(f) of the Outer Continental Shelf Act, the secretary of the army has authority to prevent obstruction to navigation in navigable waters, including "artificial structures" and "fixed structures" on the OCS. This authority might be construed to include authority to build superports, but it was really intended to block construction. Nor was there any evidence that the Congress even considered the possibility of building superports on the continental shelf at the time the act was passed in 1953. Congress used language to interpret the act narrowly. Later, the 1958 Convention on the Continental Shelf provided that the adjacent coastal state has "sovereign rights [over its continental shelf] for the purpose of exploring it and exploiting its natural resources." [95] Thus neither domestic nor international law seemed to support U.S. authority to use the continental shelf for loading or unloading.

The Interior Department's authority to build superports seemed equally shaky. Under subsection 5(c) of the OCS Lands Act of 1953, the secretary of the interior had the authority to grant rights-of-way for pipelines on the shelf, presumably to gather oil, gas, or other natural resources from the shelf. But since the language of subsection 5(c) does not explicitly limit the Interior Department's authority over pipelines built to transport oil, natural gas, or anything else from the shelf, the language could be construed to mean that the department had authority to grant pipeline rights-of-way to transship oil across the shelf. This would be oil and natural gas not produced from the continental shelf but transshipped from superport to shore. Also, although one monobuoy might be narrowly construed as part of a pipeline, there seemed to be no authority to license much larger facilities, like sea islands or artificial islands at the end of the pipeline. In brief, there seemed to be serious doubt that a court would confirm the Interior Department's authority under the OCS Lands Act of 1953 in such a way as to justify licensing superports. New legislation was needed.

[95] 15 U.S.T. 1964, paragraph 1 of Article 2.

In asserting legal justification for jurisdiction over superports beyond territorial waters, the administration was careful to take a position consistent with the U.S. negotiating position for each of the law of the sea conferences. At those conferences, an underlying U.S. principle was the right of all nations to use the high seas, restricting the right of coastal states to claim extension of their territorial waters. The task force was conscious that the U.S. negotiating position must not be undermined by any unilateral assertion of territorial jurisdiction over any part of the high seas for the purpose of constructing superports. In particular the task force contended that superport legislation should grant the authority to ensure proper operations but should avoid any geographical definitions that other nations might construe as an attempt to extend American territorial waters. Ignoring this principle, Congress in 1976 passed and the President signed a law unilaterally extending U.S. fishing rights to 200 miles offshore (see Chapter 12).

Although Article 2 of the Convention on the High Seas [96] prohibits nations from asserting sovereignty over areas of the high seas, it also notes the freedom to use the high seas—citing specifically the freedoms of navigation, fishing, pipeline- and cable-laying, and flying over the high seas. This list is expressly non-exclusive so that new uses of the high seas may be in order, provided they do not interfere with the freedom of other nations. A good case could be made that creation of superports would be an acceptable use of the high seas, provided that the superport did not unduly interfere with the navigation, fishing, scientific research, cable and pipeline laying, and so on of other nations. Also, superports could give tangible benefits to other nations (ports of refuge, sites for navigation aides, for example) and could reduce the chances for collisions and marine pollution. Inherent in the right of use of the high seas must be an adequate jurisdictional basis for ensuring safe and efficient operation of superports. Also, the right to enforce the laws and regulations, both with respect to any nationality of ships and with respect to personnel docked at a superport, was implicit in the "reasonable use" concept.

In theory, enforcement of federal regulations against foreign flag vessels at or near a superport could be difficult because of the lack of authority on any territorial basis. It appeared unlikely that there would be any enforcement problem, however, because the ability to

[96] Article 2, Convention on the High Seas, 450 U.N.T.S. 11; 13 U.S.T. 2312; T.I.A.S. 5200; Geneva 1958.

316

refuse the use of a superport should be sufficient to gain compliance with U.S. federal superport regulations.

Financing of Superports. The administration gave no serious thought to federal financing of superports. The task force study, although reviewing potential superport rates and various technologies in order to assess the general economic benefits and environmental costs, avoided specific and detailed cost comparisons for various sites and technologies. Federal planning of this kind seems to have an element of self-fulfilling prophecy so that federal analysis might lead to inhibiting or obstructing specific alternatives. A survey of active superport planning by industry in 1972 made it clear that industry was willing to finance superport construction without government aid. A consortium of fifteen oil companies was studying the feasibility of a superport in Delaware Bay inside Cape May. A ten-company consortium planned a superport (Loop Project) in the Mississippi Delta, near Southwest Pass off Louisiana, and by July 1972, a nine-company consortium was planning the Seadock Project, a mono-buoy system off Freeport, Texas, feeding by pipeline the refining centers of Texas City, Houston, Pasadena, Beaumont, and Port Arthur.

The Federal and State Authority in Licensing and Siting Superports. The administration saw no great difficulty in meshing state and federal regulatory laws within the three-mile limit, permitting states to maintain maximum authority consistent with federal regulations. However, since receiving facilities are subject to state jurisdiction, state veto power could thwart superport construction. This became one of the key issues in Congress.

One-Window Licensing. To avoid dealing with a bewildering list of agencies having partial and often overlapping authority for superports, the task force agreed that a single federal government agency should be given basic licensing authority over superport facilities, and other agencies with special expertise should be granted authority separately in the regulatory scheme. After the usual bureaucratic infighting by the agencies for leadership of the program, the White House staff and the Office of Management and Budget [97] recommended to the President that the Department of Interior should be the lead agency but ultimately the

---

[97] Peter Flanigan, John Schaefer, and the author for the White House staff, and William Morrill for OMB.

authority should reside in a proposed new Department of Energy and Natural Resources. The logic of establishing the DENR seemed overwhelming, since the relevant agencies in Interior and the Army Corps of Engineers that dealt with superports were slated to become part of DENR. Other contenders were the Maritime Administration, the Department of Transportation, and the Environmental Protection Agency.

Congress eventually decided to give the lead agency role to the Department of Transportation. It became a small issue for the administration because of the failure of Congress to act on legislation for DENR. Although the respective bureaucracies lobbied Congress on the lead agency issue, their respective cabinet officers were not particularly concerned about the lead role, so long as the legislation passed. However, the jurisdictional squabbles were much more important in the Congress. Six committees held superport hearings: Commerce, Interior, and Public Works in the Senate, and Interior, Merchant Marine and Fisheries, and Public Works in the House. The Senate established ad hoc subcommittees comprised of five members from each full committee, to hold hearings and recommend legislation to the full committees. The inevitable jurisdictional disputes in Congress over which agency would control the program and therefore which congressional committee would have oversight jurisdiction contributed to the delay in passing the bill.

President Nixon sent the legislation to Congress in April 1973, as part of an overall energy message.[98] One last-minute touch was to abandon the term *superport* for the less environmentally menacing term *deepwater ports*. But the touch was insufficient and everyone continued to talk of superports.

A year later Congress was still a long way from passing a superport bill. The House had become polarized around two bills, H.R. 11951, sponsored by the Interior and Merchant Marine committees and closest of them all to the administration proposal (H.R. 5898), and H.R. 10701, a Public Works Committee bill. The latter was opposed by the administration, principally because it permitted several states adjacent to a proposed superport to veto the project and authorized states to set "reasonable fees, tolls or charges" for superports off their shores. Since the superport was designed to benefit the whole nation, it did not seem proper for one or two coastal states to obtain all the revenues. Fees also could discourage private investment and could limit oil imports. In

[98] Office of the White House Press Secretary, Special Message to Congress on Energy, April 18, 1973.

addition, the Public Works Committee bill called for a Federal Deepwater Port Facilities Licensing Commission composed of the Interior, Commerce and Transportation departments, the Environmental Protection Agency and the Army Corps of Engineers. In the administration's view, this would destroy the one-window licensing concept and would lead to bureaucratic delays in administering the program. The Public Works Committee's bill gave the states preference over all other applicants and permitted a state to assign its license to whomever it chose. The administration viewed this as extending state authority beyond its proper jurisdiction. Finally, dredging companies were successful in inserting a provision that would require the secretary of transportation to look at the economic, social and environmental effects of dredging harbors to accommodate supertankers instead of constructing superports.

In the House Rules Committee, competing forces caused the superport issue to be considered at three long and sometimes stormy sessions—something of a record for a bill that had no significant organized opposition. Two things worked to defeat the Public Works Committee bill—what seemed to many members a grossly unfair rule (favoring the public works bill) and the dredging provision, which drew the environmentalists' fire. In the floor debate it was the powerful chairman of the Public Works Committee, Robert Jones, Democrat of Alabama, pitted against Chairwoman Leonor Sullivan, Democrat of Missouri, of the Merchant Marine and Fisheries Committee, with the administration and the environmentalists favoring the Merchant Marine Committee's bill. The floor debate indicated that there was substantial sentiment for the latter version. This indication of sentiment, coupled with a parliamentary move, brought a vote on the substitution of the Merchant Marine Committee's version for the public works bill. By a vote of 174 to 158,[99] the House struck from H.R. 10701 (the public works bill) everything following the enacting clause and substituted the wording of the Merchant Marine Committee's bill (H.R. 11951), which was then passed on a 318-to-9 vote.[100] The substitute action was destined to complicate the congressional process later, when the conference committee was called.

In the Senate, legislative action was even slower and more complex than it had been in the House. In spite of requests by President Nixon

---

[99] *Congressional Record,* vol. 120, no. 81 (June 6, 1974), pp. H4891-92.
[100] Ibid., pp. H4892-93.

for superport bill passage in his messages to Congress of June, November, and December 1973, and January 1974, the superport bill did not pass the Senate until October 9, 1974. The jurisdictional question did not generate as much heat in the Senate as in the House. Delay was simply a function of what was only marginal interest by the committees and a false notion that Project Independence objectives eliminated the need for continued importation of crude oil through superports.

The House bill gave the states veto power over the construction of a superport within ten miles of the state, a provision acceptable to the administration. But the final bill that passed the Senate gave the states veto power over superport construction: (1) if the state were connected by pipeline to the proposed superport, (2) if the state were within fifteen miles of the proposed superport, and (3) if the administrator of the National Oceanic and Atmospheric Administration (NOAA) determined that a state would incur "substantial risk of serious damage" to its coastal environment from an oil spill because of winds, currents, or whatever. This provision in particular gave the administration concern, because it could invite opposition from distant states to almost any superport proposal, and particularly from a state that would not realize a direct financial benefit. Because of the vague language, NOAA could be required to designate hundreds of miles of coastline as subject to "substantial risk of serious damage" from any deepwater port. This could be tantamount to a ban on superports for the Atlantic and New England states, which would force concentration of deepwater ports in the Gulf of Mexico, far from most demand centers. On the other hand, if superports could be properly distributed, onshore impact would be lessened and would spread refinery construction and distribution of products in such a way as to minimize the costs to the consumer. Some of the cost savings for superports would then be lost, particularly to East Coast consumers who would have to pay pipeline transportation costs from Gulf Coast superports.

A stumbling block in appointing conferees cropped up in the House. With H.R. 10701 being a Public Works Committee numbered bill, the chairman of that committee claimed the majority of the House conferees. However, the body of the bill was drafted by the Merchant Marine Committee and Chairwoman Sullivan claimed a majority of the conferees. The House leadership favored the Public Works Committee, and its members made up the majority of the conferees. With the Public Works Committee opposed to the Merchant Marine Committee's version of the

House bill, it was a foregone conclusion that the Senate version would be reported out by the conference. That is what happened and, without any changes, the Senate bill reached the White House.

Despite the several objectionable features of the bill, the President decided to sign it,[101] because a veto would cause further delay (with no guarantee the bill could be improved) at the very time the nation needed to get moving on superport construction.

[101] The Deepwater Ports Act of 1974, P.L. 93-627 (88 Stat. 2126), January 3, 1975.

12

Emerging Problems and Summing Up

If you want to discover tomorrow's problems, then look in the book stores today. The abuses to the environment and the pending energy crisis were well documented by the late 1960s, yet political leaders and government institutions were ill prepared to handle the problems when the crisis "hit." The reason was fairly simple: lack of money. Such problems cost enormous amounts of money to solve, and usually, when the crisis is not here and now, political leaders either are ineffective or see no political gain in urging voters to pay taxes for matters that do not threaten their immediate well-being. Nor are presidents usually able to find money to solve new problems by reordering priorities and eliminating expenditures on problems that for all practical purposes have already been solved. President Nixon's proposed Federal Economy Act of 1970 [1] was a classic example of how presidential leadership is impotent compared with the iron triangle of common interest linking the middle-level bureaucracy, the congressional subcommittees, and the special interest groups. Many presidents had attempted to abolish obsolete programs by taking them on one at a time and had failed, so Nixon came up with the idea of dealing with fourteen programs—all sacred cows, in his opinion, that had outlived their usefulness—in one message to Congress, hoping to embarrass the lawmakers into making some budget cuts. If all his recommendations for reductions, restructuring, or termination that required congressional action had been accepted, about $1.1 billion would have been saved. Yet, today, each of those programs still exists, and some have been restructured and even enlarged.

---

[1] *Public Papers of the Presidents, Nixon, 1970,* Special Message to the Congress on the Proposed Federal Economy Act of 1970, February 26, pp. 215-219.

Had the federal government in the 1950s and 1960s had the foresight to pass today's pollution laws before the air and water became so dirty, and the land so expensive and crowded, then the enormous burdens that will be imposed upon the taxpayers over the next twenty-five years to cleanse our environment and provide open spaces could have been avoided. If the federal government had begun judicious funding of a long-term program to develop nuclear, geothermal, and solar energy and to convert coal to gas and oil, then the taxpayers today would not have to support a crash multibillion-dollar research-and-development effort—one so large and complex as to assure considerable inefficiencies. And if the government had moved more quickly on the Alaskan Naval Petroleum Reserve #4 and the outer-continental-shelf search for oil, then the nation might be self-sufficient, instead of importing oil at a cost of approximately $24 billion annually, and rising.

It seems that the environmental revolution and the energy crisis of the 1970s could be forerunners of far more serious problems. Food, water, and mineral shortages, for example, would have even more serious ramifications than the present difficulties.

Worldwide Food Shortages. In 1972, farm prices were relatively low and federal agricultural policy, as it had been for years, centered on the problem of disposal of food surpluses. Yet by 1973, through a series of events—such as poor weather and the Soviet decision to buy 18 million tons of grain in the U.S. and 30 million tons worldwide—U.S. grain stocks were so low that the federal government embraced a new policy. Previous federal programs designed to keep land out of production were dropped as government-held stocks were virtually eliminated.

In the short run, at least until 1980, there should be expanded grain production in countries like Argentina, Canada, and the United States. But the 1975 world crop forecast did not live up to expectations because of dry weather in Canada, Europe, the Soviet Union, and the United States. Fortunately, in the critical undeveloped areas of India, Pakistan, and the sub-Sahara, weather conditions were much better. But there is still considerable jeopardy for the poor, food-importing countries because of depleted stocks and fertilizer shortages and because of the high fuel costs brought on by the price increases of OPEC and the very limited foreign exchange of these countries. Beyond 1980 the role of the United States as a major supplier of food for world markets and as an exporter of farm technology must grow significantly. The dependence of poor nations on food imports will probably continue to increase. Even so, without either a reduction in the rate of population growth in the developing countries or unforeseen breakthroughs in food production techniques, the race for an adequate food supply will continue to be a problem deserving this nation's full attention.

In giving a view that most experts agree with, Don Paarlberg, director of agricultural economics for the Department of Agriculture, said, "In the long run, looking into the twenty-first century, unless the rate of population growth is checked, there is no solution to the world food problem." [2] Even if productivity increases dramatically, some problems will persist. Bad weather and pestilence require some sort of world reserve food stocks as an insurance policy against starvation. But building these world food stocks entails difficult decisions, such as less consumption and higher food prices while the stocks are being accumulated. Both the detailed policy and the mechanics for establishing a world food reserve need to be aggressively worked out. The cost of these stocks should be borne by all countries. In the past, other countries would not incur the cost of purchasing and storing their own stocks because the stability of the world price and the availability of imports was reasonably assured by the presence of large U.S.-government-owned stocks.

Other serious questions arise about the mechanics of building a world food reserve. Should the U.S. continue to use private traders to carry stocks or should they be held by the federal government? Should barter become an instrument of building stockpiles—Soviet oil, for example, for American grain? Even if the mechanics could be worked out, the domestic political problems of building such a costly stockpile would be enormous. During the last ten years, the United States supplied 90 percent of the world's food aid. Could the President and Congress ask the voters to pay higher costs for their own food so that stockpiles can be accumulated, when this nation has no food shortage and the problem is far away? Relying on American generosity in spite of these domestic concerns, at the United Nations World Food Conference in Rome in 1974 President Ford authorized Agriculture Secretary Earl Butz to enter into an international system of nationally held food reserves. Tentatively the world stockpile would be about 30 million metric tons of grain, of which the U.S. reserve would be about 25 per-

---

2 Don Paarlberg, *The World Food Situation: Consensus View,* Remarks before the World Future Society Second General Assembly, Washington, D.C., June 3, 1975.

cent, or about $2 billion worth of grain costing about $100 million annually to store.

One can also speculate about political benefits to be derived from building a worldwide food reserve. With the United States far and away the world's largest exporter of grain, food exports could give the nation as much or even more international influence as oil gives OPEC. But could this life-or-death power be used in a positive and constructive way to achieve international stability? In times of worldwide food shortage, would the United States or other large grain exporters (Canada, Australia, New Zealand, and Argentina) use the threat of stopping exports to hungry nations as an instrument of foreign policy? A sizable worldwide food reserve will act as a safety valve, so that no nation applies that sort of coercion.[3]

Another food-supply concern is the prevention of depletion of worldwide fish stocks. Limited progress was achieved when the International Commission for the Northwestern Atlantic Fisheries agreed to reduce overall catch limitations from 923,900 metric tons in 1974 to 850,000 metric tons in 1975.[4] And after tough negotiations at the Montreal meeting in September 1975, the commission's overall catch quota off the northeast coast of the United States for 1976 was reduced further to 650,000 metric tons, a level that should result in recovery of depleted stocks to a maximum sustainable yield level in about seven years.[5]

Congress, however, became impatient with a succession of law of the sea conferences that had not acted to establish a 200-mile fishing zone and decided to take unilateral action. Atlantic, Pacific, and Alaskan fishermen had complained repeatedly that efficient and technologically sophisticated foreign fishing fleets were depleting coastal waters. In April 1976, President Ford signed a bill establishing a 200-mile fishing limit off U.S. coasts to protect American fishermen and to guard against over-fishing by foreign fleets. Stiff fines were provided for foreign fishermen who exceeded catch quotas set at various limits for different species.[6]

---

[3] For more on this interesting concept, see Vernon Guidry, Jr., "The Awesome Food Weapon May Not Be Loaded," *Washington Star,* January 28, 1976, and "Food: Potential U.S. Weapon," *U.S. News & World Report,* February 16, 1976, pp. 26-28.

[4] Department of State press release, "Multilateral Agreement Reached on Atlantic Fisheries Crisis," October 26, 1973.

[5] Press release of the U.S. delegation to the Seventh Special Meeting of the International Commission for the Northwestern Atlantic Fisheries, September 28, 1975.

[6] The Fishery Conservation and Management Act of 1976, P.L. 94-265 (90 Stat. 331), April 13, 1976.

Opponents of the bill argued that unilateral extension of fishing rights to 200 miles could hamper United Nations law of the sea negotiations by causing other nations to make unilateral assertions. Freedom of navigation for U.S. ships and planes could be affected; other nations might be encouraged to assert sovereignty over the deep seabed oil and mineral resources adjacent to their coasts; and the possibility of achieving an equitable legal regime for the oceans at the 1976 Law of the Sea Conference in New York might be reduced. In a compromise, Congress passed a bill more acceptable to the President by providing that the law would not be enforceable until July 1, 1977, to give the law of the sea conference an opportunity to work out an international agreement on fishing zones.

Domestic Water Shortages. The federal government's involvement in water resources began in 1824 with an appropriation of $75,000 to the Corps of Engineers for navigation improvements along the Mississippi and Ohio rivers. Today, the government's program totals about $2.5 billion annually. In the early years of the Nixon administration, an attempt was made to concentrate on projects to supply municipal and industrial water in the rapidly growing, but arid, western states and to cut back on irrigation projects. This proposal entailed a reorientation of the Bureau of Reclamation program in seventeen western states, which are strongly irrigation oriented. While some of the pending reclamation projects were multipurpose, most of them were not to be undertaken unless there was local pressure for irrigation projects. Reclamation projects already irrigated about 11.0 million acres at a cost for all purposes of $7.7 billion. Projects that were authorized but not started and projects still under way would add about 5.0 million acres of irrigated land at a cost of an additional $9.1 billion for all purposes. At the time, when high and increasing yields from present acreage were more than sufficient to meet food and fiber needs, it did not seem rational to continue to put vast sums into irrigation projects. Additionally, the federal government was spending several billion dollars each year on various price-support operations, land diversions, and acreage retirement programs. Some projects cost more than $1,500 per acre to irrigate, with farmers paying as little as 10 percent of this cost over fifty years, without interest, and the remaining 90 percent repaid with electric power revenues, again without interest.

As the domestic grain shortage became apparent in the 1972–74 period, western congressmen saw it as a justification for more irrigation projects, or at least for equality between irrigation and municipal and industrial water development programs. But surplus lands lying fallow and lands retired by Department of Agriculture subsidies could have been brought back into production at a fraction of the cost of newly irrigated acreage.

Also, the administration made some modest gains—politically almost as difficult as making water run uphill—on the water resources development subsidy issue. President Nixon approved new procedures in planning water resources projects.[7] Environmental costs for the first time were weighed equally with economic benefits, and the planning discount rate was increased to reflect more closely Treasury borrowing rates.[8] In theory these new practices will result in authorizing only the more efficient and environmentally sound water resources projects, with specific accounting of all economic, environmental, and social effects, both favorable and adverse. Also, an omnibus water policy review under the direction of the Water Resources Council could result in legislation increasing the share of the costs paid by the beneficiaries. At present, 100 percent of the capital costs for most flood control and navigation and an average of 75 percent of the irrigation costs (sometimes as high as 90 percent or more) are paid for by the federal government. It does not seem politically feasible to expect Congress to pass legislation that would make its constituents pay 100 percent of capital costs. However, legislation to increase the beneficiaries' costs to, say, 25 to 50 percent of capital costs and 100 percent of the operation and maintenance costs, with interest repayable at Treasury borrowing rates, does seem politically feasible, though this reform will be very difficult to get through Congress. Under the principle that the user, and not the general public, should pay, however, this kind of legislation is by far the most important and effective reform that can be undertaken.

In the arid West, even if the water project subsidies are reduced, it is likely that agricultural, municipal, and industrial uses of water, including uses for energy, will continue to increase. Hard choices—for example, between irrigation and energy needs for water—are not likely to be made as long as both food and energy markets remain high-priced

---

[7] Water Resources Council, "New Principles and Standards," *Federal Register,* vol. 38, no. 174, Part III, September 10, 1973.

[8] However, Congress passed the Water Resources Development Act of 1974 (P.L. 93-251 [88 Stat. 12], March 12, 1974) reducing the 6⅞ percent discount rate established by President Nixon to 5⅝ percent based on an earlier formula.

and profitable. Instead, there is a danger that a first-come-first-served philosophy will prevail. A more orderly approach would be to set priorities based on a limited water supply, supported by detailed and constantly updated planning, conservation of water, and construction of new facilities and expanded water research techniques. In 1960, the Interior Department estimated an additional 17 million acres could be irrigated at a cost of about $22 billion.[9] But at that time the planners did not foresee the tremendous quantities of water that would be required for energy production—electrical power and oil shale, as well as synthetic gas and synthetic liquids derived from coal. A coal liquefaction plant, for example, requires 5.3 barrels of water for each barrel of oil produced. About 12,000 acre-feet of water are consumed each year in a 1,000-megawatt coal-fired generating plant, and a 250-million-cubic-feet-per-day gasification plant, converting 8–10 million tons of coal annually into synthetic pipeline gas, would consume about 10,000 acre-feet of water. The National Petroleum Council study on water availability for energy concluded that, for a maximum energy-development scenario in the arid West, a nearly $1-billion construction program for reservoirs and aqueducts was required.[10] The Interior Department report, *Water for Energy in the Upper Colorado River Basin,* indicated that under certain projections "there could be a significant water shortage occurring in all states [of the Upper Colorado River Basin] except Wyoming by year 2000."[11] Also the Westwide Study, an extensive attempt to pinpoint water problems prepared by representatives of the eleven western reclamation states and the federal government, found that "the consumptive use of water for power generation, coal conversion, and oil shale development may be 1.0 million acre-feet from the Colorado River Basin alone by 1985."[12]

Several factors that cannot be accurately projected, however, could increase future water availability. These include large-scale substitutes of air cooling in place of water cooling in industrial plants; increased water supply through cloud-seeding weather modifications; use of ground

[9] Department of Interior, *Future Needs for Reclamation in the Western States* (Washington, D.C.: U.S. Government Printing Office, 1960), p. III.

[10] National Petroleum Council, *U.S. Energy Outlook, Water Availability,* 1973, p. 1.

[11] Department of Interior, "Report on Water for Energy in the Upper Colorado River Basin," mimeographed, July 1974, p. 62.

[12] Department of Interior, *Westwide Study Report on Critical Water Problems Facing the Eleven Western Reclamation States* (Washington, D.C.: U.S. Government Printing Office, April 1975), p. 81.

water; construction of additional storage facilities; and a hard trade-off, purchase of agricultural water rights by energy interests. Thus, as in world food supplies, the best available estimates indicate there will be a knife-edge balance between water supply and demand. The problem requires attention, and eventually a whole new conservation ethic for conserving water, like energy, will be required.

Worldwide Mineral Shortages. Following the Arab boycott and steep crude-oil price increases in 1973 and 1974, the administration began studies to assure that no foreign action could disrupt the supply of other commodities imported by the United States. In December 1974, the Council on International Economic Policy issued a coordinated federal study of critical imported materials, judging their vulnerability to foreign actions such as embargoes, cartels, and other supply disruptions.[13] Of the nineteen critical imported materials studied, only four of them—bauxite, chromium, platinum, and palladium—appeared to have market structures that would permit foreign producers to take advantage of a tight supply situation and practice price gouging, which could have an adverse short-term effect on the domestic economy.

Aside from mineral shortages that might result from actions by foreign producers, there is the larger question of the future adequacy of the world's mineral resources. As the National Academy of Sciences study *Mineral Resources and the Environment* points out, much of the thinking on this problem is dominated by two schools of thought.

> The "doomsters" see a future in which catastrophic exhaustion of resources is inevitable unless drastic measures are taken to reduce economic growth. . . . Their gloomy outlook is based on a "fixed" supply of materials and fails to recognize that the supply available changes as prices rise and technical advances make lower grade resources economically and physically more accessible.

> The "Cornucopians" on the other hand rely too heavily on the market mechanism for including the transformation of "infinite" resources into almost infinite reserves, and on the technological miracle of providing the physical wherewithal. Their hypothesis insufficiently represents the increasingly large capital costs of technological advance, the long lead time involved, the "net energy" factor (the energy cost involved in

---

[13] Council on International Economic Policy, *Special Report: Critical Imported Materials* (Washington, D.C.: U.S. Government Printing Office, December 1974).

330

the technology of increasing production), and the fact that although technology has always come up with an answer in the past, its solutions have always had their social, environmental, or economic costs.[14]

Those involved in deciding government policy naturally include "doomsters," mindful of the difficult technological obstacles that must be overcome to keep the world adequately supplied with minerals, as well as "Cornucopians," who rely upon the market mechanism and consequently resist federal subsidies to increase mineral supply. But there is little disagreement that minerals, like energy, must be carefully conserved and a great deal more information on the worldwide availability of minerals is needed.

Actions that seem likely to be undertaken over the next few years include the following.

(1) The federal government could reduce the possibility of adverse effects from foreign price gouging or new cartel actions by building, as has been suggested,[15] larger-than-normal stocks of such materials as aluminum/alumina/bauxite, chromium, platinum, and palladium, which could be privately held and financed by a tax incentive (rather than a subsidy, which would require a large bureaucratic organization and a burdensome set of administrative processes).

(2) Research and development should be undertaken to exploit alternative sources or substitutes for critical imported minerals, such as large-scale demonstration plants for the production of alumina from domestic nonbauxite sources (pilot plant work is already under way on a cooperative effort involving the Bureau of Mines and ten private firms).

(3) The number of mineral attachés serving overseas should be expanded in order to supply better data on worldwide reserves and the status of mineral technology.

(4) Tax incentives should be granted to private research and development of mineral exploration, mining, and conservation of materials.

(5) Legislation should be developed for deep sea mining, with adequate environmental protection and in concert with the United Nations law of the sea negotiations. Restraint will be necessary in order to allow time for these complicated international negotiations to reach

---

[14] National Academy of Sciences, *Mineral Resources and the Environment* (Washington, D.C.: National Academy of Sciences Printing and Publishing Office, 1975), pp. 1 and 2.
[15] Department of Interior, "Critical Materials: Commodity Action Analysis, Aluminum, Chromium, Platinum and Palladium," mimeographed, March 1975.

a legal consensus. Premature action by the United States could lead to unrestrained commercial rivalries among nations mining the international seabed without clear title and under lax environmental standards.

Besides the major problems of potential food, water, and mineral shortages, there are hosts of other environmental and natural resource problems that await resolution by Congress.

Land Use. The Ford administration made a commendable effort to obtain better understanding and coordination of federal decision making that affects land-use patterns. But this is no substitute, in the author's opinion, for a national land-use law that will fund the institution-building and learning process needed to encourage state and local officials to work together for effective land-use decisions. The key issue is how the states and the local governments will divide decision authority over the management of land. There need be no federal involvement in the decision making but only federal funds to help the planning process. The Coastal Zone Management Act is helpful in planning development in an environmentally sound way in the coastal states. Adequate land-use planning has become a nationwide problem, however, and requires a national solution through federal legislation to provide the necessary funds.

The Public Lands of Alaska. Alaska contains 66 percent of the National Resource Lands, and in December 1973, as required under the Alaska Native Claims Settlement Act, Interior Secretary Morton recommended that about 83 million acres be added to the "four systems" (National Parks, National Forests, Wildlife Refuges, and the Wild and Scenic River systems). Less than four years are left for Congress to ratify or modify this proposal. In terms of acreage, this is the largest land-use decision ever made, which irrevocably sets a development pattern for Alaska. The decision deserves the scrutiny of Congress.

Regulation of Surface Mining. In spite of President Ford's veto of strip-mining legislation, Congress and the administration should try again to design legislation that ensures environmental protection without resulting in large or unpredictable amounts of coal that cannot be mined.

In May 1976, the Interior Department published final regulations expanding environmental protection for strip mining on the public lands.[16] Because the strip-mining reclamation issue has become polar-

16 Department of Interior press release, "Surface Mining Regulations Provide Protection and Production," May 11, 1976.

ized, however, the regulations will become so controversial—without a specific federal strip-mine law—that they will probably be the subject of further legal delays and uncertainties.

Summing Up. When reviewing major decisions on environmental and natural resources development since 1969, one naturally finds things that should have been done differently. In the initial stages of formulating pollution abatement legislation, too little attention was given to developing an analytical capability to anticipate federal budget costs, consumer costs, and degrees of loss in productivity resulting from varying environmental regulatory standards. Instead, decisions were often reached, by both the administration and the Congress, without any detailed forecast of the cost or potential productivity loss. In the last few years, as the balance of public opinion has tipped toward concern about inflation, jobs, and an adequate energy supply, EPA has developed a sound capability for estimating pollution control costs. Because EPA is obviously an advocate of environmental improvement, other agencies are often suspicious that EPA's cost estimates are too low, but few other agencies have any real capability to challenge EPA's assumptions. Recognizing this problem early, the President announced in his 1971 environmental message to Congress his intention to establish an "Environmental Institute," a nonprofit foundation to be financed jointly by the government (CEQ and the National Science Foundation) and by private foundations.[17] But because of difficulties in finding the right person to direct this organization, it never was established. If it had been, perhaps it would have developed a more dispassionate analytical capability to identify cost factors for alternative pollution abatement strategies, which both the administration and the Congress would view objectively. Instead, a great opportunity was missed, and, during the early stages of the Nixon administration, there was a strong tendency for EPA and environmental advocates in Congress to understate costs while their adversaries overstated them. The administration did, however, set up what became known as a "quality of life review," coordinated by OMB. Under this system, all proposed pollution abatement legislation, and the proposed environmental regulations being prepared by EPA, underwent vigorous cost analysis by an interagency review group, bringing together whatever information was available to predict costs more accurately. As would

---

[17] *Public Papers of the Presidents, Nixon, 1971,* Special Message to Congress Proposing the 1971 Environmental Program, February 8, p. 141.

333

be expected, EPA's cost estimates were often lower than the estimates of other agencies. Usually a decision was made—particularly in promulgating regulations with some degree of administrative discretion—to endorse a regulatory scenario less costly than EPA initially proposed. More recently, EPA's pollution abatement cost analysis has improved, outdistancing the capability of other agencies performing this kind of analysis.

The administration moved much too slowly in the author's opinion in undertaking environmental studies of the frontier areas of the outer continental shelf and in expanding the pace of oil and natural gas leasing. Four precious years were lost in finding desperately needed oil and natural gas from the time of the Santa Barbara blowout in February 1969 until CEQ began the administration's first environmental assessment of the frontier areas of the Atlantic and the Gulf of Alaska, in response to the President's request in April 1973.[18] Only after that study was completed was baseline environmental monitoring systematically undertaken in OCS frontier areas. In hindsight, even under the strong opposition to offshore oil and natural gas exploration following the Santa Barbara blowout, the administration should have dramatically increased its ability to assure that offshore drilling could be conducted in an environmentally sound way and should have expanded the leasing program. It was not until 1974, however, that the administration expanded OCS frontier activity. Start-up problems and legal interventions still delay the program.

Nor should the administration have waited until 1975 to propose legislation that could ultimately develop the Naval Petroleum Reserve #4 of Alaska. Geologists believe it is the largest potential onshore oil prospect in the United States.

Still, much has been accomplished in environmental quality. The air is considerably better than it was in 1970, though by mid-1975 only 91 of 247 Air Quality Control Regions had completely met air standard levels. CEQ's *Sixth Annual Report* indicated that between 1970 and 1974 particulate emissions dropped 29 percent, sulfur dioxide declined 8 percent, carbon monoxide dropped 12 percent, and hydrocarbon emissions declined 5 percent, though nitrogen oxide increased about 10 percent over the same period. The standards for the 1975 model

---

[18] Office of the White House Press Secretary, Energy Message to Congress, April 18, 1973.

cars represented a reduction in carbon monoxide and hydrocarbon emissions of more than 80 percent from uncontrolled levels.

Burning fossil fuels in electric power plants, residential furnaces, and industrial facilities accounts for most of the sulfur dioxides, almost half the nitrogen oxides, and a significant amount of the particulate matter emitted nationwide. From 1970 to 1974 sulfur dioxide was reduced 10 percent and particulates 29 percent, while nitrogen oxide increased 9 percent. The reductions in sulfur dioxide and particulates were due primarily to better stack-gas control, to a reduction in coal burned in all sources except electric power plants, and to the burning of lower sulfur coals in electric power plants.[19]

Water quality is also improving. The CEQ *Sixth Annual Report* concludes "that the worst point sources of pollution are being effectively controlled and that our most heavily polluted waterways are being cleaned up." [20]

While all of this was being achieved, public concern for environmental quality by the mid-1970s was giving way to concern for an adequate energy supply, jobs, and inflation. In May 1975, six years after the Santa Barbara blowout, Santa Barbara County residents voted 35,507 to 34,700 in favor of constructing a $30 million plant to process oil and gas from new offshore sources. *Time* magazine said "the plant's contribution to the nation's energy supply and the local economy helped outweigh environmental fears." [21] A public opinion poll in September 1974 showed 74 percent in favor of offshore oil and gas drilling, 16 percent opposed, and 10 percent undecided.[22] A Harris poll in mid-April 1975 showed 73 percent favoring offshore drilling, 13 percent opposed, and 14 percent undecided.[23]

Land-use legislation, which President Nixon had once called his number one environmental priority, failed to pass Congress. Environmental concern had been overridden by fears that the bill might slow housing construction and other economic development projects, as well as restrict state and local planning prerogatives.

By 1973, a Congress concerned about an adequate energy supply voted to pass a bill expediting construction of the Alaska pipeline.

---

[19] Council on Environmental Quality, *Sixth Annual Report,* pp. 305-307.

[20] Ibid., p. 362.

[21] *Time,* June 9, 1975.

[22] Opinion Research Corporation, Princeton, N.J., November 13, 1974; 603 households.

[23] Louis Harris and Associates, May 5, 1975.

Congress even agreed to accept the Interior Department's environmental-impact statement and to exempt the study from review by the courts, as provided for in the National Environmental Policy Act of 1969. President Ford's veto of strip-mining legislation, another environmental issue, was narrowly sustained by Congress.

None of these events would have been likely to happen in 1970, 1971, or even 1972. But by January 1974, with the impact of the Arab boycott, the energy crisis was on everybody's mind. A few months later, inflation became the chief concern of the public. By April 1975, a Gallup poll reported that 60 percent of the public thought that the high cost of living was the most important problem facing the country, and 20 percent named unemployment. The next most frequently cited problems were the energy crisis, dissatisfaction with government, and moral decline (each named by 7 percent).[24] In spite of a sagging economy, loss of jobs, and worry over the energy problem, the *New York Times* in October 1975 reported on an Opinion Research Corporation poll showing that 60 percent felt that environmental protection was worth the cost, compared with 21 percent who wanted prices and taxes reduced, even at the risk of increased pollution.[25]

There is no inherent contradiction between Gallup's findings in the spring of 1975 and Opinion Research Corporation's poll in the fall of 1975. As the public turned to new issues, it remained *aware* of environmental issues though its *concern* about them waned. No longer was there that hopeless feeling of the late 1960s and early 1970s, particularly prevalent on the campuses, that nothing was being done and that pollution was increasing unabated. By the mid-1970s progress could be seen clearly, and an environmental ethic had become embedded in the national being. Protecting the environment had become institutionalized in federal, state, and local governments and in the judicial system.

Environmental studies are now taught in universities and high schools, and environmental-awareness field trips are offered in many elementary schools. The protection of the environment has become a way of life. The success of the environmental movement—in cleansing the air and the waterways, in providing more open spaces, in reducing noise, and in stemming the introduction of toxic pollutants—seems to be one of the few cases in which government action has succeeded in dealing with a problem. While crime and drugs plague the decaying cities,

[24] The Gallup Poll, April 13, 1975.
[25] *New York Times,* October 7, 1975, p. 34.

and inflation and unemployment persist, improvement of the environment stands out as an isolated success.

Much of the credit belongs, in the author's opinion, to Richard Nixon. Nixon was there at the right moment. He grasped the issue quickly and presented a comprehensive and broad legislative environmental agenda. A number of ingredients—including a public outcry to stop pollution, a talented and dedicated group in the executive branch to put forth legislative proposals, a Congress whose majority was ready to act, and a President ready to accept comprehensive recommendations that often ran counter to the wishes of his cabinet officers—combined to produce the best conservation and environmental record since Theodore Roosevelt. Politically, Nixon was assailed from both sides: by those who bitterly resented the costs of environmental clean-up, and by those who insisted that the movement take absolute priority over all other considerations. Between these he steered a progressive middle course, establishing the environment as a national priority, but doing so in a way that enabled economic growth to go forward—so that the nation could, in the longer term, continue to afford the cost of environmental clean-up together with the rising standard of living that the people demanded.

Index

340

341

OPEC: *see* Organization of Petroleum Exporting Countries
Organization of Petroleum Exporting Countries:
  embargo, 1973–1974: ~~101~~, ~~105~~, ~~207~~, ~~208~~, 228, ~~230~~, ~~232~~, ~~249~~, ~~252~~, ~~269~~, ~~270~~, 272, ~~274~~, ~~277~~
Outer Continental Shelf Lands Act of 1953: 261, 271, 281, 291
Outer Continental Shelf Research Management Advisory Board: 307

Paarlberg, Don: 325
Pan American Petroleum Company: 242
Parathion: 134, 139
Parks: 185–205
Passman, Otto: 46
Peck, Raymond, Jr.: 176n
Pesticides: 23, 31, 41, 125–139
Petroleum Placer Act of 1897: 237, 240
Petroleum reserves: 223, 274–275, 276
Pinchot, Gifford: 18–20
Poage, W. R.: 130, 141
Point Reyes National Seashore: 192n
Population growth, impact: 179–181, 209–210, 229–230, 304–305
Powers, Richard: 276n
Prairie National Park (proposed): 193
Predator control: 51, 139–143
Presidential vetoes: 84, 88–89, 175–176, 181–183, 217, 254–255
President's Advisory Council on Executive Organization (Ash Council): 53, 55, 56–57, 58
President's Committee on Administrative Management (1937): 58
President's Task Force on Government Organization (1964): 59
President's Task Force on Government Organization (1967): 60
Price, Don K.: 59
Price, Raymond: 30, 187
Price Task Force: *see* President's Task Force on Government Organization
Property Review Board: 30, 38, 52, 186–189
Prospecting permits (minerals leasing): 215–216, 218, 219
Proxmire, William: 75
Prudhoe Bay: *see* Alaskan oil deposits
Public lands: 149, 186–190
  mineral reserves: 207–257

Public Land Law Review Commission, report: 60, 161
Public opinion polls: 8–15, 335–336

Quarles, John: 29, 137
Quarles, Steven P.: 160

Rather, Dan: 7
Ray, Dixy Lee: 68
Reclamation of mined land: 209, 228–229
Recycling: 111, 112, 113
Reed, Nathaniel: 143
Regional planning grants: 169
Reilly, William: 159
Resource Recovery Act of 1970: 112–113
Resource Sciences Company: 244
Revenue sharing: 157, 302–306
Reynolds Metal: 3
Rhodes, John: 163–164
Rhodes-Steiger Land Use Planning Act (proposed): 163–164
Rice, Don: 157–158
Richardson, Elliot: 70, 93
River basin development: 21, 22
Rivers and Harbors Act of 1899: 169
Rockefeller, Laurance S.: 27n
Rockefeller, Nelson: 2, 234
Rogers, William P.: 31
Roosevelt, Franklin Delano: 21–22, 58–59
Roosevelt, Theodore: 19–20, 21, 337
Royalties:
  geothermal energy: 254–256
  minerals: 214–215, 218, 219, 116, 231
  petroleum: 250–251, 293–294
Royalty bidding (offshore oil leases): 283–284, 292–294
Ruckelshaus, William D.: 5, 81, 97–100
  pesticides: 133, 136–137
Rumsfeld, Donald: 187n
Rusk, Dean: 46

Sable, Edward: 276n
Santa Barbara Channel: 259, 264–272
Sawhill, John: 70
Sawtooth Range national preserve (proposed): 193

343

Schaefer, John: 317n
Schledee, Glenn: 29
Schlesinger, James: 30, 77, 250–251
Schorr, Daniel: 7
Schurz, Carl: 18
Scott, William: 5
Seidman, William: 234n
Sequoia National Park: 21
Shell Chemical Company: 137
Shell Oil Company: 232n, 236
Shultz, George P.: 69
Sierra Club: 108, 216–217
Simon, Paul: 6
Simon, William: 69
Smith, George Otis: 237–238, 240
Smog: 23, 95
Soil Conservation Service: 61n, 65
Solid waste management: 22, 111–123
Soper, Philip (quoted): 149
Standard Oil Company of California: 241–242, 244–245
Stans, Maurice: 31, 40
State Air Implementation Plans: 106, 109
State-local relations: 147–148, 149, 155–156, 158, 332
Steiger, Sam: 162–164
Stratton Commission: *see* Commission on Marine Science, Engineering, and Resources
Stratton, Julius: 56n
Strelow, Roger: 29
Strip mining: 41, 173–183, 210, 332–333
Submerged Lands Act of 1953: 261, 262
Sulfur oxides: 34, 35, 41, 106, 334–335
Sulfuric acid emissions: 102–105
Sullivan, Leonor: 319–320
Sun Oil Company: 3, 232n
Superports: 310–321
Synthetic fuels program: 235–236

Tankers: 310–314
Teapot Dome: 236, 245, 246, 252
Texas Gulf Sulphur: 3
Thallium: 140
Thomson, Harry: 276n
Tidelands: *see* offshore oil

Tocks Island reservoir: 51
Toxic substances: 143–145
Train, Russell: 51, 81, 137
    air pollution control: 102, 103–104, 108, 109
    land-use programs: 155, 157, 158, 159, 187, 205
Trent, Darrell: 30, 188–189
Truman, Harry S.: 260, 263
Tussock moth: 135–136

Udall, Morris: 163–164
Udall, Stewart: 6, 225, 226, 232, 266-267
Union Oil Company: 224, 264–266, 271
User fees: 36

Volpe, John A.: 31, 33

Warren, Gerald: 163
Waste paper recycling: 116
Water pollution control: 33–37, 73–92, 148, 168
Water resources development: 327–330
Weber, Arnold: 187n
Weinberger, Caspar: 88
Wells, Chris (quoted): 224
Whitaker, John: 275n, 276n, 277n
Whitten, Jamie L.: 46
Wild and Scenic Rivers system: 202–204
Wilderness preservation: 201–202
World Heritage Trust: 205

Yosemite Valley: 20–21

Zarb, Frank: 70, 108, 176n, 180n, 181, 234n
Zausner, Eric: 176n
Zoning: 147–149

344

Cover and book design: Pat Taylor